PRACTICAL
WATCH
REPAIRING

Practical
Watch Repairing

Donald de Carle FBHI

Illustrations by
E.A. Ayres

Skyhorse Publishing

Skyhorse Publishing books may be purchased in bulk at special discounts for sales promotion, corporate gifts, fund raising, or educational purposes. Special editions can also be created to specifications. For details, contact the Special Sales Department, Skyhorse Publishing, 555 Eighth Avenue, Suite 903, New York, NY 10018 or info@skyhorsepublishing.com.

www.skyhorsepublishing.com

10 9 8 7 6 5 4 3 2 1

Library of Congress Cataloging-in-Publication Data

De Carle, Donald.
    Practical watch repairing/Donald de Carle; Illustrations by E. A. Ayres.—3rd ed.
      p. cm.
    Includes index.
    ISBN 978-1-60239-357-8 (alk. paper)
    1. Clocks and watches—Repairing. I. Title.
    TS547.D38 2008
    681.1'140288—dc22
                    2008018956

Printed in the United States of America

CONTENTS

CONTENTS—*continued.*

PREFACE

THE ABSORBING and everlasting subject of watch repairing has been dealt with in books in many languages. At first glance the production of yet another would appear superfluous ; even one in addition to my own previous book on the subject, published by Pitman's under the title of *With the Watchmaker at the Bench*. Readers of the present volume will be able to judge. The work of producing PRACTICAL WATCH REPAIRING occupied all my spare time for some three years, and I do not regard it as less than a valuable investment in experience and a humble effort to be of service to my fellow craftsmen.

My publisher, Arthur Tremayne, from whom came the inspiration for the work, convinced me in the early stages of writing it that perhaps the majority of textbooks took too much prior knowledge for granted, and that only a book about watch repairing which did not disdain to explain even the most simple processes and operations could give the student full return for his outlay.

" I want a textbook," said Tremayne, " that a watchmaker can understand, even if he can't read." A fairly tall order, needing a throw-back to hieroglyphics or picture writing to carry out to the letter, but as a student of many textbooks, indeed, of as many as I could lay hands on since I first aspired to be a craftsman horologist, I understood exactly what was required. Although some readers of this book may consider parts of the subject laboured, I feel sure that many more, among them those of the younger generation, will appreciate the fact that I have left so little to guesswork, and will pay tribute to the publisher's prodigious and insatiable appetite for drawings and blocks, to say nothing of the skilful labours of my friend E. A. Ayres, the illustrator.

The several charts and tables, most of them being original and specially compiled for the purpose, should attract particularly the attention of experienced craftsmen. In constructing them I have endeavoured to provide useful information by the most direct and compact method in a form to encourage quick reference as routine.

The preliminary publication of the book as a serial from June, 1943, to December, 1945, in the pages of the HOROLOGICAL JOURNAL gave it a preview of inestimable value, bringing to light errors and omissions which wickedly dog the author of any work calling for accurate description of mechanical detail. It has also brought valuable criticisms of both the letterpress and drawings, all of which have been received most gratefully and corrections made where necessary.

As the work proceeded it was realised that a job had been started which need never end, because the designing of watches has not stood still since the first watch was made and will go on developing and progressing until the end of time itself. But the fundamental design of the lever watch may be regarded as stable, with future development more likely to be by way of the introduction of new materials or the elaboration of mechanisms which add other functions than timekeeping to the watch. The motive power with the train and escapement combine to make a very highly developed piece of mechanism, and it is mainly to this that I have devoted the book, wishing and hopeful that it will assist in creating an aspiration for fine craftsmanship, giving very practical help in its attainment.

Acknowledgments and thanks are due to my early teachers in the craft, to writers of innumerable existing textbooks and articles, to my illustrator, Mr. E. A. Ayres, to Mr. Hillyard T. Stott for his special assistance in the chapter devoted to magnetism, to Professor D. S. Torrens for reading the proofs and for kindly help and criticism at all times and, finally, to Mr. Arthur Tremayne, the Editor of the HOROLOGICAL JOURNAL, who, in his rôle of publisher, has supplied the driving force without which the book would never have appeared.

PINNER, MIDDLESEX.   D. DE CARLE.
May, 1946.

PREFACE TO SECOND EDITION

IT GIVES great satisfaction to any author to know that his book has been successful and I am no exception. Since 1946, PRACTICAL WATCH REPAIRING has run to four impressions in this country ; it has been published in America and translated into Italian and Spanish.

This second edition has been designed to bring the book completely up-to-date. Corrections have been made and the latest information added, particularly in relation to watch timers.

Again I should like to record my thanks to horological friends who have taken so much trouble to offer helpful criticism and suggestions.

PINNER, MIDDLESEX.   D. DE CARLE.
August, 1953.

PREFACE TO THIRD EDITION

THE WORLD of horology is moving fast, in fact almost in step with other sciences and technologies, such as space travel and surgery.

It behoves the watch repairer to take notice of what is happening around him. There is little doubt that in the future watches will be wholly electronic. It may be some years yet—it is anybody's guess—but I would say within the next 25 years. If the Swiss do not go ahead the Japanese will.

With this in mind, a chapter on the tuning fork electronic watch has been added, and watch repairers should start to become interested.

In addition a revised chapter on timing machines has been included in this new edition.

PINNER, MIDDLESEX.   D. DE CARLE.
June, 1969.

CHAPTER ONE

WORKSHOP AND WORK-BENCH

THIS BOOK is specially written for the beginner who intends to make watch repairing and adjusting a life study, as should all who hope to get a living by it. It will describe the first steps of the work in a manner which may appear too simple ; but even if the reader has already travelled some way along the road to proficiency he is requested not to skip the elementary preliminary details, for these are the foundation upon which the more advanced practice is built. The information given is based on my own practical work, the knowledge acquired in the appreciative study of all the currently available horological literature, and the experience gained while responsible for an important horological repair shop handling many thousands of watch repairs a year. The theories and practices to be explained have been tested and approved by the many readers of my previous book on the subject, *With the Watchmaker at the Bench*, and their helpful correspondence has been of great assistance.

Watch repairing is work which calls for a vast amount of intelligently concentrated application. It must be understood from the start that it cannot be picked up ; it demands the most careful study.

Although it is essential that the advanced repairer has a complete knowledge of the theory of the lever escapement, it is not necessary for the beginner to acquire this knowledge before starting practical work. It is impossible to learn the adjustments of a watch movement without first being fully acquainted with the form and function of each component. Modern watch movement design is still a long way from standardisation, but provided it contains no complications, such as chronograph, calendar or repeater actions, each movement design follows the same straight-forward plan despite many differing layouts, and it is therefore safe to assume that a useful repairing technique can be successfully acquired by practical application. Theoretical knowledge, without which no advanced work can be done, will be gained just as quickly as the student can grasp it. Let him put his heart into his practical work, and the necessary theoretical knowledge will be easily and quickly absorbed.

Every watch repairer must aim at acquiring keen sight and a deft touch. He must have the fullest muscular control of his wrists and fingers, and be capable of peering closely at his work through an eye-glass for long periods at a stretch without tiring. These attributes of the repairer, if they are to be employed successfully, call for a high degree of bodily comfort, a clear head, a contented mind and a determination to succeed.

It may be said that all mechanical work calls for similar personal characteristics and application. It does ; but if one compares an aptitude for work on large mechanisms, such as a motor car engine, with heavy tools and adjustments which are readily measureable, with the aptitude required for work on a watch movement, where the clearances and adjustments cannot be measured except by the eye or by a delicate touch, and when these adjustments are made to parts which, when dismantled, can be dispersed with a breath or crushed with a fingernail, it becomes evident that it is a highly specialised type of work.

Therefore I warn the beginner at watch repairing that he must be prepared to study closely, to sit close to the bench and to work to close limits. If he is prepared to do this and has a keen sight and a cool temperament then, with the necessary study and practice, he can succeed.

The key-word is PRACTICE. Study is necessary, but practice is essential.

The first points to consider are the surroundings of the workman, his workshop, his lighting, both natural and artificial, his bench, and his seating accommodation. Next will be the tools he works with. Throughout this book the tools to be used on each job will be described when that part of the work is under discussion. In this trade, as no doubt in many others, no workman, be he ever so skilful, has every possible tool for every possible job ready to hand, and the watch repairer will discover ideas for tools of his own conception and will delight in making them.

The essentials for success are scrupulous cleanliness, a clear bench and good light. A clear bench is contrary, perhaps, to the ideas of the majority of watch repairers, who seem to accumulate on the bench many tools, some in use, and others of no immediate use, together with a confused collection of litter consisting of old material, work in hand, oil pots and a host of other things. The result is that tools get damaged or lost, and the time taken in rectification and search mounts up to many costly hours in the course of a year.

The beginner at the job has a fair chance of forming better habits and it is hoped that he will determine to keep a clear bench with trays, drawers and boxes to hold his various tools, keeping each in its regular place, out of the way of his current work yet within easy reach when required.

When one is engaged on a job demanding close, almost intense, mental and physical application, the immediate surroundings of the work-bench are of prime importance. One finds watch repairers given very poor quarters in many establishments, accommodated at the rear of shops behind screens, or poked into dusty, ill-lit corners with insufficient room, a prey to draughts and petty distractions that militate against the concentration and application necessary to such exacting work. In such conditions it is no wonder that repairs are often costly and unsatisfactory.

The small calibre wristlet watch has produced changed conditions in the manufacturing processes in the factories ; new conditions must be also introduced in the repairers' workshops to enable the finer, closer work to be done.

The vogue of the small watch movement is certain to persist. It is certain that many more small watches will be used in the future than in the past, with every prospect of their becoming flatter than hitherto. If watches are not small they will be complicated by actions other than timekeeping. The point here is that watch repairing is passing out of the realm of mechanics into that of a mechanical science, and this feature should be taken into consideration in planning and fitting-up the workshop and bench. It is a vital point for the beginner and of primary importance to the employer.

To sum up : Banish damp, dirt, draughts and distraction. Encourage comfort, warmth, quiet. Provide good light, good ventilation, good tools and a liberal supply of materials. Good and *profitable* work should result.

Although I am going to describe working conditions of an ideal character, it does not prevent the beginner from making a start in a simple way. But do not think that any good can come of trying to do work on the corner of an odd table. Take the job seriously and at least fit up a shelf to serve as a bench. Fix it across a window, let it be at least 36 to 38 inches from the floor and from 15 to 20 inches wide. The length is immaterial so long as it provides room to rest the elbows while at work.

Fig. I. An ideal work-bench.

An ideal bench is illustrated in Fig. 1. This provides a roomy bench protected from sudden draughts, and with a bead along the front edge, a comfortable foot-rail, a shelf for the heavier tools which are kept in wooden cases or boxes, and drawers for tools and equipment, with a cupboard for the lathe.

Set the bench facing the light, which should be a window open to the sky and, for preference, facing due north. A northern aspect gives a soft white light which, for the watch repairer's purpose, is practically shadowless. If a north light is impracticable, means for shading strong sunlight should be provided. An eyeshade is an added advantage.

An articulated fitting should be employed for artificial light as this enables the light to be brought close to the work. Furthermore, it can be arranged at any suitable angle and, once set, will maintain that position. It is an advantage to be able to bring the light close to the work as this allows a comparatively small lamp to be used, which means less heat near the eyes and head. It also costs less to run. A good type of fitting which is finding favour with repairing horologists, as with other workers, is the Terry *Anglepoise*, as illustrated in Fig. 2. For ordinary drop pendants, the shade I prefer is made of metal, green enamel on the outside and white on the inside. Green and white lined card shades are obtainable but

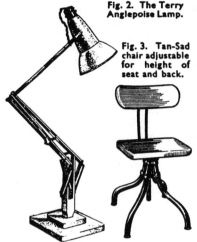

Fig. 2. The Terry Anglepoise Lamp.

Fig. 3. Tan-Sad chair adjustable for height of seat and back.

they turn a dirty white or even brown on the inside in a short period and the light is not then so well reflected.

The height of the stool is important. No general rule can be made, but it should enable the watch repairer to sit comfortably without the necessity of crouching down at the work. He should feel quite at ease. No two people are alike in this respect and it is well worth spending some time to accomplish the desired result. You will find that it has not been time wasted. The Tan-Sad Chair Company, London, E.C.1, make a very useful adjustable seat with a convenient back rest (see Fig. 3).

If there is more than one man in the shop I still advocate the type of bench described and illustrated above, as it promotes steadiness. One man may wish to file or hammer, while another, who may be engaged in touching a balance spring, will require the bench to be absolutely steady. In the Swiss factories, where there are several men in the same shop, they employ a long narrow substantial bench about 15 inches wide, firmly fixed in just one long run against the window ; but here all the men (or women) may be doing the same type of work, so that if one makes the bench vibrate they will all be doing the same, and nobody will be inconvenienced. In an ordinary repair workshop, where every variety of watch passes for repair and various operations to each watch are carried out, it is far better for each man to be a separate working unit.

Attention should be paid to the floor. A composition flooring with a radius where it meets the wall is ideal. Good plain brown linoleum with a wooden bead nailed round the skirting is the next best. Most of the parts of a watch are light in colour, gilt or white plates, gilt wheels and white pinions, blue screws are the exception, but the majority of the parts are light and they will show up well on a dark background, and should they fall to the floor they will be more readily discovered.

CHAPTER TWO

ESSENTIAL TOOLS

So much for the workshop and bench. Now for a few words about your tools, or rather the manner in which to obtain the best results from screwdrivers, tweezers, pliers, nippers and other simple but very essential universal equipment.

Four screwdrivers are usually sufficient for all ordinary purposes and the most useful sizes are those with blades made from wire or rod of 2.5mm., 2mm., 1.25mm. and .75mm. diameter. Some manufacturers give sizes to their screwdrivers but the numbers do not seem to bear any relation to a measurement and are not universal, so that the measurements I have given are the best indications of the sizes. The blades of the screwdrivers should receive constant attention. The business end must be shaped, not to a knife edge, but with an edge as illustrated in Fig. 4. The taper of the blade should be reasonably long so that when it is inserted in the slot of a screw it will not, when a little pressure is exerted either to unscrew or screw up, have the tendency to slip up out of the slot and so maul the screw head. Fig. 5 shows a screwdriver blade as it should not be.

Fig. 4. The correct shape for screwdriver blade.

The blades should be hardened and tempered. This is usually the case with tools which are purchased from the tool shop, but should you find when filing to remake that they are soft, do not hesitate to remove the blade and harden and temper it. Eventually you will find that this is time well spent.

Fig. 5. The wrong shape damages screw heads.

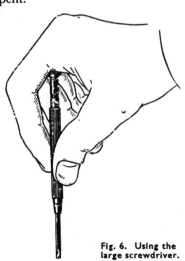

Fig. 6. Using the large screwdriver.

The manner of holding the screwdriver should be obvious, but some watch repairers handle tools so awkwardly that a word of advice may not be out of place. The large 2.5mm. driver is used for large pillar plate screws and such like, and a certain amount of power is necessary to give greater control over the tool. The best way to ensure both these points is to hold the screwdriver as illustrated in Fig. 6. The other three screwdrivers are used for lighter work, and better control can be exercised if a lighter or more delicate touch is exerted. To ensure this hold the screwdriver as demonstrated in Fig. 7.

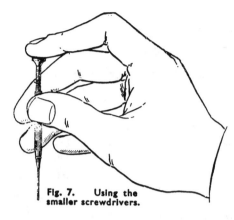

Fig. 7. Using the smaller screwdrivers.

We all have likes and dislikes about tweezers. I prefer Dumont Swiss-made tweezers, or at least something of a similar design ; they are the solid type. Three pairs of flat tweezers meet most requirements : two stout pairs and a fine pair for balance spring work, see Fig. 8. For balance spring over-coil forming I suggest two pairs to start with. As will be seen from a glance at Fig. 9, they vary in curve.

There are dozens of various types of tweezers, and it is fascinating to peruse the tweezers section of a good tool list—indeed, the whole catalogue, for that matter. There are tweezers for almost every conceivable job. In fact, you may be persuaded that the tools do the work but, as you will find in practice, that is far from the truth, so start off with the essential tweezers first, indulging in fancy types later.

Tweezers require an occasional overhaul. A good test by which it can be ascertained whether the tweezers are in good condition or not is to place a human hair on a sheet of glass. If the tweezers are in good trim it should be possible to pick up the hair with them without any difficulty. A further test, and an important one, is to grip a thin piece of metal, such as a mainspring, exerting some considerable pressure, and the points of the tweezers should not curl up. See illustration (Fig. 10a). If the tweezers do not comply with these tests they must be trimmed up, and the best way to do this is with an Arkansas slip. It may be necessary

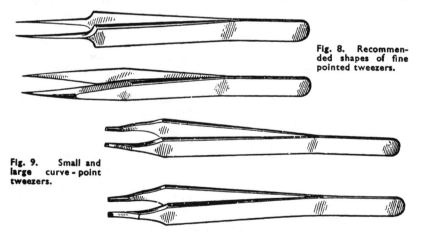

Fig. 8. Recommended shapes of fine pointed tweezers.

Fig. 9. Small and large curve - point tweezers.

in the first place to bend the nose of the tweezers slightly ; if they are parallel there is the danger that when something is gripped tightly the points curl up, which may result in the piece snapping out, which may either damage it or cause it to be lost (Fig. 10b).

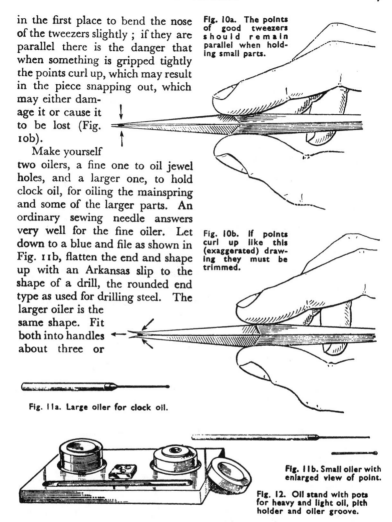

Fig. 10a. The points of good tweezers should remain parallel when holding small parts.

Make yourself two oilers, a fine one to oil jewel holes, and a larger one, to hold clock oil, for oiling the mainspring and some of the larger parts. An ordinary sewing needle answers very well for the fine oiler. Let down to a blue and file as shown in Fig. 11b, flatten the end and shape up with an Arkansas slip to the shape of a drill, the rounded end type as used for drilling steel. The larger oiler is the same shape. Fit both into handles about three or

Fig. 10b. If points curl up like this (exaggerated) drawing they must be trimmed.

Fig. 11a. Large oiler for clock oil.

Fig. 11b. Small oiler with enlarged view of point.

Fig. 12. Oil stand with pots for heavy and light oil, pith holder and oiler groove.

four inches long. I find that long handles are more convenient than shorter ones. Wood handles are quite good but the ideal, in my opinion, and the type I use, are made of bone. A mapping pen holder is ideal, and I find it very comfortable. A hexagonal collar on the handle keeps the point safe and stops rolling. The Swiss and Americans favour oiling trays consisting of two or three oil pots fitted on a stand with a rack for the oilers. An excellent system this, the oilers thus being always at hand.

In the illustration (Fig. 12) a holder is shown fixed to the tray which contains pieces of pith to clean the oilers or to act as repositories when in use.

Two or three eye-glasses are necessary ; a double lens glass with a ¼ inch focus is essential for examining jewel holes and pivots. It is a mistaken idea to assume that the wearing of an eye-glass weakens the

sight. Look round amongst your horologist friends and see if there is a predominance of men wearing spectacles. I do not think you will find there is a greater percentage than the rest of the community, and the reason is that we do not strain our eyes to observe something small without adequate assistance. I do not advocate the regular use of a strong glass as this

Fig. 13. 3″ focus eye-glass.   Fig. 14. ¼″ focus eye-glass.

tends to render it less effective when the real necessity for its use arises, but I am definitely of the opinion that the general eye-glass is far from harmful.

A two-inch glass is useful when examining depths, adjusting the balance spring, etc., and a three-inch glass for general use. The double glass obviously reveals itself by its shape, but it is advisable for the others to be of different colours or one, say, of the open wire collapsible type, so that you readily distinguish the glass you wish to use. Like other tools, eye-glasses need some attention to make them more serviceable. The solid frame type of glass is inclined to steam up when the heat of the eye is greater than that of the atmosphere, and to prevent this three or four holes about $\frac{1}{16}$ inch in diameter should be drilled in the sides. If this is not effective, wave the glass in the air to cool the inside : it is better and quicker than wiping it.

Two pairs of nippers are necessary, one fine and the other a little heavier. Nippers when purchased from the tool shops have the cutting edges shaped as illustrated in Fig. 15. That is quite in order for the heavier pair, but the fine pair should be filed up as illustrated. We are then able to get up close for cutting or when removing a close fitting tight part such as a short pin from a plate. A little time occasionally spent in keeping such tools in good trim saves a lot of time eventually.

Four pairs of pliers are necessary and these should be as illustrated in Fig. 16. A pair with a square nose for general use, the narrow tapered nose for more delicate work, round

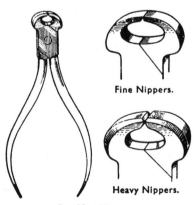

Fine Nippers.

Heavy Nippers.

Fig. 15.   Nippers

nose for manipulating wire, etc., and a pair of brass lined pliers for holding finished surfaces, such as are encountered when removing a snap-on cannon pinion.

Pliers when new are usually left with the inside of the jaws very rough. In watch work generally such a rough surface is not necessary, so file or stone at least the majority of the ridges away.

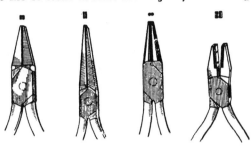

Fig. 16. Pliers.
Square nose.
Tapered nose.
Round nose.
Brass lined.

Three hammers are necessary, all of distinctly different types : an ordinary flat face type, one with a rounded face for riveting, and the third either all of brass or having the face lined with brass. A hammer such as this last is useful when tapping a finished surface to ensure that a burr will not be made. If it cannot be bought, a brass pad should be screwed into a steel hammer head.

Fig. 17.
Hand-lifting levers,
with enlarged
detail.

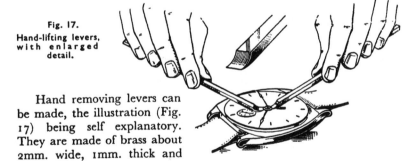

Hand removing levers can be made, the illustration (Fig. 17) being self explanatory. They are made of brass about 2mm. wide, 1mm. thick and 4 to 4½ inches long.

Fig. 18.
Bluing Pan.

Fig. 18 illustrates a bluing pan. This is an indispensable tool and is useful not only for bluing screws, etc., but also for heating pallets when adjusting the stones.

Every watch repairer's bench should be provided with a pith container, such as an old French clock barrel (Fig. 19) cut down to half its original height, packed tight with pieces of pith placed in endwise. The container should be something reasonably heavy ; pith itself is very light and if it is not securely held by packing tightly into the container it will be picked up by the tool during cleaning and so defeat its object. Pith is useful for cleaning the blades of screwdrivers, oilers, points of tweezers, etc., the habit—and it can become a good habit—being to stab such tools into the pith before using. This practice is much to be preferred to the usual habit of twirling screwdriver blades and oilers on the pad of the little finger (Fig. 20). I have even seen men wipe an oiler on the lapel of the coat, probably picking up more foreign matter than they remove, and then using it to apply oil ! Bellows (Fig. 21) should always be available and also one or two glass dust shades. for which broken wine glasses do very well. I shall refer frequently to all these things in their proper place, and numerous other tools in addition will be described as we proceed.

There is no doubt in my mind that knowing *which* tool to use and *how* to use it, is to be well on the road to success.

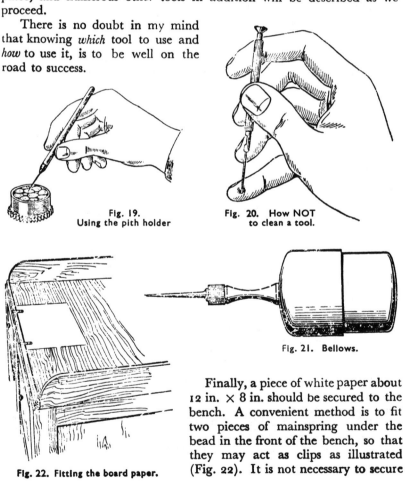

Fig. 19.
Using the pith holder

Fig. 20. How NOT
to clean a tool.

Fig. 21. Bellows.

Fig. 22. Fitting the board paper.

Finally, a piece of white paper about 12 in. × 8 in. should be secured to the bench. A convenient method is to fit two pieces of mainspring under the bead in the front of the bench, so that they may act as clips as illustrated (Fig. 22). It is not necessary to secure the paper further, the oil pots and dust shades hold the farther side flat. A supply of tissue paper cut to size, about four inches square, should be at hand together with a supply of pegwood and pith.

Just a personal word here before we start work. Watches are fine delicate instruments, and one of our main objects is to make them as clean and dust-free as possible, so see your hands are clean. I have seen watchmakers handle movements with enough dirt under one finger nail to stop a dozen watches. With short nails, and nice clean hands (our finest irreparable tools, and they are worth looking after) we shall stand a better chance of success.

CHAPTER THREE

CASE, DIAL AND HANDS

WE ARE now ready to commence work. For convenience let us examine a movement together. It best suits our purpose to take a popular type as being more likely to be commonly encountered in the general run of repair work, and a 13 ligne wrist watch (1 $\frac{3}{16}$ inches diameter) with a modern Swiss straight-line lever movement is undoubtedly the best choice. During the examination or repair it may be necessary to fit new pieces, such as a balance staff or a guard pin, and these items will be dealt with under their separate headings.

As considerable confusion is caused by the lack of a recognised standard list of names for watch parts, large scale drawings of a movement are reproduced on pages 21 to 26. These consist of views of the complete movement from the back and under the dial, and also of each part (except jewels and screws) drawn separately. All parts are clearly named.

All that part of a watch which is not the case is known as the movement. It includes the dial and hands and also the winding shaft and the winding button.

When the watch is received for repair it is advisable first to make an intelligent general examination of the watch as a whole, both case and movement. By *intelligent*, I mean that we must examine the movement with the intention of diagnosing the cause of the watch's failure to give good service. If it is just a matter of cleaning to re-oil, because the watch has been running beyond the prescribed time, then the cause is obvious, but for deeper trouble than that we must proceed first to examine the case. If it is bruised, make a special examination of the escapement and balance staff pivots ; the watch may have had a blow. Make sure the glass gives ample freedom for the hands. Failure to ensure that the hands are free of the glass and of each other is the cause of a high percentage of watch failures, the remedy is obvious. If when the case is opened you find the movement has an abnormal amount of dust in it, examine the case to find the reason ; it is useless to clean the movement and then replace it in a dust trap. A test made some time ago proved that dust penetrated what appeared to be a perfectly fitting case. The test was this : a watch was brought to a temperature of about 86 deg. F. (the average temperature of the pocket) and while still warm it was placed in a bin containing flour and allowed to remain there until the watch cooled down to the normal temperature in the bin, which was about 65 deg. F. The watch was then removed and the case opened, and upon examination the movement was found to be covered with flour. What happened was that with the heat the air had expanded. During the cooling off the air had contracted and to replace that lost, fresh air was sucked into the case and, with it, as we have seen, dust. So take particular care to examine all cases, and if they appear to be a good tight fit and, notwithstanding that, the movement was covered with dust, steps must be taken to render it more dust proof before the wearer finally takes delivery.

These observations apply also if it is desired to improve the water resisting properties of the case. Most watch cases will resist the entrance of water for momentary periods. That is, if a good watch is dropped into water and recovered immediately, very little harm may come to the movement, but continual soaking or use in a damp atmosphere, such as that encountered in the tropics, or in laundries and factories, is extremely detrimental to the movement, and a simple treatment applied to the case will greatly improve the resistance of the watch to climatic conditions.

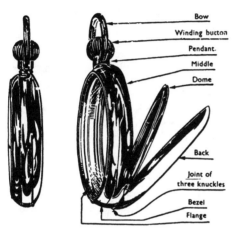

Fig. 22a. Pocket watch case.

When the final regulation is finished and it is not necessary to open the case again, mix a little beeswax with vaseline or petroleum jelly, one part beeswax to four parts vaseline, heated to make a stiff mixture, and smear this on the edges of the bezel and the back, so that when the back and bezel are snapped on, they close on to a film of wax. Also apply wax to the winding button so that when it is fitted on to the pendant it works in wax, and run wax round the edge of the glass.

Before proceeding to the subject of opening cases, which it is advisable to study before going much further, it should be mentioned that the metal frame in which the glass is fitted is known as the bezel, the body of the case into which the movement goes is termed the middle, while the back of the case is obvious. The back and bezel of the case will be fitted to the middle in one of three ways. They will snap on, be jointed, that is, hinged on, or they may screw on. Cases will frequently be found with a combination of these methods of fitting. Although it was a regular practice in the old days, it is now rare to find a bezel jointed to the watch ; it is snapped or screwed on.

Sometimes there are two backs to a case, one inside the other, the inner case being known as the dome. Many cases are now made so that the back and middle are in one piece, the movement fitting into the case

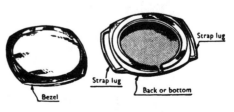

Fig. 22(b). Two-piece case.

from the front, the bezel being the only detached part. These are known as two-piece cases and, because they reduce the crevices through which dirt and damp can enter, are being favoured for wristlet more and more by designers.

The shapes of watch cases are legion. Undoubtedly the round case is the best from the aesthetic point of view as well as being the easiest to make and the best in use, but fashion must be served, and shapes will continue to vary. The application of the watch to the wrist is the primary cause of variation in the shape of cases and has also called for fittings for bracelets and wristlets, which have come to be known as lugs. The small tube through which the winding shaft enters the case is called the pendant, a term existing from the days when only pocket watches were known and the pendant carried a bow, to which the swivel of the watch chain was attached.

Leaving style for a moment and the very important question of waterproof cases, to which a whole chapter is devoted, let us now consider the safest method of opening the watch case. The first step is to determine the *method* of opening, and if it is not obvious do not start right away with a knife blade or screwdriver without having decided if the case actually snaps on. It may screw on or, if it is a waterproof case, have a special method of attachment.

Examine the edge of the back or the bezel for signs of previous opening. If it is a plain snap-on it is probable that a small portion of the case is filed away to give room for the knife or case opener to enter or for the thumb-nail to bear on. Sometimes there is a small lip provided for the same purpose. If a screwed-on case is suspected, lay the watch flat on the palm of the left hand glass down, place the palm of the right hand on the back and, with firm even pressure, apply an unscrewing motion with both hands. This usually moves the tightest screw. Some considerable force may be necessary but let that force be intelligently applied.

If you are satisfied that the back is not screwed on then proceed to open it with a blade. Hold the watch firmly in the left hand and the opener in the right as in Fig. 23. Insert the blade at the right place, that is, in the file mark or behind the lip. If there is no lip or mark, insert it opposite the joint ; but if there is no joint, then near the winding button, but not in such a manner that the blade when twisted causes pressure on the button. When the blade is well in between the back or bezel and the middle, give it a turn over so that the bottom edge of the blade levers on

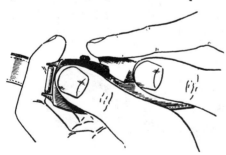

Fig. 23. The correct way to open a watch case.

to the snap-edge or rim on

the middle and the side of the blade pushes off the part you are endeavouring to remove. Do not turn the blade lengthwise so that the sharp edge cuts into both the parts being disengaged, doing this will only mark or damage the case and will not open it so easily.

Opening a case should be such a simple matter, but I have seen men gouging away with a screwdriver as if trying to bore a hole in it—and almost succeeding ! Often watches are found with cases badly damaged through clumsy attempts at opening. Screw cases sometimes bear evidence of attempts to force them open with a knife, and in such circumstances the thread is usually ruined. Joints are frequently strained, especially in shaped cases, because the opener has not been inserted opposite the joint. Opening a case without retaining full control over the opener often causes that instrument to slip across the back of the movement, badly scratching the plate in the process. *Damage such as this must be avoided, and it can be avoided*

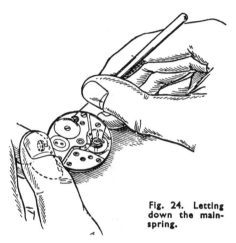

Fig. 24. Letting down the mainspring.

with just a little forethought and care. If the opener is held, as in the illustration, with the first finger as near the top of the blade as possible, it will act as a guide and a stop, and also give considerable pressure at the right spot with perfect safety.

The case being open, the movement can now have attention. Having opened the bezel let us next remove the hands, not only for safety but also because it is more convenient to do so before taking the movement out of the case. Make a pair of small levers as illustrated in Fig. 17 (page 9) ; they will remove the tightest hands without any risk of damage to the dial, even if it is made of delicate enamel. When using the levers on a metal dial it is advisable to place a small piece of paper under them to prevent marking the surface. Should there be a seconds hand it can be removed with the levers if there is sufficient space between the boss of the hand and the dial. Usually these hands fit so closely to the dial that it is not possible to get the levers underneath, and it is very dangerous to force a lever under one side, or to attempt to prise off a tight hand with the tweezers or screwdriver. It is better to remove the dial and the seconds hand in one operation. When the dial has been loosened ready for removing, prise it up with the blade of a knife near the seconds hand, and the hand will come away with it quite easily and safely on both metal and enamel dials. So far, the movement is still in the case, so that if it is not possible to remove the seconds hand with the levers it is advisable to let it remain until the movement is out of the case.

To take the movement out of the case, first loosen the pull-out piece screw 1 to 1½ turns and draw out the winding shaft. At this point it should be noted that there are two systems of fitting the winding shaft. The *positive*, with a long wind-

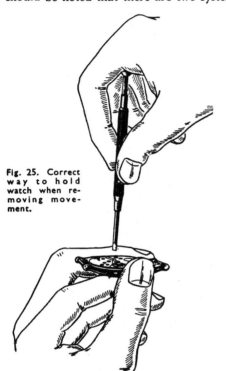

Fig. 25. Correct way to hold watch when removing movement.

ing shaft, is used almost invariably by Swiss manufacturers and is the type mostly met with in Great Britain. American manufacturers favour the *negative* system where the winding stem is short and fits into a small square hole in the top of the movement. Therefore, in American cases the winding shaft will not be removed but the button will be pulled out to the set-hands position. Having removed the winding shaft or pulled the negative-set button to the set-hands position, take the watch in the left hand as Fig. 25, with the joint of the first finger resting on the dial and the second and third fingers holding the case. Release the movement by removing the case screws, or giving them a part turn if they have half heads, so that they are free of the case. Case screws with half heads are usually called dog screws. If you now ease the first finger of the left hand the movement may be free ; I say may, because more often than not the movement sticks. If the movement is tight in the case turn the watch over, place a piece of tissue paper over the movement and apply a little pressure on the back plate at the extreme edge of the movement immediately opposite the pendant. Sometimes a steady-pin is located near the shaft. Hold the watch down on to the bench while doing this so that the released movement will just roll over on to its dial. See Fig. 26.

With the modern two-piece case, the movement is merely laid in and the bezel snapped or screwed on over it. The procedure with these watches is first to remove the bezel, then to pull the winding button into the set-hands position, and carefully ease the movement out by means of the winding shaft. Should it jam at any point a careful levering

Fig. 26.
Removing a
tightly fitting
movement.

up with the small screwdriver, making sure that the screwdriver is under the shoulder of the plate and not just under the dial, will help it out.

With the movement out we next remove the dial. Many modern watches are fitted with side screws to hold the dial in position. Do not remove them, but unscrew sufficiently to allow the dial to come away without exerting any force. It is important that force should never be used on a dial. If it is enamelled cracking is almost inevitable, and if the dial is made of metal, pressure will cause the dial to show a bump or indentation where the dial feet are fitted. When the dial has been removed, screw the dial screws up again directly to prevent them from working out and being lost.

The correct handling of a movement is a special technique which should be practised from the start so that even in moments of crisis—and many arise in the life of the watch repairer—the movement will be held without danger. It is a bad practice to allow the fingers to touch the plates or the dial (see Fig. 27) for not only does it stain and mark but, in the case of a finished movement so held, the oil may be sapped away from the pivots. Make it a definite habit always to hold the movement

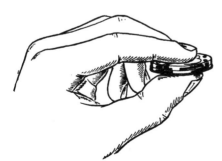

Fig. 27. How NOT to handle
a watch movement.

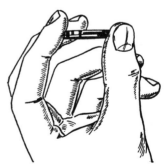

Fig. 28. The correct method.

correctly, and when the work is finished take the further precaution of holding the movement not only by the edges but in tissue paper also. There may be moisture or dust on the fingers, so slight as not to be visible but, as the barrel teeth project so that the fingers can come into contact with them, this moisture, dust or perspiration can be conveyed thereby to the centre pinion. Rusting centre pinions are sometimes encountered, and I am of the opinion that this is the cause.

When they are removed it is advisable to place the dial and hands away in a safe place as they are so easily damaged. Put them in a box or drawer, one of those miniature nests of drawers kept on the bench is most useful for this and many other purposes. The dial and hands will not again be wanted until the movement is finally reassembled.

When speaking of the main parts of the watch movement, the plates and bridges (which, when single ended, are known as cocks) are together called the frame. When viewing the movement in the case from the back, the plate visible is called the top plate. The plate which is actually the foundation of the watch movement and to which the dial is attached is known as the bottom plate.

CHAPTER FOUR

THE MOVEMENT, COMPONENTS AND DISMANTLING

WHEN the dial and hands are removed the face of the bottom plate carrying the motion work is visible. The motion work is the small reduction gear between the hour and minute hands. Remove these wheels and place them for the time being under a glass cover on the board paper. Old wineglasses broken at the stem make excellent work covers, and the watch repairer should make a point of collecting several of these in various sizes as and when he is able. *All parts as they are removed should be placed under cover.* It saves them from getting lost, damaged, damp or dirty, and even if the parts are in need of cleaning, it is still advisable to place them under a cover. It is a good habit, and one well worth cultivating.

Now turn the movement over and proceed to remove the balance. Be careful when the movement is on the bench with the bottom plate down, there will be two important parts projecting : the centre arbor which holds the cannon pinion and, if the watch has a seconds hand, the fourth wheel pivot, which projects through the plate. Keep these in mind when working on the movement from the back plate. Therefore hold the movement by the edge with the thumb and fingers so that it is bedded on the fleshy parts of the fingers, touching the bench only at the point where pressure is to be applied. With a screwdriver of the correct size, that is, one to fit the full length of the screw slot, take the screw out of the balance cock and with the stout tweezers carefully prise up the cock at the foot end. You will see a small slot cut out of the bottom of the foot to allow the point of the tweezers to enter. Hold the cock with the tweezers while you carefully prise it up and, when it is free of the steady pins, lift it off with the balance still attached. Take care that no undue force is employed. When the cock is free, the balance may be inclined to stick owing to the safety roller catching up on the lever fork, so that it is imperative that the balance be not pulled away for fear of distorting the balance spring. Should there be any inclination for the balance to stick, hold the balance cock still, keeping the right hand steady, and give a slight turn of the left hand to rotate the movement ; this should disengage the lever. It may be necessary to rotate the movement both to the left and to the right before the balance is free.

When the balance is free of the movement do not let it dangle at the end of the balance spring, but lower it steadily to the bench and, as the bottom pivot touches the bench, carefully turn the balance cock over with its index downwards, so that it rests flat. The balance will be inclined to turn over with the cock and it will facilitate matters if when turning the balance over you gently draw the balance along sideways a little while it still touches the board paper. If the balance does not turn over in the manner described, lift it carefully with the tweezers and place it so that the top balance pivot, now at the bottom, rests in the jewel hole.

This procedure of turning the balance is perfectly safe with the great majority of watches, but not all ; some watches are fitted with a soft balance spring. These soft springs are usually white in colour and if there is any doubt as to the hardness of the spring place the movement aside on the bench for a moment. Lower the balance so that the bottom pivot rests on the bench, then, holding the cock firmly with the left hand, loosen the balance spring stud screw, and the balance may fall away. Sometimes the curb pins will continue to hold the spring, and this is brought about by the downward pull of the balance causing the spring to twist between the pins and so become wedged. To release the spring give it a gentle turn with the fine tweezers held as near the pins as possible. There is also a type of balance spring stud which is secured to the top side of the balance cock, the stud lying along the top of the cock. Some Swiss, and most English watches, are made in this way, and in such instances the stud is unscrewed first while the balance cock is still in the movement, and upon the balance cock being lifted up, the balance and balance spring are left behind. The majority of watches with this type of stud are pocket watches, but there are a few wrist watches employing this principle to be found.

Assuming that the balance and cock have been removed complete and now lie on the bench upside down, take the foot of the balance cock between the thumb and first finger of the left hand, still holding it on the bench, unscrew the stud and lift the balance off the cock. It is not necessary or advisable to lift the balance cock during this operation. When lifting a balance away from a jewel hole, whether the balance is in the movement or just lying on the upturned balance cock, always give it a straight-up lift in order to avoid injuring the balance staff pivot. After releasing the balance spring stud retighten the screw.

Now turn the movement over and release the cannon pinion. For this operation hold the movement firmly in the left hand by the edges of the bottom plate and lightly grip the pinion with the brass lined pliers, giving it an anti-clockwise twist and a slight pull at the same time.

Turn the movement over again (be careful of the fourth wheel pivot) to commence dismantling the train, but before going any further make sure that the mainspring has been let down or, if it has not, wedge the train with a piece of pegwood. It is important always to test the mainspring tension of a watch train before touching the pallet cock. This is simply done by light pressure on the cross arm of the centre wheel or by gently touching over the lever.

The experienced man will remove the pallet cock and lift out the pallets, allowing the spring to run down under control of a finger brake on the edge of a wheel, but the safest method of letting down the spring is to hold the watch as Fig. 24 (see page 15) so that the button is lightly gripped between the thumb and forefinger, then release the click with the pointer and allow the button to revolve slowly between the fingers. When you feel you are losing control of the button release the click in order that it may re-engage the ratchet. The mainspring must never

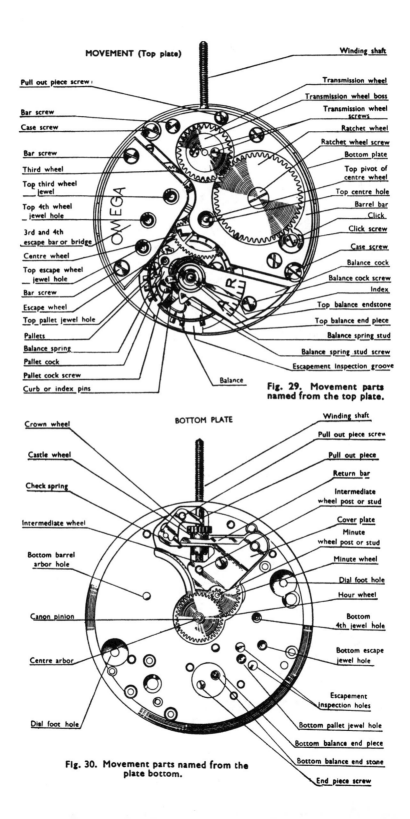

MOVEMENT (Top plate)

Winding shaft
Pull out piece screw
Transmission wheel
Bar screw
Transmission wheel boss
Case screw
Transmission wheel screws
Bar screw
Ratchet wheel
Third wheel
Ratchet wheel screw
Top third wheel jewel
Bottom plate
Top 4th wheel jewel hole
Top pivot of centre wheel
3rd and 4th escape bar or bridge
Top centre hole
Centre wheel
Barrel bar
Top escape wheel jewel hole
Click
Bar screw
Click screw
Escape wheel
Case screw
Top pallet jewel hole
Balance cock
Pallets
Balance cock screw
Balance spring
Index
Pallet cock
Top balance endstone
Pallet cock screw
Top balance end piece
Curb or index pins
Balance spring stud
Balance
Balance spring stud screw
Escapement inspection groove

OMEGA

Fig. 29. Movement parts named from the top plate.

BOTTOM PLATE

Crown wheel
Winding shaft
Castle wheel
Pull out piece screw
Check spring
Pull out piece
Intermediate wheel
Return bar
Bottom barrel arbor hole
Intermediate wheel post or stud
Cover plate
Minute wheel post or stud
Canon pinion
Minute wheel
Centre arbor
Dial foot hole
Hour wheel
Bottom 4th jewel hole
Bottom escape jewel hole
Escapement inspection holes
Dial foot hole
Bottom pallet jewel hole
Bottom balance end piece
Bottom balance end stone
End piece screw

Fig. 30. Movement parts named from the plate bottom.

BOTTOM PLATE
(From inside the movement)

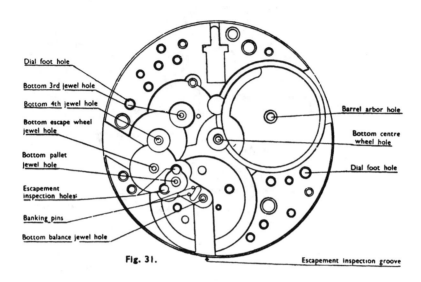

Dial foot hole

Bottom 3rd jewel hole

Bottom 4th jewel hole

Bottom escape wheel jewel hole

Bottom pallet jewel hole

Escapement inspection holes

Banking pins

Bottom balance jewel hole

Barrel arbor hole

Bottom centre wheel hole

Dial foot hole

Escapement inspection groove

Fig. 31.

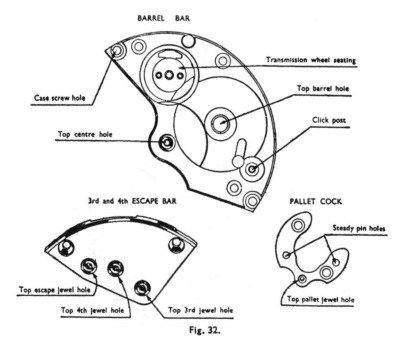

BARREL BAR

Transmission wheel seating

Case screw hole

Top barrel hole

Top centre hole

Click post

3rd and 4th ESCAPE BAR

PALLET COCK

Steady pin holes

Top escape jewel hole

Top 4th jewel hole

Top 3rd jewel hole

Top pallet jewel hole

Fig. 32.

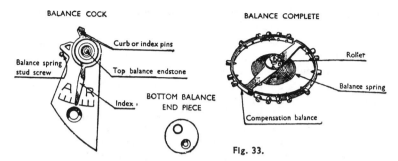

Fig. 33.

be let down with a jerk or the centre of the spring will be injured.

If the pallets are removed and the train allowed to run out its power with a rush, it is quite possible that a pivot may be ground off. I have known watches to run down when they have been dry and in so doing rip off an escape wheel pinion pivot. Having let down the spring, unscrew the pallet cock screws and remove them. I specially emphasize *remove the screws*, because a screw often appears quite free yet, when you attempt to lift the cock or bridge with the screw in position, it may still catch. Prise up the pallet cock and lay it aside. This will expose the pallets, which should be lifted straight up and away from the movement. The train may still have a little power left and run down for a few turns when the pallets are finally removed ; it is not always possible to let the mainspring down fully but so little power remains that no harm can come of this action. Having removed the pallets, replace the pallet cock screws in the holes in the pallet cock. To save constant reiteration it should be stressed here that every screw as it is removed should be associated with the part to which it belongs, thus saving considerable time when reassembling and sometimes preventing incorrect assembling. Screws which may be similar in size and thread are sometimes just a little different in length in order to clear springs of the keyless work, etc., and to use a screw that is too long may cause damage to another part, or prevent it from functioning correctly. These remarks more particularly apply to old watches. It is impossible to tighten fully a screw which is too long, and this will inevitably lead to a loose plate or part.

Now unscrew the escape third and fourth wheel bridge and remove the escape wheel. Next remove the ratchet wheel followed by the centre bridge, and take out the centre, third and fourth wheels. Next remove the barrel bridge and lift out the barrel. We are now left with the bottom plate with the hand setting mechanism attached to the underside. Usually the crown and castle wheels can be lifted straight out. It is not advisable to remove the pull-out piece screw yet. The pull-out piece may be held down by a check spring. Should this be so, remove the check spring and then unscrew the pull-out piece screw and remove the pull-out piece. Next remove the balance end piece. Sometimes this end piece plate sticks owing to the adhesion of the oil : to free this revolve the end piece a little so that if a point is placed in the screw hole from the other side the end piece can be pushed out. Returning to the barrel bridge, the transmission wheel can now be removed. This wheel is usually held with a left handed screw which must be turned clockwise to unscrew, though sometimes two right hand screws are used. Treat this screw with respect and try it gently in both directions without undue force until it moves. There have been many suggestions in the trade that left handed screws should carry some easily identifiable indication of the fact, such as a small spot on the head or two cuts, or other plain marking. Until the manufacturers reach a wise standardisation of marking it is as well to give every screw likely to be left handed the benefit of the doubt before applying force to remove it.

Carefully unscrew and remove the click and click spring.

Now turn your attention to dismantling the barrel. Insert a screwdriver blade in the slot in the cover and carefully lever it off. It should come away quite easily but if it sticks it can be loosened by brushing a little benzine round the edge and leaving it for a short period. Exercise great care when removing the barrel arbor. Hold the arbor with the stout tweezers and give it a slight clockwise turn to unhook the spring. The arbor should then draw away from the barrel.

Even greater precautions should be taken when removing the mainspring as—and this should be thoroughly apprehended—much trouble can be caused by clumsiness at this point. If the mainspring is forcibly extracted from the centre so that it has the shape of a cone when it is out, the spring is ruined. Once the mainspring adopts this shape it cannot be got back to the flat and will always give trouble by creating unnecessary friction against the barrel cover. To remove the spring in the correct way, hold the barrel in the tips of the fingers and with the strong tweezers give a slight pull at the centre. Do not pull more than is absolutely necessary ; in fact the word pull does not convey the correct action, we want rather to coax the spring out. When it starts to move, place the barrel in the palm of the left hand and carefully manipulate the spring with the fingers of the right hand. Do not let it come out suddenly. It is such a simple operation, yet so often badly done.

The movement is now in pieces and the parts are laid out on the bench under the glass dust cover. This is not the usual practice but, as I have mentioned before, the process of dismantling has been carefully explained step by step ; what to do with the parts will be fully explained in a later chapter on cleaning. At the moment we are now more or less familiar with the shape and function and, particularly with handling, all the various parts of the movement. Assume that the watch is being dismantled in the orthodox manner and examine the various actions as it is taken down.

If the student has been carefully following the instructions up to the present it is not bad practice, in the initial stages of study at any rate, to endeavour to replace the parts in the correct position, keeping in mind that

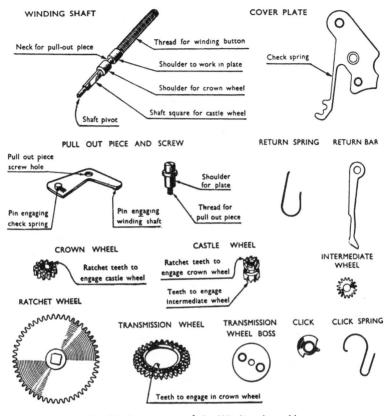

Fig. 34. Components of the Winding Assembly.

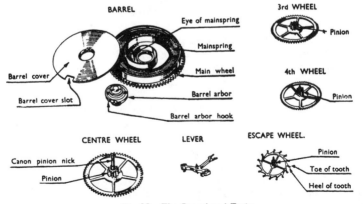

Fig. 35. The Barrel and Train.

in no case is force ever required for fitting up ; if a screw or a part does not fit easily it may be in the wrong position. Any student of average technical intelligence, having reached the stage of taking down the movement,

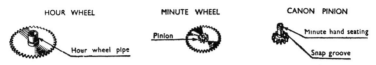

Fig. 36. The Motion Work.

should be able to replace the parts without any further instructions, so that if the watch were going before being dismantled it would be in going order when re-built. In the case of a watch stopping before being taken down it is not to be expected that simple dismantling and re-assembling will put it in going order. Something must be done to it and this something can only be discovered by careful testing and examination of each separate part, which is preferably done while the movement is being dismantled. Therefore the next section of the instructions will deal with the work in this way.

Before the dial is taken off examine the shake of the hour hand. Hold the hour hand near the collet with the tweezers and try to lift it up and down. The hour wheel, with the hand on and the minute hand in position, must have endshake. If it has none, remove the minute hand and try again ; if it then has endshake, it indicates that the hour hand needs to be let down further on to the wheel, or the top of the hour hand boss needs to be turned away. If, on the other hand, the hour wheel still binds, with the minute hand off, then the hour wheel pipe needs to be turned down. Usually you will find that the hour wheel has too much endshake, and if this is so, place an hour wheel collet on the hour wheel when re-assembling.

We now test the side play of the hour hand, i.e., the depth of the hour wheel in the minute wheel pinion. The hour hand must be perfectly free. Want of freedom may be due mainly to three faults : (a) Deep depth with the minute wheel pinion ; (b) Tight fit of the hour wheel pipe on the cannon pinion ; (c) Hour wheel pipe binding in the dial.

With the movement out of the case, and the dial either removed before or after this operation, examine the underside of the dial at the position immediately above the minute wheel to check the clearance between the minute wheel pinion and the dial. If there is lack of freedom at this point a rubbing mark will be observable. If the mark is of the very slightest, or there is any doubt, smear the top of the minute wheel pinion with oil, replace the dial and, with the button in the set-hands position, rotate the hands two or three times. Remove the dial and look for a trace of oil on the underside. This is an important test, because through it we discover whether the minute wheel is free when the movement is assembled and the dial in position. The freedom of the hour hand can easily be checked but this does not give any clue as to the freedom of the minute wheel.

A minute wheel which binds may not cause the watch to stop but it will have a detrimental effect on the timekeeping. The wheel may bind only at certain positions in its revolution but it may cause sufficient loss of power to bring about intermittent stoppage. Should there be evidence of fouling some means must be found of giving the right clearance, and there are two ways in which this can be effected. If the dial is enamelled a carborundum pencil will reduce the thickness at the back, or if the dial is metal a scrape with a knife may be sufficient. Should this fail, reduce the length of the minute wheel pinion. A carborundum pencil for grinding away enamel can be purchased from the tool shop, and is about the thickness of a lead pencil and 3 inches long.

Lay the dial face downwards flat on a piece of chamois leather on the bench—an old chamois watch bag answers well. Hold the dial down steady with the thumb and finger and, with the pencil in the right hand, moisten the end and rub at the spot indicated. Move the pencil in small circles and with a fair amount of pressure. Carborundum cuts quickly so it will not be long before the copper of the dial shows through ; it is not advisable to cut deeper. Sometimes it may only be necessary to grind until the mark made by the pinion is erased. Clean off the dirt which the carborundum pencil has made and, after smearing the minute wheel pinion with oil as before, try the dial on the movement. If there is still

Fig. 37. Scraping a metal dial.
A—Cork.
B—Chamois.
C—Tissue Paper.

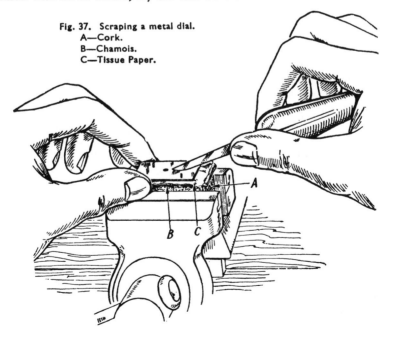

a sign that the pinion touches the dial, the length of the pinion will have to be reduced.

In the case of a metal dial, take a large cork, cut the top flat, and clamp it in the vice. Place the chamois leather on the cork, and over this a piece of tissue paper. This extreme care must always be taken in order not to mark the very delicate front surface of the dial as many dial finishes are bruised at the slightest touch. Hold the dial as before and scrape the affected part with a sharp knife, using diverse movements. Hardly any pressure should be used otherwise a bruise will appear on the face of the dial. It is better to make many light cuts than a few heavy ones. (See Fig. 37.) When all the pinion marks have been removed, scrape away a little more, and replace the dial, testing as before to see if the pinion is now free.

If the height of the minute wheel pinion is such that no amount of shaving or grinding on the back of the dial will give sufficient clearance, place the minute wheel on an arbor and turn down the top surface. Test in the movement again and, if quite free, finish off the top of the pinion in manner to that fully explained in *Making New Parts*, under-hand polishing. (See page 174.)

Before removing the hour wheel examine its depthing with the minute wheel pinion. Depths are dealt with in detail in Chapter 7, for the moment we will carry on with our examination of the motion work. It is advisable to cause the motion work to rotate so that the depthing can be checked at the four quarters. Several points must be looked over, the hour wheel may be out of round a little or the centre out of upright or the centre arbor may be bent. All these faults will result in a variation of the depths, which may be correct at one part and deep or shallow at another. Should it not be possible to correct the depthing and the hour wheel is still so deep at one part that it is likely to cause binding, it must be " topped " in order to free it. The use of the topping tool will be dealt with later. Topping the wheel may make a shallow depth at another part, but it will clear the part which binds, and I am of the opinion that a shallow depth is the least harmful. In any case, the discrepancy is not likely to be much in the case of the shallow depth, but it is important that the depthing should not be too deep, otherwise it will cause trouble when timing.

Now remove the hour wheel and examine the minute wheel depth with the cannon pinion. The same remarks apply exactly as for the hour wheel. Remove the minute wheel and hold the pinion in the tweezers, trying to turn the wheel with the fingers, in order to ensure that the wheel is tight on the pinion. Make a habit at this stage of testing the minute wheel post or stud with the tweezers to see that it is firm. Very occasionally you may find the minute wheel pinion or, more frequently, the stud loose. Both these points can give a great deal of trouble and can easily be over-looked if their examination is not made part of your habitual routine.

CHAPTER FIVE

LEVER ESCAPEMENT, EXAMINATION AND CORRECTION

AT THIS point it is advisable to consider means of holding the movement. Many experienced repairers prefer to hold the movement in the finger tips, while others, equally expert, prefer to use a little stand called a movement holder. Movement holders of various sizes are required and for the various shaped movements special devices can be obtained. In any event, it is preferable to acquire an aptitude to hold the movement in the fingers. With the top-plate uppermost, first check up the endshake of the balance staff. Here let us insert two small definitions :

Endshake is the movement available when the distance between the endstones is greater than the length of the staff; sideshake is the movement available when the diameter of the jewel hole is greater than the diameter of the pivot.

Necessarily the distance between the endstones and the diameter of the jewel holes must be greater than the length of the staff or the diameter of the pivot and these differences in the measurements give working freedom.

It is difficult to say how much endshake a staff should have ; it must be perceptible and the staff must move freely, but the clearance should be the minimum which would comply with these requirements. If one says that the staff should be free to move, the statement indicates what is necessary rather than defines it. Naturally the size of the escapement has much to do with it and a large staff will have more freedom of movement than a small one. In this case the freedom is a matter of proportion. No doubt the manufacturers have methods of measuring the clearance, but such methods are not available to the repairer ; he must depend on his experience in this small but extremely important matter. Some watch repairers compare the amount of endshake with some other part of the watch, such as the thickness of the balance spring, others give a definite measurement, whilst some content themselves with saying that it must be perceptible. If we are examining a 13 ligne watch a suitable amount of endshake would be .02 of a mm. As a rough indication of what this distance means, the thickness of the paper on which this book is printed averages 0.1 of a mm. You will see from the foregoing that there is considerable latitude in the matter and the same observation can be made about the sideshake, that is, the freedom of the pivot in its hole. Therefore lightly hold the balance arm with the tweezers, move it up and down to feel the endshake, and decide whether it is perceptible or whether it has too much movement. Generally speaking, if the movement is measureable it is far too much.

A very closely fitting pivot, either in endshake or sideshake, is likely to stop the watch or affect the rate for, although the pivot might move freely when tried, it does not allow a full thickness of lubrication. In addition, and this is decidedly more serious, the balance staff may not be dead upright.

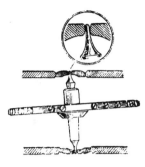

Fig. 38. Balance staff out of upright and binding the pivots.

Most watches, including many of good quality, are full of very minor errors ; it is a condition which has to be tolerated, and one of the most frequent of these slight faults is the question of upright generally. The inclination of a pinion from the vertical may be so slight that it is not perceptible and hardly measureable, except by means of a very fine instrument made specially for the job. Microscopic faults of this character are checked at the factories on projection machines the parts of movements are enlarged many times by projection so that such a fault as slight variation from upright of a pinion would then be observable. Since there must always be clearance between the pivots and the jewels it may be taken for granted that perfect uprightness is never achieved. Therefore, if the pivots of the staff, or any of the pinions in the train, fitted dead into the jewel hole the binding condition illustrated in Fig. 38 (which is exaggerated) could, and in all probability would, arise, quite apart from the question of lubrication.

The above statements may at first glance appear hypothetical, but in fact they are not. What I wish to convey is that if the pivots are an exact fit—and by exact I mean real precision—and if the holes are absolutely upright, then, and only then, would the part be free. Such a degree of precision does not exist in a watch, so in order to accommodate for this we must be just a little generous in our fitting.

The application of oil between two surfaces has the effect of introducing a series of molecular rollers between those surfaces. If these rollers or layers are too thin, by reason of the close fit, the full advantages of lubrication would not be obtained. If, on the other hand, the close fitting of the staff pivots became our whole concern, then more or less elaborate arrangements would be made to achieve this object. But tight fitting is obviously not required, so that when finishing a pivot make it a smooth sliding fit in the jewel hole, just fitting, so that the jewel hole will drop off of its own weight, and then give the pivot a final polish of two or three strokes with the burnisher to obtain the required little bit of extra freedom.

To test the balance staff pivots for sideshake the watch should be held as in Fig. 39, with the tip of the first finger steadied on the edge of the plate and the fleshy part lightly touching the arm of the balance. Now with the slightest movement the balance can be rocked from side to side, thus testing freedom of both the top and bottom pivots. Rock the balance very slowly, and with a strong glass examine

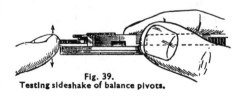

Fig. 39.
Testing sideshake of balance pivots.

the top pivot by looking under the balance cock. Then give the same examination to the bottom pivot by looking through to the side of the pallet cock. The pivots cannot be seen, but the staff should be carefully observed as near to the pivots as possible. I mention this because there is a temptation to attempt the examination of sideshakes by looking through the endstones ; this is not satisfactory even if all the oil has been removed. The ends of the pivots are small and rounded, and unless there is an excess of sideshake the amount of movement is not pronounced enough to be able to judge whether it is correct or not. To my mind it is not a good test. There is latitude here, just as there is in the amount of endshake, but it must be borne in mind that too little sideshake may cause the watch to stop or affect its rate, and too much sideshake would certainly give a bad rating in positions. Another test of sideshake is to place the balance as Fig. 40 : it should be possible to rock it approximately 5° from the perpendicular on each side.

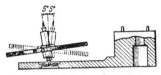

Fig. 40. Sideshake of the balance staff should not permit a movement of more than 5 degrees from the vertical.

As a further method of testing the endshake of the balance staff, light pressure can be applied to the top balance endstone when the watch is finally assembled and going in its case. With a pointed piece of pegwood press lightly on the top endstone ; if the balance stops or the vibration of the balance falls off immediately this slight pressure is applied, then the endshake is too close. If, on the other hand, considerable pressure can be applied without effect on the balance, then the endshake is too generous. A proviso to be borne in mind, however, is that the strength of the balance cock must be considered. A thin or weak balance cock will not stand the same pressure as a stouter one, and here again we must rely on discretion and experience.

If the foregoing instructions have conveyed insufficient indication as to the correct amount of endshake required, examine a watch which has been passed as correct by an experienced watch repairer. Just a final word : the endshake of the balance can be tested by listening intently when the movement, in its case, is turned over. Press the watch flat against the ear and move the head smartly from side to side, when you should hear the balance staff pivots fall on their respective endstones. This test is possible with

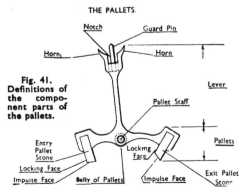

THE PALLETS.

Notch

Guard Pin

Horn

Horn

Fig. 41. Definitions of the component parts of the pallets.

Lever

Pallet Staff

Entry Pallet Stone

Locking Face

Pallets

Locking Face

Impulse Face

Belly of Pallets

Impulse Face

Exit Pallet Stone

watches from about 10½ ligne size and upwards. In smaller watches the balance is too light to be heard. The test serves a dual purpose. It indicates if there is any endshake at all and with experience it is possible to determine if the endshake is of the requisite amount and whether the pivots are free in the jewel holes.

If the case is held with the back to the right ear and the head moved smartly to the left, the top balance pivot will be heard striking the end-stone. Now if the head is moved slowly back again and the fall of the pivot is not discernible, it will indicate that the pivot sticks in its hole. It requires a little practice to become proficient, and to know immediately if the endshake is correct or to ascertain if the pivots are free or which pivot is sticking or binding, but this operation can be practised quite simply until proficiency is attained.

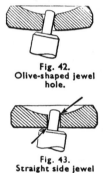

Fig. 42.
Olive-shaped jewel hole.

Fig. 43.
Straight side jewel hole.

The advantage of the olive-shaped jewel hole (Fig. 42) is that if the hole is slightly out of upright it will not have a tendency to bind and, furthermore, a greater reserve of oil is possible. The straight side hole (Fig. 43) would cause the pivot to wedge, as it were, at top and bottom if out of upright. Quite apart from the great advantage of the foregoing, which in itself is sufficient to commend it, the surface friction of the olive hole is considerably less than that of the straight side hole.

The next important feature of the escapement to be examined and checked is the position on the locking face of the pallet stone where the escape tooth rests when the pallet arrests the wheel. To examine this the balance, complete with balance cock, must be removed from the movement, and this is the point at which to test the endshake and the sideshake of the pallet staff. Remarks, and tolerances, applicable to the balance staff apply also in this instance, with the exception that the pallet staff should have a little less endshake than the balance staff. Also, unless a pallet staff is fitted with endstones, the endshake will be controlled by the shoulders of the pivots.

Some control over the movement of the lever is essential when examining the locking, and this may be obtained by folding a small slip of paper and placing it under the lever to act as a wedge (see Fig. 45). The thickness of the paper required depends on the distance between the lever and the bottom plate, some movements will take a piece of notepaper while others require only tissue paper. The slight springiness of the paper will act as a brake to steady the lever and keep it in the required position.

Fig. 45. A piece of thin paper folded and inserted under the lever forms a convenient brake.

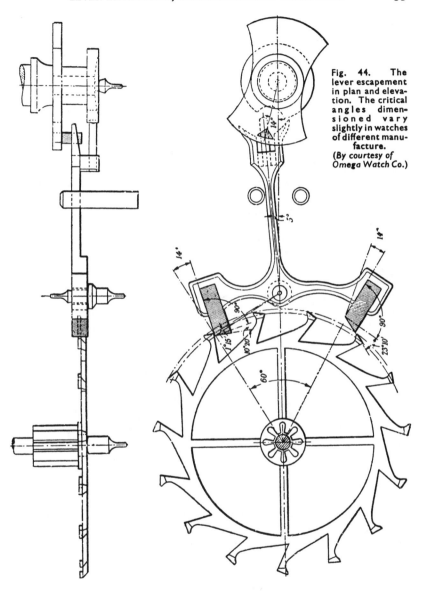

Fig. 44. The lever escapement in plan and elevation. The critical angles dimensioned vary slightly in watches of different manufacture. (*By courtesy of Omega Watch Co.*)

Let the mainspring right down. With a pointed piece of pegwood move the lever over and so arrange that an escape wheel tooth rests on the impulse face of the entry pallet stone. The pallet stones are named entry and exit, the reason being obvious (Fig. 41). As the escape wheel turns the entry stone is struck on its outside face by the heel of the escape tooth, whereas the exit pallet is struck on the inside face, these two faces being known as the locking faces. The ends of the pallet stones which are ground off at an angle are called the impulse faces. The action of the escape tooth on the pallet surface is first to hit it, which stops the wheel revolving ; but there is power behind the wheel which continues to exert pressure on the locking face, and the locking face must be at such an angle to the teeth that this pressure tends to draw the pallet further into mesh with it. This is called the draw. The slight movement which drawing down the pallet stones gives to the lever is called the run to the banking. The next action is the swing of the balance freeing the pallet stone from the lock and allowing the escape wheel to continue its revolution. In doing this the tooth passes along the impulse face of the pallet stone and escapes entirely from the control of the pallet. Meanwhile the opposite pallet has been brought into position for another tooth of the escape wheel to lock on its inside face, when exactly similar operations of draw, run to the banking, and impulse, are repeated. This rough description of the functioning of the lever escapement is introduced here in order to define the various terms which will be used in the next few paragraphs. Study Fig. 48.

To return to our examination of the locking of the entry pallet : gently move the escape wheel forward with the pointer so as to cause the lever to travel as the tooth slides along the impulse face. When the tooth drops off the pallet stone, observe very closely with the double eyeglass the exact position where the corresponding tooth rests on the exit pallet.

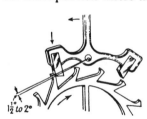

Fig. 46. Correct locking should not exceed 2 degrees.

There are two inspection holes immediately beneath the pallet stones, and if the movement is held two to three inches away from the board paper on the bench so as to light up the escapement by reflection, the amount of locking can be checked. To be correct, it should be approximately two degrees of the arc of a circle of which the pallet staff is the centre (rather less than more), drawn from the pallet staff as indicated in Fig. 46.

Without an elaborate instrument it is not possible to measure 2° but you will be able to carry in your mind's eye the correct depth of locking, after studying Fig. 46. Now move the lever in the reverse direction a shade so that the tooth is on the impulse face of the exit pallet and apply a forward pressure to the escape wheel to impel the lever, at the same time very closely observing the locking of the entry stone. Repeat this test on each stone fifteen times, that is with each separate tooth of the escape wheel, to ensure that all the teeth lock safely ; there is a danger that the escape wheel may be a little out of round. If this method of testing is adopted a more accurate inspection is obtained than by simply winding the mainspring and moving the lever backwards and forwards to examine the locking under power. On the other hand, if the watch has passed through your hands before and you have made a meticulous examination of the locking, and the watch comes to you with a good record, then testing the locking under the power of the mainspring should suffice.

If on any tooth the entry stone mislocks, i.e., the escape tooth drops direct on the impulse face instead of first dropping on the locking face, the repairer's reaction may be to draw that stone out to make it deeper. But before making this considerable alteration to the adjustment of the escapement, consider the position of the exit pallet as well.

Increasing the depth of the entry stone automatically increases the lock on the exit stone, and it is therefore necessary, when drawing out the entry stone, to compensate this by pushing in the exit stone an equivalent amount. But consider the case where the entry stone is too deep and the exit stone on the deep side, but not too deep. This fault can be checked simply by moving the entry stone back a little, which will correct the exit stone without actually touching it. So before moving either stone always study them as a pair, and visualise what will happen before any movement is made.

The stones are secured in their slots by shellac. They should just fit in the slot to leave room for the film of shellac to hold them. This being the case, the stones become movable when the shellac is softened by heating.

It will be noticed that, except in very fine watches where the stones are accurately fitted, there is a slight plate or shield of shellac on the back, or underside of the pallets. Place the lever on the bluing pan (see Fig. 18, page 9) shellac side uppermost, and close to the work, by the side of the pallets, place a small loose piece of shellac to act as a guide to the amount of heat required. Hold the pan over the flame of the spirit-lamp until the test piece of shellac is soft. It is important not to go beyond this point or the shellac will run. Shellac swells when heated, and if it is made too hot the stones are forced out of position. When sufficiently warm place the pan on a piece of wood or some other material to insulate it from the bench, and with a pair of stout tweezers in the left hand hold the lever steady on the warm pan as Fig. 47, and with another pair of tweezers carefully move the pallet stones as required. It is advisable to apply only the minimum of heat necessary to enable the stones to be moved, and thus ensure that the adhesive properties of the shellac are not destroyed. The test piece of shellac can be examined and touched to find when the stones can be moved in preference to touching the shellac of the pallets. It may be necessary to make one or two alterations before the locking is correct, and it is essential to replace the pallets

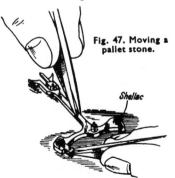

Fig. 47. Moving a pallet stone.

Shellac

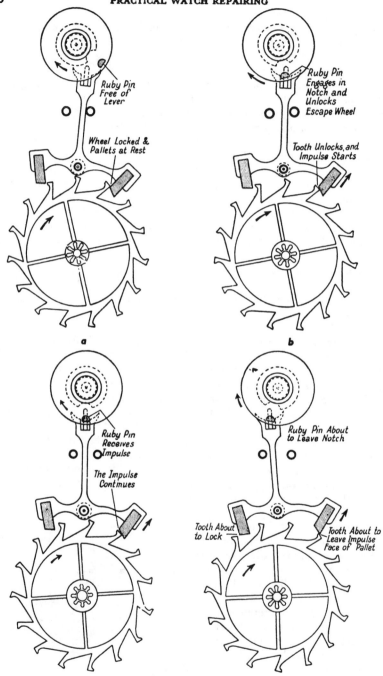

Ruby Pin
Free of
Lever

Wheel Locked &
Pallets at Rest

a

Ruby Pin
Engages in
Notch and
Unlocks
Escape Wheel

Tooth Unlocks, and
Impulse Starts

b

Ruby Pin
Receives
Impulse

The Impulse
Continues

c

Ruby Pin About
to Leave Notch

Tooth About
to Lock

Tooth About to
Leave Impulse
Face of Pallet

d

Fig. 48. A series of diagrams showing what happens at every point of the escapement
except the balance spring, within 1/5th of a second.

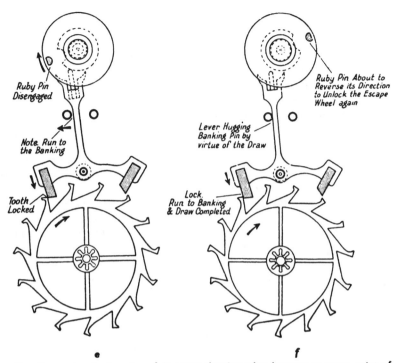

Fig. 48—*continued.* A series of diagrams showing what happens at every point of the escapement except the balance spring, within 1/5th of a second.

e With the lever hard against the banking pin the escape wheel is locked against the exit pallet ; ruby pin is about to enter the lever fork. Balance is free and is swinging in the direction of the arrow.

b Balance continues its movement, guard pin is brought opposite the crescent, ruby pin engages notch in lever fork which lifts exit pallet enough to unlock escape wheel ; pressure of escape wheel tooth on face of exit pallet starts impulse.

c With train now driven by mainspring, escape wheel revolves ; continued sliding pressure on impulse face of exit pallet gives full impulse which is transmitted to balance via lever fork and ruby pin.

d The lever pivoting about its arbor now brings the entry pallet within reach of the next operative tooth of the escape wheel.

e The escape wheel locks on the edge of the entry pallet and if the banking pin were so positioned as to permit no further movement of the lever, no further action would take place. But the position of the banking pin purposely permits a slight further movement, so the continued pressure of the escape wheel tooth continues the movement of the pallet, until the lever is arrested by the banking pin. This movement of tooth and pallet is the " draw," and the movement of the lever during the duration of the draw is the " run to the banking." The balance is again free and continues its swing.

f The escapement is now locked and the balance continues its swing until arrested and reversed by the balance spring.

in the movement each time in order to check off each alteration. Finally examine the locking and impulse faces of the pallets for traces of shellac; if it has spread, it can readily be chipped off with a screwdriver blade. Also, before making any alterations, examine the locking and impulse faces and the locking corner, with the strong glass, for chips or pits due to wear. If the impulse face is pitted it is due to mislocking, a heavy escape wheel, or possibly, a heavy train. Should the surface be defective, the stones must be replaced without hesitation or the timekeeping will suffer.

New pallet stones are supplied by the tool shops ready for setting ; it is necessary to send the lever for fitting, as the stone must fit the slot. Fitting a new pallet stone is a very similar operation to that already explained for adjusting the pallet stones. Place the pallets on the bluing pan, and push the stone into position, making sure it is the right way up, and on top of the stone, at the back end, place a small piece of shellac. Now hold the pan over the flame until this piece of shellac melts and flows over the top surface of the stone. Remove the pan from the flame and set it down on a piece of wood on the bench.

Hold the lever with the tweezers in one hand and, with a pair of tweezers in the other hand, draw the stone in and out so as to work the shellac between the stone and the sides of the slot. When finally pushed into position see that the shellac has formed a plate over the stone. If the movement of the stone has disturbed the plate, re-heat to make the shellac flow again. Replace the pallets in the movement and check their position. If it is necessary to make adjustments, as it most likely will be, proceed as previously explained. Finally remove all traces of shellac from the stone and the metal part of the pallets other than the plate of shellac on the underside. Of course, with the finer quality of movement, where no shellac shows on the original stones because they fit particularly well, all visible traces of shellac should be removed.

Having achieved a satisfactory locking, that is, having set the pallet stones exactly at the required depth, the run to the banking must next be checked. As explained earlier, this is the movement of the lever towards the banking pin immediately after the locking. Unlocking involves a slight recoil of the train. With this test the mainspring is wound up one or two turns and the lever wedged, as before, with a piece of folded paper. Move the lever slowly but steadily until the tooth has just fallen on the locking face of the pallet stone. Note the distance the lever is now away from the banking pin and continue to move the lever until it is stopped hard against the pin. This movement should be perceptible and Fig. 49 indicates the approximate amount. To give a rough physical idea of the amount of movement between the lever and the banking pin, it should be equal to about the thickness of the balance spring. The run to the banking should be equal on both bankings. This run deepens the locking and is actually a wasted effort since it increases the amount of

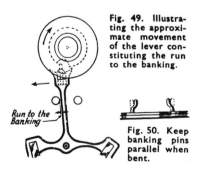

Fig. 49. Illustrating the approximate movement of the lever constituting the run to the banking.

Run to the Banking

Fig. 50. Keep banking pins parallel when bent.

power required to unlock. It is essential to the action of the escapement, however, to provide for the freedom of the guard pin. It allows for draw to ensure the free entry of the ruby pin into the lever notch, as we shall presently see.

If there is too much run to the banking, the bankings obviously must be closed, that is, the banking pins must be brought nearer together. Where banking pins are fitted, this is a simple matter, as they can easily be bent inwards, *but it is essential that the pins be kept parallel*, as shown in Fig. 50, or the run will vary in the dial-up position. In the case of solid bankings it is not quite so simple. A cut is made near the banking face to form a post or pin which can be bent inwards (see Fig. 51). This cut can be made with a screw-head file. If there is not sufficient run the solid banking can be cut away as indicated in Fig. 52. American watches are usually provided with banking pins set eccentrically in the ends of screws, so that by simply turning the screws the bankings can be opened or closed and yet remain parallel. Should there

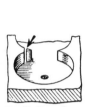

Fig. 51. To reduce width of solid bankings.

Fig. 52. To widen solid bankings.

be insufficient run to the banking then bend the pins outwards if they are not fitted into screws, still taking care to keep them parallel.

There are other forms of bankings fitted in diverse models of watches but the principle of opening and closing is always the same.

When the great English watchmaker and inventor, Thomas Mudge (1715–1794), invented the lever escapement in the year 1765, he endeavoured to make it a dead beat escapement, and did not discover the necessity for the " draw ". The result was that he made about two samples and was not encouraged to proceed. It is possible that he found something of far more interest to occupy his time since he did a considerable amount of research work on the marine chronometer.

It was not until Josiah Emery (1770–1805), a Swiss watchmaker resident in England, introduced the " draw " that the lever escapement was really detached. Until then, about 1780, the lever escapement was not in general use. Some authorities attribute this improvement to A. L. Breguet (1747–1823)

As we have previously explained, if the locking face of the pallet is inclined a little from a radial line drawn from the centre of the escape wheel, the pressure of the tooth draws the pallet down, forcing the lever against the banking pin, see Fig. 54. To test the draw, give the mainspring a couple of turns, remove the paper wedge, and carefully move the lever so that a tooth of the escape wheel is just about to leave the locking face of the pallet, and then, at this precise moment, if the lever is suddenly released, it should fly back to the banking on which it originally rested. Test both pallets in this fashion. This test is very important as it ensures that the guard pin is kept free of the safety roller. Without draw the watch would function satisfactorily if it were kept stationary in a horizontal position, but as such a condition is not practicable in use, it is essential that the lever should have draw.

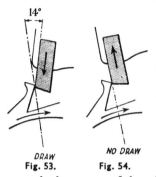

14°

DRAW
Fig. 53.

NO DRAW
Fig. 54.

What would happen if there were no draw, is that a slight jar would jerk the pallets, so that the guard pin would rub on the safety roller. It will be seen that the run to the banking facilitates the draw.

Fig. 54 shows a pallet stone set radially and it can at once be realised that the tendency of the escape wheel tooth is to push the pallet up and away from the wheel. Glancing at the other condition, Fig. 53, with the stone set at an angle, it is readily understood that the pallet will be drawn towards the centre of the wheel.

If there is no draw, or if it is weak, that is, if the lever does not fly back smartly to the banking when tested according to the above instructions, proceed as follows : Let the mainspring down and remove the pallets from the movement. Place them on the bluing pan, shellac side up, again place a small piece of shellac by the side of the pallets as a heat guide. Heat until the test piece of shellac is soft, remove the pan from the flame and place it on the bench ; then while holding the lever steady on the bluing pan with a pair of tweezers, push the pallet stone needing adjustment to one side, as indicated in Fig. 55, with the clock oiler. Still holding both the tools in position, blow on the pallets to cool and set the shellac.

It is not sufficient merely to push the stone to one side and take the lever off the bluing pan. The amount it is necessary and possible to move the stone to correct the draw is so slight that if the stone is not held in position until the shellac sets, it is likely

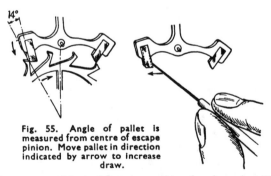

Fig. 55. Angle of pallet is measured from centre of escape pinion. Move pallet in direction indicated by arrow to increase draw.

to return to its original wrong position. If upon testing the draw is still not sufficient, the pallet stone must be changed for one very slightly narrower. In some pallets it may be possible to open the slot a shade ; the best tool with which to do this is the lever notch polisher, which will be described later. I have never yet come across a pair of pallets that have too much draw, so that I do not think the question of correction in this direction arises.

The next test is to make sure that the escape wheel is of the correct size. The test is made by checking it for inside and outside shake. With the lever in position, give the mainspring one or two turns and replace the paper wedge. Move the lever so that a tooth of the escape wheel is resting on the locking face of the entry pallet. Now *very carefully* move the lever so that the tooth is just about to unlock and, when in this exact position, try the shake of the escape wheel. The heel of one tooth will be arrested by the entry pallet, and the toe of the fourth tooth from it will be arrested by the back of the exit pallet; see Fig. 56, where the amount

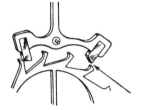

Fig. 56.
Arrow
indicates
outside
shake.

Fig. 57.
Arrow
indicates
inside
shake.

of freedom is indicated. This is known as the outside shake. Now move the lever over so that the exit pallet arrests a tooth, arrange matters so that the tooth is just about to unlock, and check again. Here we have only three teeth spanned by the pallet stones, and Fig. 57 indicates where inside shake should be checked.

The apparent freedom of the outside shake and the inside shake should be equal. Little or no outside shake and an excess of inside shake shows that the escape wheel is too small. An absence of inside shake, and an excess of outside shake means that the escape wheel is too large, and the only remedy in both cases is to change the escape wheel for one the correct size. Fortunately, the necessity for changing the escape wheel owing to its incorrect size does not often arise. If the outside and inside shakes are not the same (there may be a little more freedom to the outside than the inside, or vice versa), it is not necessary to go to any trouble to correct it unless, of course, there is any indication of binding because of the lack of freedom or shake, when the wheel must be changed.

Another term which requires definition is the angle. In reality it is the alignment of the lever. The term has been handed down from the old English escapement makers whose levers, being made separately from the pallets, were pinned to them at a definite angle. (See Chapter 18, page 237.) The term, angle, also refers to the angular movement of the lever, and we hear of " high angled " or " low angled " escapements. We are not concerned here with the manufacturer's problem of which type of escapement he uses in designing his watch, so that when the term angle is used in these instructions it refers to the alignment of the lever.

To test for angle place the lever in position, give the mainspring one or two turns, and replace the folded paper wedge. Move the lever with the pegwood pointer, and directly a tooth of the escape wheel drops off the pallet, hold the pointer away, carefully noting the position of the tip of the guard pin in relation to the outer edge of the bottom jewel hole ; it may just be pointing to the extreme edge or perhaps a little inside the edge. Now move the lever over to the other side and repeat the procedure, again noting the position of the guard pin. For the lever to be in angle it should be in the exactly corresponding position with relation to the jewel hole, see Fig. 58. In other words, the lever should move an equal amount on both sides of the centre of the bottom balance jewel hole. This test may appear somewhat crude but it answers satisfactorily.

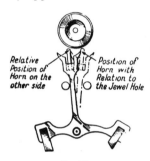

Relative Position of Horn on the other side — Position of Horn with Relation to the Jewel Hole

Fig. 58.
Test for angle of the lever.

The correct test is to place the balance in position without the balance spring but with the mainspring partly wound and the lever wedged. Make the balance bind by placing a bristle from the watch brush under the back of the balance cock. The bristle takes up the endshake of the balance staff and thus holds the balance slightly friction tight. Now move the balance round carefully until a tooth of the escape wheel has dropped and, at that precise moment, rotate the balance more slowly than before, noting the amount the lever is moved by the ruby pin after the tooth has dropped off. Reverse the motion of the balance and repeat the procedure in the opposite direction of rotation. To be correct, the movement on each side should be equal, though in a fine escapement there should be no movement of the lever at all. Even in a fine movement it may not always be possible to carry out the angle test in this manner with the straight line lever escapement. Some movements are so designed that it can be done; but in the majority you will find that it is difficult to observe the lever when testing.

For the above test the balance spring must be dismounted from the staff and in doing this the balance is bound to come in for a certain amount of handling. When holding the balance *always grip it at the opposite ends of the arms,* and avoid any pressure that is likely to distort the rim if it is a cut balance, see Fig. 59. Now take a tool similar to the clock oiler illustrated in Fig. 11a, page 7, and insert the blade in the slot of the balance spring collet. Hold the balance firmly and

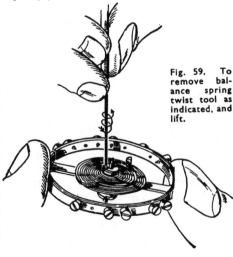

Fig. 59. To remove balance spring twist tool as indicated, and lift.

give the tool an anti-clockwise twist, at the same time pulling away from the balance. You will find that this slight movement will release the tightest collet with perfect safety. Sometimes you may find that the slot in the collet is so wide that the blade of the oiler will not be effective. In this case use a tool with a thin sharp edge that can be inserted under the collet. A flat needle file with the end stoned sharp answers quite well, as is indicated in the sketch, Fig. 60.

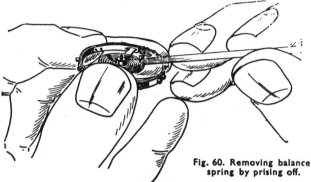

Fig. 60. Removing balance
spring by prising off.

Let us study a definite case for correction of a faulty angle. The escape tooth has just dropped on to the entry pallet and the guard pin points to the outer edge of the jewel hole. On the other side the guard pin points beyond the outer edge, indicating that the lever needs to be bent towards the centre of the jewel hole. To do this proceed as follows : Remove the pallets and ascertain whether the metal of which they are made is hard or soft. The brass and bronze coloured levers are obviously soft, but some of the white coloured levers need testing. Just try to dig the point of a needle into the metal from the underside : if the needle sticks or drags the metal is soft, but if the needle slides the metal is hard, or at least too hard for us to bend with safety. This method of discovery is something like the gemmologists' hardness test for precious stones, but in place of a diamond point we are utilising a steel needle as a standard of hardness. If the lever proves soft, it can safely be bent with the tool illustrated in Fig. 61.

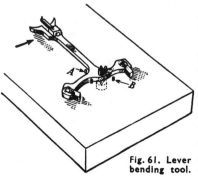

This tool is not procurable ready made but is quite easy to make. A piece of brass about 2 inches square and 2 mm. thick forms the base. Drill a hole through the centre large enough for the pallet arbor to drop into and also allowing sufficient freedom for the lever to be moved over

Fig. 61. Lever so as to contact the pins, four of
bending tool. which should be fitted about 2 mm.

away from the hole and about 2 mm. high.   The illustration should make this perfectly clear.   The pallets should be placed upside down on the tool, as indicated, and the lever pushed over as required with a piece of peg-wood.   In the case in point the lever must be bent as indicated by the arrow, and the pins A and B on the tool will take the pressure.   When bending pressure is applied to the lever the force *must* be taken by the pins and not by the arbor in the hole.   It is most advisable to make only slight alterations at a time and test the lever frequently in the movement.   When using this simple tool we have no great control over the bending movement of the lever, therefore *care and caution must be exercised* lest we may be bending the lever backwards and forwards to no good purpose.

If the lever is of hard metal it must be peaned, that is, the metal is caused to curl by dispersal and compression at a certain point.   To do this, hold the lever on a stake, or punch, held in the vice, and with another chisel-shaped punch (with a well rounded edge) tap the side of the lever as indicated in Fig. 62.   This will cause the lever to curl upwards.

Fig. 62. Peaning the lever. The lever will curl up as indicated by the arrows.

By using this method we have considerable control over the movement of the lever, but even so it is advisable to make very slight alterations at a time, and to test the movements frequently. The punch may mark the side of the lever, but the marks can be readily removed with a polisher and oilstone dust and oil.   Instructions on using the polisher will be given later, when dealing with making new parts.

Testing for angle will also reveal if the lever is of the correct length. After an escape wheel tooth has dropped off the pallet stone, note the amount of movement of the lever before the ruby pin is free of the notch. It was said that in a well designed and well made escapement the movement would be nil or negligible, and if it prove so it indicates that the lever is of the correct length.   Should there be con-siderable movement of the lever before the ruby pin is free of the notch, the lever is too long.   To help decide whether to shorten the lever or not, it should be pointed out that it is usually safe for the lever to move a little after the escape wheel tooth has dropped on to the locking face and the ruby pin is still in contact with the lever notch, so that when the ruby pin is quite free of the notch it is possible for the pointer to move the lever still further to the banking. The amount it is possible to move the lever after the ruby pin is free of the notch is the run to the banking.   If this movement is negligible the lever should be shortened.

On the other hand the lever is too short if, when making the balance move round so that the ruby pin engages in the notch, it disengages before the escape wheel tooth has locked. Such a condition is quite possible and the watch will still function. This action of impulse takes place at some speed, and if the momentum of the balance moved the lever so that locking took place, the balance would not receive its full impulse, with consequent weak vibration and subsequent effect on the timing.

Should it be decided that the lever is too long, proceed to shorten it in the following manner. Remove the guard pin which is fitted in from the pallet stones end and should be pushed out towards the pallet stones. It is advisable to cut the pin short before attempting to remove it. The tool illustrated here (Fig. 63) is useful for this purpose. Use an old pair

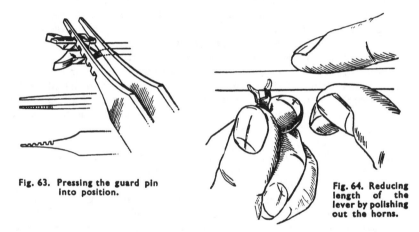

Fig. 63. Pressing the guard pin into position.

Fig. 64. Reducing length of the lever by polishing out the horns.

of tweezers and cut notches in the side of one blade only. The illustration shows the tweezers in use, pressing the guard pin into position. Reverse the tool and the pin can safely be removed.

Hold the lever in the left hand, as indicated in Fig. 64. In the right hand hold a round, soft steel or iron rod, the diameter of which is equal to the curve of the lever horns, Fig. 65. With the left hand resting on the edge of the bench, and the polisher charged with oilstone dust and oil, proceed to polish the lever in order to shorten it. Use short, steady strokes, revolving the rod at the same time. At this point the lever is thin and will not require much polishing to remove the metal ; so after every few strokes try it in the movement again. It is not necessary to replace the guard pin for every test but only when the work is finished. When satisfied that the length is correct, wipe the polisher clean of the oilstone dust and file the surface with a fairly fine file, raising a circular cut grain as if you were filing a pin on a filing block. Recharge the polisher with diamantine and repeat the operation of polishing,

Fig. 65 Section, view of polisher same diameter as curve of horns.

using quicker motions both lengthwise and circular. This will give a good polish to the surface of the lever horns. When doing this, and any other adjustments where metal is removed, make perfectly certain that the right action is being taken before any cutting away is done. *It is easy to remove metal but not quite such a simple matter to put it on again. Think well before you act.*

It will be noted that the rod used is round and the horns will therefore be made circular. This may not be quite correct, but it is accurate enough for the repairer. The curve of the horns should be equal arcs of equal circles struck from the axis of the balance staff with the lever locked alternately against each banking pin. In some Swiss factories they make the horns flat in order to free the ruby pin, so it will be seen that the curve is unimportant provided the ruby pin is free.

Having shortened the lever it is not usually practicable to replace the old guard pin, so it will be necessary to file up a new one. Instructions for this will be found in a later paragraph.

If it is found necessary to lengthen the lever, place it upside down on the smooth surface of a flat stake held in the vice in a similar manner to that illustrated in Fig. 62. With a flat chisel-ended punch lengthen the lever, employing the method used when peaning the side. Used carefully the flat ended punch will not cause the lever to curl. Another way to overcome the trouble if the lever is too short is to make the ruby pin lean forward a shade. To do this refer to instructions given under length of ruby pin ; but keep in mind that it is only a temporary method of dealing with the trouble and is not the correct thing to do.

There is yet another shake, or freedom, to test and, if necessary, correct, should it be found faulty. This is known as the shake on the banking, referring to the freedom of movement of the guard pin between the banking on one side and the roller on the other. While the balance is in position, still without the balance spring, and the mainspring slightly wound, lead the balance round so that the ruby pin is free of the lever notch. Hold the balance in this position, and with the fine tweezers or pointer try the shake of the lever. If the lever is pushed towards the roller it should fly back to the banking perceptibly. Try this on both sides of the lever. It is difficult to convey here the exact amount of freedom required ; but, as an indication, it should approximately equal the run to the banking movement. Fig. 49 on page 38 gives some idea of the required amount of freedom.

If the shake of the banking is tight on both sides the guard pin must be shortened. *On no account alter the bankings to correct faulty shake on the banking. This correction is effected from the guard pin only.*

As its name implies, the guard pin is merely to ensure that the lever notch is in the correct position to receive the ruby pin as the balance rotates. It is not a functional part of the escapement and the watch will go quite well without it, provided it is kept in a stationary position. To shorten the guard pin, hold the lever as in Fig. 66 and with an Arkansas slip stone away the pin, leaving the end V shaped as Fig. 67. The angle of the end of the guard pin should be something less than 90°.

Should the shake on the banking be found excessive on one side, and tight on the other, the guard pin can be bent to equalise it. Excessive shake on the bank-ing is corrected either by drawing the guard pin out a little or fitting a new and longer one. It is usually quicker to fit a new guard pin. File up a brass pin with a long gradual taper, well burnish with a flat burnisher and insert in the lever from the pallet side. See Fig. 68. Cut the back end off with the fine nippers leaving a percept-ible projection and

Fig. 67. Enlarged view of guard pin. Point should have angle of rather less than 90°

Fig. 66. Reducing length of guard pin with 3-square Arkansas slip.

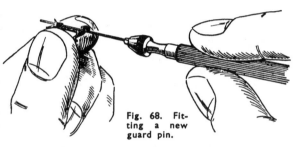

Fig. 68. Fitting a new guard pin.

trim the active end to length ; finish off with the Arkansas slip as previously explained.

The corrected or new guard pin is now tested in position. Set up the movement as for the previous test and hold the guard pin hard against the roller with the pointer, and while so doing rotate the balance until the ruby pin enters the notch. To be correct the ruby pin should enter quite freely without touching the horns of the lever. If it should touch, it may be possible to make the necessary correction by lengthening the guard pin slightly, but do not lengthen it sufficient to affect materially the shake on the banking. If this is not possible, owing to the amount it is necessary to extend the guard pin, reduce the horns of the lever slightly. Use a polishing rod a little larger in diameter than the one used in Figs. 64 and 65, so that the length of the lever is not affected more than is absolutely necessary but the radius of the horns is increased. Only just touch the corners of the notch during polishing.

When holding the guard pin against the safety roller to test the free entry of the ruby pin into the notch, take the opportunity, while holding the guard pin against the roller, to check that the escape wheel is not unlocked. If the escape wheel tooth has unlocked and started to jam, the run is too great or, alternatively, the shake on the banking is excessive.

The ruby pin should not project from the impulse roller beyond the top face of the safety roller, see Fig. 69. With some movements it is difficult to see the action of the ruby pin, while others have a groove cut along the bottom plate under the balance, to allow for this inspection.

If the ruby pin is too long, place the balance, roller side up on the bluing pan (without the balance spring), with a test piece of shellac by its

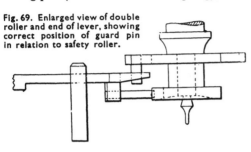

Fig. 69. Enlarged view of double roller and end of lever, showing correct position of guard pin in relation to safety roller.

side. Hold the pan over the flame of a spirit lamp and, when the test piece of shellac is soft, gently press the ruby pin down a shade with the blade of the bench knife. Hold over the flame a little longer so that the shellac floods the fixed end of the ruby pin again. Apply the minimum of heat to soften the shellac, and there will be no fear of bluing the staff.

Another method of moving the ruby pin is to apply heat by means of the tool illustrated in Fig. 70. It is simply made : two pieces of brass or copper wire are twisted together and held in a light handle, the prong ends are flattened by hammering and then bent inwards so that the ends meet. The extreme ends are then filed on the inside to form a lip, so that when the tool is pushed on to the impulse roller the jaws will open and

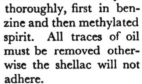

Fig. 70. Tool for warming shellac holding ruby pin.

grip it. To use, heat the whole of the wire part of the tool. Hold the balance in the left hand, and slip the tool on the impulse roller near the ruby pin. Hold the balance close to the bench so that the handle of the tool can rest on it, thus freeing the right hand to pick up the tweezers and adjust the ruby pin, see Fig. 71.

When applying new shellac it is advisable to clean the parts

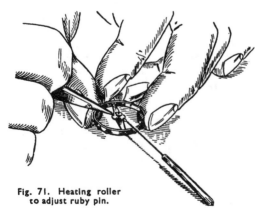

Fig. 71. Heating roller to adjust ruby pin.

thoroughly, first in benzine and then methylated spirit. All traces of oil must be removed otherwise the shellac will not adhere.

Ruby pins which are faulty in size should be corrected. If there is insufficient freedom of the ruby pin in the notch, the lever notch is opened, and to do this the tool illustrated in Fig. 72 should be employed. It is simply made from a stout piece of brass wire bent like a bow, having for a bowstring a piece of mainspring, which has been softened, and a hole drilled at each end. The wire is bent outwards so that it is strained inwards to fit the piece of mainspring, the stress thus created holding the spring taut. The piece of spring is buffed crossways with a fairly coarse buff. Charge it with oilstone dust and oil and use as shown in Fig. 73. Give two or three strokes to both sides of the notch, keeping in mind, if the roller notch is thin, that the polisher cuts quickly. Clean off with pith and try the ruby pin in the notch. When almost sufficient freedom has been given, clean the polisher off with a rag and rebuff the surface as before. Charge the polisher with diamantine and polish both sides of the notch. The amount of curvature caused by the give of the polisher imparts a slightly rounded surface to the side of the notch, which is desirable.

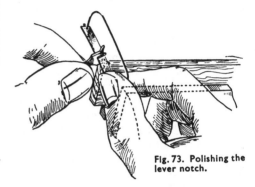

Fig. 72. Tool for opening lever notch.

Fig. 73. Polishing the lever notch.

Should there be an excess of freedom in the lever notch, change the ruby pin for one slightly larger, which may entail opening the ruby pin hole in the roller. On the other hand, the alteration we want to make is comparatively slight, and the roller may take a larger pin. To open the ruby pin hole, file up a piece of iron or soft steel wire to the shape of the ruby pin, usually a little more than half round, but smaller, so that the wire will enter the hole freely. Charge with oil stone dust and oil and polish the hole to increase the diameter. It will not be necessary to use diamantine afterwards. Some authorities recommend closing the lever notch to correct this fault and have devised special stakes for that purpose. *I do not recommend this as I feel that it is a dangerous practice with grave risk of fracturing the notch, or at least of distorting it, and also a possibility of putting the lever out of angle.*

The relative angles of the impulse planes of the pallets and the impulse faces of the escape teeth are determined by the manufacturer. American horologists regard the point as of considerable importance, but I consider that the repairer cannot do much about it, other than change the pallet stones should they be incorrect. The angles of the planes on pallet and teeth are complementary to each other, and should be so designed that at no time during the whole action of impulse do the faces coincide. If they do there is a decided drag due to what may be termed suction or, more correctly, oil adhesion. Therefore, other than changing the stone, or stones, the repairer has no remedy.

It is possible to lap the faces on a copper wheel charged with diamond powder, but it does not appeal to me as being either practical or economical for the watch repairer.

If the double eyeglass is used to observe very closely an escape wheel tooth as it travels along the impulse face it may be possible to see the light between the tooth and the stone. The heel of the escape tooth should be the only part in contact with the stone, see Fig. 48, and it is as the tooth leaves the pallet stone that the toe of the impulse face of the escape tooth contacts the pallet stone. I have in mind a well-designed escapement where the escape teeth are cut at an angle of three degrees, the entry pallet stone impulse face at an angle of 10° 20′, and the exit stone 23° 10′, see Fig. 44.

To test if the escapement is in beat is very important but easy of accomplishment. For the escapement to be in beat the ruby pin should be in the centre of the lever notch when the balance is at rest and the mainspring unwound. This is not always a convenient way to make the test ; *neither is it always accurate.* The beat is a compromise depending upon slight inaccuracies in the escapement (and there are many, as I have observed before). The best method of testing for beat is to wind the mainspring two or three turns with the escapement fully assembled. Hold the movement in the left hand and with the pointer in the right try to stop the balance vibrating. In a well proportioned and correct escapement it will be found that it is not possible to stop the balance. *If it will not " set," the escapement is in beat.* In many watches it will be found that the balance will set, and the test then is to see if the balance sets on one side more than on the other. The escapement is in beat if the balance sets an equal amount on both sides. That is, during the operation of both pallets. To instance a definite case, lead the balance round by holding the pointer so that the arm of the balance rests against it. The balance is travelling so that the entry pallet locks on the tooth and the balance sets ; move the pointer to the other side of the arm and move the balance to unlock, the balance will then swing smartly round a half turn arrested by the pointer. Continue to lead the balance round until it sets on the exit pallet. Move the balance to unlock again and we note that it was necessary to move the balance further to unlock on the exit pallet than on the entry pallet, indicating that the balance spring collet must be moved towards the exit stone. The necessary amount of movement to give the collet can only be discovered by trial.

It is always better, and safer, to remove the balance from the movement when attempting to move the collet. Insert the blade of the clock oiler in the collet and give it a slight twist which should turn it on the staff. Place the balance on the stake and press the collet down tightly, as the correction may cause the collet to rise a little, with the possibility of its running out of flat when it is again assembled in the movement.

At this point it would be advantageous to make a general survey of the escapement. Start by examining the impulse roller to make sure it is free of the top side of the lever notch, as in Fig. 69. If not, the roller

Fig. 74. Bending lever on wood block.

should be let on to the balance staff a little further, and it may even be necessary to turn back a little the underside of the back slope of the balance staff, Fig. 76. Another method is to bend the lever, first taking the precautions already given for ascertaining its hardness. Assuming it is required to bend the lever down, remove the lever from the movement, place it upside down on a wood block on the bench. The block should have a hole drilled in it to accommodate the pallet staff. With the round back part of the tweezers or a small oval burnisher, stroke the lever as indicated in Fig. 74, using some little pressure ; this will cause the lever to curl. Should it be necessary to bend the lever up, reverse it on the block and stroke the top side. When the lever is turned over it will be found that an additional hole is required to free the guard pin block. The amount of pressure required depends entirely on the hardness of the metal from which the lever is made.

The next point is to check that the guard pin is free of the crescent (Fig. 75) of the safety roller ; but it is not always possible to see this in a modern escapement. When making the test to see that the guard pin functions correctly, hold the lever over so that the guard pin touches the safety roller, and then lead the balance round to ascertain that the

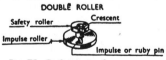

Fig. 75. Definitions of component parts of Double Roller.

ruby pin enters the notch satisfactorily. If, during the test, a sticking effect is found, it may be due to the guard pin either touching the corner of the safety roller crescent or rubbing on the bottom of it. If there is any doubt, smear the end of the guard pin with rouge and oil, and repeat the test, then remove the balance and inspect the safety roller. If there is any trace of rouge on the crescent, it should be made wider or deeper. If the corners foul, or the guard pin bottoms, the position of the rouge will indicate where the freedom is required.

As the escapement is taken to pieces inspect the various parts for tightness of their components : make sure that the balance staff is firm in the balance, the roller firm on the staff, and the ruby pin secure in the roller. See that the balance spring collet fits tightly on the balance staff. Check over the pallets, making sure that the pallet stones are quite firm, that the staff fits tightly, and that the guard pin is firm. Next see that the pinion is tight in the escape wheel. Closely scrutinise the jewel holes and endstones to see if they are secure. The slightest sign of loosening of any of the parts mentioned will have a serious effect on the timekeeping of the watch, and it is as well to cultivate the habit of testing them, as an undetected fault of this nature may lead to serious consequences which can be very troublesome to eradicate.

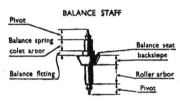

Fig. 76. Definitions of parts of the Balance Staff.

Examine the pallet stones and ruby pin for chips ; if these stones are damaged, especially the actual operating faces, they should be changed without hesitation. Check over the endstones for pits, as it sometimes happens that the pivot has worn a dent or small pit in the centre of the stone. The remedy is to change the endstone for a new one. Examine the edge of the safety roller to see that it is well polished. There should be no burrs or ridges, and the corner of the crescent, too, must be free from burrs. If there is any roughness on the edge of the safety roller there is a risk of the guard pin catching when it comes into contact with the edge through the watch receiving a jolt.

What happens when a watch receives a jolt is this : the lever leaves the banking and the guard pin contacts the edge of the safety roller, and the lever is then safe for the free entry of the ruby pin into the notch, that is, if the jar comes when the ruby pin is about to enter the notch. If the jolt comes when the ruby pin is some distance away from the notch, the draw of the pallets will have time to operate, and the lever is drawn or pulled back on to the banking by the escape wheel, and all is well.

Check that the teeth of the escape wheel are free of the belly of the pallets. If you have any doubt—the escape wheel may hesitate occasionally during the drop—smear the teeth of the escape wheel with a mixture of rouge and oil and try again. If the belly shows traces of rouge then that part of the pallets must be reduced. Make sure to remove the rouge as it is a dangerous substance if left in a watch.

Inconsistency of rate in a watch when worn can be caused by want of poise in the lever. The draw may not be over-strong and a slight jar may cause the lever to fall away from the banking, and so allow the guard to foul the safety roller. The remedy is to improve the poise of the lever and also to make the draw a little more definite.

To poise the lever is sometimes quite impossible. Some fine quality watches have counter-poise pieces attached to the pallets for this purpose. If we cannot poise the lever, we can at least improve it so that the excessive predominance of weight in one part is considerably reduced.

Escapement makers use a test which is known as running to half time to determine the correct weight of the balance before springing. It is generally a good indication that all is well with the escapement if the watch will run to half time. It is assembled without the balance spring, and the mainspring is wound up ; when the balance is given a light swing it should unlock the escape wheel and receive sufficient impulse to carry it round, and the other parts of the escapement will function without the balance spring. The balance should continue to vibrate backwards and forwards in this manner until the mainspring has run down. If the balance is of the correct weight the watch will run to half time, i.e., the watch will register one hour in two.

Oiling the lever escapement plays a very important part in its correct functioning, and this subject is fully dealt with in Chapter Nine, page 94.

See that the ruby pin is upright ; if it is not, warm a piece of flat steel rod, similar in shape to the pivot end burnisher, and hold this against the ruby pin until the heat softens the shellac and enables you to press the ruby pin upright.

This reminds me of an old Clerkenwell finisher, the man who used to turn the pinions in, who cleaned a watch for a friend. The watch afterwards failed to function, so he sought the advice of another friend, an escapement maker. The escapement maker heated a piece of wire and placed it in the movement with the miraculous result that the watch functioned, so ever afterwards the finisher placed a heated wire in the movement of every watch he repaired ; he was convinced that he had discovered the " mysterious art." No doubt the escapement maker just made the ruby pin upright. There is a moral to this story : *there is no short road to success in watch repairing,* no mysterious touch or trick ; you must *know* what you are doing and why. There are certain functions in connection with the escapement that must be learned by close study, they cannot just be picked up.

Readers may think the examination of the lever escapement is a very lengthy business and that the average watch would not warrant the expenditure of time. To the experienced man the examination as I have given it takes less than 10 minutes. Corrections or alterations will take longer. It is all time well spent ; a watch cannot give the best service unless that vital part, the escapement, is functioning correctly.

CHAPTER SIX

PIN PALLET ESCAPEMENT

MOVEMENTS FITTED with the pin pallet escapement play an important part in the horological industry today, and we cannot afford to ignore them. This form of escapement is not associated with a high-grade watch and fine results are not expected from it, but at the same time, reasonably good results are obtained for a low price. I have known of a test of 10,000 watches fitted with pin pallet escapement, in which the required result was to be 1 minute in 24 hours dial up and pendant up, with only 9 failures. There is nothing here to cause us to turn our horological noses up. Fortunately this escapement is simple ; I say fortunately, because the original cost would not justify much expenditure of time on it. It is, in fact, from the production engineer's point of view, a very cleverly designed and efficient escapement. Its straight-forward design, rugged construction and good clearances make it especially suitable for mass production.

From the repairer's point of view the examination is a very simple procedure as there are but few special features to be looked for, and any reasonable adjustments can speedily be made with sufficient accuracy to ensure satisfaction.

As in the case of the lever, before attempting an examination of the escapement, the condition of the case and general appearance of the watch should be taken into consideration. This type of watch suffers much from amateur tampering and signs of this are usually observable on the case. The case, from its dents and scratches, can often give a guide to the age of the movement. Always look for any signs of rough usage, accidental dropping and other damage which may give a clue to the reason for the watch stopping, or for its bad performance, and following this clue the cause of the trouble may, perhaps, be located immediately, and a subsequent examination be based on what it is assumed or can be discovered has happened to the watch.

Assuming that there is no major breakage or disturbance due to outside causes, an examination of the escapement will start with a test of the locking. It is not necessary to remove the balance. With the mainspring partly wound, lead the balance round so that a tooth of the escape wheel is released, and observe that the pallet pin drops on to the locking face of the escape tooth, as in Fig. 77 at A. Continue to hold the balance and lead it a little further so that the escape tooth draws the pallet to the root of the tooth. Carry out this test on both pallets and round the wheel on all 15 teeth.

If the locking is faulty, that is, if the pallet pin drops on the impulse face of the tooth, bend the tongue A (Fig. 87, page 58 and Fig. 91, page 60) towards the escape wheel. To do this hold it with the long, flat-nosed pliers and give them a twist. This can be done quite safely whilst the pallets are in position in the watch. The clearances of the pin pallet escapement being ample, the degree of accuracy required in the ordinary jewelled lever escapement is unnecessary but, naturally, every escapement must be correct, whatever its design, if acceptable results are to be expected from it. Bending the pallet hole tongue may put the pallets slightly out of upright, as there is seldom a means of adjustment from the pallet cock end, but this is immaterial, the amount being very small.

It is important when examining the locking to see that the tooth of the escape wheel drops on to the pin at a point above the line of centre of the pallet pin, see Fig. 77. If the tooth drops on to the pin as in B the escape wheel will push the pallet forward so that the guard pin rubs on the roller, and this is equally as faulty as a complete mislocking which is illustrated in C. The next test is to see that the drop of the escape wheel is equal on each pallet pin. Move the balance round to unlock an escape tooth, and note the distance the tooth dropped before it was arrested by the pallet pin. Reverse the motion of the balance until a tooth has dropped on to the other pallet pin, and note the amount of

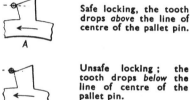

Safe locking, the tooth drops *above* the line of centre of the pallet pin.

A

Unsafe locking; the tooth drops *below* the line of centre of the pallet pin.

B

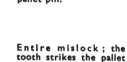

Entire mislock; the tooth strikes the pallet pin on its impulse face.

C

Fig. 77.

Fig. 78. Tool with prong end for bending the lever.

Fig. 79. Showing the prong end tool in use bending the pallets to lessen the drop.

drop. If the drop is unequal, bend the arm of the pallet to which the offending pin is attached. If, for instance, it is found that the exit pin allows more drop than the entry pin, bend the pallet arm of the exit pin towards the entry pin. Some designs of pin pallets are so made that the arms carrying the pallet pins can be bent quite easily. Make a tool as Fig. 78. Take a piece of steel about 4 in. long and 1 mm. round, file up the end as illustrated, and fit the tool into a small handle. When using it, place the prong end straddlewise over the arm (see Fig. 79) and give the tool a slight twist. Here, again, it is not usually necessary to remove the pallets from the movement to make this alteration, provided that the arm is thin and can easily be bent. Always bear in mind that the pivots of the lever staff are generally very thin, and may also be soft, so discretion must be exercised as to whether it is

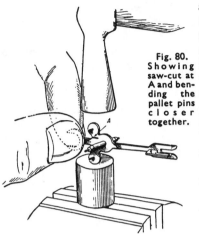

Fig. 80. Showing saw-cut at A and bending the pallet pins closer together.

advisable to remove the lever from the movement to make the adjustment. Some pallets are more robust as in Fig. 87, page 58, and for these it will be necessary to remove the pallets and bend them with the flat-nosed pliers. Where this is not possible, make a saw-cut with a fine screw-head file as at A in Fig. 80, and tap the pallet as indicated to close it up.

To examine the shake on the roller move the balance round so that the impulse pin is free of the lever notch and try the shake. In most designs of this type of watch banking pins are omitted, the lever banking on the root of the escape wheel teeth. Reverse the direction of the balance and again try the shake ; it should be the same on each side.

It is a simple matter to correct the shake on the roller. Should it be found that there is little or no shake on one side, and an excess on the other, bend the lever towards the side that has excess. To do this

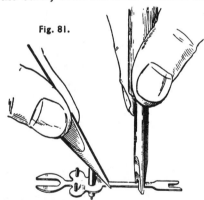

Fig. 81.

use the same bending tool as Fig. 78, employing it as shown in Fig. 81. This correction also can usually be carried out without removing the balance. If it is found that there is little or no shake on the roller on both sides, shorten the guard pin a little. If there is too much shake on both sides then the guard pin must be lengthened. The guard pin, if made of wire, can be lengthened by bending it first down and then up so that it engages on the roller, as demonstrated in Fig. 82. Some guard pins are solid and in this case the pin should be stretched to lengthen it. Use the chisel-shaped punch with the flattened end ; fit up on a punch held in the vice as Fig. 83, and one light tap with the hammer is usually sufficient.

See that the impulse pin engages securely in the lever notch. During the course of repairs the lever is easily bent, and if it is found that the lever is either too high or too low to engage the impulse pin safely, bend the lever up or down, as required, using the bending tool in the manner

shown in Fig. 84. Try the shake of
the impulse pin in the notch ; it must
be quite free. To test the draw, move
the balance round so that the impulse
pin is free of the notch and hold the
balance in that position. With the
pointer move the lever so that the
guard pin touches the safety roller, and
then suddenly release the lever. If the

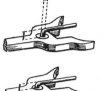

Fig. 82. Showing procedure of bending guard pin to lengthen it.

draw of the escape wheel operates, the lever will fly smartly back
from the roller. The draw is due to the angle of the locking face of the
escape wheel teeth. Should there be no draw this angle is not sufficiently

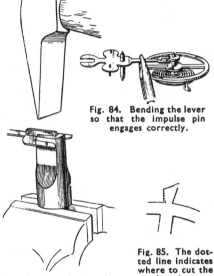

Fig. 84. Bending the lever so that the impulse pin engages correctly.

Fig. 85. The dotted line indicates where to cut the tooth to increase the draw.

Fig. 83. Lengthening the guard pin by stretching it.

acute, see Fig. 85. The best
method to correct it is to change
the escape wheel with the hope
that the teeth of the new
wheel are more accurately cut.
Another way is to cut each
tooth as indicated by the
dotted line, with a flat needle
file. This is rather a long job
for an inexpensive watch repair
but it may be the only remedy.
The draw is essential if the best
results are to be obtained.

Try the draw on both pallet
pins, and test each pin on all
15 teeth. I am convinced that
sufficient attention is not paid
to the draw, not only in the
pin pallet escapement but in
the solid pallet escapements as
well. The draw is as important
as the locking. My experience

is that most watch repairers know something about the locking, but very
few realise even the existence of the draw, and they certainly overlook
its prime importance.

If the pallet pins are worn it may be more economical to fit new
pallets, but if this is not possible new pins can be fitted. The original
pins are only driven in and held friction tight so, if we are to fit new pins
they must be a shade larger in diameter to hold in the pallets. The
fact of the pins being slightly thicker than the original does not affect
the working of the escapement. Knock out the old pins and select a
piece of steel the correct diameter. An ordinary sewing-needle answers
quite well ; it is hard, and has a good polished surface. Cut a piece to
the exact length required; place the pallets on a steel stake, hold the pin

in the tweezers as Fig. 86, and drive the pin into the pallet hole. No further finish is necessary. Some pallet pins are turned from a piece of steel of much larger diameter, the larger end being fitted to the pallet arm. When a new one is to be fitted this is not quite so good from the repairer's point of view.

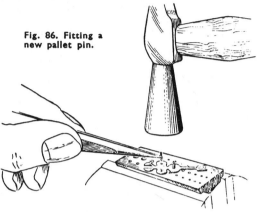

Fig. 86. Fitting a new pallet pin.

It is not worth the time to turn up a new pin, so it is quicker to file off the old pin and drill a hole in the stump to receive the new one.

The modern Ingersoll pocket watch has pallets of the robust type as in Fig. 87, banking taking place on the root of the escape wheel teeth. The clearances are large, and the watch will function quite satisfactorily with reasonably large holes to the escape wheel and pallet staff bearings. The balance staff has conical pivots, the endshake being controlled by a screw. The pivots work in Vee bearings, one in the end stud and the other in the end of a screw.

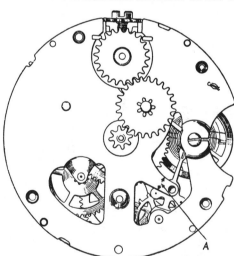

Fig. 87. The Ingersoll pocket movement and the pallets (double size).

When repairs are necessary to the watch the staff pivots should be dressed or sharpened. To do this, remove the balance spring and fit the staff up in a split chuck in a lathe. While revolving at some speed, stone the pivot with an Arkansas slip at an angle of 45°, see Fig. 88, the maximum resistance to wear with the minimum of friction is then secured. Some authorities are of the opinion that a stronger pivot is made if the cone is slightly curved, as illustrated. It is argued that when in the vertical position the curved or rounded part of the pivot comes into operation and not the extreme point.

When dealing with a watch and a very small pivot, surface friction must be taken into account and of the two evils, the more delicate pivot may be the less objectionable. When all signs of wear are removed and

Fig. 88. The top shows the conical pivot with straight sides and the lower with slightly curved sides.

the point has a smooth conical surface, finish off with a sharp flat burnisher, holding it at the same angle as the Arkansas slip. Treat both pivots in this manner. The action, or vibration, of the balance is greatly improved if care is given to the balance staff pivots.

The illustration, Fig. 89, shows part of a 13 ligne Swiss movement with the balance and cock removed to show the banking pins.

There is no means of readily adjusting this escapement should the locking be faulty. The balance staff pivots are of the usual shape associated with a hole and endstone, and the same precautions are taken to see that they are polished and the ends burnished round and smooth. The movement is designed on the Roskopf model.

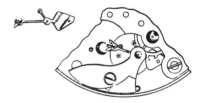

Fig. 89. Showing the Banking Pins. Inset, the pallets.

Fig. 90 illustrates a 10½ ligne Ingersoll of Swiss manufacture, and Roskopf design ; it has no banking pins. The system of the lower pallet hole offers a means of adjustment should the locking be faulty. Yet another Swiss movement, marketed under the trade-mark " Ebosa," has an adjustment screw by which the position of the lower pallet hole can be set.

Fig. 91 is the pin-pallet 10½ ligne movement made by The Medana

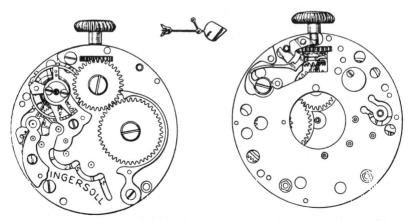

Fig. 90. The 10½ Ligne Ingersoll Movement (double size) ; showing *left*, the top plate ; *right*, under the dial ; and *inset*, the pallets.

Watch Company. This is not a Roskopf design movement. The train, motion work, etc., are normal, but the pin pallet escapement has banking pins. The balance staff pivots are of the hole and endpiece type, and it has a means of adjustment should the escape wheel mislock. It should be explained that the great enemy of the pin pallet escapement is dust, and in order to avoid this the movement has as much protection as possible ; it is equipped with a little brass dust cover over the movement, fitting tightly round the edge.

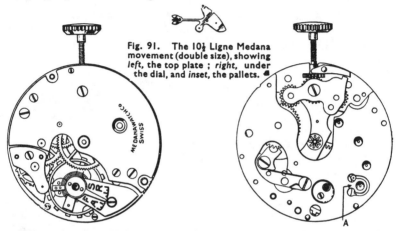

Fig. 91. The 10¼ Ligne Medana movement (double size), showing *left*, the top plate ; *right*, under the dial, and *inset*, the pallets.

When cleaning the pin pallet escapement there are one or two points to observe. There is a tendency for the pallet pins to force all dust and dirt that come their way into the roots of the teeth of the escape wheel. This applies particularly to the type that banks on the wheel. The continual hammering of the pallet pin at this one spot can cause matter to collect there and form a hard core. If this core is not removed during cleaning it will seriously affect the shake on the roller, and even cause the guard pin to rub on the roller. Ordinary cleaning may not remove the hard core, so hold the wheel between the first finger and thumb of the left hand, and just draw the blade of a sharp bench knife along the root of

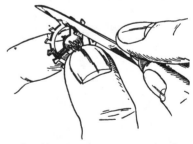

Fig. 92. Showing the method of removing the hard core likely to be found at the roots of the teeth

each tooth, not sufficiently hard to remove any metal, but firmly enough to remove the dirt and make the corner bright. See Fig. 92.

See that the pallet pins are free from congealed oil ; clean them well with pith dipped in benzine. The same applies to the impulse pin and the lever notch.

The pivots are oiled in the usual manner. The pallet pins are oiled when the watch is wound. Apply a little oil when the watch is locking on a tooth of the escape wheel. Allow the watch to run for about three teeth, then arrest the balance and apply a little more oil as before, and so on, until all the escape wheel teeth have a supply of oil. Unlike the solid pallet lever escapement, the impulse pin is oiled slightly, or rather just greased. Place a little oil on the thumbnail with the watch oiler, cut a piece of pegwood to a chisel shape and grease this with the oil on the thumbnail and, in turn, apply the greased end of the pegwood to the impulse pin. Quite sufficient oil for our purpose will thus be imparted.

The oiling of the pins and escape-wheel of pin pallet watches that are not of the Roskopf type is a controversial point. Through the introduction of a centre wheel and finer wheelwork the distribution of power to the escapement is better controlled. Consequently a mainspring of a less coarse type can be employed and, together with this power-control of the centre wheel, the life of the watch is extended. The lubrication, however, is of great importance, and a special grease has been put on the market in Switzerland suitable for the pin pallet escapement. This lubricant has a two-fold advantage, (a) it does not spread, remaining constant longer than oil, and (b) it is claimed that it does not mix with particles of dust to the same extent as oil. This grease does not clog ; it forms a thin film over the highly polished surface of the pins. It is as well to use oil sparingly on this type of watch.

CHAPTER SEVEN

THE TRAIN : GEARS AND TOOTH FORMS

AFTER ESCAPEMENTS, the train is the next part of the movement demanding study. The first thing to consider in connection with it is the count ; that is, the number of teeth in the wheels and the number of leaves in the pinion. If the wheels have : centre, 80 teeth, 3rd 75, 4th 80, escape 15, and the pinions have 10 leaves in the 3rd, 10 in the 4th and 8 in the escape, then $\dfrac{80 \times 75 \times 80 \times 15 \times 2}{10 \times 10 \times 8} = 18000$. The escape wheel has 15 teeth, so that number is doubled because each tooth operates on both pallets.

From the foregoing it is obvious that the balance must vibrate 18000 times each hour. When counting a train to ascertain the number of vibrations that the balance is to make, it is not necessary to take into consideration the number of teeth in the barrel or the leaves in the centre pinion ; the time is registered from the centre wheel. If the watch is fitted with a seconds hand then the calculation is as follows : $\dfrac{80 \times 15 \times 2 \times 60}{8} = 18000$. 80 equals 4th wheel, 15 multiplied by 2 equals the escape wheel, divided by 8 leaves in the escape pinion, and the result multiplied by 60 (as the 4th wheel rotates 60 times in an hour), and we get 18000. We can determine, by proportion, the number of teeth in a wheel or leaves in a pinion. If we have a movement with the 3rd wheel missing, then $\dfrac{80 \times x}{10 \times 10} = 60$ $\therefore$ $80 \times x = \dfrac{60 \times 10 \times 10}{80} = 75$ the number of teeth required in missing 3rd wheel.

Should the wheel and the pinion both be missing we can find the ratio of the teeth in the 3rd wheel to the ratio of leaves in its pinion by $\dfrac{x \times 80}{10 \times c} = 60$ $\dfrac{x}{c} = \dfrac{60 \times 10}{80} = \dfrac{7.5}{1}$ which indicates that the wheel should have $7\frac{1}{2}$ times as many teeth as the pinion has leaves. Taking into consideration the count of the rest of the train, a wheel of 75 and a pinion of 10 would be selected.

It is not proposed to give lengthy details of train calculations here.

I must just say here that watchmakers sometimes take the train too much for granted, thinking that it is not necessary to examine it closely. If you have not seen the particular watch you are working on before, or if you have reason to believe that the watch has been in other hands since you last repaired it, take nothing for granted and examine all the depths. If the train is perfectly free and you allow it to run down after winding the mainspring a little, the train should reverse its motion at the very end of the mainspring In other words, before the escape wheel stops it should run backwards for perhaps one revolution or two. This is due to the rebound when the eye of the mainspring butts on the hook of the barrel arbor. It is perhaps a crude test, but it forms a general indication that all is well with the freedom of the train. So before we discuss the very important subject of depths or gearing, we must take a glance at the train generally.

First of all examine the cannon pinion ; if it is the snap-on type, make sure it is tight enough to carry the hands. It is much to be preferred to tighten it now, if necessary, rather than to wait until the watch is assembled complete with the dial, only to find the hand work is loose and may be so loose that the hands do not carry. Another fault the cannon pinion is heir to is riding up, and for a better understanding of why these weaknesses exist refer to the chapter on *Making New Parts* (Fitting Cannon Pinion). Examine the wheels of the train by holding the movement up level with the eyes to see that they are upright ; it is vital that the centre and the fourth wheels (if fitted with a seconds hand) should be perfectly upright. If you have any doubts, proceed as follows : Replace the cannon pinion, hour and minute wheels and then replace the dial and make secure. Fit the winding shaft and button in position. Now fit on the hour, minute and seconds hands. Move the minute hand round and observe the tip to see if it travels at the same distance from the dial all round ; if it is up on one side and down on the other then the centre wheel is out of upright. Try the same with the seconds hand by making the watch go for about one minute. The third and escape wheels should be upright also, but it is not so essential provided they are quite free of other parts of the movement and carry out their functions correctly. I do not for one moment advocate any wheel being out of upright, but from an economical point of view it would not be wise to spend a lot of time uprighting wheels in an inexpensive movement ; the important thing is to know what is safe to leave. If you find that the minute hand travels

at the same distance from the dial all round, but the hour hand rides up on one side and down on the other, then the centre arbor is bent. Find out which way it is bent by spinning in the callipers, and lay the arbor on a flat steel stake (Fig. 93) with the bend pointing downwards, then lightly tap with the pean end of the hammer as indicated in the illustration, and this will cause the arbor to curl upwards. If this method is adopted, there is very little fear or breaking the arbor and it is not necessary to soften it, or lower the temper.

To make upright these wheels—if they are faulty—is quite a simple matter. Dealing with the centre

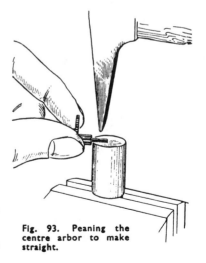

Fig. 93. Peaning the centre arbor to make straight.

wheel first, there are two ways in which this error may be rectified : one is to rebush one of the centre wheel holes, the other is to plug one of the holes and drill correctly in an uprighting tool. As a rule it is better to rebush or plug the top hole, because by so doing we shall not to any extent alter the depths of the barrel and centre pinion. If the top hole is jewelled it may be economical to deal with the lower hole, but it must be realised that the cannon pinion as well as the barrel depths may have to be adjusted as a con-

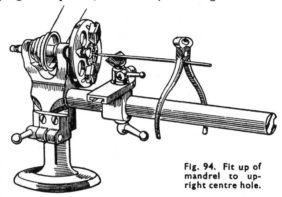

Fig. 94. Fit up of mandrel to up-right centre hole.

sequence. We shall assume the top hole is to be rebushed. Fit the lower plate up in the mandrel, bringing the centring rod up so that its conical end engages in the centre hole, and tighten down the dogs. Bring the T-rest up to within about an inch of the plate, broad side parallel to the plate (Fig. 94). Sharpen a piece of watch pegwood to a long point. Withdraw the centring rod, place the pegwood in the hole, and make the face-plate revolve quickly, meanwhile holding the peg ; this is to wear the peg to the shape of the hole. Now place on the end of the peg-wood a pair of nippers, or something similar, straddlewise, as indicated in the illustration. Without holding the pegwood, make the face-plate revolve slowly and watch carefully the extreme end of the pegwood ; if the centre hole in the lower plate is fitted up centrally on the face-plate —as it should be—there will be no movement of the peg, but if the hole is out of centre, however slightly, the end of the pegwood will work up and down. We carry out this test as a check on the truth of the centring rod, and if it is not true there must be something wrong with the tool.

If the tool is a little out of truth, the conical end of the centring rod may not be quite true. Tap the edge of the plate lightly with a hammer (without loosening the dogs). For instance, when the end of the pegwood is at its lowest point give a light tap to the top edge of the watch plate so as to bring the end up. When quite true, without removing the plate from the tool, place the centre bar in position on the plate, complete with screws. Repetition of the test with the pegwood

Fig. 95. Cutting tool, made from an old file.

in the top centre hole will disclose some considerable movement. Now proceed to catch the hole true with the tool illustrated in Fig. 95, which can be made from the handle of an old file. Some term this operation boring. When the hole is quite true remove the plate from the mandrel and proceed to fit a bush to the top centre hole.

Select a piece of bush wire with the hole a little smaller than the size of the pivot which is to fit into it. Cut off a piece three or four times the length of the finished hole, place on a turning arbor and turn down true to a taper equivalent to the taper of a broach. Open the hole of the centre bar with a cutting broach, just sufficient to give

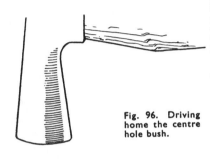

Fig. 96. Driving home the centre hole bush.

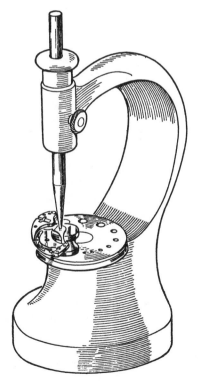

it a taper, from the inside. Turn the bush down until it fits the hole, push in as far as possible, not using undue force. Mark the top end with a knife flush with the bar, also mark the underside in a similar manner. Turn the bush to length, a little below the mark on the top side, and the same with the underside ; this will allow a tight friction fit when driven home with the hammer. Undercut the top end to form the rivet. Slightly chamfer the upper side of the hole in the centre bar to receive the rivet. Place the bar on a polished stake, underside uppermost, with the bush in position, and drive home with a polished flat-ended punch and hammer (Fig. 96). Replace the bar right side up on the stake and, with a polished rounded-end punch and hammer, rivet the chamfered end slightly, giving the punch frequent light taps. If care has been exercised in turning the bush to the correct length no further finish should be necessary. If, however, the bush was left too long, and you wish to reduce it in order to give the necessary endshake, two methods can be employed. One is to fit up the plate on the mandrel, and turn the excessive metal away with a cutter held in the slide rest. The other is to file the metal down and then stone with a piece of Montgomerie stone (an ordinary slate pencil answers quite well). Both these methods are explained in *Fitting New Parts*. Lastly, open the hole to size, finishing off with a round broach to harden and polish the hole. It will be necessary to chamfer slightly both sides of the hole to remove the burrs thrown up during broaching. The end of an old rat-tail file whetted pyramid shape makes an excellent chamfering tool (Fig. 97).

Fig. 97. Chamfering tool made from a rat-tailed file.

To upright the fourth hole we select the hole furthest away from the pinion, so as not to interfere with the escape pinion depth. If the holes are jewelled, push the jewel hole out and fit up and catch true as for the centre hole, resetting a larger jewel. Should the hole be of brass, proceed as follows, assuming that the top hole is being rebushed : Open the hole to a fair size and plug with a piece of brass wire ; the fitting and riveting are the same as when fitting the centre wheel bush. Fit the lower plate in the uprighting tool, adjusting the centring rod in the lower hole (Fig. 98). Make secure with the dogs. Without removing the plate from the tool, screw on in position the 4th wheel bridge. Lower the top centring rod down on to the bridge, and pin-point mark the position of the new hole ; by making the centring rod revolve and

Fig. 98. Centring the 4th hole in the uprighting tool.

using a little pressure a sufficiently deep mark will be made. With the type of uprighting tool illustrated, the fourth wheel bar can be placed in position on the bottom plate as soon as the plug is fitted and the centre obtained with the lower rod. Drill the hole smaller than will be ultimately required. It is not necessary to remove the plate from the uprighting tool for this operation. Replace the centring rod with a female rod ; hold the drill in a stock fitted with a ferrule and, by using the

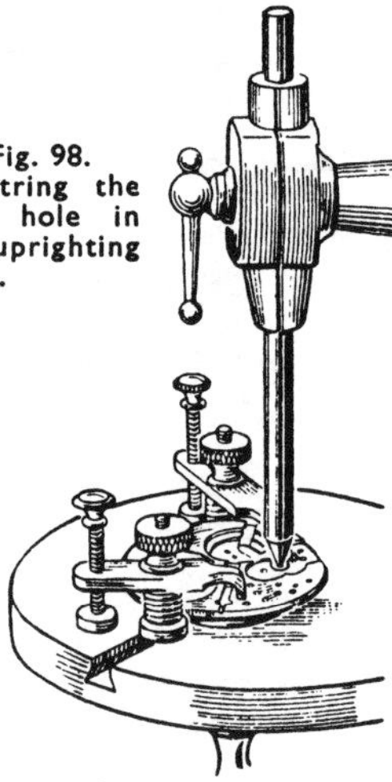

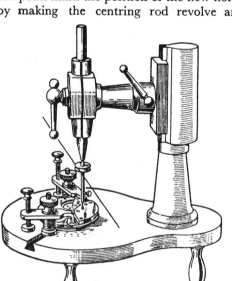

Fig. 99. Drilling the new top 4th hole.

bow, the new hole can be drilled upright (Fig. 99). Open from inside with a broach to size, finish with a round broach. Chamfer the top of the hole to receive the oil, and very slightly chamfer the under side to remove the burr. To fit a new jewel hole refer to the chapter on *Fitting New Parts*.

Now that the train wheels are upright, try all the endshakes, and see that the sideshakes are not excessive. Endshake and sideshake are perhaps debatable ; in other words there is a certain amount of latitude. The first factor to bear in mind is that all parts must be free, the watch, unlike most machinery, has only limited power at its disposal, the limit being imposed by necessity, as too much force will cause knocking. Limited power is perhaps not the correct term ; meticulous, or an accurate degree of power, would perhaps be more correct. Be that as it may, we have at our disposal a definite force, and it is because of this that all friction must be reduced to a minimum, and the small amount of friction which is tolerated—and we must tolerate some—should be as constant as possible.

The centre, third and fourth wheels need more endshake than the escape wheel and balance staff, and the pallets need less. To give the exact amount of endshake is difficult, unless measurements are given ; I feel that to do so would be misleading and would afford no general guide. To consider our 13 ligne movement, the centre, third and fourth wheels should have endshake equal to about the thickness of three pieces of tissue paper (which together approximate .03 mm.). The escape wheel endshake should equal about two thicknesses of tissue paper, (.02 mm.) and at the pallets the endshake should be just perceptible. The sideshake should not be perceptible, but to test, take the movement in the left hand and hold it sight-high and square, i.e. parallel, with the bench. Lift up each wheel with the tweezers. When released, the wheels should, by virtue of their own weight, fall into their original positions, provided the holes are clean and free from oil. This test is to ensure that the pivots are free in their holes. Another test to ascertain that the pivots are free is to hold the movement sight-high as before and observe the space between the pivot shoulders and their holes (which is the endshake). Turn the movement upside-down and again hold sight-high, observing the space between the pivot shoulders as before. They should be the same. In other words, the wheels should drop of their own weight.

Now for the important question of depths. You must know what a correct depth is before we can proceed to examine the movement further, so we will discuss this matter now.

In the first place imagine two discs mounted on arbors and placed so that their edges just touched. Motion given to one would make the other rotate, and this means of conveying motion from one part to another is the perfect form. The friction generated to give motion is rolling friction only, just one surface rolling upon another. Rolling friction is the least objectionable of all forms of friction, and this simple statement is of the greatest importance, as will presently be seen. Not only is the method just mentioned the perfect one because of the rolling, but also because the power so transmitted is even, i.e., the speed of such wheels during the transmission of power is regular.

The other forms of friction met with in a watch train are engaging friction and disengaging friction. Engaging friction is the resistance set up when a point of a stick is pushed forwards over a surface ; disengaging friction is the resistance set up when the point of the stick is drawn over a surface (Fig. 100). It should be readily understood that the resistance of engaging friction is higher for a given force than disengaging, therefore, in gearing, rolling friction is the ideal ; disengaging friction has to be tolerated, but engaging friction must be avoided if at all possible.

Fig. 100. Rolling, engaging, and disengaging friction.

Reverting to the toothless wheels : if power were applied for any length of time the two surfaces would slip, and to prevent this it would be necessary to force the discs or wheels harder together ; serious complications would then arise, setting in motion another problem of pivot friction with its consequent wear. To overcome this difficulty teeth made to a mathematical shape known as epicycloidal are formed on the wheels.

An epicycloidal curve is a line traced by a point in the circumference of a circle rolling on the exterior of another circle.

So the perfect toothed gearing tolerates rolling friction only. But there are certain limitations to carrying this theory into effect in practice.

It has been established that in the case of a wheel of less than 21 teeth gearing with a pinion of less than 11 leaves, engaging friction must take place.

It is not required to go into the theory of gearing here, but it may suffice to say that a wheel is generally known as the driver and the pinion the driven, and that if the driven is less than half the diameter of the driver, a new set of conditions come into operation to determine the hape of the leaves of the pinion. To those who wish to study further the theory of gearing—it is a vast subject—I would refer them to *Lessons in Horology*, Vol. I., by Jules and Hermann Grossman (now out of print), and *Practical Treatise on Gearing*, by Brown & Sharpe Mfg. Co. The illustration (Fig. 101), gives the definitions of the various parts that compose the wheel and pinion. The shape of the leaves of the pinion are determined in the following manner. The acting parts of the leaves are the flanks or sides, so it is with the shape of the flanks that we are concerned. A circle half the diameter of the pinion pitch circle—and equal to that used when tracing the shape of the teeth of the wheel to gear with the pinion—is rolled inside the pinion pitch circle. The line traced by a point on the circumference of the small circle is, it so happens, straight and therefore the flanks of the pinions are straight and radial. The line so traced is called a hypocycloid curve. If these conditions are complied with, the motion transmitted will be even, i.e., at the same speed, throughout the action, from the time the tooth engages with the flank of the pinion until it has transmitted the power and is

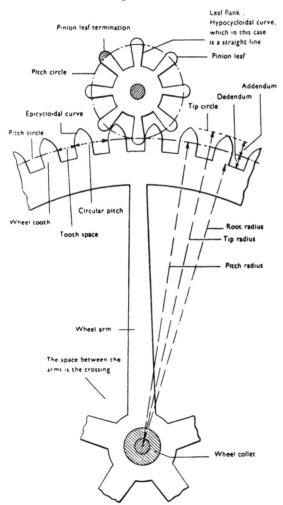

again free. In practice this is not wholly correct, because we have the freedom of the pivots to contend with, and there seems little doubt that even with an ideal gear—ideal as regards the correct pitch and the correct tooth and lear form — disengaging friction is generated, because of the movement of the bearings. To revert to the discs, teeth are made to project above the original circle and clearance is made by cutting into the circle, so the original circle is important because, when examining a depth, these two imaginary circles, the pitch circles, should coincide (Fig. 102). *In actual practice it is better, that is safer, for a depth to be a shade on the shallow side,*

Fig. 101. Definitions of the parts forming the wheel and pinion.

rather than too deep. Most pinions in watches have less than 11 leaves, usually 8 or 10, and disengaging friction is bound to be present, even if only to a very slight degree. With a pinion of 6 leaves and a wheel of less than 176 teeth, engaging friction takes place. In watches it is usual for a pinion of 6 leaves to engage a wheel of 60 or so teeth, and it follows that there must be considerable engaging friction in such a gearing ; hence if the watch has been running for some time pinions of 6 invariably become badly worn, due solely to the reason just stated.

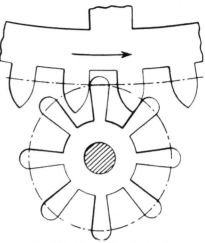

Fig. 102. Dotted lines indicating the pitch circles.

Sometimes it is found that the pinion is not of the correct ratio to the wheel, and it is not possible to make a correct gearing, no matter how you adjust the distance between the centres. Even if the pitch circles coincide as we have noted, there is still engaging friction, i.e., the incoming leaf of the pinion makes contact with the wheel tooth some distance before the line of centres. When this occurs the size of the pinion is not suitable to the wheel or, conversely, the wheel is not correct for the pinion. Therefore, it will be seen that if the engagement takes place before the line of centres (see Fig. 103), engaging friction takes place. The theoretically perfect gear is obtained with a wheel of not less than 96 teeth and a pinion of not less than 12 leaves. Provided the wheel and pinion are correctly proportioned, with the distance of centres accurately set, the wheel teeth will roll over the surface of the flanks of the pinion leaves. There will be no disengaging friction and certainly no engaging friction. When the tooth that is in engagement has finished its function it will have propelled the pinion so that the succeeding tooth will engage the succeeding leaf of the pinion on, or a little after, the line of centres, and we shall have an even regular motion of the moving parts. See Fig. 104.

Fig. 103. Showing the point at which engaging takes place.

The combination of a pinion of 12 and a wheel of 96 has been established as the minimum number for a perfect gear, but we all know that there is no such thing as perfection, and present-day authorities would debate the above statement. I am not talking about a good *commercial* gear but rather a mechanical ideal, so for my purpose I can stick to my idea of a perfect gear. Gearing is a study in itself; several books have been written on this one subject alone, but other than in the Grossman book, I can find little about the epicycloidal and hypocycloidal gears, the forms of gear that

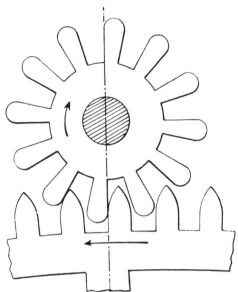

Fig. 104. The perfect gear : action takes place *on* the line of centres.

interest us most. It is a debatable subject, so I think it best to leave it at that. We must, however, bear in mind the question of the necessary freedom of the pivots (sideshake and endshake) in their holes, and the consequent effect this has on the gearing. If the pivots were without freedom the theoretical conditions would be complied with, but the watch would stop for reasons that have been stated elsewhere.

Here is an instance where theory does not work out in practice. I do not for one moment deprecate theory because of that. On the contrary, watchmakers have a great deal for which to thank mathematicians and scientists.

In the majority of watches the engagement takes place after the line of centres and a slipping or disengaging friction takes place, or engagement is slightly before the line of centres, or a mild form of engaging friction is present which is not usually detrimental. The illustration (Fig. 105) shows the depth too deep and (Fig. 106) too shallow.

Before we leave the subject of mathematically correct gear forms we must look at the Involute gear, Fig. 109; and also the Circular Arc form, Fig. 109a.

The involute curve is the line traced by a cord being unwound from a cylinder, Fig. 108. This form of gear is not much used in watch work, other than in some of the keyless wheels. A composite between the involute and cycloidal is, however, used extensively in Switzerland. Some factories have their own formula to form the curves, while others use the formula of the makers of the wheel cutting machines. Such a tooth form is known as the Mikron and is used in several Swiss factories. A very important step forward in gear cutting in England was made when the British Standards Institute standardised a tooth form known as the Circular Arc form, Fig. 109a.

Its introduction was primarily to assist manufacturers to reduce the quantities of cutters or hobbing tools in use ; originally it was necessary

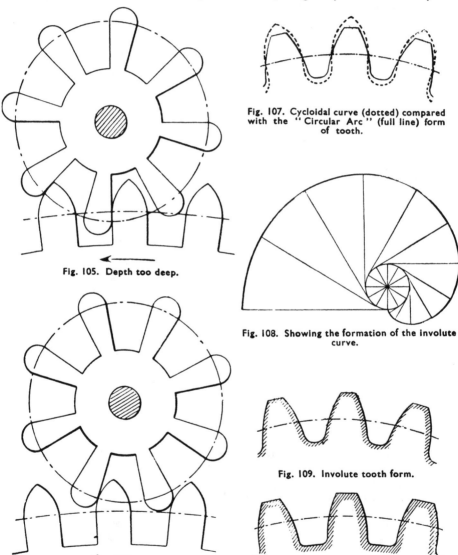

Fig. 105. Depth too deep.

Fig. 106. Depth too shallow.

Fig. 107. Cycloidal curve (dotted) compared with the " Circular Arc " (full line) form of tooth.

Fig. 108. Showing the formation of the involute curve.

Fig. 109. Involute tooth form.

Fig. 109a. Circular Arc tooth form.

to have large numbers made to comply with the conditions laid down for the cycloidal gearing. The foreword of the British Standard Specification says : " it has the advantage that a single hob of any pitch can be used to produce gears of any number of teeth of that pitch, whereas the cycloidal form requires at least eight hobs for each pitch." The shape of the pinion leaves is the same as that of the wheel teeth and they are cut with the same cutter.

The instructions which follow, however, apply equally to the circular arc form, and also the composite iorms mentioned, when the question of determining a correct depth is discussed.

To revert to our cycloidal gearing : if you have any doubt as to the size of the wheel check it up in the sector, which is a proportional gauge, see Fig. 110. Open the sector, insert the wheel and close it in on the wheel to correspond with the number of teeth in the wheel. Say the wheel has 64 teeth, then adjust the arms of the sector so that when the wheel is placed between at its *widest* part 64 will be registered on the scale (Fig. 111). Make the arms secure by means of the binding screw placed there for that purpose. At the lower end of the sector is a steel

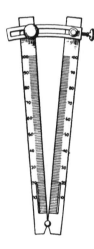

Fig. 110. The sector.

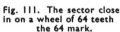

Fig. 111. The sector close in on a wheel of 64 teeth the 64 mark.

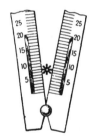

Fig. 112. The lower end of the sector with pinion of 8 registering 8.

gauge, which is for the pinion. We now place the pinion between the arms, slide it down, and observe at what figure it registers ; if it is correct it should stop at the 8 mark, as this pinion has 8 leaves. Make sure you gauge the widest part of the pinion, i.e., from the ends of the opposite leaves as shown in Fig. 112. If the pinion will not slide down so far it is too large and may have to be changed for one of the correct size. Conversely if the pinion registers lower than the 8 mark, then the pinion is too small. Manufacturers usually err on the side of fitting pinions too large. Jules and Hermann Grossman, in their book *Lessons in Horology*, Vol. I., say "it is best to make a deep gearing when the pinion is too large. Reciprocally, a gearing whose pinion is too small should be relatively shallow."

To be theoretically exact the sector is not absolutely correct. It cannot take into account the various forms of pinion leaf terminations ;

some are half round, some more elongated, like a Gothic arch, and various other considerations ; but for all practical purposes it is sufficiently accurate to give a good depth of gearing. Further, the sector is not suitable for high ratios, such as 12 to 1, here the allowance would be insufficient, the pinion would have to be larger than the number on the scale ; for a lower ratio, 4 to 1, the allowance would be too great, and the pinion would have to be smaller than the number indicated on the gauge. Wheels and pinions in watches are usually 7 or 8 to 1 proportionally, and so for our purpose the sector is sufficiently accurate.

If you wish to check the size of a doubtful pinion and have no access to a sector, and assuming the wheel has 64 teeth and the pinion 8 leaves, then the pitch diameter of the wheel must be 8 times the pitch diameter (ratio of 8 to 1) of the pinion. As we have seen, it is not convenient to mark on the parts their pitch diameters, so we must estimate the amount of the tooth above the pitch diameter, the addenda, and bear in mind to double this amount, as the projection is equal on both sides of the wheel. The same calculation must be made for the pinion.

You will see that our gauging is only an approximation, but at the same time it is accurate enough for our purpose. The best tool to use for such a check would be the micrometer or the Vernier gauge.

To use the micrometer, hold the tool in the right hand and open to the size of the wheel at its widest part, Fig. 113 ; this is most important. Micrometers are made to measure in inches or millimetres, but the actual method of reading is the same. We shall here consider the millimetre gauge. The diameter of the wheel reads, say, 9.55 millimetres. The millimetres are shown on the fixed arbor or barrel of the gauge and the number visible is counted. The last millimetre division is partly covered by the rotating " thimble," and on this thimble is engraved the decimal points of a millimetre. If the 0 on the thimble is in line with a millimetre on the barrel, then a full millimetre is indicated, as one complete revolution of the thimble is equal to half one of the millimetres marked on the barrel so, if half a millimetre is exposed on the barrel and the marking on the thimble indicates 5, then the reading is .55 millimetre as shown in the illustration, Fig. 114, i.e., 9 millimetres, five tenths millimetre and five hundredths on the thimble.

$$9.5$$
$$.05$$
$$9.55 \text{ millimetres.}$$

The Vernier gauge is read as follows (see Fig. 115) : open the jaws to engage the wheel and say we read 14 millimetres and something over. Now count the divisions on the sliding Vernier section of the gauge until you come to the one which exactly coincides with a division mark on the main part of the gauge. Say it is 7, then the measurement is 14.7 millimetres as indicated by the arrow in Fig. 115.

To continue with our wheel and pinion size calculation. The wheel has 64 teeth and measures 9.55 millimetres in diameter. The ratio is 8 : 1. So the diameter of the pinion should be approximately 1.2 millimetres, less 0.05 to 0.15 millimetres, depending on the shape of the pinion addendum.

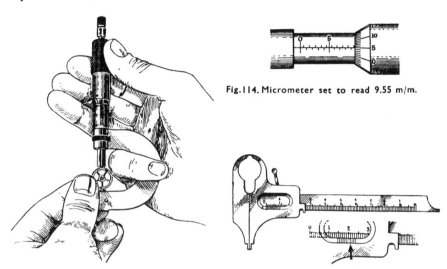

Fig.114. Micrometer set to read 9.55 m/m.

Fig. 113. The micrometer and the correct way to hold it.

Fig. 115. The Vernier gauge. The lower division reads 14.7 m/m.

It is difficult to examine the depths in most watches, so we have to improvise to a certain extent. Starting with the third wheel and fourth pinion, sharpen a piece of pegwood to a blunt point and press this on to the top of the fourth pivot, then with another pointer try the shake of the third wheel teeth in the pinion. Test the other wheels in the same way (Fig. 116).

A little practice will soon accustom you to judging if the depth— or gearing—is correct. If, however, there is any doubt about a particular depth, proceed as follows. Say it is the fourth wheel and escape pinion depth that is doubtful : fit these two parts up in the depth tool. First of all remove the wheels from the movement. Place the pointed runners in the depth tool, Fig. 117, both at one end with the points outward. Make one runner secure with the screw placed there for that purpose (B), leaving the other runner loose for the present. Now place the fixed runner in the pivot hole of the fourth wheel (it is usual to use the hole nearest the pinion head). Hold the tool perfectly upright—this is important—and adjust the screw (A) so that the loose pointed runner can be inserted in the escape wheel hole ; when this is

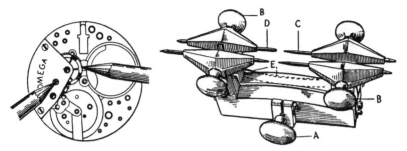

Fig. 116. Showing method
of trying depths.

Fig. 117. Depth tool. (A) Depthing screw.
(B) Screws to tighten runners. (C) Male
runner. (D) Female runner. (E) Spring to
make limbs follow up.

achieved make that runner secure also. Hold the movement at a
distance, with the runners in the holes, to make sure that the depth
tool is upright. If the tool leans to one side or the other the distance
between the centres is not correct. On no account touch the screw
(A) from now onwards. Now place the fourth wheel and escape wheel
in the depth tool and adjust the runners so that the wheel engages at
the end of the pinion. Female runners must be used so that the pivots
will fit into them. We are now able to examine the intersection clearly
(Fig. 118). Carefully make the escape wheel bind between the centres
by holding the finger on the end of the runner, exerting a little pressure
before making it secure. We now have exposed to view the depth as
it was when in the movement : move the fourth wheel with the finger
very slowly, and you will be able to see the whole cycle of the function
of the tooth and pinion leaf, which should appear as Fig. 104. If it is
as Fig. 105 it is too deep, and as Fig. 106, too shallow.

If the depth is too shallow, the wheel must be stretched and to do
this use the stretching tool, Fig. 119. Before actually using this tool,
first select a cutter of the topping tool that just fits the wheel, you will
see the reason for this presently. Hold the wheel as shown, Fig. 119,
lower the top punch and tap the top with a hammer, making the wheel
revolve while so doing. It is better to give the stake frequent light
blows while rotating the wheel several times. In this manner the wheel
will not be marked, and a more even distribution of stretching assured.
After the wheel has been treated in this manner it will be necessary to
pass the wheel through the topping tool.

Before we talk about the topping tool, there is another wheel stretching
tool I should like to mention. It consists of two narrow steel rollers,
like wheels. The wheel to be stretched is passed between these steel
rollers, operating at the roots of the teeth. A screw adjustment enables
the rollers to close together ; a handle is turned to make the wheels
rotate and, with the other hand, the train wheel is guided so that the
rollers operate on the same diameter all the way round. This system

has the advantage that it is not necessary to top the wheel, as the shape of the teeth had not been altered ; but it has the disadvantage of marking the wheel. See Fig. 120.

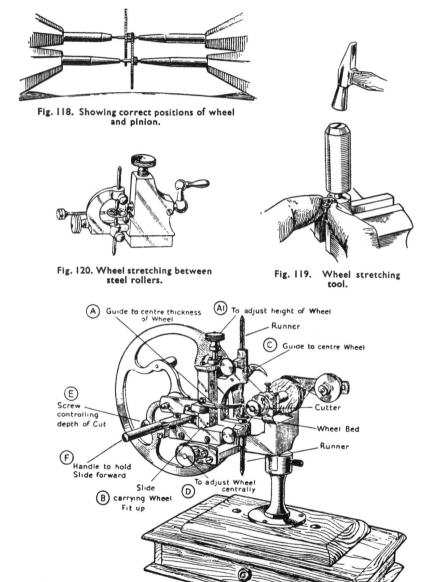

Fig. 118. Showing correct positions of wheel and pinion.

Fig. 120. Wheel stretching between steel rollers.

Fig. 119. Wheel stretching tool.

A Guide to centre thickness of Wheel
A1 To adjust height of Wheel
Runner
C Guide to centre Wheel
E Screw controlling depth of Cut
Cutter
Wheel Bed
Runner
F Handle to hold Slide forward
To adjust Wheel centrally
Slide
B carrying Wheel Fit up
D

Fig. 121. Topping tool.

To revert to the topping tool, Fig. 121 ; having stretched the wheel, the punch will have altered the shape of the teeth a little. A cutter was selected before we stretched the wheel. In order not to alter the original dimensions of the teeth, the cutter is selected in the following manner. To avoid making the teeth thinner a cutter of exactly the same thickness as the distance between two teeth is used. Hold the wheel in the left hand and with the right try the cutter between the teeth as in Fig. 122. Draw the cutter through as if it were cutting the teeth. To place the cutter between two teeth and draw out again may result in using a cutter which is too large ; also make sure, when gauging, to try with the widest or thickest part of the cutter, that is, the part that actually does the cutting.

Having selected the cutter, fit up as follows. Some cutters have an adjustment to operate the guide which moves the wheel forward one tooth at a time. If it has, adjust it so that when the thickest part of the cutter is in between two teeth, the thin part of the cutter, where there are no cutting teeth but just a knife edge, is *exactly* central in the next space (Fig. 123). Fig. 124 shows a close up of the cutter. The spring part from A—B is controlled by the screw shown. Some cutters are quite plain with no spring guide attached. In this case the cutter fits on to a brass bed which has the spring guide attached to it. Other than this the adjustment is exactly the same as the one just described.

Now secure the cutter in the tool. Select a brass bed, the diameter of which gives the fullest support to the wheel, but leaves the teeth free (Fig. 125).

Fit the bed in the machine (see Fig. 121) and adjust the wheel between the centres so that the wheel rests lightly on the bed. Secure the lower centre and apply a little pressure to the upper one, so that it binds the wheel, and make that secure also. Discretion must be exercised as to the amount of pressure used to cause the binding, we want the wheel to stay in place during topping and little

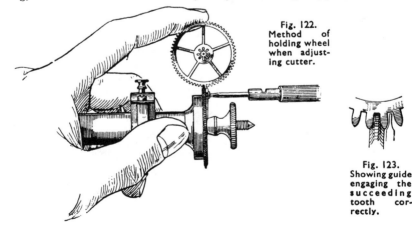

Fig. 122. Method of holding wheel when adjusting cutter.

Fig. 123. Showing guide engaging the succeeding tooth correctly.

Fig. 124.
Close up of
cutter. A-B
forms the
spring con-
trolled by
the screw.

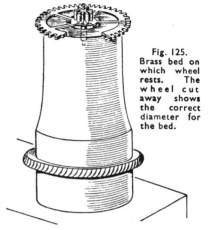

Fig. 125.
Brass bed on
which wheel
rests. The
wheel cut
away shows
the correct
diameter for
the bed.

more ; it must not drag unduly,
otherwise the shape of the teeth will
be affected. Attached to the tool is a
hook shaped guide (A) which we
now swing over, and it should point
to the centre of the thickness of the
wheel. The screw A1 will raise
or lower the wheel as required. An
adjusting screw attached to a slide (B), (which carries the wheel fit up),
enables us to centre the wheel, should it require it. Another guide (C)
is brought into operation to ensure that the cutter operates radially,
i.e., the teeth are cut upright. The adjusting screw (D) will bring the
cutter central with the centre of the wheel. The screw (E) forms a
stop to adjust the distance it is possible for the cutter to enter into the
wheel. As the wheel being topped needs the teeth re-shaped the stop
is adjusted so that the cutter cannot cut any further than the bottom of
the tooth. Adjustments are now complete and we are ready to start
cutting.

Bring the cutter on to the wheel. Make sure the guide part on the
cutter contacts the wheel first and that it enters between two teeth. Do
not engage the cutter by chance and commence turning the handle,
this action may spell disaster. We may have to move the wheel a little
with the finger so that it receives the cutter correctly.

Make the wheel revolve very slowly and watch closely with an eye-
glass to see that the guide and cutter are functioning correctly and that
the guide is moving the wheel forward one tooth at a time. When you
are satisfied that all is in order, proceed to cut until all the teeth have
been re-shaped. Hold the cutter part of the tool firmly forward by
means of the handle (F) provided for that purpose during the whole of
the cutting operation. It is not necessary to apply lubricant to the
cutting teeth of the cutter. The tool itself needs oil occasionally at all
the bearings and surfaces where friction occurs.

You will be able to tell when the cutting is complete by the free
running of the cutter. Remove the wheel from the tool and try the
depth. It may be necessary to recut with another cutter, the next size
wider ; it is always better to cut the minimum away at first. It is far
safer to make two, or even three, cuts to ensure a satisfactory result.

While talking about the topping tool we may as well mention other operations which can be performed with its aid. Should it be necessary to reduce the diameter of the wheel, owing to the depth being too great, use a cutter of the same width between the teeth and no other than the fit

Fig. 126. Making the wheel smaller in diameter. Dotted lines indicate the cut.

up adjustments referred to above ; the only adjustment necessary is to bring the cutter deeper into the wheel, a little at a time, and test the depth between each full cut (see Fig. 126).

Another operation may be to make the teeth thinner (see Fig. 127). For this we use a cutter of a thickness to fit between two teeth as a gauge and then select the one a size *larger*, otherwise the procedure is as for re-shaping the teeth. Some topping tools are supplied with cutters which have no guide adjustment. In such a case a separate guide piece is supplied, and this has two screws operating on guide springs. The cutter is fitted up in the tool with this guide piece and made secure. The guide adjustment is made when the wheel is fitted up in the topping tool. One screw in the guide is to bring the spring so that it engages

Fig. 127. Making the teeth thinner. Dotted line indicates the cut.

the succeeding tooth, and the other screw to bring that end of the spring upon which it operates to the middle of the cutter, so that when a cut is complete the guide follows on and moves the wheel round one tooth in precisely the same manner as the combined cutter and guide.

There are one or two important points to watch when using the topping tool : one is to make quite sure the cutter is central to the wheel, otherwise the teeth will be cut out of upright. The other is to see that the wheel is bound slightly, if there is too much friction there is a tendency for the wheel to drag unduly, which may result in a step being cut on one side of each tooth. On the other hand, if the wheel is left free between the centres, the tendency will be for the cutter to make a cut wider than it should.

The motion work must come under the heading of the train and receive attention as to the depths of its wheels. It is equally important that the motion work should gear as freely as the rest of the train, though it may not be so important that it gears accurately, i.e., at a theoretically correct depth. Examine the depth of the minute wheel with the cannon pinion, then the hour wheel with the minute wheel pinion. The hour wheel must be perfectly free on the cannon pinion (a matter we shall talk about again in the chapter on cleaning). An important point to watch is the liability of the cannon pinion to ride up. This may be due to one or two causes ; it is dealt with fully in the chapter on new parts dealing with fitting a cannon pinion.

CHAPTER EIGHT

THE BARREL AND MAINSPRING

WE NOW come to the barrel and mainspring and will start the examination with the mainspring removed. Place the barrel arbor in position with the spring out and the cover on. The arbor should have endshake.

Hold it in the sliding tongs, or pin vice, slightly tilted to one side so that the top of the jaws act as a guide (Fig. 128). First of all give it a spin to ensure that it is quite free. Then revolve it with the fingers and examine to see if it runs flat and upright ; here the jaws of the tongs come in useful. If the holes are too wide, causing the barrel to wobble, do not hesitate to rebush because, when in the watch and wound up, the mainspring will tend to cock the barrel to one side and cause fouling. If the barrel runs out of upright, that is up on one side and down on the other, rebush one hole. The cover hole is usually the better, because it is further from the teeth and altering

Fig. 128. Barrel held in pin vice to test its truth.

its position a little is not so likely to upset the centre pinion depth, Fig. 129.

When uprighting the barrel arbor in the barrel proceed as follows : Remove the barrel cover and the arbor and shellac the barrel on to a wax chuck in the lathe, Fig. 129. First secure the wax chuck in the lathe and apply heat to the chuck with a spirit lamp ; when sufficiently warm, smear over the surface a little shellac (shellac can be purchased in sticks similar to sealing wax) and stick the barrel in position on the chuck. Quickly bring the T rest into position as Fig. 129. Revolve the head-stock, and while so doing hold a piece of pegwood in the barrel arbor

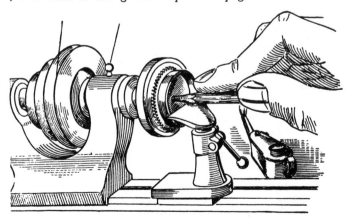

Fig. 129. Catching the barrel true on a wax chuck.

hole.   The pegwood should be larger than the hole and the end is made
round with a file.   Hold the pegwood firmly on the T rest so as to bring
the barrel central on the wax chuck ;   a little more heat may have to
be applied.   When the barrel is running *perfectly true*, cool it and set the
shellac by blowing, and leave for a minute or two to make quite sure the
barrel is secure.   Move the T rest out of the way.   Snap the barrel
cover on without removing the barrel from the lathe ;   this is important.

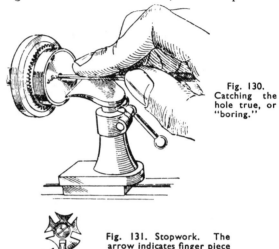

Fig. 130.
Catching the
hole true, or
"boring."

Bring the T rest into
position again and with
the cutter, Fig. 95,
catch the hole in the
barrel cover true, Fig.
130, as we did the
centre wheel hole,
when uprighting that
wheel.   Rebush the
hole in the same way
as for the centre wheel
hole.

If the barrel is fitted
with stopwork (Fig.
131) place the star
wheel and the finger
piece in position and
give the barrel a light
spin.

Fig. 131. Stopwork.   The
arrow indicates finger piece
"butting," fully wound.

It should revolve quite freely for all the four turns of the finger piece
(four turns is the usual number) until the finger piece banks on the
block of the star wheel.   Move the barrel round with the fingers and
occasionally try the shake of the star wheel when the finger is quite free
of it, and also during the function of the finger piece moving the star
wheel.   The star wheel should be perfectly free at all phases.   Remove
the finger piece and the star wheel should revolve quite freely if moved
with a fine pivot broach, we are then able to give it a more delicate
touch.   In fact, a fine pivot broach is a very useful guide while testing
the train wheels for freedom.

Now test the barrel in the frame to see that the holes are not too wide,
and also that the barrel is upright.   If the holes are wide fit new ones,
and if out of upright fit a new hole furthest from the barrel teeth, which
is usually the lower hole.

The same instructions apply when fitting new holes or uprighting
as were given when dealing with the centre wheel.   It is not necessary
to have any endshake of the barrel arbor at all between the plates or,
at most, very slight.   The barrel arbor does not revolve when the watch
is going, it revolves only during winding.   Wearers often complain that
after a watch has been repaired the winding is stiff, so see that the barrel

arbor is quite free ; this facilitates easy winding. Other than this, endshake to the barrel arbor between the plates is a danger. There is not much room as a rule for the barrel in the frame, the manufacturer quite rightly uses a mainspring as high as possible, with the result that with the endshake of the arbor in the barrel, and then endshake of the arbor in the frame, there is grave risk of the barrel fouling.

The mainspring of the average 30-hour watch should make 5½ to 6 turns in the barrel, i.e., you should be able to wind the barrel arbor for 5½ to 6 revolutions. To achieve this there are certain conditions to be complied with, and I think the simplest is to see that the spring occupies one third of the barrel space, the barrel arbor one third, and the remaining one third to be empty for the spring to occupy when fully wound round the arbor (Fig. 132). To be correct, the unwound mainspring should occupy rather less than one third of the width between the barrel arbor and the inside of the barrel wall. When wound, of course, the spring occupies the centre third, shown as B in Fig. 132. For all practical purposes then, one third each of the width allocated to the mainspring, empty space and the arbor answers quite satisfactorily.

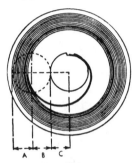

Fig. 132. The correct amount of space the mainspring should occupy in the barrel.

A = Position occupied by unwound mainspring.

B = Position occupied by spring when wound.

C = Radius of arbor.

A ready means of determining the correct position for the mainspring to occupy in the barrel is to take a pair of dividers, one leg of which has a trumpet end. Place the trumpet end in the barrel hole and open the other leg so that it touches the outer wall of the barrel. Transfer this measurement to a piece of brass or paper and divide it into three, then take two of these thirds and adjust the dividers to that size ; place the trumpet end in the hole of the barrel again and score a circle. The outer circle is the space to be occupied by the mainspring when unwound or, to be correct, the spring should take up a little less than the space so defined.

The correct length of mainspring is very important because the work, or force, of a spring is inversely proportionate to the length ; i.e., a spring twice as long as another will exert only half the force, provided it is bent through the same arc. The reason is that the long spring is not bent so much as a shorter one. By having the barrel too full the maximum number of turns are not obtained, which affects the number of hours run, and the maximum power is not achieved.

The strength of the mainspring is directly proportionate to its height, i.e., a mainspring twice as high as another will exert twice the force. The strength of the mainspring is proportionate to the cube of its thickness ; i.e., a mainspring twice as thick as another will exert 8 times the force.

It will be seen from the foregoing that there are certain limitations regarding the strength and height of the mainspring. If too high it will bind, if too strong we may not be able to get sufficient turns from it, with the result that the watch will run short of the required number of hours, quite apart from exerting too much force.

The height of the mainspring should be such that when the barrel cover is snapped into position the mainspring should have endshake. If the barrel cover is not recessed, the spring should stand in the barrel just below the shoulder on which the cover rests. If the cover is recessed, the spring can stand as high as this shoulder, and the recess of the cover will give it the necessary freedom. A mainspring too low, one having too much endshake, has the tendency to buckle or cockle when partly run down, causing excessive friction, and the spring will rub both the bottom of the barrel and the cover excessively.

A very important point to watch, especially with weak springs, is to see that the diameter of the barrel arbor, that is the part around which the mainspring wraps, is larger than the boss of the barrel and the cover.

To put it another way, the boss of the barrel and the cover must be a little smaller than the body of the barrel arbor (Fig. 133). Lack of

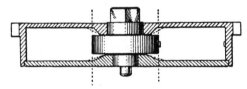

Fig. 133. The vertical dotted lines indicate the position of the mainspring, the dotted lines cutting indicate where the mainspring is liable to bind.

attention in this direction can be a constant source of trouble as this condition may cause the watch to stop when fully wound. If you try the spring in the barrel out of the watch it may seem quite free, with no signs of the arbor binding, but when going in the watch this fault develops. We must remember that the spring unwinds very slowly when the watch is going normally, there is no momentum or sudden jerk to overcome this extra friction, so if you have any doubts about the freedom here, reduce the size of the bosses.

There are numerous forms of mainspring hooking. Fig. 134 shows those most popular today ; the system most commonly used is the riveted on piece ; it is simple and very effective. The 13 ligne wrist watch we are now examining is fitted with such a spring.

To fit a new mainspring proceed as follows : It is better, before hooking, to wind the mainspring in the barrel to see if it is of the correct length. Alternatively, it may be possible to gauge

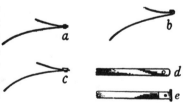

Fig. 134. (a) riveted on piece. (b) bent over end and a loose piece. (c) stud and loose piece. (d) eye to engage hook in barrel. Bottom ; (e) brace hooking.

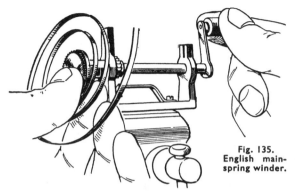

Fig. 135.
English main-
spring winder.

the length from the old spring. If you are able to obtain a spring as supplied by the maker of the movement, it will be broken down to the correct length and already hooked. Failing this, break to the correct length (springs are usually left too long), and use a piece of the broken spring for the piece to be riveted on.

Just a word here about winding the mainspring into the barrel. Use the tool illustrated in Fig. 135, but before winding take hold of the end of the spring near the hook with the brass nosed pliers and draw the spring through a clean linen rag. Draw out to as near the eye in the centre of the spring as possible, without causing distortion. (See Fig. 136.)

There are two methods of using this mainspring winder (Fig. 135). First, secure the tool in the vice. One method is to hold the mainspring between the thumb and first finger of the left hand and wind the spring up as small as possible ; hold the spring thus and with the right hand present the barrel to the wound spring ; the spring will be smaller in diameter than the inside of the barrel. By careful manipulation the mainspring is slowly released and the hook on the spring will engage the hook in the barrel. The barrel is now held and allowed to revolve slowly until the spring is safely in position. This method can be employed with the larger sizes, say from 10½ ligne upwards.

When winding mainsprings into their barrels the finger must come into contact with the spring and there is a very real risk of rusting. I am of the opinion that rust is the cause of a high percentage of mainsprings breaking. The moisture conveyed to the spring may be so slight as not to be perceptible to the naked eye, but the *slightest* spot of rust on the spring is an invitation for it to break at that point. Sometimes it is

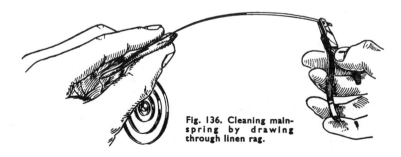

Fig. 136. Cleaning main-
spring by drawing
through linen rag.

possible to hold the mainspring with a linen rag during the winding, and wherever possible I should strongly recommend this being done. Usually the procedure is only practicable with a pocket size spring, and then care must be exercised : first, to use a rag without fluff and, secondly, during the unwinding, see that the coils of the spring as they close in tightly together do not nip the rag. If these precautions are not taken we are likely to have pieces of linen left between the coils of the spring.

Another way in which to overcome, or partly to overcome, the difficulty of avoiding moisture, is to draw the mainspring through a piece of oiled tissue paper. The disadvantage of this is that the fingers become oily, and the barrel is liable to become oily as a result.

I am convinced that watchmakers do not give enough serious thought to this problem of touching and manipulating mainsprings with the fingers. Unfortunately, I know of no tool which entirely obviates manual contact, but such actual contacts should be reduced to an absolute minimum. No hard and fast rule can be laid down, and it is, therefore, a case for employing one's own discretion or, rather, initiative.

The second method of using the same winder is first to hook the mainspring eye to the hook of the tool, then hold the barrel in the left hand and present it to the unwound spring ; hold the spring with the first two fingers and the barrel with the thumb (Fig. 135) ; wind the main-

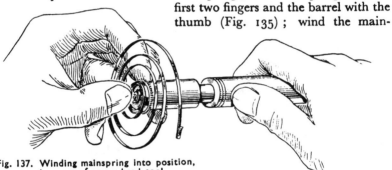

Fig. 137. Winding mainspring into position, using part of screw-head tool.

spring up and, when the diameter is small enough, you will feel the barrel jump forward a little. The hook of the spring will engage the hook in the barrel. Now hold the barrel and allow it to revolve slowly until the spring is in position. This method usually has to be adopted with small barrels and springs.

Another method, and one quite satisfactory for very small barrels, is to place the barrel arbor in the barrel, and hold the arbor (in a brass chuck) in the rolling stock of the screw-head tool. Hold the mainspring over the arbor (Fig. 137), and wind until the barrel arbor hook engages in the eye of the mainspring ; continue winding, using the thumb to hold the spring in contact with the barrel. You will feel when the spring has hooked to the barrel, and when this occurs immediately grip the barrel, allowing the rolling stock to reverse slowly so that the spring unwinds into position.

The other form of mainspring winder is illustrated in Fig. 138. The mainspring is wound into a box or toothless barrel, of smaller diameter than the watch barrel. The mainspring is then pushed, by means of a plunger device, from the winder barrel into the watch barrel. This is quite a good system but it does not obviate the possibility of rust.

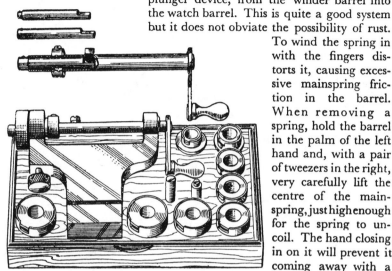

To wind the spring in with the fingers distorts it, causing excessive mainspring friction in the barrel. When removing a spring, hold the barrel in the palm of the left hand and, with a pair of tweezers in the right, very carefully lift the centre of the mainspring, just high enough for the spring to uncoil. The hand closing in on it will prevent it coming away with a rush and eliminate the possibility of distortion.

Fig. 138. American mainspring winder.

With some of the very small barrels this is not possible, so we employ the same principle, but using only the thumb and first two fingers of the left hand. *The point to watch in either method is not to pull the spring out, thereby distorting it so that it assumes a conical form.*

To return to the hooking of the mainspring. Heat the extreme end of the spring to a distance of not more than a quarter of an inch ; let the extreme tip down to a greenish colour. Drill a small hole as indicated in illustration (Fig. 139). The best way to make the hole is to use the chamfer tool (Fig. 97, page 66). Place the spring on a hard wood block, such as a filing block, and chamfer where the hole is to be made.

Fig. 139. Mainspring showing shape of end with small hole for rivet.

A bump will appear on the reverse side of the spring ; file this flat and a small hole will be left. Having filed the end up to shape as indicated (Fig. 139), do the same to the piece to be riveted on.

Clean the spring with a No. 0 emery buff, leaving a straight grain, that is, one running lengthwise. Clean the discoloration from the end of the mainspring, both sides and edges. Now hold the spring and the small piece together and broach the holes open at the same time, and remove the burrs thrown up by the broaching with the chamfering tool. File a pin of soft steel to fit the holes tightly and fit up in a vice as illustrated in Fig. 140. While still in the vice cut the pin close to the spring with the nippers ; file so that a very slight portion of the pin projects, and rivet this portion with a round faced hammer. Remove from the vice, cut the other end of the pin close to the spring and file down as before, and rivet on a steel stake.

If you are dealing with a low mainspring, such as would be used in a flat watch, it is not always advisable to drill a hole in it as this tends to weaken it. The best procedure is to bend the end over. The illustration (Fig. 141) shows how this is done.

Fig. 140. Method of holding in vice to rivet end into position.

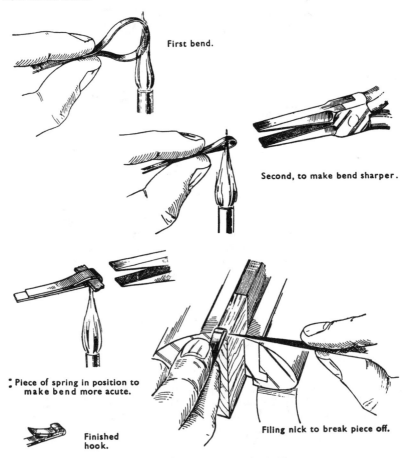

First bend.

Second, to make bend sharper.

Piece of spring in position to make bend more acute.

Finished hook.

Filing nick to break piece off.

Fig. 141. Forming a mainspring hook.

It is better not to break the spring down to size at first. If the spring is very much too large, then break some away, leaving 2 or 3 inches for convenience of bending. Bend the spring over at about the position of the length ultimately required and, while holding the spring, apply heat as indicated in the illustration. The spring will at once start to move. Hold the end so folded over close to the main part of the spring between the thumb and first finger of the left hand. In the right hand heat a pair of flat-nosed pliers (the long narrow ones are useful for this purpose). Now apply more heat at the fold of the mainspring and when it moves give the fold a slight nip with the hot pliers, not too severe at first or the spring will fracture. Repeat this once or twice. When the fold is getting close, break off a short piece of the superfluous spring and slip it inside the fold ; apply heat again, with this piece of spring in position. Now give it a final nip with the hot pliers, fairly hard this time, and hold it for a moment or two. The result should be a neat bend over. Nick the top surface of the spring near the fold with a three-cornered file, and if the folded piece of spring is lifted up it will break away. File square the end of the hook thus formed and finish with an emery buff as previously explained. Finally, a short length of mainspring is filed to shape and inserted as shown in the last illustration in Fig. 141 so as to engage the hook in the barrel.

When it is necessary to fit a new hook to the barrel, I am not in favour of the pressed-in type of hook ; tools are made to carry out this work in one operation.

I prefer the steel screw-in type of hook. The hole in the barrel should be at a slight angle, in a direction against the pull of the mainspring. This makes for increased strength and adds a little to the thread of the screw. File up a piece of soft steel wire and tap it to suit the hole. On the end of this tapped piece of steel file the hook. The illustration (Fig. 142) shows the procedure. Remove from the screw plate when finished and screw it into the barrel from the inside. Hold the end projecting on the outside in the pin tongs and unscrew, and this will draw the hook inwards towards the inside of the barrel wall.

Make sure the hook is facing the correct way and, when in the correct position, remove the pin tongs and cut away the portion not required with the nippers, as close to the barrel as possible. File closely to the barrel without touching and, finally, stone flush with the barrel with an Arkansas stone slip.

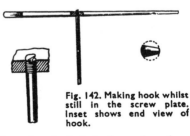

Fig. 142. Making hook whilst still in the screw plate. Inset shows end view of hook.

The hook and eye form, a hook in the barrel and a hole in the mainspring, is only suitable for barrels fitted with stopwork ; usually such watches have no form of recoiling clickwork. It is not necessary, because the stopwork prevents the mainspring from being fully wound.

To fit a new spring with a hole break the spring down to size ; heat the end as before and make the hole. Now open the hole fairly large so that it will fit freely over the hook in the barrel. The final broaching is carried out with the broach held at an angle as shown (Fig. 143), this gives an undercut to the edge of the hole that contacts the hook. Remove all burrs and clean up this end with the emery buff. To ensure that the

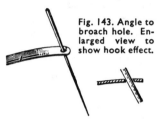

Fig. 143. Angle to broach hole. En-larged view to show hook effect.

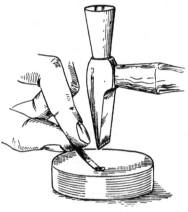

Fig. 144. Peaning end of mainspring.

spring hooks safely, give the end of the spring a curve similar to that of the inside of the barrel. To do this, place it on a lead block and pean the end as shown in illustration (Fig. 144) ; this will cause the end to curl up with little fear of a fracture.

The pivoted brace form of hooking is met with in American and some Swiss watches. The virtue of this system is that the end of the mainspring is allowed to swing round when fully wound. It is claimed that a better spring development is assured. This system needs a recoiling click. When fitting a new spring, the points to watch are that the pivoted brace should not be higher or wider than the mainspring, otherwise when fully wound, and the spring pulls the brace round, it may bind between the bottom of the barrel and the cover and not return. The other point to check is that the pivots do not project beyond the thickness of the bottom of the barrel and the cover, otherwise the projections may foul another part of the watch.

There are several other systems of hooking which I think do not concern us here, and there are slipping-spring systems developing in Switzerland. Here are three systems of slipping mainsprings. The one as illustrated (Fig. 145) is used by the Rolex Co. in some of their models ; it is quite simple. The three notches cut into the sides of the barrel allow the spring to cling to one of them until the watch is fully wound, when, if extra pressure is exerted, the spring slips to the next notch, and so on.

Another system (Fig. 146), is used by the Movado Watch Co. A stiff spring is inserted into the barrel first, it has a small hook end, and on to this hook a stud riveted on to the mainspring engages. When the spring is fully wound the spring clip slips round the inside of the barrel and the friction of the expanding ring comes into action.

Fig. 145. Rolex Watch Co. slipping mainspring device.

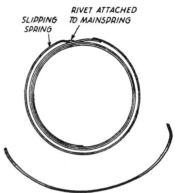

Fig. 146. Slipping device used by the Movado Watch Co.

The system illustrated in Fig. 147, devised and patented by the author, has several advantages over some other systems. All the available space in the barrel is given to the mainspring ; no sudden jerk is experienced when the spring is fully wound and starts to slip ; an indicator shows when the spring is actually being wound. The action is quite simple :—

The ratchet wheel (A) is recessed to receive the spring (B) and a large round hole is made in the place of the usual square hole of the ratchet wheel. A boss (C), with a square hole (D) fits on the barrel arbor, and the tongue engages on the spring. The action is that as the watch is wound the ratchet wheel carries the spring (B) and this spring makes the boss (C) revolve, and so the mainspring is wound. When fully wound the boss (C) remains stationary, but the ratchet wheel can be made to revolve ; the spring (B) slips in the recess of the ratchet wheel. Fixed to the barrel arbor by means of an extended pivot is a hand which revolves while the mainspring is being wound, remaining stationary when fully wound.

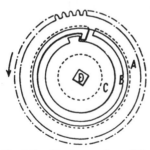

Fig. 147. Slipping ratchet. (A) Ratchet wheel ; (B) Slipping spring; (C) Boss with tongue square on to barrel arbor.

While talking about the mainspring we will for a moment look at the recoiling click. The object is to prevent the final pull of the mainspring on the hook when tightly wound. The recoil of the ratchet (usually the equivalent of about two teeth), allows the mainspring to unwind a little and so prevent that extra tight wind which can cause the watch to knock, with the consequent excessive gaining during the knocking ; *i.e.*, the excessive arc of vibration of the balance which causes the ruby pin to hit, or knock, the outside of the lever fork. There are one or two systems of the recoiling click ; one is an elongated hole in the click, which allows

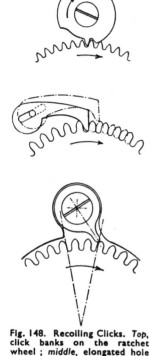

the click to travel forwards during the winding and then backwards a little upon release of the winding button. Another system is to employ a click with a large angle of movement and a part of the plate so cut as to allow it to bank against it when the winding is released, or sometimes the click locks on the ratchet wheel itself. (See Fig. 148.)

A new form of mainspring is now being made both in America and Switzerland. Instead of the usual flat ribbon, a segment of a circle section is employed (Fig. 149). The advantage of this is at once apparent. A thinner spring can be employed which will give a greater number of turns in the barrel. This facilitates rating over a given number of hours.

The spring, being weaker, is less likely to break. The reason is that the molecules on either side of the neutral axis are not subjected to the strain experienced in a thicker spring. Fig. 150 shows what takes place during tension of a spring. The reason for the increased power exerted by a curved section spring is that to a certain degree we are utilising the thickness of the spring as the height. For instance, if we take a mainspring of say 1.5 mm. height and .1 mm. thick, and instead of coiling it in the usual manner, coil it edgeways, it would become a spring of .1 mm. in height having the strength of a spring 1.5 mm. in thickness. Such a spring (if it were practicable, which it is not) would exert considerably more force than if coiled in the conventional manner.

Fig. 148. Recoiling Clicks. *Top*, click banks on the ratchet wheel ; *middle*, elongated hole in click ; *bottom*, click banks on plate.

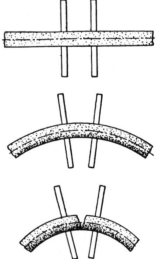

Fig. 149. The new curved section mainspring. Inset shows curve. This sketch much exaggerates the curve.

Fig. 150. Breaking mainspring. *Top* : dotted line indicates the neutral axis. *Middle* : density of dots below neutral axis indicates compression and above the axis the stretching. *Bottom* : so much compression below axis and stretching above that the spring snaps, the limit of elasticity has been exceeded.

The reason for mainsprings breaking is often debated and, to summarise, it seems there are five main causes :

(a) Rust, even minute specks.

(b) Cross grain scratches, i.e., scratches that run against the grain of the metal.

(c) Barrel hook projecting too far into the barrel.

(d) Barrel arbor hook longer than the thickness of the mainspring.

(e) The thickness of the mainspring should not be thicker than a 32nd part of the diameter of the barrel arbor. It has been established by Roye, Sen. and Jnr. (Swiss), in 1857, that the thickness of a mainspring must not exceed one thirty-second, or at most one thirtieth part of the diameter of the barrel arbor ; for instance, if the barrel arbor is 5 mm. diameter then the spring should be between .160 to .166 mm. (approx.).

CHAPTER NINE

HAND CLEANING AND OILING

THERE ARE two methods of cleaning in use today, one by using benzine and brushing, and the other by the machine especially made for that purpose. The benzine method will be discussed first. In the third chapter was a description of taking the movement to pieces in order to become familiar with the various parts and the manner of handling. It is necessary, in order to make this chapter more complete, to assume that the movement has yet to be taken to pieces, so that advice can be given as to what to do with the parts when they are dismantled. First take the movement out of the case and remove the hands and dial. Dust the dial with the watch brush. A dial needs to be treated with respect : if it is made of enamel, brush carefully. Sometimes an unseen crack will show up after brushing, due to the dust on the dial being brushed into the crack. To remove the dust and thus make the crack invisible again, hold the

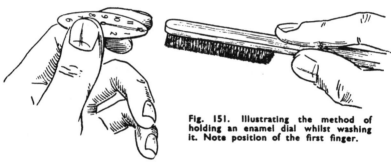

Fig. 151. Illustrating the method of holding an enamel dial whilst washing it. Note position of the first finger.

dial as Fig. 151 so that the crack or cracks run lengthways. Exert slight upward pressure with the first finger which opens the crack slightly. While holding the dial thus, place under a tap of running water—warm water for preference—and, with a soft clean watch brush and a little soap, brush the dial lengthways of the crack. Brush until all soap disappears, withdraw from the flow of water, dry off all water with tissue paper and not until the dial is perfectly dry on the face do we release our hold. Do not brush the face of the dial again, but dry off the back and ensure that all traces of moisture are removed. Generally speaking it is not advisable to touch silver dials. Some of the surfaces are lacquered and do not respond even to mild treatment, and if any form of abrasive is used the lacquer is liable to skin off, and with it may come the figures. Some of the dull silver dials can be improved by rubbing carefully with a little cream of tartar made just damp and used on a piece of linen or the inside of an old chamois leather watch bag. Usually metal dials are best left alone other than for a light brushing. If such a dial needs reviving and it is the owner's wish, then it is a matter for the dial restorer.

Having removed the dial, put it in a safe place ; it will not be needed again until the movement is finished. Place the hands in the benzine pot. Just a word about the benzine pot. It should be cleaned out at least once a week or more frequently if the benzine is dirty. It is advisable to empty the pot into a container kept for that purpose and this benzine used for clock work. Do not pour fresh benzine into a pot containing dirty benzine. Clean the pot out with a duster and then pour in the fresh benzine to a depth of about half an inch, not more. Now remove the hour and minute wheels and the cannon pinion, and place them in the benzine. Remove the balance cock and the balance from the cock. Remove the balance spring from the balance and clean the balance. If the balance is cut, buff the top edge with a leather buff charged with dry diamantine. Dry diamantine is better than rouge for this purpose as it is sharper. Immerse the balance, suspended on a piece of brass wire, in a solution of cyanide of potassium and swirl it about for a few moments.

The solution is made up by dissolving a piece of cyanide about the size of a walnut in a teacupful of warm water, and should be kept in a glass jar with a glass stopper. Needless to say it is a deadly poison and should not be kept on or near the bench as the solution quickly rusts steel work.

Well wash the balance in clear water, remove and blow on it to rid it of all superfluous water. This is the single exception where it is permissible to blow with the mouth on a part of the watch. Charge a soft watch brush with plenty of chalk and give the balance a good brushing on the top and under side and the edges where the screws are, until it is quite bright. Then drop the balance in either box-wood dust or killed lime and leave it there until the rest of the watch has been cleaned and assembled, by which time the balance will be perfectly dry.

A useful container for the box-wood dust is easily made. Procure two tins about 2 inches diameter and 1 to 2 inches deep and fitted with lids. Cut the bottoms out of both tins, and solder them together with a piece of gauze wire between. The result is a short tin tube with gauze half way down, see illustration (Fig. 152). To use this box, replace bottom lid and fill the top half with box-wood dust or killed lime; bury the balance in the dust and replace the lid of that half. Leave the box standing on the bench thus until wanted. When ready to deal with the balance, shake the box gently, and this will cause the dust to sieve through to the lower half of the box and leave the balance exposed on the gauze. Reverse the box gently, and open the lid when

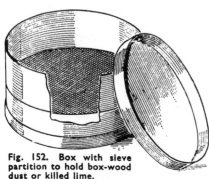

Fig. 152. Box with sieve partition to hold box-wood dust or killed lime.

next wanted. If it is not convenient to make such a box, a tin about 2 inches diameter and 1 to 2 inches deep can be used, burying the balance in the dust. When the balance is again required, a few slight taps with a knuckle on the underside of the tin before removing the lid will quickly bring it to the surface of the dust.

Take the balance cock to pieces and place the parts and the balance spring in the benzine. Now remove the pallet cock and the pallets and place them also in the benzine. Leave the pallets in the benzine only for a few moments. Some shellac stands up to benzine well and some does not ; the pallets we are cleaning may not so, to be on the safe side, remove them after a few moments. A word about watch brushes. Some watchmakers employ the stiff kind, but generally speaking the soft kind are to be preferred. To clean the brush it is best to rub it occasionally on a burnt mutton bone : the bone from the leg is best. When preparing the bone, all meat should be removed and the bone placed in a clear red fire and left there until it will no longer burn. Upon removal from the fire it will be found to be white. When cold it should be used as you would use chalk, finally brushing the brush on clean tissue paper. You will find that a brush cleaned in this manner is free from dust, and the brush comes cleaner than one that has been cleaned with chalk. To clean the pallets, hold them down on the bench with the tweezers while still wet with benzine and brush well with a soft watch brush. Brush both sides of the pallets and on no account hold the pallets in the bare fingers.

To clean the pallet stones, hold the lever in tissue paper between the first finger and thumb of the left hand and brush carefully, finally wiping each stone with a piece of soft pith. (See Fig. 153.) Continue to use the pith until the stones glisten, especially the locking and the impulse faces. Now reverse the pallets in the fingers—still between the tissue paper— and pith the notch, rubbing it backwards and forwards. It is quite safe so to do provided you are using soft pith. Sharpen a piece of pegwood to a long chisel shaped end, and well peg each side of the notch, drawing the peg backwards and forwards along each side. Finally, lay the pallets on the bench, hold down with the tweezers and lightly brush again with the brush to ensure the removal of pieces of pith and pegwood. Give a puff or two with the bellows and place under a glass shade. The illustration, Fig. 154, shows the method of holding down pieces on the bench while cleaning.

Fig. 153. Holding pallets when cleaning the stones.

While these detailed descriptions may cause cleaning to appear to be a lengthy business, it is not so in practice. The actual cleaning of a movement can be carried out in about three-quarters to one hour.

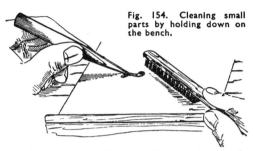

Fig. 154. Cleaning small parts by holding down on the bench.

It is advisable to place on the bench a small square of tissue paper and to cover this with the glass shade. Place the parts as they are cleaned on the tissue paper. In this manner it is convenient, when all the parts are cleaned, to remove the glass shade and draw the tissue paper towards you with the parts ready to hand for assembly. We next remove the centre, third, fourth and escape wheel bar, or bars if some of the wheels are under separate bars or cocks. It is advisable to brush the centre, third, fourth and escape wheels with a soft watch brush (kept especially for that purpose) dipped in the benzine. Well brush the teeth and then place the wheels in the benzine pot. Treat the bar or bars in a similar manner. Before dismantling the movement further, finish cleaning the parts that are in the benzine pot. Remove the balance spring and place it on a clean piece of tissue paper and dab it with a clean soft watch brush. Move the spring on the tissue paper frequently so that the paper absorbs the benzine. Finally, fold a dry part of the tissue paper over the spring and dab the paper so that the spring is cleaned by direct contact with the paper on both sides (see Fig. 155). Place the cleaned balance spring on the tissue paper under the glass shade. To save repetition, it should be understood that all parts, after being cleaned, are puffed with the bellows and placed under the shade. No part should be left exposed after cleaning. It becomes a habit to place everything under cover and it is a good habit to cultivate.

Remove the balance cock from the benzine and dry it with a piece of linen rag. Then hold it in tissue paper and brush well. If the piece is gilt, give the brush a circular motion ; it is then not so inclined to scratch

Fig. 155.

the surface. Nickel finished parts are best cleaned by brushing with the grain of the finish. If the finish is circular or damascened, brush with a circular motion as for the gilt finish. Brush the balance cock well on both sides and also the edges. Clean both surfaces of the jewel hole with a sharpened pegwood, rubbing the surfaces until they glisten.

Sharpen the pegwood to a fairly long point and peg the hole from both sides, scraping the pegpoint with the bench knife to keep it clean. Finally, lightly brush the cock to remove pieces of pegwood and dust. Remove the index, end piece and screws from the benzine, hold these parts down on the bench with the tweezers and brush well while still wet.

Next deal with the end piece. Well clean the endstone, both sides, with pegwood. Brush the screws ; do not endeavour to clean them by rolling them on the board paper with the finger as moisture may be imparted, which will result in the screw rusting in its hole. This equally applies to all screws. Reassemble the balance cock, sharpen the pegwood to a chisel shape and clean well between the index pins. All traces of oil or grease must be removed. It is a good practice to keep a piece of pegwood sharpened chisel shape, and the end charged with rouge, especially for cleaning index and banking pins. Clean the balance cock screw and drop it in position. Make it a habit to associate all screws with their respective parts.

The rest of the parts are cleaned in a similar manner. Pieces too large to hold with the tweezers during cleaning are held in tissue paper. The escape wheel is well brushed and then held in tissue paper as were the pallets. Draw soft pith across all the teeth, brushing the teeth, as it were, with pith. Hold the wheel in the tweezers and dab with the brush,

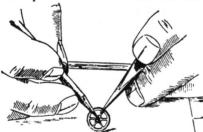

especially the leaves of the pinion. Sharpen the pegwood and clean the leaves of the pinion, work the peg up and down in the leaves until they are quite bright (Fig. 156). Clean all the pinions in this manner, finishing with a light brush. The teeth of the other wheels are cleaned by brushing, holding them as we did the escape wheel. The pivots

Fig. 156. Illustrating method of holding wheel whilst cleaning the leaves of the pinion.

are cleaned with pith. Select a fairly hard piece and press the end on to the pivot right down to the shoulder and then twirl the pith round. This will clean both the pivot and the shoulder. Treat all the pivots in this way. Sometimes you will find that pivots are brown, due to a chemical action of the oil on the steel pivot. It is advisable to remove all discoloration and to do this quickly, proceed as follows. Cut the end of a piece of pegwood chisel shape and just damp one of the flats with diamantine. Hold and arrange so that the pivot to be treated rests on the box-wood filing block, held in the vice. Proceed to polish the pivot with the diamantine charged pegwood, revolving the wheel while so doing (see Fig. 157). Well peg the hole in the hour and minute wheels.

Having cleaned all the parts that were in the benzine, we proceed to finish the dismantling. Remove the barrel bar from the bottom plate and take off all the parts attached to it, brush all the large parts with the benzine brush and place all in the benzine. Take the barrel to pieces and place all but the mainspring in the benzine. It is not advisable to benzine the mainspring, as they break so mysteriously, and it seems to me

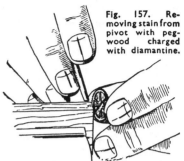

Fig. 157. Removing stain from pivot with pegwood charged with diamantine.

rather to invite breaking by removing every trace of oil. To clean the mainspring, hold it near the hook with the brass nosed pliers and carefully draw the spring between a clean linen rag held between the first finger and thumb (see Fig. 136). While so cleaning the spring, do not hold it in such a manner that the shape or curve of the spring is varied. *The form of the spring must not be altered.* A piece of metal bent backwards and forwards will ultimately break, due to the molecular disturbance at that point. It must follow, therefore, that if you alter the form of the mainspring, that is beyond the natural flexing of the spring (not to be confused with the limit of elasticity, following which the spring breaks), you are making it one step nearer to breaking.

Remove all the pieces from the bottom plate, including the balance endstone and other endstones if they are fitted. Well brush the bottom plate with the benzine brush and place it and all the other parts in the benzine. Finish cleaning the parts still in the benzine in the manner already described. Dry the large pieces with the linen rag and brush the smaller pieces while wet. The bottom plate calls for special attention. Having dried it, brush well, and then clean all the countersunk parts with a piece of pith ; clean the surfaces of the jewel holes, peg all the holes from both sides. Peg large holes with pegwood sharpened to a long point. Peg the pull-out piece screw hole ; remember the pull-out piece screw revolves in its hole each time the hands are set and must, therefore, be free. Clean the bankings with the chisel peg as we did the index pins. Having cleaned all the parts, we are now ready to reassemble.

First of all brush the board paper off with a dusting brush. A painter's dusting brush is useful for this purpose. Then remove the glass shade and draw the tissue paper with the cleaned parts on it towards you ; give all the parts collectively a few puffs with the bellows. Always replace the glass shade over the pieces when not working on them. First assemble the barrel. Wind the mainspring into the barrel and apply about two clockoilerfuls of clock oil to the top edges of the mainspring. Work the oil over the whole of the top edges. Place the arbor in position and see that the eye of the mainspring engages on the hook of the arbor. The centre of the mainspring should hug the barrel arbor, so it is necessary to push the spring to one side to admit the arbor. If you find that this is not so, bend the centre in with the brass nosed pliers, otherwise there is a risk of the spring unhooking at the centre when the spring has fully run down. Snap the cover in position ; the cut out notch of the cover should come opposite a dot on the barrel.

Sometimes the cover and the barrel both have dots and, if they have, the dots should come opposite. This is an important point to observe, because the barrel is made to run true when the cover is in that particular position. To snap the cover on, do not use a tool but hold against the edge of the bench (Fig. 158), and with a little pressure the cover will snap into position. Hold the barrel arbor with the brass nosed pliers and try the endshake. The arbor should have little endshake ; it must, however,

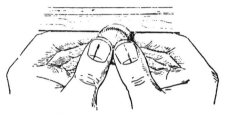

Fig. 158. Snapping the barrel cover into position.

be free. If it has none, consider which way the barrel can be moved, up or down ; if there is room for it to come up a little, place the assembled barrel on a brass stake and give the top of the barrel arbor a slight tap with the brass hammer. This will cause the barrel cover to bulge very slightly and thus free the arbor (Fig. 159). Apply a little clock oil to both the arbor pivots that work in the barrel.

There are various forms of movement holders, two of which are illustrated here (Figs. 160, 161), though, personally, I prefer to hold the movement

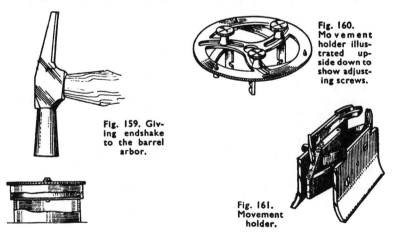

Fig. 160. Movement holder illustrated upside down to show adjusting screws.

Fig. 159. Giving endshake to the barrel arbor.

Fig. 161. Movement holder.

in tissue paper. Take the bottom plate and place the barrel in position ; next, position the pull-out piece screw and the centre wheel, first applying a little clock oil to both centre pivots, then the 3rd, 4th and escape wheels. Screw the barrel bar and the centre bars into position. Replace the click and spring ; first applying oil to the click post and just a trace to the click spring where it engages the click. Slightly oil the transmission wheel seating, and screw the wheel in position —not forgetting that if this wheel is held in position with a single screw, that screw will be left-handed. Invariably the transmission wheel is over-oiled, a little oil on the seating and a trace to the boss contacting the wheel is all that is necessary. Apply a little clock oil to the top barrel pivot working in the barrel bar. It is not necessary or advisable to apply oil to the under side of the ratchet wheel. Occasionally one meets with a watch that has both ratchet and transmission wheels flooded with oil, which is quite unnecessary.

Screw the ratchet wheel in position. Now turn the movement over and replace the rest of the keyless work ; apply a *little* oil to the acting surfaces of the various moving parts. Only clock oil has been used up to now. Place the winding shaft in position and wind the mainspring up two or three clicks, and while the train is running down, puff with the bellows into the movement, not hard, or we shall cause the oil of the centre wheel and barrel pivots to spread ; but just sufficient to ensure absolute freedom from dust. Replace the pallets and the pallet cock ; try all the endshakes. Wind the mainspring up about half a turn.

Now comes the very important operation of oiling the movement proper. I am convinced that watch repairers as a whole are given to over-oiling, and to guard against this, proceed as follows. First of all clean the oil pots out occasionally, both the watch and the clock. Make it a habit when putting out fresh oil to put it into a clean pot. One drop as it drops from the large watch screwdriver is sufficient watch oil for one helping. Make sure to clean the screwdriver well before inserting it into the oil.

Some watch oil pots are made with a flat portion as Fig. 162 and on this flat part place as much oil as you are able to pick up with the watch oiler,

Fig. 162. Watch oil pot. The lower illustration indicates the oil and also the spot of oil on the flat part of the pot.

and no more. From this one spot of oil, oil the top and bottom escape wheel pivots and also the top and bottom pallet pivots. It is a good habit to dry the oiler in the pith, as mentioned previously, every time it has been used and before taking up more oil. Not only does this ensure that the oiler is clean but also that it is dry. A dry oiler will pick up an exact amount of oil more accurately than an oily one. Oil, as we all know, creeps, and if an oily oiler is used, some of the oil intended for the movement will have crept up the stem of the oiler; the oil already there will have enticed it. So keep your oilers dry. Do not be tempted to apply more oil to these four pivots just mentioned; I know that it is a weakness with watchmakers to revel in oil, they do not feel " safe " unless they see the pivots swimming in oil. It is a mistake, and a big mistake, to apply to watches up to 11 lignes more oil than I have prescribed, and very little more for watches up to 18 lignes. I have proved on numberless occasions that poor rating in positions has been due to over-oiling these four pivots.

When the escape wheel and pallets have conical pivots, and they run on endstones, the question of the quantity of oil is not quite so vital, but when these pivots work on square shoulders, it is another matter. There is then adhesion to contend with, and if the watch has to be submitted to a low temperature test, the trouble is aggravated. The illustrations (Fig. 163) much exaggerated will help to show my point. It must always be borne in mind that it is not possible to control the amount of oil deposited by an oiler once it has made contact. All the oil leaves the point of the oiler directly it touches anything; you cannot say " I shall use half the oil," so the only safe alternative is to see that the oil the oiler picks up is the correct amount.

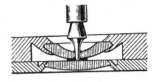

Now oil the pallet stones, apply a little oil to the locking face of the entry pallet stone, and with the pointed pegwood move the lever backwards and forwards so that the oil is transferred to the escape wheel teeth. A second spot of oil *may* have to be applied to the same stone, for all the teeth to receive their share. The teeth will carry the oil

Fig. 163. Top : the correct amount of oil for a conical pivot. Centre : an escape or pallet pivot over oiled. Bottom : the correct amount of oil for an escape or pallet pivot.

to the exit stone ; here again guard against over-oiling. Oil collected on the metal part of the pallets does no good, it tends to draw the oil away from the acting surface. Do not use the oiler to move the lever backwards and forwards, there is a risk, and a very real one, of carrying oil to the bankings or the ruby pin ; use a pointed pegwood for this purpose. On no account should the ruby pin be oiled. Few repairers admit oiling the ruby pin, yet many are found with oil on them. The cause may be one of three things : (1) deliberate oiling ; (2) oiling accidentally with the oiler when moving the lever ; (3) when removing the balance after the balance pivots have been oiled, the lower pivot carrying the oil to the notch as it passes and so to the ruby pin.

Fig. 164. Illustrating capillary attraction. The oil is held at one point by this property.

Oil is held in position at the pivot by capillary attraction, and the illustration (Fig. 164) shows that if one surface is curved, the oil collects better at the apex of the curve. If jewel holes with curved surfaces are used the oil is better retained at the point or acting surface.

Now direct your attention to cleaning the balance and, while so doing, place the partly assembled movement under the glass shade. By now the balance is quite dry. Remove it from the lime or box-wood dust, hold in tissue paper and well brush ; it should present a bright appearance. Place in the benzine for a few moments to remove oil, and then brush until quite dry. Hold the balance in the left hand and press a *soft* piece of pith over the bottom pivot and beyond until the impulse roller is embedded in it, then give the pith a twist or two so that the ruby pin is cleaned with the pith. At the same time the safety roller also will be well cleaned. It is quite safe to clean the ruby pin in this manner provided a soft piece of pith is selected. Well pith

the top pivot and, before we replace the balance spring, see that the ends of the balance staff pivots are smooth and free from facets. To test this draw the finger-nail over the end of the pivot and if it has facets you will find that it will scratch the nail (Fig. 165). Finally, before replacing the balance spring test the poise of the balance. Although you may have poised the balance before, cleaning it may have thrown it out. This necessity to test for poise after cleaning applies only to the cut balance. Plain

Fig. 165. Testing the end of balance staff pivot for smoothness. Note the nail of the third finger is used for this purpose.

Fig. 166. Stake to hold balance while replacing spring.

or uncut balances need to be poised, but they are not affected in this respect by cleaning. To replace the balance spring use the stake (Fig. 166). The balance is usually marked so that the spring can be replaced in the correct position. The balance spring stud should come opposite the mark, which may be a small dot on the top surface of the balance or a slight scratch on the side. Press the balance spring collet well down with the stout tweezers held as illustrated (Fig. 167). By using both hands a very steady firm pressure is assured with no danger of slipping. Do not oil the balance holes yet.

Replace the balance on the balance cock, and carefully turn the balance cock over. With the balance hanging down, manipulate it into position in the movement. Make sure that the ruby pin engages in the notch ; to achieve this hold the balance cock steady and turn the movement so as to present the notch to the ruby pin. Screw the balance cock down very carefully. The watch should start to function before the cock is screwed home ; if it does not, test the balance

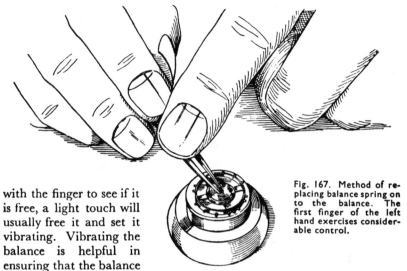

with the finger to see if it
is free, a light touch will
usually free it and set it
vibrating. Vibrating the
balance is helpful in
ensuring that the balance

cock is not being screwed down on to the top of the balance staff
pivot. When the balance cock is securely fixed, check up the endshake
and then try the beat. It may be necessary to move the spring round,
and to do this the balance must be removed from the movement, and it
was against this contingency that the staff pivots were not oiled. Had we
oiled them and it had proved necessary to remove the balance once or
twice, the condition and the amount of oil at the jewel holes would not be
as required. Slight particles of dust may be picked up by the staff pivots
and a certain amount of oil is removed from the holes as they are withdrawn. The pivots also come into contact with the board paper. There
is the further risk of transferring oil to the notch and so to the ruby pin as
mentioned before.

When the escapement is satisfactorily in beat, remove the balance cock
and the balance with it ; apply a little oil to the lower hole, turn the
balance cock over, lift the balance up a little and apply oil to the top hole.
Some repairers favour the method of introducing a feeler into the balance
holes so as to work the oil through to the endstones. I have not found it
necessary to do this, and am of the opinion that the balance pivots carry
the oil through quite satisfactorily. Having oiled the balance staff holes,
replace the balance in the movement. Turn the movement over and
give the plate one or two light puffs with the bellows.

Slightly oil or rather grease with clock oil the centre wheel arbor and
press the cannon pinion into position. It may be necessary to hold it with
the brass nosed pliers and slightly twist it backwards and forwards to
snap it home. Apply an oiler of watch oil to the 3rd and 4th holes and the
merest trace of watch oil to the minute wheel post. Replace the hour
wheel without oil, and then the dial. Do not oil the top plate until the

movement is in the case, or if the movement fits into a two-piece case or something similar, not until it is ready to be finally cased up.

It is better to fit the hands on, where possible, when the movement is in its case. The hour hand is pressed onto the hour wheel pipe with a piece of clock pegwood. The pegwood has a hole drilled in the end by means of a watch screwdriver. In this manner the hand is not marked. The minute hand is pressed on to the cannon pinion with the back of the handle of the watch brush, placing a piece of tissue paper over the ball or boss of the hand first, so as not to mark it. The seconds hand is fitted by pressing it on the 4th wheel pivot with the end of a piece of watch pegwood. Oil the winding shaft with clock oil. I have seen repairers dip the end of the shaft in the oil pot, trusting to chance that the oil found its way to where it was wanted. Needless to say, this is wrong : the correct method is to apply a little oil to the shaft pivot, then a little to the square, all the four sides, the crown wheel shoulder, and the ratchet teeth, the pull-out piece groove, and finally the shoulder working in the plate.

The oiling chart (Fig. 168) will help as a guide to oiling. W—Watch oil. C—Clock oil. XXX—As much oil as the oiler will pick up by holding it upright in the oil pot, not sideways. XX—Oil only half way up the flattened end of the oiler. X—As much oil as the oiler can pick up from the spot of oil. O—no oil at all. The amount of oil suggested on the chart is for a $10\frac{1}{2}$ ligne movement and this applies to movements larger than $7\frac{3}{4}$ lignes. For movements smaller than $7\frac{3}{4}$ lignes use a little less oil to all the pivots except the escape wheel and pallet pivots. Use less oil to the mainspring. Some of the factories in Switzerland advise no oil at all to the pallet pivots for movements of $8\frac{3}{4}$ lignes and smaller. I cannot quite see eye to eye with them yet. I should not feel *safe* with no oil at all. For movements larger than $10\frac{1}{2}$ lignes use your discretion, but as a general guide I should recommend that for an 18 ligne movement C.XXX (two or three) for the mainspring and the escape wheel and pallet pivots W.X. (twice).

The Swiss practise a method of oiling by the speed with which the oiler is removed from the part being oiled. Some control can be exercised in this manner but the foregoing is more certain.

The movement is now ready for casing. After the case has been polished and before fitting the movement in, make it a habit to pass the inside of the case through the flame of a spirit lamp. If the case has joints to the back, dome or bezel, see that they are touched by the flame. Do not make the case hot ; it is only necessary to linger long enough for the flame to burn any hairs, short pieces of wool, a fine bristle from the brush or pieces of lint or fluff that may be lodged in the case or the joints. The piece may be so fine that it is hardly visible, but if it came into contact with the balance it could have a serious effect on the timing, and become a troublesome fault to elucidate. Replace the movement in its case, and finally give a light puff or two with the bellows to the top plate and then apply a little oil to the top 3rd and 4th pivots. The watch is now ready for timing.

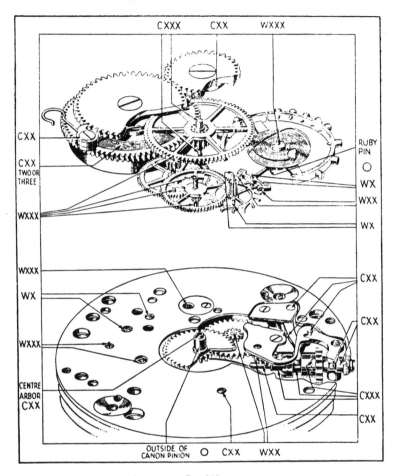

Fig. 168.
WATCH OILING CHART.

Indicating the type and quantity of oil to be applied to movements from 10½ lignes to 7¾ lignes. Larger movements need more. Smaller movements need less.

W—Watch oil.	X—Slight touch.
C —Clock oil.	XX—Oiler half full.
O —No oil at all.	XXX—Oiler full.

Size of small oiler 0.3 mm., for use with WATCH oil.
Size of large oiler 0.6 mm., for use with CLOCK oil.

CHAPTER TEN

THE CLEANING MACHINE

WHEN USING the cleaning machine, the movement is dismantled as instructed when cleaning in benzine. In fact it is advisable to dismantle it still further. All screws should be removed, including the dial screws. There are one or two points to note when using these machines. The most important is that though the No. 1 solution does not cause rust, if it is allowed to dry on the metal parts it will undoubtedly spot or stain them. Normally No. 2 solution will not cause rust, but it has been proved that sunlight affects the chemical composition. If the No. 2 solution is used when quite fresh and it has not been exposed to sunlight, there seems little risk of rusting. The precautions to be taken to prevent rusting are to see that the No. 2 solution is not exposed to sunlight ; it is not likely to be so treated while in the tin in which it is usually supplied by the manufacturers, but the glass jars supplied with the machine are transparent and it is here that the trouble may occur. It is a good plan to paint jars Nos. 2 and 3 with a flat black paint : it will not be so easy to see the solution and determine by its colour when it is necessary for it to be renewed, but this can be overcome by pouring a little into a transparent glass jar. This little extra trouble is worth while to obviate the risk of rust.

The procedure then is this : The machine (Fig. 169) is supplied with three glass jars and they are numbered 1, 2, 3. No. 1 contains the cleaning solution ; No. 2 the rinsing solution ; No. 3 is the same solution as No. 2 but cleaner. The reason being that a certain amount of No. 1 cleaner is carried into No. 2 rinse, and the liquid in that jar becomes contaminated with the cleaning solution from No. 1 jar. To a lesser degree No. 3 also becomes contaminated with No. 1 liquid as a certain amount of No. 2 liquid is carried to the No. 3 jar. All the solutions have to be changed periodically. No. 1 cannot be used again, so when it becomes dirty and beyond further use, throw it away. Clean the jar out and supply fresh liquid. No. 2 liquid can be passed through a filter and used again. A satisfactory system is to use laboratory filter paper ; fit up a funnel, line it with the paper and

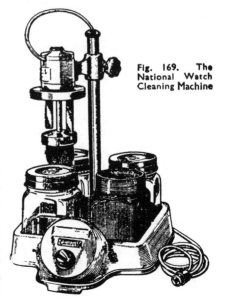

Fig. 169. The National Watch Cleaning Machine

leave to filter through. The No. 3 liquid is usually fairly clean, and it is economical to turn this into No. 2 jar and use it without filtering, and to use the filtered solution in No. 3 just adding a little fresh solution to make up loss due to evaporation and working.

The amount of liquid placed in each jar is important. If too little is used, the liquid does not reach all the parts in the basket. As the basket revolves it creates a vortex, and vanes are fixed to the basket support so that as the liquid swirls up the sides of the jar it is thrown back into the basket. If less than the correct amount of liquid is in the jar, the quantity thrown up will be insufficient to cover the basket. This is a very important point to watch, as too little liquid, especially Nos. 2 and 3 solutions, may cause rusting. If the jars are too full, they will overflow as the basket gathers speed, so this condition is quickly brought to notice.

The basket consists of the main container and a tray with indentations or recesses and a flat cover fits over the tray to hold it firmly down. The large parts of the watch, such as the bottom plate, bridges, bars, cocks and the barrel, are placed at the bottom of the basket. It is essential to spread them out so that they do not overlap. When the basket revolves, centrifugal force may cause them to collect at one side, but this does not always happen. The small wheels are placed in one of the recesses of the tray with the screws and click. It is not advisable to pass the mainspring through the solutions for the reasons mentioned when discussing cleaning with benzine. Some types of shellac are affected by the solution, and to be on the safe side it is better not to clean the pallets or the balance in the machine. Quite apart from the shellac securing the ruby pin, there are also some balances and balance screws which are affected by the solutions. I have met cases where the watch has gained considerably after cleaning in the machine, and upon investigation it has been found that a chemical action has taken place on the metal of the balance and on the screws and so reduced the weight. There are also instances on record where the balance spring has been affected, causing the watch to lose, so without accurate knowledge of what quality of shellac the manufacturer uses, or the exact nature of the balance, balance screws and the balance spring, these parts are better left out of the basket. They should be cleaned in benzine.

The usual practice is for the basket containing the movement to revolve for half a minute at a slow speed in the No. 1 solution ; the basket should then be lifted out of the solution and allowed to revolve in the air for a few seconds at high speed in order to throw off superfluous fluid. Immerse in No. 2 solution, repeat the same operation for a minute, and again in No. 3 solution. Finally, the basket is lowered into the heat chamber and allowed to revolve there slowly for one minute. No time should be lost in transferring the basket from No. 1 to No. 2 jar, because if the No. 1 solution dries on the parts before the rinse, they are liable to spot. The lid of the basket fits loosely, and it is a good idea to fit a steady pin into the seat for the lid and cut a small notch in the lid to engage the pin and so prevent the lid from turning independently of the basket. If the lid moves slightly, it may catch the parts in the tray and cause damage. It is claimed that it is not necessary to peg the holes after cleaning in the machine, but, to be on the safe side, it is advisable that the holes should be pegged. There is a lot to commend the cleaning machine system, but it *must* be used with knowledge of its working and with extreme care.

CHAPTER ELEVEN

KEYLESS WORK

THE DESIGNS of keyless work in watches are multifarious, but most of them are of the crown and castle wheel type—the same object achieved in differing ways. It is proposed to deal with only one or two of the best known designs. Broadly speaking, the functioning of keyless work is obvious ; there are one or two points to consider, and in the main they are these :— the keyless work must not slip ; the shaft must not pull adrift ; the keyless work should be free to facilitate the easy winding

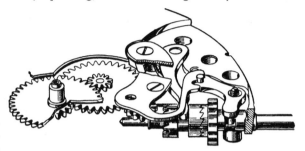

Fig. 170. The return bar and spring keyless mechanism.

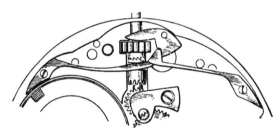

Fig. 171. The return bar and spring combined.

up of the mainspring. We shall consider these points in turn. The illustration (Fig. 170) shows a typical keyless mechanism of the crown and castle wheel type with the return bar actuated by a separate spring. Fig. 171 shows a design where the return bar and spring are combined. Whatever the design under examination, they are all heir to the same faults and weaknesses.

Slipping keyless work may be caused by the teeth of the crown wheel failing to engage correctly with the transmission wheel. Apply pressure to the shaft and observe closely the gearing of these two wheels. Continue the pressure, or the operation of winding, for a longer period than that occupied during the normal winding, because slipping is sometimes intermittent and it may be that the wearer makes longer contact which manifests the slipping. If the winding slips at this intersection the crown wheel teeth can usually be seen to move *underneath* the teeth of the transmission wheel. The cause may be due to two or three reasons. The transmission wheel may have too much up and down shake. Try it with the tweezers as (Fig. 172). If it appears loose the remedy is to lower the boss that holds it down, though it may be due to the fact that the boss is not screwed down tightly enough, so try this first. If the boss is screwed as tightly as possible (it may be held by one left-handed screw or two right-handed screws) we must proceed to lower the boss.

Some of the bosses are solid and form the bearing for the wheel, while others are just a plate and the wheel takes its bearing from the boss formed on the barrel bar itself. In the case of the former the boss is reduced by stoning the underside as demonstrated in Fig. 173. In the

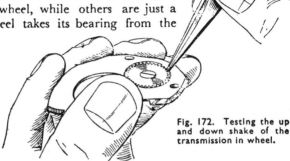

Fig. 172. Testing the up and down shake of the transmission in wheel.

Fig. 173. Method of stoning down the transmission wheel boss.

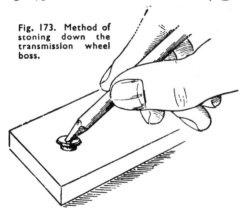

latter instance the height of the boss or post is reduced, and for this the barrel bar is fitted up in the mandrel and a light cut made across the top (Fig. 174). In either case the reduction must be slight, otherwise the wheel will be made to bind and difficulty in winding will be experienced. Should the boss be screwed down tightly and with little or no up and down shake, and slipping is still evident, look to the fitting of the crown wheel on the shaft, which should be a close fit—just free, with no perceptible side play. See that the shaft itself fits the plate closely; there should be no

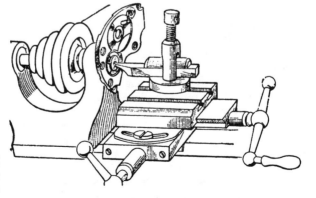

Fig. 174. Reducing the transmission wheel seating.

perceptible play here.   If the crown wheel fits the shaft badly the remedy is to fit a new wheel or a new shaft.   If the shaft is a poor fit in the plate the

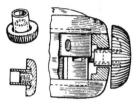

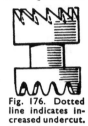

remedy is to fit an oversize shaft. When economy has to be considered, an effective method is to fit a sleeve or collar to the winding button (Fig. 175), so that the winding button holds the shaft rigidly in position by virtue of the close fit of the sleeve in the case.

Fig. 175. Collar fitted to button to take up play.

Fig. 176. Dotted line indicates increased undercut.

Examine next the ratchet teeth of the crown and castle wheels to see if the slipping originates there.   It may be due to the crown and castle wheels fitting loosely on the shaft or the castle wheel only.   The remedy is to fit either new wheels or a new shaft.   On the other hand the fault may rest with the shape of the ratchet teeth.   Sometimes these teeth can be undercut a little (Fig. 176), but generally this is not satisfactory and a pair of new wheels is the only permanent cure.

Now comes the question of the shaft coming adrift.   This may be due to one or two reasons, but the immediate cause is that the pin or nib of the pull-out piece disengages with the groove in the shaft.   A worn plate allowing the shaft to fit in a slack manner may be the trouble, and the remedy is either to fit an oversize shaft (meaning that a shaft must be turned in especially, an interchangeable one would not suit) or re-bush the shaft hole.   It is not practicable to fit a new hole as this hole is in two parts, half in the bottom plate and half in the barrel bar, so a peg or plug is fitted to the barrel bar as (Fig. 177).   The peg is filed so that it bears on to the shaft, allowing the requisite freedom.   Such a repair takes up the wear in one direction only, downwards, but it is in the right direction to cure the fault we are seeking to correct, as it causes the shaft to press towards the pull-out piece.

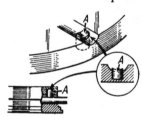

Fig. 177. Fitting a bush to the shaft hole. (A) indicates the bush or peg.

Another cause of the shaft pulling out is lack of freedom of the pull-out piece screw.   When the shaft is withdrawn to set the hands the pull-out piece is made to revolve slightly, and the pull-out piece screw should be screwed to the pull-out piece so tightly, and the screw itself free, that the screw revolves *with* the pull-out piece.   Should the screw be bound, the pull-out piece will revolve on the thread of the screw and the shaft may be safe, but if the screw is only partly bound it may become unscrewed by the withdrawal of the pull-out piece a few times, with the result that the shaft will come adrift.   This unscrewing of the pull-out piece may be due to the pull-out piece screw actually binding in the plate and the remedy is to free it.   Another reason, and a common one, is that the shoulder of the screw does not project through the bottom plate, so that when the screw is tightened it causes the pull-out piece to bind on the plate instead of binding on the shoulder and being held free of the plate.

The illustrations (Fig. 178) show one binding and the other free as it should be. The remedy for binding is to turn the shoulder of the screw back a little so that the full thread and a little of the shoulder projects through the plate.

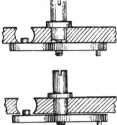

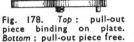

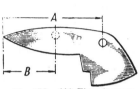

Fig. 178. *Top* : pull-out piece binding on plate. *Bottom* : pull-out piece free.

Fig. 179. (A) This distance can cause the pull-out piece to become too flexible, whereas (B) is not so susceptible.

Another cause of the trouble is that in some watches the position of the screw in the pull-out piece is not correct. If the screw hole in the pull-out piece is some distance from the pin or nib (see Fig. 179) the tendency is for the pull-out piece to become too flexible and allow the shaft to be pulled right out. Unfortunately there is no remedy for the watch repairer, other than to make a new pull-out piece of stouter material. This fault in construction, however, is seldom met with in the modern movement. Examine the pin or nib of the pull-out piece and see that it is square on the edge and also that it is long enough and that the groove in the shaft is square. Otherwise there will be a tendency for the pull-out piece to slide out of the groove. The illustrations (Fig. 180) show how the fitting should be, and also the incorrect way.

Fig. 180. *Top* : Nib on pin of pull-out piece square, as it should be. *Bottom* : The fitting liable to come adrift.

Stiff winding may be due to : (a) The transmission wheel binding; (b) lack of freedom of the barrel arbor : (c) wide holes of the barrel arbor in the plates, which allow the ratchet wheel to touch the barrel bar (see Fig. 181) ; (d) the barrel arbor shoulder may not project sufficiently to keep the ratchet wheel free of

Fig. 181. Barrel arbor hole wide (A), allowing the ratchet wheel to touch the plate at (B).

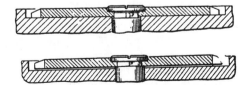

Fig. 182. Ratchet wheel bound because the arbor shoulder does not project through to plate. *Top* : bound. *Bottom* : free.

the barrel bar (see Fig. 182), which causes the ratchet wheel to bind ; and (e) bad depth between the ratchet and transmission wheels, which is unlikely unless at some time a change has been made here.

Sometimes slipping is experienced when setting the hands and this may be due to a wide shaft pivot hole. Occasionally this hole bursts open and it is a troublesome matter to rectify, as fitting a new shaft does not meet the case. I am reluctant to use soft solder in watches, but we must resort to it here if the repair is to be carried out in an economical manner. First select a piece of bouchon wire that fits the shaft pivot accurately, turn this down so that it fits the shaft pivot hole and cut it to the exact length. Sometimes it is advisable to open the shaft pivot hole a little before rebushing. To do this select a round rat-tailed file and use it as you would a broach. Place the bush on the end of a piece of aluminium wire, taking care that the wire does not project through to the other end of the bush. Heat over the spirit lamp and apply a little flux (the wax type of flux) and then a small piece of soft solder, making sure the solder adheres and runs all round. While still hot brush the solder off. This should leave the bush with a thin film of solder covering it. Apply a little more flux and while still on the aluminium wire place in position in the plate, apply heat to the end of the wire until the solder runs. Remove from the flame and the bush will be held securely in position. Carefully remove the aluminium wire ; soft solder will not adhere to it. If care has been exercised in making the bush the correct size, and the minimum of solder has been used, no further finishing is required. Fig. 183 clearly illustrates the procedure.

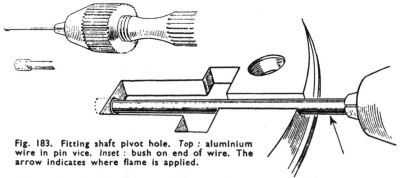

Fig. 183. Fitting shaft pivot hole. *Top :* aluminium wire in pin vice. *Inset :* bush on end of wire. The arrow indicates where flame is applied.

General points to observe when examining keyless mechanism are to turn the shaft so that a tooth of the castle wheel is as near the intermediate wheel as possible ; the intermediate wheel must be quite free during the whole function of winding. Sometimes the teeth of the castle wheel catch the teeth of the intermediate wheel (Fig. 184). This can be an elusive fault ; during winding the hands may be moved one or two minutes and the keyless work not suspected. The remedy is to change the castle wheel for one a little shorter. If the return bar rides over the castle wheel and the shaft is a good fit, pean the return bar downward. If this work is carried out as demonstrated in Fig. 185, it will not be necessary to lower the temper of the part, unless it is dead hard,

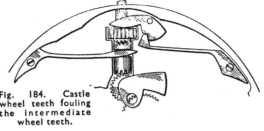

Fig. 184. Castle wheel teeth fouling the intermediate wheel teeth.

which is hardly likely. See that the return spring rides safely as it is at times apt to ride up out of position. To correct this, the return bar should be stoned at a slight angle on the edge where the spring operates. This will cause the spring to bear down (see Fig. 186).

Fig. 185. Peaning return bar downwards.

If the pull-out piece is hard to operate, i.e., if difficulty is experienced in withdrawing the button to the hand-set position, examine the end of the pull-out piece which operates on the return bar and also that portion of the return bar upon which the pull-out piece impinges. If the acting surfaces meet the pull-out will be stiff and jumpy. To obviate this, the angle of the return bar should be stoned as indicated by dotted lines in Fig. 187.

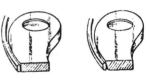

Fig. 186. Return bar undercut to hold return spring down. *Left*: before stoning. *Right*: the undercut made.

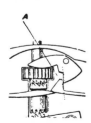

Fig. 187. Dotted line indicates angle to stone to facilitate easy hand setting.

Great care must be exercised because, in the first place we cannot replace what is removed and, secondly, the part marked A must not be stoned, otherwise the return bar will not carry the castle wheel far enough into the intermediate wheel. Conversely, if the pull-out piece will not hold the return bar in the hand-set position when once placed there, stone a *slight* flat at A on the return bar, being careful not to take away too much or it will affect the intermediate wheel depth. The check spring materially assists the retention of the pull-out piece in the desired position, but its primary object is to act as an " All-or-nothing piece," the name given to a device in repeating watches to ensure that the action strikes the correct number of hours or not at all.

The check spring controls the position of the pull-out

piece ; without it, the button can be partly pulled out, neither engaging the crown wheel nor the intermediate wheel, with the result that slipping may result during winding. A peculiarity with some wearers is that they are inclined to pull the button out during winding.

With the shaft in position, pull it out and in, at the same time observing closely the head of the pull-out piece screw ; it should rotate a little. This will indicate that the pull-out piece screw is free and not likely to give trouble and unscrew as already mentioned.

CHAPTER TWELVE

SPRINGING AND TIMING

BEFORE TALKING about springing and timing it is best to establish the signs used, so as to avoid any confusion.

+ = Fast or gaining.
− = Slow or losing.
± = No error.
DU = Dial up.
DD = Dial down.
PU = Pendant up.
PR = Pendant right.
PL = Pendant left.

When regulating a watch by moving the index, the index is moved to Fast or A (*Avance*) if the watch is losing, and to Slow or R (*Retard*) if it is gaining. Setting a watch to the exact time is apparently a very simple matter but it takes a little practice.

To set the watch to time proceed as follows : Do not at first wind the watch. Make a mental note of the position of the seconds hand, say, for instance, it is 10 seconds. Observe the standard time keeper, which may be a regulator or a chronometer, and when the seconds hand of the standard reaches 10 seconds, give the watch a slight circular twist to set the balance in motion and at the same time give the winding button a turn. Then hold the watch quite firmly and still, and wind up the mainspring fully. Do not, as so often happens, work the hand holding the watch backwards and forwards, assisting the winding, as it were. By so doing, you are liable to cause the ruby pin to strike the back of the lever. In the first place this may break the ruby pin off and secondly it will cause knocking—known as " knocking the banking "—which results in the watch gaining a few seconds in as many moments.

Having set the seconds right, now set the hour and minute hands. It is advisable to set the hands forward ; setting the hands backwards, if the hand friction is a little stiff, is liable to reverse the train and thus set the seconds hand back. On the other hand, moving the hands forward slowly may cause the watch to knock the banking. It is better therefore to set the hands forward fairly quickly.

When the hour hand is to time, bring the minute hand forward slowly for the last five minutes and see that it points to the correct minute and that as the seconds hand reaches 60 seconds the minute hand indicates the minute *exactly*. It should point precisely to the minute stroke on the dial. If, after the watch has been set to time, you observe that the seconds hand does not synchronise with the standard, on no account touch the seconds hand itself to set it right. It is better to note the error on paper, but if for some reason you want the seconds right, then open the watch and stop the balance. If the watch is a few seconds fast, stop the balance for that period, noting mentally the number of seconds it is fast and counting the seconds of the standard immediately the balance is stopped, releasing it immediately after the expiration of the required period. A camel hair brush is useful for stopping the balance. Should the watch be a few seconds slow, say 5 seconds, then hold the balance for 55 seconds and set the minute hand forward 1 minute.

The experienced timer will give the watch a circular twist or two deliberately to cause the balance to strike the banking. This will make the watch gain rapidly and so pick up the required number of seconds. It is, however, a dangerous practice and if used should only be done by those who thoroughly understand what they are doing. For instance, if the balance is a heavy one and the ruby pin relatively thin, the chances are all in favour of the pin breaking off.

Here is an example of the way in which you should record your observations on paper. We will take it that the watch is five seconds fast : your entry should then read :—

		M.	S.
Date	Time set	+0	5 DU.

After 24 hours the watch is observed to be 15 seconds fast, and your second entry should therefore be :—

Date	Time set	M.	S.
„	„ „	+0	10 DU.

10 seconds only are recorded because the watch was set 5 seconds fast.

The watch is then placed PU and after another 24 hours it is observed to be 35 seconds fast. Remember it was 15 seconds fast when placed PU, so it has gained another 20 seconds, thus :—

Date	Time set	M.	S.
„	„ „	+0	10 DU.
„	„ „	+0	20 PU.

Say we now test DD and after 24 hours it reads fast 15 seconds. Again it was 20 seconds fast when placed DD so it has lost 5 seconds, thus :—

Date	Time set	M.	S.
„	„ „	+0	10 DU.
„	„ „	+0	20 PU.
„	„ „	−0	5 DD.

NOTE :—To find the total error: Add the + signs together and add the − signs together, subtract the smaller sum from the larger and give your answer the sign of the larger.

The next part of the watch to receive attention has been the subject of more research than any other in recent years. The balance and its spring have been the special care of the mathematicians and the scientists (physicists), and as this subject is pursued, the colossal task undertaken and the wonderful results achieved will be more readily appreciated. The results are not the fruits of one brain alone, far from it ; every generation for the last hundred years has added something, and perhaps the most important contributions have been made during the present generation. Strange to relate there is nothing spectacular in the modern improvements ; no new balance with an imposing array of screws. The improvements have been in the material used to make the balance spring, the shape of the overcoil, and various adjustments that are not apparent. The balances have received little attention other than the metal from which they are made. On the whole, the modern watch, from the balance and balance spring point of view, looks a dull piece of work, but (and this is a big but) we get as good results as with the older styles, and a more robust article at a lower cost of production. The advantages of the modern systems are legion.

Watchmakers generally are not as well versed in this subject as they should be. I have known men able to turn a first class balance staff or pinion, but they regard the balance and spring as just another part of the watch. We shall see there is something more to it than that. I have seen watches perfectly repaired and cleaned, but if, during regulation, the watch did not respond as was expected, it was regarded as just another bad timekeeper. We shall see that this need not necessarily be so. There is, however, one very important thing to remember and that is that the escapement with its balance spring is dependant upon the rest of the watch for its accuracy. It is hopeless trying to rate a watch with a poor or faulty mainspring, faulty train resulting in bad transmission of power, or faulty escapement. On the other hand, if the rest of the movement is correct and the balance and spring adjustment faulty, poor rating must result.

Taking the balance first, it is proposed to discuss several types, and to digress generally on this subject. The balance and spring as fitted to the 13 ligne movement at present under examination will form part of the study.

The balance is to the watch what the pendulum is to the clock, with the difference that the balance spring controls the balance. Many years ago the balance or foliot, as it was then known, had no spring. Later a hog's bristle was added to act as a spring and, later still, the steel spring. The balance spring was invented by an Englishman, Dr. Robert Hooke. The steel spring, if used with a plain (non-compensating) balance, will cause the watch to lose as much as $1\frac{1}{2}$ minutes in 24 hours for a change in temperature of $10°$ F. To overcome or compensate for this error a bi-metal balance of steel with brass fused on the outer edge is used. The balance is cut, and screws or sliding weights fitted to facilitate adjustment. The usual proportion is two parts brass to one part steel.

The necessity for a compensating balance, when steel is used for the balance spring, is that steel loses its elasticity in heat, which, in turn, causes a loss in rating. The steel spring also increases in length under heat, but this is more than compensated by the other dimensions (thickness and width) increasing proportionately. Loss of elasticity is the real cause of a loss in rating when speaking only of the spring. If a plain metal balance is used, and by plain I refer to an uncut balance,

whether of one metal, or one of steel and brass, the balance will expand in heat, which will cause losing. But still the loss of elasticity of the balance spring is the major cause of the error. Brass has a greater coefficient of expansion than steel and when it is fused, or secured by partial melting to steel, and the balance is cut, as illustration (Fig. 188), heat will cause the limbs to curl inwards, thus making the watch gain. The dotted lines indicate the position of the limbs in heat and cold—

Fig. 188.
Compensation Balance.

the outside line in cold and the inside line in heat. As weights are fitted to the arms of the balance, an accurate adjustment can be made, so that the balance can compensate for the loss of elasticity in the steel spring. The diagram (Fig. 189) shows the definitions of the cut balance components.

> Move screws towards the FREE end of the balance rim and the watch :
>   Gains in heat ; Loses in cold.
> Move screws towards the FIXED end of the balance rim and the watch :
>   Gains in cold : Loses in heat.

Watches are usually tested in two extremes of temperature, 85° F. and 32° F., and the errors are compared with the rating in the normal temperature 60° F. to 65° F. If the balance has been adjusted so that the watch functions accurately at 85° F., 32° F. and is then tested at, say, 60° F., another error will appear, the middle temperature error. This error amounts to approx.

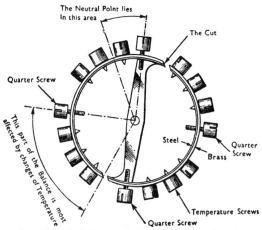

Fig. 189. Definitions of the parts composing the compensation balance.

2 sec. in 24 hours for a change of 40° F. *It is not possible to make an adjustment to correct this error with an ordinary balance.* Several devices, known as auxiliary compensation, have been invented to overcome this middle temperature error, but balances incorporating these devices are costly to make and the benefits to be obtained debatable. The new monometal balances with one of the composition balance springs

definitely minimise this error, and we shall discuss these balance springs later. When " accurately " is mentioned regarding the rate at 32° F. and 85° F. this refers only to the absence of variation in the rate, and has no regard for the mean time. To put it another way : if the watch is gaining 3 seconds per day at 85° F. it will also gain 3 seconds per day at 32° F., there being no *variation* in the rate.

To cite a definite test : first of all bring the watch as near to time as possible in workshop conditions, then run the watch for two or three days and make a note of the rate. No further alterations are made to the regulation. Now submit the watch to the heat test at 85° F. Special ovens are made for this purpose ; they are usually heated by gas through the medium of a water jacket surrounding the compartment for the watches, and are fitted with some form of thermostat or temperature control, which automatically keeps the chamber at an even temperature. Today, watchmakers in the repair shop are not often called upon to make temperature adjustments, and an oven may not be available. In these circumstances an excellent substitute can be made by using an ordinary wooden box with a door fitted to it. The interior is heated with a 25-watt electric bulb and a convenient fit-up is as illustrated (Fig. 190), which is self-explanatory. A thermostat could also be fitted which switches the current off and on as necessary to maintain a given temperature.

Fig. 190. A useful, electrically-heated oven.

Suppose that in normal temperature the watch gains at the rate of 5 seconds in 24 hours, and in the oven it loses 20 seconds in the same time ; as the watch was already gaining 5 seconds, this is equal to a loss of 25 seconds in the oven. Unfortunately, there is no definite rule regarding the amount of adjustment necessary to correct this error ; adjustment is by trial and error. For a start, move the screws from the holes B and 1B (Fig. 191) to the holes A and 1A (Fig. 192). Screws are always moved in pairs ; if a screw is moved on one side to a certain hole the screw exactly opposite to it must be moved to correspond. This is most important, not only does it keep the balance in poise, but it ensures that the balance is not thrown out of poise when in the oven, temperature tests being more often than not required to be made pendant up. Test the watch again and move the screws round as dictated by the rating.

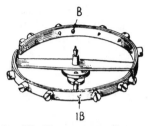

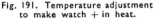

Fig. 191. Temperature adjustment
to make watch + in heat.

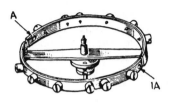

Fig. 192. Temperature adjustment
to make watch + in heat.

Test the watch in cold at 32° F. An ice box or an ordinary domestic refrigerator does well ; usually if the balance has been adjusted for heat the cold test is satisfactory. That is as well because if, for instance, the watch lost in heat, and we moved the screws towards the free end and found that the watch lost in cold, it would mean that the screws would have to be moved away from the free end and therefore our heat adjustment would be ruined. If, however, you find that the watch does lose in cold, then the balance is either not constructionally correct, or, as is more likely the case, the oil is at fault, but more about this presently.

As has already been stated, no hard and fast rule can be made as to where to move the screws. If you find upon re-testing that the adjustment is not sufficient, i.e., the watch still loses in heat, then move the screws A2 and A3 to the holes AII and AIII (see Fig. 193). On the other hand, if the watch gains in the heat, move the screws B2 and B3

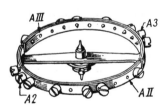

Fig. 193. Further temperature
adjustment to make watch + in
heat.

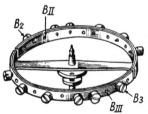

Fig. 194. Further temperature
adjustment to make watch − in
heat.

to the holes BII and BIII (Fig. 194) and so on until the error is reduced to the region of 2 secs. in 24 hours. A diversity of movement of screws has been chosen to indicate the necessity for trial.

When you are satisfied with the heat test, proceed with the cold test, bearing in mind that the normal error is + 5 sec. in 24 hours ; we shall calculate our readings from that figure. Generally speaking, the cold test does not reveal an error greater than the heat. For instance, if the balance was adjusted in heat to + 2 secs., i.e., a reading of + 7 secs. adding the 5 secs. normal error, and we found that in cold the error was + 7 secs., i.e., a reading of + 12 secs., this would mean that to correct it, it would be necessary to move the screws towards the free ends of the balance ; if we were to do this, our error in heat would then be greater than + 2 secs. Such a discrepancy would indicate that the balance is faulty, maybe the proportion of brass is in excess, so much so that the steel is not sufficiently strong or powerful to open the balance out far enough ; or, to put it another way, the brass is too strong for the steel. There may be a fault in the fusing of the two metals ; or a slight fracture in the steel. The remedy is to change the balance, as it is not usually economical to remedy faults in a balance.

It is as well to mention here that the screws on the balance from the quarter screws, or the position of the quarter screws if there are none actually fitted, to the free end, are the effectual temperature screws. Positions from the quarter screws to the fixed end have little effect on the balance in temperature. In fact, there is a point, somewhere near the balance arm, that remains stationary in temperature. The arms, or centre bar of the balance, expand in heat and contract in cold, so that the quarter screws at the fixed end move, but at a certain distance from there, there must be a point that does not move, the " neutral point," as it is known.

Quarter screws differ from the temperature screws in that they have a long thread, which enables them to be drawn in or out when making mean time adjustments. Screwing in will cause a gain, and drawing out a loss. In some balances you will find that the quarter screws at the fixed end are a little distance from the arm, towards the free end, and this is usually the calculated neutral point. The object is, that when a mean time adjustment is made, using those two screws, it has no effect on the temperature adjustment. This refers to very fine timing, and need not be considered commercially.

Sometimes, when adjusting for change in temperature, it is necessary to change the screws for others of a heavier metal. For instance, if all the holes near the free end of the balance are occupied by screws, and the watch still loses in heat, then the screws at the free end must be changed for heavier ones. The average watch to-day is fitted with brass screws to the balance, and in this case, gold screws, which are heavier than brass, would be used, and if they were not heavy enough, platinum screws would be employed.

A useful tool to use when changing screws for others of different weights is the comparative balances or scales here illustrated (Fig. 195).

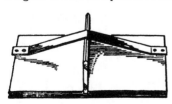

Fig. 195. Balance Screw Scales.

We shall refer to them as scales in order not to confuse them with the balance of the watch. These scales are simply made : Take a piece of brass about 1 in. by 2 in. and 2 mm. thick and slot a piece of steel ½ in. wide and 1 in. long into it. File the upper edge to a V-shape with a knife edge ;

now procure a piece of mainspring about .25 mm. thick, 3 mm. wide, and 3 in. long.   Soften the centre and both ends and with a screwhead file cut a slight nick in the centre.   Bend the spring as shewn in the illustration.   Drill two holes in each end of the spring, and bend up so

that they are parallel with the base.   Place the spring on the knife edge and make it balance by filing as necessary.   To use the scales, we shall cite a definite instance.   The watch loses so much in heat that it is necessary to change the screws 1 and 2 (Fig. 196) for heavier ones, made of platinum.   Remove the screw No. 1 from the balance and place it on the scales ;   on the other side of the

Fig. 196. Changing temperature screws for heavier ones.

scales place the new platinum screw ;   it will be much heavier.   We next make the scales balance accurately by placing the screw No. 3 from the balance on to the scales besides the screw No. 1, and if this makes the scales balance accurately, it indicates that an entire screw must be removed from each limb of the balance to keep the balance to its original weight and so maintain the same time.   So we remove the screws No. 1 and No. 2 and fit in their places the new platinum screws.   We also deal with screws Nos. 3 and 4 in order to maintain the poise of the balance.

The temperature adjustment will have been satisfied, and the watch will run to time, or very nearly so.   Sometimes the temperature adjustment can be made by adding washers or collets to the screws Nos. 1 and 2, and in this instance, to maintain the original weight of the balance, proceed as follows.   Remove the screw No. 3 and place on the scales, and beside it place say two balance collets.   On the other side place the screw No. 1 ;   we now reduce the screw No. 3, either by cutting the slot deeper with a screw slotting file, or file the head down, if the slotting is not sufficient.   Screw No. 4 is treated in the same manner to keep the balance in poise.   If the head is reduced, finish off with an Arkansas slip and polish the head.   Other methods of reducing the weights of balance screws are : bevelling the inside of the screw slot at the top (Fig. 197).   This little operation is known as breaking the edge and is effected with a fine three-square needle file. A second method, practised by the Americans, is to recess the under side of the screw (Fig. 198).   This recess is cut by placing the screw on the rose type cutter and making it revolv with a screwdriver.   These rosecutters are made in various sizes and the set of cutters are fixed in a box and

Fig. 197. Reducing weight of balance screw.

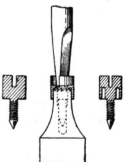

Fig. 198. Undercutting balance screw.

are not removed, but are used while in the box. The advantage of this system is that the appearance of the screw is not altered and also the operation is very speedy. This recessing can only be carried out on reasonably large screws, screws as used on the balance of a 13 ligne watch and upwards.

Another method is to chamfer the end of the balance screw as shewn in Fig. 199. This system may at first sight appear objectionable, as it certainly mauls the end of the head of the screw, but the method is used extensively in the Swiss factories. It can be used on screws of all sizes and is very speedy as the screw is not

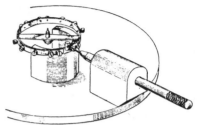

Fig. 199. Chamfering end of balance screw.

removed from the balance. One would not use this method on a fine quality balance but for ordinary commercial types of balances I can see no objection. The tool used to chamfer the heads of balance screws is illustrated in Fig. 199 and is self explanatory. The balance must be raised slightly if the head of the screw is large and lowered if very small, otherwise the chamfer will not be made centrally. The tool is

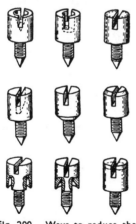

usually made for the average size balance screws. Fig. 200 demonstrates nine methods of reducing the weight of a balance screw, the first showing the chamfered head.

Proceeding with our temperature adjustment, we place the screw No. 1 in its original position on the balance with the two collets under it, and the reduced screw, No. 3, is also returned to its original position. We carry out exactly the same procedure with screws Nos. 2 and 4, with the difference that before replacing screw No. 3 on the balance, the screw No. 4 is reduced to match it, so that eventually we have two collets under the heads of screws Nos. 1 and

Fig. 200. Ways to reduce the weight of a balance screw. See also Figs. 197 and 198.

2, and screws Nos. 3 and 4 have been reduced a corresponding amount. All this may appear rather involved, but in practice it is very simple and speedy and saves a great deal of time by obviating retiming after each adjustment, or at least minimising it. It is imperative that after these adjustments, no matter if you have changed the screws, added collets, or reduced the weight of the screws, the balance must still be in perfect poise. It is advisable to test on the poising tool after each alteration.

The ease with which oil can be applied to a watch invites the fault

TEMPERATURE ADJUSTMENT CHART

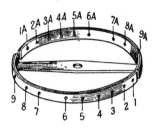

24-HOUR TEST.		24-HOUR TEST.	
	92° F.		32° F.
— 5 sec.	Move screws 7 and 7a to holes 4 and 4a.	— 5 sec.	Move screws 4 and 4a to holes 7 and 7a.
— 10 sec.	Move screws 7 and 7a to holes 2 and 2a.	— 10 sec.	Move screws 2 and 2a to holes 7 and 7a.
— 15 sec.	Move screws 8 and 8a to holes 1 and 1a.	— 15 sec.	Move screws 1 and 1a to holes 8 and 8a.
— 20 sec.	Move screws 8 and 8a to holes 1 and 1a and also screws 7 and 7a to holes 2 and 2a.	— 20 sec.	Move screws 1 and 1a and screws 2 and 2a to holes 8–8a and 7–7a.
— 25 sec.	Remove screws 3 and 3a and replace with screws made of platinum.	— 25 sec.	Move screws 1–1a and 2–2a and 3–3a to holes 9–9a—8–8a —7–7a.
— 30 sec.	Remove screws 1 and 1a and replace with screws made of platinum.	+ 5 sec.	Move screws 7 and 7a to holes 4 and 4a.
+ 5 sec.	Move screws 4 and 4a to holes 7 and 7a.	+ 10 sec.	Move screws 7 and 7a to holes 2 and 2a.
+ 10 sec.	Move screws 2 and 2a to holes 7 and 7a.	+ 15 sec.	Move screws 8 and 8a to holes 1 and 1a.
+ 15 sec.	Move screws 1 and 1a to holes 8 and 8a.	+ 20 sec.	Move screws 8 and 8a to holes 1 and 1a and also screws 7 and 7a to holes 2 and 2a.
+ 20 sec.	Move screws 1 and 1a and screws 2 and 2a to holes 8–8a —7–7a.	+ 25 sec.	Move screws 9–9a and 8–8a and 7–7a to holes 1–1a and 2–2a and 3–3a.
+ 25 sec.	Move screws 1–1a and 2–2a and 3–3a to holes 9–9a— 8–8a—7–7a.		

of over-oiling, and over-oiling increases the difficulty of adjustment for temperature. For instance, when the escape wheel pinion and pallet staff are fitted with square shoulders instead of conical pivots running on endstones, it is important that no more than the correct amount of oil be applied to the escape wheel and pallet pivots. It is better to err on the side of insufficiency ; less, rather than enough, is the criterion.

Fig. 168 demonstrates the clinging or retarding effect of an excess of oil on the pallet pivots, and this retarding effect is accentuated in the cold test. When regulated at ordinary temperature a watch may be adjusted to gain in order to overcome the resistance caused by an excess of oil, yet, when tested in heat, the oil is eased and the watch will register a relative gain. The same adjustment in normal temperature would give an apparent losing in the cold test.

If satisfied that the oil is as it should be, and the watch continues to lose in the cold, the balance screws must be adjusted as explained on page 122. Always make the first temperature test dial up as a balance is sometimes thrown out of poise in heat. If a start is made pendant up in heat we shall not know whether the error is due to temperature or position. Position testing in temperature comes last, after the positional test in normal temperature, and we shall come to positional timing later and come back again to the oven then.

The illustrated chart is not put forward as an accurate table, but rather as a general guide. As we have seen, no two balances are exactly alike when it comes to timing in temperatures, so it would not be practicable to effect a definite alteration and then expect an accurate result. The table should give an indication of the possible benefits of moving the balance screws, and some indication of the effect on the rate.

For the sake of simplicity no regard has been taken of the existing position of the screws in the balance and it has been assumed that it would be possible to move a pair of screws to the holes as tabulated. In practice one would have to move the screws to the nearest holes available.

There are two methods of poising the balance : one is to use the ordinary callipers and the other is to employ the poising tool. In the first method, the balance is placed in the callipers, as if we were going to true the balance, but the balance is not gripped so tightly ; the balance must

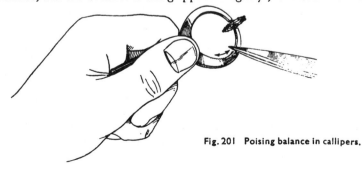

Fig. 201 Poising balance in callipers.

be free and have endshake. The callipers are held in the left hand and down on the edge of the bench, so that the balance is suspended over the bench at an angle of approximately 45°. The inside edge of one of the limbs of the callipers has notches filed in it (Fig. 201) and if these notches are stroked with the round back of a pair of tweezers or a screwdriver it will cause the balance to revolve slowly. When the balance has been set in motion cease stroking. We shall now be able to observe the heavy point of the balance. For a balance to be in poise there should be no heavy point. When testing in the callipers, the balance, once set in motion, should continue to revolve in the same direction until it finally stops. It should not revolve backwards and forwards, as this would indicate a heavy point.

The other method is to use the poising tool, Fig. 202. There are several designs of these tools, some have agate jaws and others steel jaws. Personally, I prefer steel jaws, they can be polished to keep the knife edges keen. If the agate jaws get chipped or damaged they are more difficult to repair, and the agate jaws are usually thicker than the steel ones. An important point to watch with the steel jaws is to see that they are free from magnetism. Test them occasionally with the small compass, if they are magnetised pass the tool through the de-magnetising machine. Agate jaws are set in bronze as a rule and therefore not subject to magnetism, but even this does not weigh me in their favour.

Fig. 202. Poising tool.

To use the poising tool, first of all wipe the knife edges with a piece of pith ; these edges must be perfectly clean. Place the balance on the tool and touch it lightly with the tweezers to make it revolve. On no account should you blow with the mouth on the balance to set it in motion: blowing with the mouth on the movement or any part of the watch is greatly to be deplored, as there is a risk of slight imperceptible specks of moisture being introduced. Make the balance revolve slowly, and if it gathers speed adjust the poising tool by means of the screws running through two of the legs, to make the tool level on the bench. Some tools are fitted with spirit levels but I prefer the balance itself to tell me when the tool is level. Having adjusted the tool, if necessary, watch the balance carefully : as with the callipers, the balance should revolve in one direction only until it stops.

To poise a balance is quite a simple operation but it is a matter which cannot be hurried. When you have decided which is the heavy point, reduce the weight of the balance at that point. If the balance is fitted with screws, the screw at the heavy point can be lightened by one of the methods already explained. Sometimes the heavy point is between two screws, then slightly lighten both these screws and so on. A cut balance should not be held in the hands and then tested for poise immediately. The temperature of the hand may affect the balance and so upset the poise and if an adjustment is made for that condition, it will not be correct when normal. This does not necessarily mean that the balance is out of poise in heat, the heat applied by holding in the fingers cannot be equally distributed throughout the whole balance.

If the balance is of the solid type with no screws, then the underside of the balance itself should be chamfered with the tool illustrated in Fig. 97. This tool is made by whetting the end of a round rat-tail file pyramid shape. Exercise care, as we cannot weight these plain balances if they are made too light. The only remedy is to let the balance spring out. It is essential that the balance be poised with the roller in position.

The monometal or plain balance is usually made from brass or, when used in conjunction with a beryllium steel balance spring, of an alloy of beryllium. There are two metals in common use today for the balance spring, Elinvar and beryllium steel. We shall speak of Elinvar first. Elinvar (the name is derived from " *El*asticity *invar*iable ") is an alloy of nickel-steel with a percentage of chromium. It is a decided improvement on Invar, which is a nickel-steel. As its name denotes it is invariable to changes in temperature. Elinvar is harder than Invar, and therefore supersedes it on this account. In addition to being unaffected by changes in temperature, or practically so, it is non-magnetic and rustless, making three very desirable properties.

It has been found in practice that sometimes a temperature error is present and there is no adjustment to correct it. If an Elinvar balance spring is used with a brass balance a losing rate may be observed in heat, due to the expansion of the balance, so an Elinvar or Invar balance should be used. On the other hand some Elinvar has a $+$ rate in heat so the expansion of the balance is compensated. Elinvar is not as hard as steel and greater care must be exercised when handling a balance spring made of it. Elinvar can generally be recognized by its whitish colour, it is almost grey and sometimes of a dull finish. It must not be confused with Invar which is whiter and has usually a bright finish. Palladium also is white with a bright finish ; but palladium springs are, or should be, used with a cut balance, their virtues being only twofold, in that they are non-magnetic and rustless only.

In recent years beryllium has come into prominence. It appears to be a metal with a history. As far back as 1797, the Abbé Haüy, the mineralogist, found that the minerals beryl and emerald have the same physical properties. In the years that followed many scientists sought to isolate metallic beryllium and in 1921 it was for the first time formed in the shape of large buttons. This metal, beryllium, alloyed with copper, iron, and a number of other metals, is a discovery of major importance to us. After a certain heat treatment it is as hard as hardened and tempered steel.

I am of the opinion that in the future the monometal balance will supplant the compensation balance. I can see no case for the cut balance ; the monometal balance fitted with either Elinvar or beryllium steel balance springs has everything in its favour. Especially is this true of beryllium steel. Elinvar is moderately hard but beryllium steel is harder. With soft metal for the balance spring, it is not possible for the watch to maintain its rate after the oil deteriorates slightly. The soft spring has little elasticity, and when the power of the mainspring becomes sluggish due to the oil becoming thick, after some time, then the soft balance spring does not help matters, in fact, the reverse is the case.

Beryllium steel is an alloy of iron, nickel, beryllium, etc., and is marketed under the trade name of Nivarox. Unless you know from the manufacturers it is a little difficult to recognise in a watch. Sometimes it has a distinct coppery tint, while some specimens appear a grey or slaty colour. This alloy has a low co-efficient of expansion, and does not change its modulus of elasticity up to a temperature much above that likely to be met with in watch work. It is non-magnetic and rustless.

I know of watches fitted with Nivarox springs which have passed the Kew tests with very good marks. The balance used in conjunction with the springs is usually made of an alloy of beryllium to suit the Nivarox spring. Whilst beryllium does not change its modulus of elasticity in heat, up to a certain limit, it has a co-efficient of expansion which, although low, has an appreciable effect on the rating when the balance is made from it, but the metallurgist is able to make an alloy of beryllium to match or suit the Nivarox spring, with excellent results. The manipulation of Nivarox is very similar to the steel balance spring with regard to its hardness.

A study of the chart will reveal that the cut balance and steel balance spring is superior to the monometal balance and alloy spring as a whole. If we consider the 1st grade monometal and Elinvar the temperature error can be from no error to 9 sec. for a change of 32° F. and the cut steel and brass balance and steel spring from no error to 1·8 sec. under the same conditions. But both can have no error and, considering the physical properties of both, I am of the opinion that the credit is in favour of the monometal balance and the alloy balance spring.

Springing and timing is one of the most interesting operations in our business. It calls for some considerable skill in the initial stages, and still greater thought and study later. It is not wholly a mechanical operation, no two instances being alike ; each watch has its particular problems. We all know, sometimes only too well, that no two watches rate alike and here, maybe, is the source of the interest. We shall together, you and I, spring and time a watch. It is the usual practice to send to the tool shop for a balance spring. When you send the balance to the tool shop state the count which is ascertained either by (a) counting the vibrations of the old spring, or (b) counting the train as explained when dealing with the train in Chapter Seven. Also state if for a Breguet spring or flat. If for a flat spring, send the balance cock so that the distance of the index

BALANCE SPRINGS FOR BI-METALLIC CUT BALANCES

Type of Balance Spring	Compensating Balance to be used	Quality	Colour	Temperature error over a range of approx. 32 deg. F. in 24 hours	Middle temperature error in 24 hours	Physical Properties
				Sec.	Sec.	
Tempered steel	Guillaume	Highest	Blue	0 to 0·36 approx.	0 to 1	Subject to magnetism and rust.
Tempered steel	Steel and brass cut	1st grade	,,	0 to 1·8 ,,	0·5 to 3	,, ,, ,,
First tempering	,, ,, ,, ,,	,, ,,	,,	0 to 1·8 ,,	0·5 to 3	,, ,, ,,
Hardened steel	,, ,, ,, ,,	Fair	,,	0 to 1·8 ,,	0·5 to 3	,, ,, ,,
Soft steel	,, ,, ,, ,,	Inexpensive	,,	0 to 1·8 ,,	1 to 4	,, ,, ,,
X-A-M	,, ,, ,, ,,	1st grade	Yellowish	0 to 1·8 ,,	0 to 3	Non-magnetisable and rustless.
Melius	,, ,, ,, ,,	Medium	,,	0 to 5·4 ,,	0·5 to 3	Only slightly magnetisable, rustless, good elasticity.

BALANCE SPRINGS FOR MONO-METALLIC BALANCES

Type of Balance Spring	Balance to be used	Quality	Colour	Temperature error over a range of approx. 32 deg. F. in 24 hours. Sec.	Middle temperature error in 24 hours. Sec.	Physical Properties
Elinvar 1	Glucydur "affixes" With attachments	1st grade	White or blue	0 to 9·0 approx.	0 to 3	Only slightly magnetisable and rustless.
Elinvar 1		,, ,,	,,	0 to 9·0 ,,	0 to 3	,, ,,
Elinvar 2	Glucydur	Medium	,,	9·0 to 36 ,,	0 to 3	,, ,,
Elinvar 3	Nickel	Fair	,,	36 to 72 ,,	0 to 4	,, ,,
Parelinvar 1	,,	Inexpensive	,,	72 to 108 ,,	0 to 5	,, ,,
Parelinvar 2	,,	,,	,,	90 to 108 ,,	0 to 5	,, ,,
Melior		,,	,,	90 to 108 ,,	0 to 5	,, ,,
Metelinvar 1	Glucydur	1st grade	White or blue	0 to 9·0 ,,	0 to 3	Almost non - magnetisable and rustless. Very good elasticity.
Metelinvar 2	Nickel	,, ,,	,,	9·0 to 36 ,,	0 to 3	,, ,,
Metelinvar 2		Fair	,,	36 to 72 ,,	0 to 4	,, ,,
Nivarox 1 from 10½ ligne	Glucydur	Highest grade	Blue	0 to 9·0 ,,	0 to 4	Non - magnetisable and rustless.
Nivarox 1 small movements	,,	1st Grade	,,	0 to 18 ,,	0 to 8	,, ,,
Nivarox 2	Nickel	,, ,,	Red brown	0 to 36 ,,	—	,, ,,
Nivarox 3		Fair	,, White	36 to 72 ,,	—	,, ,,
Nivarox 4	,,	,,	White	72 to 108 ,,	—	,, ,,
Nivarox 5	,,	Inexpensive	,,	108 and over	—	,, ,,

pins can be seen as this determines the diameter of the new spring. Breguet springs are usually about half the diameter of the balance.

It is also advisable to examine the balance before sending the balance to have a spring picked out or before starting to fit the new spring. First see that the quarter screws, if there are any, are screwed in at a reasonable distance. If they are screwed well out, run them half way in, otherwise it may be necessary to weight the balance after the spring has been fitted because it has been found that the screws are unsafe so far out. If the balance has been packed with timing collets, remove them. Make a fresh start. Poise the balance first, it may be considerably out of poise and we may wish to reduce the weight of some of the screws. Before a new spring is fitted our opportunity has arrived to clean up the balance, as it were.

The average watch repair workshop handles so many various types and makes of movements, and the percentage of watches needing a new balance spring is so small, that it is not economical to hold a stock.

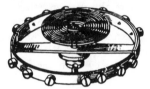

Fig. 203. Beeswax to hold balance spring for initial counting.

Having selected or had selected a spring of the correct strength, check up before starting to fit. To do this take a small piece of beeswax, about the size of a pin-head, press it on the top balance pivot, and on to this press the balance spring. See illustration (Fig. 203). The wax will hold the spring firmly enough for us to count the vibrations of the balance. The majority of watches have an 18,000 train, i.e., the balance vibrates 18,000 times in an hour; which is equal to 300 vibrations per minute, or 150 alternate vibrations. To make a rough check of the strength of the new spring, grip the outer coil

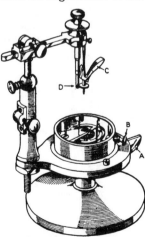

Fig. 205. Balance spring vibrating tool.

with the tweezers and hold on the glass of a watch which is fitted with a seconds hand, as illustration Fig. 204. Make the balance oscillate or vibrate, not too large an arc, and count as the half arm of the balance swings toward

Fig. 204. Counting the vibrations of the balance on a watch.

you. These are the alternate vibrations and should count 150 to the minute for an 18,000 train. In the initial stages of counting count 75 alternate vibrations to the half minute. In fact, for the rough selective counting half a minute may be sufficient. When you are satisfied that the spring is correct, transfer to the vibrating tool. The vibrating tool

(Fig. 205), is very useful and speedy ; the base is fitted with a tested balance vibrating 18,000. Usually these tools are provided with two extra boxes complete with balances, which can be interchanged, giving vibrations of 16,200, 18,000, 22,000.

The spring to be tested is gripped in the spring tweezer-like attachment by the outer coil. Adjust it so that the bottom balance pivot touches the glass and see that at the same time the balance is square or parallel

with the glass. Bring the bottom pivot in position so that it is immediately above the top pivot of the test balance. Move the lever, which causes the test balance and the one being tested to start vibrating together. Observe the two balances. For our balance to be correct it should vibrate in step with the master balance. If it is slow, as it is likely to be, release the grip and pull the balance spring through a little, thus shortening the spring. Continue thus until the tested balance vibrates at a rate synchronised with that of the master balance. Break away most of the superfluous spring, not too close to the grip, but far enough to make an allowance for the distance from the stud to the index pins. Where the grip held the spring is the position at which the index pins will operate when in the movement.

Fig. 206.
Tool for
breaking
away cen-
tre of
balance
spring.

Having broken down the spring to size, remove it from the tool, and also remove the spring from the balance. The object of reducing the diameter of the spring as much as possible is that it facilitates manipulation. Lay the balance spring collet on the board paper and place the balance spring over it, noting how much is to be broken away in the centre to free the collet when the spring is pinned to it. To break the spring, use the tool illustrated in Fig. 206, which is an ordinary sewing needle with about half the eye stoned away, leaving a forked prong. Hold the spring as indicated in the illustration (Fig. 207) and working the needle backwards and

Fig. 207.
Method of break-
ing centre of
balance spring.

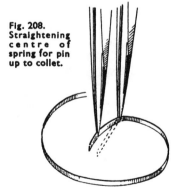

Fig. 208.
Straightening
centre of
spring for pin
up to collet.

forwards will break the spring quite easily. Bend a piece of the spring inwards and straighten it. Fig. 208 illustrates the procedure.

Place the collet on the tool, as in the illustration (Fig. 209). This tool is easily made : the first requisite is a steel rod tapered at one end. A plate or tray is fitted to a piece of brass tube which forms a sleeve and is split to give it a friction-tight grip so that it can be moved up or down on the rod. On top of the tray shellac an old enamel seconds dial ; one of the plain white ones from an old English watch answers well. Failing that, one with the seconds marking on will do. The hole in the centre must be opened considerably and this can be done quite safely with the aid of a carborundum pencil. Chamfer the hole first to cut the enamel and then widen the hole with a fine rat-tail file. Push the file in and away from the enamel, cutting on the inward stroke only ; by so doing we shall not chip the enamel. Use the carborundum pencil when more enamel is to be cut. It is immaterial if the enamel chips on the back of the dial.

File up a pin for the spring, giving it a long gradual taper to fit the hole in the collet, and to ensure that the spring does not rock when pinned up ; well burnish it with a flat burnisher. Stone with an Arkansas slip a flat of about one-third of the diameter. Take a piece of the spring broken away when breaking down to size and straighten it, place this in the collet hole and fit the pin for length, insert it flat side towards the spring. Pin up tightly, marking with a knife on both sides where the pin is to be cut. Remove the pin and cut through with a knife at the point end only. If the pin is held on the box-wood filing block and pressure applied to the knife, the pin will sever quite easily. Trim up the end of the pin with the Arkansas slip to remove the burrs thrown up by the knife. At the other mark, which determines the length of the pin, partly sever with the knife ; do not break off. We now have a short pin on the end of the wire.

Fig. 209.
Tool to hold balance spring collet.

Take the spring mounting tool and place the collet on it—make sure it is the right way up—using a little pressure to make it grip tightly, but not so hard that it will fit the balance staff loosely afterwards. Draw the tray up to the collet and place the balance spring in position ; manipulate the end of the spring into the hole in the collet, making sure not to bend the spring so as to cause it to set. Arrange the spring as illustration (Fig. 210) and pin up, but not too tightly. Break off the pin. With the aid of the tray it can be seen if the spring is flat ; it should lie parallel with the tray. Should it be necessary to adjust it to make it flat, it will be found that the

Fig. 210. Spring ready to pin to collet.

spring can be lifted or depressed, and it will turn in the hole with the pin. When you are satisfied that it is flat, press the pin home with the aid of a pair of stout tweezers or a joint pusher. Make sure it is very firm ; *it is vital that no movement whatsoever be possible between the collet and the spring.*

If you have been careful in the pinning up, the spring will run fairly true in the centre. This is where the white background comes in useful ; we can follow the convolutions of the spring with the eye and, by working to the sketch (Fig. 211), it will be a simple matter to make it perfectly true. That is, when pinning in at its centre, if we arrange so that the original convolutions of the spring are not bent, but only the comparatively sharp inward bend, the spring can be made to run perfectly true in the round, as we shall see in a moment. Before we proceed further, place the spring on the balance and fit

Fig. 211. Correct pinning at centre to ensure truth.

it up in the vibrating tool again ; time it closely and break down accurately to length, bearing in mind the additional piece required from the index pins to the stud. If a vibrating tool is not available, the method described on page 133 and illustrated in Fig. 204 can be used.

This time count for the full minute, but still only the alternate vibrations or swings of the balance need be counted. It is important to make this count as accurate as possible ; an error of 1/10th second is easily made and 1/10th second for each minute equals $2\frac{1}{2}$ minutes in 24 hours. When the spring is fitted into the watch other conditions will alter the count, such as the interference of the escapement, friction of the balance staff pivots in the holes, etc. These are, however, corrected by altering the weight of the balance, but we want the error to be as small as possible. If the spring is to be flat, not Breguet, allow about one stud length extra so that the spring can be let out if necessary.

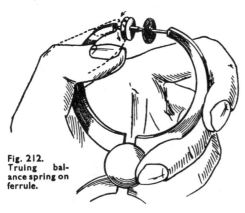

Fig. 212. Truing balance spring on ferrule.

The next step is to place the colleted spring on an arbor with a ferrule (Fig. 212) and spin in the callipers. We are now able to make the spring run perfectly true in the round and in the flat ; by making the spring as small in diameter as possible we have minimised the tendency to flop about. Practice alone is required to make the spring run true ; the acme of perfection is that, when fitted up in the watch and the watch wound and going, the 4th or

5th coil from the centre should remain motionless with the inner and outer coils opening and closing without a ripple.

Here are a few hints on how to make the spring run true in the centre. The first is not to bend the original volute at the centre. If, for

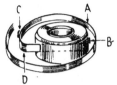

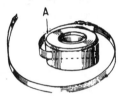

Fig. 213. Truing balance spring in centre.

Fig. 214. A twist at (A) to make spring central.

instance, you find it necessary to bend the spring at (A) in the illustration (Fig. 213) to bring the spring central with the collet, place the blades of the stout tweezers at (B) and (C) and apply a little pressure, this will cause the spring to bend at (D). On the other hand, if the spring is as Fig. 214, place the clock oiler as indicated at (A) and give it a slight twist ; this will cause the spring to bend outwards. It takes some considerable practice to pin up a spring well in the centre. The beginner is well advised to try his hand with some old springs first, not only to make himself perfect, but because balance springs will not stand continual bending backwards and forwards.

If the spring is for a flat index it remains only to pin up to the stud, and we proceed as follows. File up the pin first, as we did for the collet, but leave it longer, so that a little projects from both sides of the stud. The best way to do this is to place the stud in position on the balance cock, do not fit the spring on to the balance ; first the spring alone, and when the spring has been made secure, *very secure*, to the stud, adjust it so that the collet comes exactly over the centre of the balance jewel hole, the outer coil at (*a*) (Fig. 215) must be bent outwards a little so that the second coil of the spring is free of the stud and the index pins. This bend should be gradual. There are instances where the stud is further from the centre than it should be : to be correct it should be concentric with the index pins. The best procedure

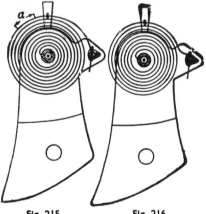

**Fig. 215.
Bend spring at (a) to free stud.**

**Fig. 216.
Bend at stud, when stud is out of position.**

is to bend the spring as illustrated in Fig. 216. The method of pinning to the stud is discussed further on when pinning up the Breguet spring.

CHAPTER THIRTEEN

BREGUET OVERCOIL

To MAKE the Breguet overcoil, named after its inventor A. L. Breguet (1747–1823, Swiss born, but practically all his life was spent in Paris), proceed as follows :—

Before actually pulling up the overcoil it is as well to have in mind what the theoretically, or mathematically, correct terminal looks like. Fig. 217 shows the curve as calculated by M. Phillips and designed by

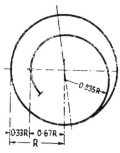

Fig. 217. The Lossier overcoil.

M. L. Lossier, and known as the Lossier curve. Although one can keep this curve in mind, the correct thing is to draw the curve to size to suit the diameter of the balance spring and this will determine the correct position for the index pins. This is not always practicable, so if you have some idea of the shape, so much the better. For those who wish to be more accurate, draw a circle the diameter of the balance spring, then draw 83° of a circle with the radius equal to the distance of the index pins from the centre. Bisect the distance from the 83° segment to the outer coil on the opposite side of the balance spring. This gives us the centre a, see Fig. 218c. Using this new centre, with a radius a–b, describe a semicircle connecting the outer circle with the 83° segment, and the resulting figure is the shape of the outer coil of the balance spring.

The design as evolved by Lossier requires that the 83° segment shall be ·67 of the radius of the circle, i.e., the outer coil of the balance spring. Then to bisect as we have just done. To make this quite clear draw a

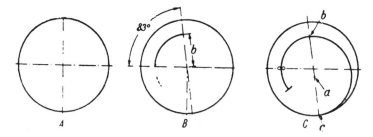

Fig. 218. Showing how to draw the Lossier curve.

circle the same size as the balance spring. We have selected the new spring and checked its strength, so this diameter is a known quantity (Fig. 218A). Suppose the diameter of the spring is 10 mm. then the radius is 5 mm. We now take ·67 of the radius, which is 3·35 mm. (b in Fig. 218B). Draw 83° of a circle of this diameter as Fig. 218B. Divide the distance between b and c (Fig. 218C) to find point a. Set your compass at *a* and join up *b* and *c*, forming a half circle as in Fig. 218C, and we have the Lossier curve. The fraction ·67 is a little more than half, so for all practical purposes we could take this measurement as half; as I have said, although an accurate curve may be formed it does not follow that the results will be perfect.

You will see, therefore, that our curve made to suit existing conditions may not be mathematically correct, but for all practical purposes—repair workshop purposes—it is accurate enough. If you have a special job in hand and you wish to obtain the maximum results, draw the curve as directed by Lossier, and then drill and fit index pins to the determined measurement obtained. It is quite a good plan to draw a series of curves of various sizes as defined by Lossier, and when the occasion arises select the one suitable. The spring should be placed over the selected curve and carefully bent to shape.

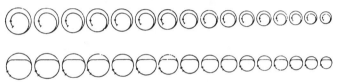

Fig. 219. *Top* : Lossier curves. *Bottom* : Phillips curves to suit the balance cock made for a flat spring if it is desired to fit a Breguet spring.

The illustrations (Fig. 219) give a series of overcoils which should suit most sizes of watches likely to be encountered. If the *exact* size is not shown, use the nearest as a guide.

Another curve which is useful where the index pins are far from the centre, or should it be necessary for some reason to fit a Breguet spring to a watch originally made for a flat spring, is illustrated in Fig. 220. The index pins are, or should be, at a distance from the centre equal to the radius of the balance spring. Draw two circles with diameters equal to the radius of the original circle. Connect these two circles with a straight line, which should be extended at both ends by an arc in the circumference of each of the small circles until it merges with the outer circle. The sketch should make this quite clear. The index pins will operate on the

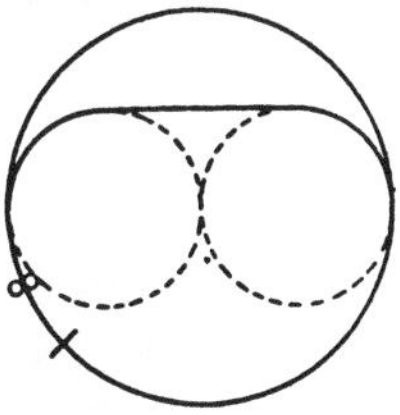

Fig. 220. Design of overcoil to suit balance cock made for flat spring. (Diameter of dotted circles should equal radius of spring.)

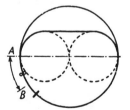

Fig. 221. Indicating where the index pins operate (A to B).

segment AB, and this portion of the spring is manipulated so that it is concentric with the centre of the index (see Fig. 221). Should this not be done, the spring will move as the index is moved. This curve is also a kind of Phillips curve, but to comply with the mathematical conditions the index pins should be at the point (A), Fig. 221. If this were so, there would be danger of disturbing the spring when the index is moved upwards when viewed as the illustration.

The same Lossier curve can be used for the inner terminal as for the outer. One would only use this curve on a high grade movement which was required to pass some stringent positional test. The curve must be accurately formed for the spring to run true in the centre and much time can be expended on this operation alone. However, if the correct inner terminal is adopted the " natural " vertical error will be considerably reduced.

Now comes the actual process of pulling up the overcoil and forming the curve. There are two or three methods in practice ; the one I favour is to place the spring flat on the board paper, hold the outer coil with a pair of stout tweezers about three-quarters of a coil round from the free end, and grip the extreme end of the spring with another pair of stout tweezers. Now hold the first pair of tweezers down on the bench firmly and quite still, so that the points slightly dig into the board paper ; lift the other pair of tweezers *straight upwards*, considerably higher than the finished overcoil is to be (Fig. 222). The spring should now look something like Fig. 223. From the point where the spring begins to bend upwards, measure as near as possible 25° to 30°, and grip the spring there with the stout tweezers, Fig. 224, and at about 10° to 15° from where the first pair of tweezers are, grip the spring with the second pair of stout tweezers, as indicated in Fig. 224. Gripping both pairs of tweezers very firmly, hold the first pair quite still and move the second pair downwards so as to bend the spring. The spring should now appear as Fig. 225.

Fig. 222. First pull-up when forming overcoil.

Fig. 223. Appearance after first pull-up.

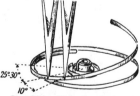

25°-30°
10°

Fig. 224. First bend down when forming overcoil.

Fig. 225. Appearance after first bend down.

It is necessary to go back for a moment. The height of the overcoil is controlled by the distance between the balance and the balance cock ; that is, when the spring is in position on the balance the overcoil should be, *without doubt*, free of the underside of the balance cock ; and the spring should engage about half way up the index pins, and should be on a level with the stud hole. When making the first pull-up, carry in your mind's eye the height the overcoil is to be. If the stud is a good distance from the balance, the first pull-up should be greater than if it is quite close. The object of not bending the spring down for 25° to 30° is to ensure that when the watch is functioning the elbow or bracket of the pull-up does not rub the body of the spring.

Now to resume : we are left with the spring as shown in Fig. 226. Move the tweezers round as indicated in Fig. 227, hold the left-hand tweezers stationary and sway the right-hand tweezers towards you. Do not make this bend in one move but work the tweezers along the spring, swaying the tweezers and nipping the spring the while. You may have seen a hairdresser using the curling tongs when dressing a lady's hair ; they run the tongs along a wisp of hair, opening and closing the tongs rapidly during the operation. It is a somewhat similar movement we employ, only not so fast, just persuading the spring to bend by a series of gentle curves or twists. Occasionally move the left-hand tweezers further towards the end, and eventually we shall bring the overcoil up and parallel with the body of the spring. Sharp bends are to be avoided as they are liable to cause fractures in the metal. The fractures may only be visible under a microscope, but their effect would be apparent when rating the watch. Not only that, but a better result will be obtained if the bends are gradual.

Fig. 226. Ready to make overcoil parallel with body of spring.

Fig. 227. Method of manipulating the over-coil upwards.

Fig. 228. Appearance of overcoil before curve is formed.

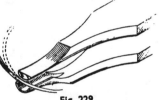

Fig. 229. Tweezers used for forming the curve.

The overcoil now has the appearance of Fig. 228. The next move is to form the curve of the overcoil, and the tweezers illustrated in Fig. 229 should be employed for this purpose. These tweezers have curved ends, and if the spring is gripped as shown, it will bend as indicated by the dotted lines. The curves of the tweezers need not necessarily be the desired curve of the spring : the extent of the bend depends upon the amount of pressure applied to the tweezers, and it is important to see that the tweezers are the correct way round before applying pressure.

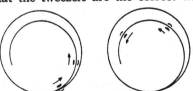

Fig. 230. Indicating the position of tweezers when forming the curve of the overcoil.

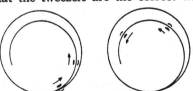

Fig. 231. The finished overcoil, showing the gradual bend up and the final coil parallel.

Practice alone can teach the amount of pressure and the points at which to apply the tweezers. The series of sketches in Fig. 230 will, however, give some indication of the procedure. These tweezers are procurable in various sizes.

During the forming of the curve the overcoil may move up or down ; it may so happen that pressure will be applied where the spring was bent or twisted, or a series of slight twists given, to make the overcoil parallel. This will cause the overcoil to bend up or down, but continue to form the curve, placing the spring over the drawing, if you have made one or are using one of those given in Fig. 219. If no design is being used, continue to form the curve until the shape is satisfactory.

It may be necessary, later on, to manipulate the overcoil again in order to make it flat or parallel ; this may, in turn, throw the curve out a little, and so by gradual manipulation, first of the curve and then to make parallel the overcoil, the aim is achieved of the overcoil being both parallel and true in the curve. Some considerable patience is necessary, but with practice an overcoil can be pulled up and made true with reasonable speed. I have seen girls in the factories in Switzerland, and in one factory in England, pull up an overcoil and make true in a very short space of time, but such operatives are continually carrying out the same operation day in and day out, and here practice makes perfect.

Fig. 232. Special tweezers to form overcoil. Bending overcoil up.

The Fig. 231 shows the finished overcoil. Mention must be made of two other methods in use. In the first method the spring is placed in the tweezers as Fig. 232, pressure is applied, and the spring is bent up more or less suddenly. The tweezers are then moved along to the next position and the operation repeated, but in the reverse direction, whereupon the spring is bent down at the same acute angle. The illustration (Fig. 233) shows the bend down.

This method is speedy and quite safe provided the spring is made of some soft metal,

Fig. 233. Bending overcoil down with the special tweezers.

such as Invar, Elinvar or beryllium, that is, something softer than the best hardened and tempered steel. To use this method on a first-class hardened and tempered steel spring needs considerable skill, and even then it is tempting providence. The curve is formed in the same way as in the first method mentioned. The other method, quite a good one, can be used with safety on a steel spring. It is carried out with the aid of the tweezers illustrated in Fig. 234. The diameter of

Fig. 234. Tweezers with pin to form overcoil.

the brass or ivory pin in the end of the tweezers determines the acuteness of the angle of the bend. So that if a pin of reasonably large diameter is used, the angle will not be as acute as it will be if a smaller pin were used ; the angle also depends upon the pressure applied.

To use these tweezers the balance spring is placed right side up on a piece of soft wood—the handle end of an emery buff answers well. Hold the spring at the point (A) where the first bend up is to be (see Fig. 235). Close the tweezers firmly on the spring, but not so tight as to make it impossible for the spring to move between them : when bent, the spring must slip between the tweezers. Then carefully and slowly force the points of the tweezers into the soft wood, which will cause the spring to bend up. Fig. 236 clearly shows what happens. Determine where the next bend is to be,

Fig. 235. First bend up, with pin, using tweezers.

reverse the spring and repeat the operation. This will bend the spring down again, and make the upward bent piece parallel with the body of the spring. Fig. 237 shows the bend down. (A) is the first bent up and (B) where we are now bending down. As the elbow is more acute than the one formed when pulling the spring up, it is not necessary for the actual bend up to occupy so large an arc as 25° to 30°. The connecting piece of spring between the body of the spring and the overcoil is now more or less upright, and is therefore not so liable to rub the outer coil of the body of the spring when functioning (see Fig. 238). The same remarks apply equally to bending up by the special tweezers described previously. Unless great care is exercised when using both the last mentioned methods, there is some risk of fracturing the spring. The bending is acute and, in the last instance, the

Fig. 236. Showing bend up being formed.

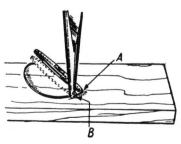

Fig. 237. Forming the bend down.

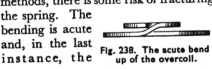

Fig. 238. The acute bend up of the overcoil.

height or width of the spring is bent over a very short arc. With soft springs the risk of fracture is greatly minimised.

Having formed the overcoil, it is now necessary to pin up to the stud. Secure the stud to the balance cock and fit the spring on the balance. Place the balance in the movement with the cock screwed on ; it is not necessary to fit in the pallets, in fact it is better to work without them. Now lead the balance round so that the end of the balance spring passes between the index pins and enters the stud hole ; it will require lifting just slightly to take up the natural sagging, otherwise no other assistance should be necessary. If the spring will not pass between the index pins, do not persuade it by pulling the spring over, but remove the balance cock and manipulate the curve smaller or larger, as the case may be, so that it is in alignment with the index pins. The foregoing instructions also apply where the stud hole is not in alignment with the index pins. If the spring passes through the index pins without assistance, but fails to come exactly opposite the stud hole, then we must bend the spring (as near the stud as possible) so that it will enter the hole. The spring must not be pushed over because by so doing the whole spring will be thrown out of centre, which will cause side friction on the staff pivots, and set up a host of other complications. Apart from this, all the careful work put into forming an accurate terminal will be utterly wasted.

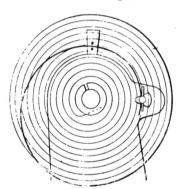

Fig. 239. Correct alignment of the index pins and stud hole.

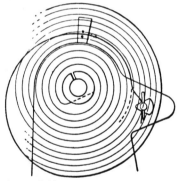

Fig. 240. Adjustment to the spring when the index pins and stud hole are out of alignment.

Fig. 239 shows the spring entering the stud hole when in alignment, or in circle, with the index pins, and Fig. 240 shows the necessary adjustment of the end of the spring, should the stud hole not be in circle with the index pins.

When all these adjustments have been made the spring can be pinned to the stud. Remove the balance from the movement and also the balance spring from the balance. With the stud in position on the balance cock, prepare a pin as for pinning to the centre, but in this case the pin is left longer (see Fig. 241). Other than this carry out exactly the same procedure, leaving the pin on the end of the wire and breaking it off when the spring has been actually pinned up. Lay the balance cock flat on the bench, manipulate the balance spring into the stud hole and pin up, but do not break off. Hold the balance cock up in the fingers, and with an eye-glass see if it is parallel with the cock. If it is not, it can be made so by twisting the pin tongs holding the pin. When you are satisfied that all is in order, break the pin off and finally press it home tightly with the stout tweezers as Fig. 242. The short straight hole of the stud may throw the spring slightly out of circle. If this is so, bend the spring as near the stud as possible to rectify.

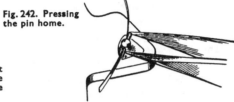

Fig. 242. Pressing the pin home.

Fig. 241. Correct length of balance spring pin at the stud.

While talking about the balance spring, a lot could be said about truing up a distorted balance spring, but no good purpose would be served. Some damaged springs can be made serviceable, and if you practise fitting new ones as explained here, I do not think you will have much difficulty in rectifying a damaged one. If the spring is much damaged, such as when the spring has been pulled up, it is a waste of time attempting to true it. It is much quicker, and certainly more satisfactory, to fit a new one. I have read somewhere that a speedy way to straighten a spring such as I have just cited is to place it between two plates and apply heat to re-set it flat. I have never attempted it, but it sounds most impracticable. With balance springs, as with all other parts of the watch, there is no short cut, you must just apply your practice and, in some sections of the craft such as springing, long practice. Balance spring work is one requiring long practice, in fact, one is never finished learning about it, and when I meet a man who says he knows all there is to know about springing and timing, I doubt whether he knows much at all.

CHAPTER FOURTEEN

TIMING IN POSITIONS

HAVING FITTED the balance spring we now come to the timing and, in order to embrace as much as possible, consideration will be given to a watch timed in positions. Temperature adjustment has already been discussed. Before starting the timing it is essential that the watch should vibrate well, that is, the action of the balance should be $1\frac{1}{2}$ to $1\frac{3}{4}$ turns when in the dial up or horizontal position.

Sometimes the arc of vibration of the balance is referred to as the " action," and sometimes one hears the expression that " it swings out well." It is not possible, or at least not practicable, to measure the arc of vibration of the balance accurately. However, it can be estimated, and to do this proceed in the following manner. Some point on the balance is taken as the standard, usually one side of the arm or centre bar of the balance. Wind up the watch, then stop the balance and, on releasing it, note carefully the arm as it swings backwards and forwards. Observe the extent of the swing or vibration ; after 20 to 30 seconds it should have reached its maximum. If it takes very much longer than this period to reach its maximum arc, it is possible that something is amiss with the movement as the full power of the mainspring is not coming through to the balance.

It can be taken as a standard that if the watch is to function satisfactorily, the arc of vibration of the balance should not be less than $1\frac{1}{2}$ turns or more than $1\frac{3}{4}$ turns, dial up or down, and not less than $1\frac{1}{4}$ turns PU or in the vertical position. If the arm under observation reaches to the other side, that is half a turn, then the balance is said to be crossing or vibrating one turn. One turn, because it must take half a turn backwards as well as forwards. Therefore if the arm reaches another $\frac{1}{4}$ turn further on, that is $\frac{3}{4}$ of a turn in one direction, it is equal to $1\frac{1}{2}$ turns, or it crosses $1\frac{1}{2}$ turns. The illustration (Fig. 243) will help you to ascertain the

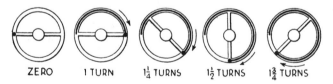

ZERO 1 TURN $1\frac{1}{4}$ TURNS $1\frac{1}{2}$ TURNS $1\frac{3}{4}$ TURNS

Fig. 243. The arc of vibration of the balance.

arc of vibration of the balance. A little practice is necessary before being able to determine the extent of the arc quickly. First, note the position of the arm with relation to some part of the watch, say the balance spring stud. Then hold the pegwood pointer at the point of commencement—that is the arm—and move the pointer round as the balance increases its arc, so that at each swing the balance arm reaches the pointer. When the balance arm has reached its maximum, the position of the pointer with relation to the balance spring stud will give us the arc of the balance. With a little practice you will be able to dispense with the pointer.

Although a timing tool was used when fitting the balance spring, the watch will need regulating to bring the watch to time dial up over a period of 24 hours. It must be borne in mind that the timing tool gives the count of the balance when perfectly free, not even the friction of the balance pivots are taken into consideration. In addition to this, the interference of the escapement, the action of the ruby pin, unlocking, etc., all have their effect upon the rate of the vibrations of the balance. Another point to consider is that the timing tool gave us the " perfect " time at one particular time ; when the balance is in the watch the power of the mainspring will vary, and with it the arc of vibration of the balance, and the extent of the arc of the balance influences the timekeeping. So, as you see, the timing over a period of 24 hours is another story to the timing on the vibrating tool—and this equally applies to timing machines.

Should it be found necessary to make an alteration for a considerable error, the adjustment must be done by altering the weight of the balance. On no account may the balance spring be et o ut or taken in, as this will alter the theoretical terminal—this does lnot apply to a flat balance spring—nor should the index be moved to any extent, for the same reason. In order to simplify matters, bring the watch to within a few seconds in 24 hours, we shall then not be confused with lengthy calculations. Say the watch is running to 5 seconds fast in 24 hours, test for 2 or 3 days to see if the rate is consistent. The daily rate of a watch is its daily error and a good rate does not necessarily take notice of the extent of the error but of its departure from its error, i.e., 15 seconds fast per day would read 30 seconds fast at the end of 2 days and 45 at the end of 3 days and so on ; that is to cite a particularly good rate. A rate is considered good if it does not depart more than 3 seconds from its previous reading. If it were + 15 seconds one day and then + 5 seconds the next (having lost 10 seconds since the previous day) and then + 15 seconds on third day (having gained 10 seconds since the previous day) the rate would be poor although the net result may look good : for a rate to be good the watch must not vary from its rate to a great extent. The rate will vary, however. One of the greatest difficulties when timing is the " variation of rate." It may be due to anything, the escapement, the train and perhaps the mainspring, but until we progress with the tests a varying rate even dial up only cannot be established.

After temperature adjustment comes positional adjustment, i.e., rating the watch in various positions. The usual positions are dial up (DU), dial down (DD), pendant up (PU), pendant right (PR) and pendant left (PL). For ordinary pocket watches, it is usual to rate dial up, dial down and pendant up only. With fine watches, however, such as those to be submitted to the " Kew " tests, or to comply with some specification— as required, for instance, by the Admiralty chronometer watch—the other two positional tests are made. Wrist watches are usually tested dial up, and pendant down ; pendant down because most people wear the watch on the left wrist, and when the hand is hanging down by the side, the pendant or button is also down. Wrist watches, no doubt, suffer from change in position much more than pocket watches, but it is not possible to test watches in all positions, so a compromise is made in the pendant down. If the wearer carries the wrist watch on the right wrist, then the positional test should be pendant up ; this is the exception rather than the rule. There are seven or eight methods of correcting the variation in rate due to change of position. It is proposed to discuss them all, and to refer to the merits of each individual method of adjustment.

The correct pinning point, i.e., the correct position of the balance spring to develop from the collet at the centre. For simplicity, the pendant up position will always be referred to for a pocket watch. If a wrist watch is being adjusted, pendant down, reverse the procedure.

Draw an imaginary line passing through the pendant and the 6 o'clock. Then draw a line at right angles to this line and passing through the jewel hole of the balance cock. The balance spring should

develop up from this last mentioned line, see Fig. 244. The balance spring may emerge from the collet on the left or the right, depending upon the position of the balance spring stud, but from whichever side it is, it should be *up*. The discovery of this is attributed to Jules Grossman. In other words, it is possible, by arranging the position of the pinning point, to correct a positional error. It has been remarked before that no two watches are alike, and this goes for the pinning point also. If two watches are sprung so that the spring develops up exactly on the line, it does not follow that both those watches will behave in exactly the same way.

Fig. 244. The correct pinning point.

Jules Grossman discovered that if this condition is complied with, the natural vertical position error will be thrown into the pendant down position, one in which the watch is not generally worn. It has been established that an error of 30 seconds slow exists between the horizontal and the vertical positions, and this is known as the natural error.

If, when testing a watch in positions, it is found that this 30 seconds slow does not exist pendant up, and it may even turn out that the error is +, it does not follow that the foregoing conclusion is incorrect. It means that one or more of the adjustments about to be discussed already exists, maybe by accident. For example, new balance spring may be fitted, and certain conditions which should be observed unintentionally complied with, such as the correct pinning at the centre. However, it is possible to correct a positional error up to 30 seconds by means of the pinning at the centre. To cite a definite case : the watch is tested dial up and the error is found to be + 5 seconds in 24 hours. The watch is then placed pendant up.

A word here about the racks in which watches are tested in the vertical positions. It is not advisable to hang the watch on a hook or nail, it may set in motion the whole watch due to the vibration of the balance : it is essential that the watch be firmly held. A simply made rack is illustrated in Fig. 245. It is useful for both pocket and wrist watches and is made of wood.

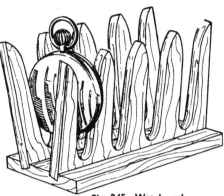

Fig. 245. Watch rack.

If the error pendant up is slow 30 seconds, that is, a difference between the DU and PU of 30 seconds, open the case of the watch, let the mainspring down and stop the balance. Observe the position of the pinning of the balance spring at the centre. It is not possible to draw a line as explained when discussing the correct pinning point, but the point from whence the spring should develop can be visualised, and it may be found as Fig. 246A, which is the reverse of what it should be.

A   B

Fig. 246. Correcting the pinning point by bending the balance spring.

To verify the accuracy of the foregoing, note where the spring develops from the collet and turn the watch round so that it develops up from the centre line, and call that position PU. It will be in this case approximately 5 o/c., practically pendant down. We now test the watch with the 5 o/c. up and we shall find that the positional rate is vastly improved.

There are Swiss watches with the balance cock quite circular. The balance cock is held in position by screws which bind on the edge of the cock, so that it can be turned round and made a fixture in any position. The balance cock carries the balance spring stud, and in this way the pinning point at the centre of the balance spring can be placed in any position, and the roller is then moved to put the escapement in beat. It is not suggested that all watches should be made in this manner, it is not necessary ; but such a device is admirable for experimental work.

From the foregoing it will be seen that it is possible to arrange the pinning at the centre to correct the error. It is known that at some point between the spring developing *up* from the centre line to the spring developing *down* from the centre line 30 seconds can be accounted for, or, in other words, the 30 seconds can be thrown into another and unwanted position. In practice it is not always convenient, when fitting a new balance spring, to pin the spring to the collet so that it develops up from the centre line. If after the spring has been fitted and the overcoil formed, it is decided to make the spring develop up, there are two methods of carrying it out. If the alteration is great, the spring must be broken away at the centre and repinned. Such a procedure will not affect the temperature adjustment (assuming the balance is cut), but it will be necessary to weight the balance, as cutting the spring away will make the watch gain. The other method, if the alteration is not great, is to bend the spring close to the collet and then bend it out again, as if it were leaving the spring hole in the collet (see Fig. 246B).

The dotted line represents the original position of the spring. This procedure may not enjoy the full benefit of the correct pinning point as the portion hugging the collet will come into operation when the balance travels in the unwinding direction of the balance spring. As an example, a watch with a flat balance spring was DU + 10 seconds PU − 15 seconds, a difference of 25 seconds. An alteration was made to the spring by bending to make it hug the collet, as explained, and the error was then DU − 7 seconds PU − 9, a difference of 2 seconds between DU and PU. Another similar watch was DU + 4 seconds PU − 30 seconds, a difference of 34 seconds. After a similar alteration to the spring at the centre the reading was ± (no error) PU + 7, a difference of 7 seconds.

Here are definite instances of theory brought into speedy, and therefore commercial, practice. We have seen that if the spring develops *up* from the centre line, there *should* be no error. Should is in italics because, as we shall see later, there are so many other conditions to be observed if this result is to be obtained. The chart (Fig. 247) gives the errors with reference to the pinning point, always bearing in mind that the pinning point is the *only* consideration at the moment.

This adjustment is permanent, inasmuch that if the watch is taken down, cleaned, and reassembled, it does not affect the adjustment. Always assuming that the spring is not damaged by accident or carelessness.

If the curve of the overcoil has been

	PU (PENDANT UP)	PR (PENDANT RIGHT)	PL (PENDANT LEFT)	PD (PENDANT DOWN)
 ⊕	+	+/−	+/−	−
 ⊕	−	+/−	+/−	+
 ⊕	+/−	+	−	+/−
 ⊕	+/−	−	+	+/−
 ⊕	−	+/−	+/−	+
 ⊕	+	+/−	+/−	−
 ⊕	+/−	−	+	+/−
 ⊕	+/−	+	−	+/−

Fig. 247. Pinning point chart.

formed to comply with some theoretical curve, the long and the short arcs should be performed in the same length of time. The long arcs refer to the long or big arcs the balance traces, i.e., when the balance vibrates or oscillates to its fullest extent, such as when dial up or dial down. The short arcs of the balance are when the watch is placed in a vertical position such as pendant up, right or left, or when the power of the mainspring is not so great. The balance then does not vibrate so fully. When the long and the short arcs are performed in the same length of time, the period of the balance is said to be isochronous. The isochronism test will be dealt with later.

As we have said before, it does not always follow that if a watch is fitted with a balance spring with a correct overcoil, it will function correctly in positions. Generally speaking, if the watch loses in the vertical position it indicates that the overcoil must be moved or shaped nearer to the centre. This can be effected in one or two ways. One is to make a kink in the overcoil as indicated by the dotted line, Fig. 248, which has the effect of stiffening the overcoil. Another is to shape the curve as indicated by the dotted line in Fig. 249, so as to bring the curve nearer to the centre. It might be argued that if the correct pinning at the centre corrects the positional error, why alter the shape of the overcoil?

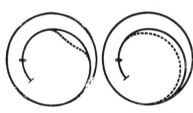

Fig. 248. Altering the curve of the overcoil.

Fig. 249. Another suggestion for altering the curve

The answer is that, when adjusting watches in positions, you cannot always achieve your object with one particular form of adjustment. Sometimes several minor adjustments are necessary, all made to different parts of the balance spring and even to other parts of the escapement. With this form of adjustment it is not possible to say how much the spring should be bent, it is purely a matter of experiment. The advantages are that it does not affect the mean time and, as with the correct pinning at the centre, it is permanent.

The two methods of adjustment just discussed are the ideal, and should be practised when dealing with a fine quality watch. A point worth mentioning here is that the theoretically correct curve is only *correct* if the *exact* curve starts at the index pins and the index is *not moved*, otherwise the shape of the curve will be either lengthened or shortened. Further, the pins must be close, there should be no movement here. From this point of view, the free spring, i.e., without index, is the ideal. There is no such thing as perfection, however, and it is therefore necessary to make use of imperfections.

It has been noted that more friction is experienced when the watch is in the vertical positions, with the subsequent decrease in the arc of vibration of the balance. Advantage can be taken of this when adjusting a watch in positions. Say the watch loses pendant up ; if the friction is decreased when pendant up, the error will be reduced. Or, alternatively, the friction can be increased in the DU position so as to give the relative lessening of the friction PU. There are two ways of doing this. One is to reduce the diameter of the balance staff pivots and fit new and smaller jewel holes. This will give greater freedom to the balance when in the vertical positions with the consequent reduction, or even elimination, of the losing rate. If this alteration is made it will be permanent. The other method is to blunt or flatten the ends of the balance staff pivots. By flatten it is not meant that they should be left dead flat, but rather less rounded. This will cause more surface friction when the watch is horizontal, and to a certain extent will make the friction when DU equal to that when PU. Friction is dependent upon pressure, and, in the case of the balance of a watch, upon the weight of the balance ; so that we cannot actually reduce the friction unless we change the weight of the balance ; but the surface friction can be reduced, or more correctly, the adhesion

Fig. 250.
Altering the end
of the staff pivot.

can be lessened. In watch work this adhesion is referred to as friction.

This latter form of adjustment (flattening the pivot points) is not as permanent as the former. The amount of flattening of the balance pivots may be very slight, it all depends on the requirements of the watch, and as the ends of the pivots wear during the running of the watch, the adjustment may in time be lost, or partly so. The dotted line (Fig. 250) shows the blunting or flattening of a balance pivot.

It is generally acknowledged that the acme of perfection is for the index pins to be close. There should be no movement of the balance spring between the pins. The spring should, however, be quite free, so that if you lift the spring up at the pins, it will return to its original position. Also, if the spring is pressed down at the pins, it should return, so that if the watch receives a jolt or jar, the balance spring will always return to its correct position. That is the ideal condition, and the adjustment we are going to consider now departs from that, but it is quite legitimate. Some of the most advanced springers and timers in Switzerland use the index pins as a means of correcting a positional error.

In order to make the procedure clear, an exaggerated case will be considered. Open the index pins so that, say, three thicknesses of the spring will pass between the pins. Now ease the spring over at the stud so that it bears against one pin, say the inside pin, it does not matter which. The result of this will be that when the watch is horizontal, and the arc of vibration of the balance at its greatest, the balance spring will leave the index pin it has been hugging, and will to a certain degree use part of the spring between the index pins and the stud. When the watch is placed in the vertical position, the arc of vibration of the balance is not so great, and the spring will not, to the same extent at least, leave the index pin. In effect, the balance spring has been shortened during the short arcs.

This means that the watch is made to lose DU and gain PU. The extent of this loss and gain depends upon the amount of pressure the spring is made to bear on the index pin, and also the extent to which the index pins have been opened. It is possible to bend the spring so hard on to the index pin, that it would not leave the pin at all during the PU position, and also possible to leave the pins so wide that the spring would not touch the other pin when DU.

There is at our disposal a very wide range of adjustments, but there are limits within which it is advisable to use it. An error of up to 90 seconds in 24 hours can be corrected in this way but, generally speaking, it is not desirable to utilise it to correct an error of more than 30 seconds. Much, however, depends upon the quality of the movement, and for a low grade movement it may be safe to use this system to correct an error of up to 90 seconds. If this form of adjustment is used to excess, the danger is this : Say the pins are opened fairly wide, and the positional error is corrected when the watch is fully wound, it will be found that towards the end of the run of the mainspring, when the action or the arc of vibration of the balance decreases the reverse error may be created. For example, say that an alteration is made to the index pins to such an extent that an error of 100 seconds has been corrected. This would mean that the balance spring would have to be adjusted fairly hard on to the index pin, with the consequence that when the arc of vibration of the balance is large the spring would leave the inner pin, but would not touch the other, it being bent out too far.

When the watch is positioned vertically, the balance spring would not leave the index pin at all, and the watch will have been made to gain considerably in the vertical position. Assume the rate before the adjustment was + 5 seconds DU − 95 seconds PU, and after the adjustment + 10 seconds DU, + 10 seconds PU. What *may* happen as the mainspring runs down and the arc of vibration decreases is that the watch will gain more DU, say 10 seconds, during the last 3 hours and PU it will lose during the same period, because the natural vertical error will predominate ; by comparison the DU will gain more than the PU position with the relative loss PU.

The ideal arc of vibration of the balance is from $1\frac{1}{2}$ to $1\frac{3}{4}$ turns. Under $1\frac{1}{4}$ turns a watch fitted with a Breguet balance spring will gain on its rate, and less than 1 turn it will lose. These are general observations ; they may not apply to all watches, but mention is made of them in connection with the index pin adjustment, as the possibilities of correcting an error are considerable, but it must be used with discretion, bearing in mind other conditions. The illustration (Fig. 251) shows the index pin adjustment in its various stages. (A) Hugging inside index pin. (B) About to leave inside pin. (C) Just touching outside pin.

The advantage of the index pin adjustment is that it can be made without removing anything from the watch, and is therefore very speedy. If used in moderation the mean time will not be affected much beyond

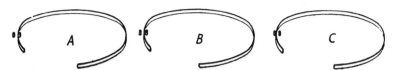

Fig. 251. Index pin adjustment.

what can be rectified by a slight alteration to the index itself. The disadvantage is that it is not permanent. If the balance cock is removed from the watch, the adjustment is almost sure to be lost. It is practically impossible to replace the balance spring *exactly* where it was before its removal.

Just a mention of two interesting examples of index pin adjustment. What, at first sight appeared to be a free sprung watch (a watch without an index or index pins), in fact had one index pin drilled into the balance cock, and the object of this pin was to correct the positional error. Another watch had one index pin fixed to the index in the conventional manner, but the other pin was fixed to a spring which looked like a compensating curb, but the spring was of one metal only, steel, not bi-metallic. The positional adjustment was made by causing the spring on which the pin was fixed to bear heavily or lightly on the balance spring, so that when the balance spring opens and closes during the vibration of the balance, the pin on the spring gives way. A nicely conceived idea, and, it would appear, permanent. Mention is made of these two instances to show that the index pin adjustment is not botch work, as it may appear at first sight, to contravene the laws of springing.

The ideal condition is for the balance to be in perfect poise, but the possibilities of adjustment by throwing it out of poise must be considered. It must be borne in mind that *absolutely accurate* poise is indeed very difficult to obtain when testing the poise of the balance on the poising tool. It may appear to be in perfect poise, with no dead point, but the watch may reveal an inaccuracy. The functioning of a watch is very searching. If the watch loses PU, it is possible to make the watch gain by making the balance heavy at its lowest point. As an example, open the back of the watch and note the position of the ruby pin when the watch is pendant up and the balance at rest ; the ruby pin will be, or should be, engaged in the lever notch, but the position to be noted is where does it stand with relation to the balance ? Is the ruby pin at the bottom, right or left side, etc. ?

Having noted the position of the ruby pin, remove the balance from the watch and place it on the poising tool (without the balance spring, of course). As the watch was losing PU, the low point must be made heavy. If it were noted that the ruby pin was to the right when the watch was PU, then throw the balance out of poise, still keeping the ruby pin on the right. It is not always possible to make the balance heavier, a plain balance for instance, but the same correction is secured by making the top or opposite side of the balance lighter. If the balance is fitted with screws, then a balance collet can be placed under one of the screws at the low point. The amount it is necessary to make the balance heavy to throw it out of poise can only be ascertained by trial.

There are one or two drawbacks to this form of adjustment. If the balance vibrates 1¼ turns or over, the reverse effect will result, and instead of the watch gaining PU, or at least not losing so much, it will lose still more. The illustration (Fig. 252) will help to explain this reason : (A) Heavy point at rest. (B) at 1 turn. (C) at 1¼ turns. If the watch vibrates 1¼ turns or over, the top of the balance must be the heavy point to make the watch gain PU, and this form of timing is known as " timing in reverse." Although positional timing, by throwing the balance out of poise, is permanent, inasmuch as taking the watch to pieces does not destroy it, it is not stable. As the arc of vibration of the balance varies,

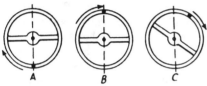

Fig. 252. Poise for positional adjustment
(A) Static. (B) One turn. (C) 1¼ turns.

so must the result of the heavy point vary, wherever it may be.

Centrifugal force positional adjustment is little resorted to today, and can only be used on the cut balance. Centrifugal force has the tendency to throw from the centre. The limbs oi the cut balance are constantly being thrown outwards during vibration, and the long arcs therefore tend to be slower than the short arcs on this account alone, that is, with no regard to other conditions. If the screw holes (A), one at each bar, are opened with a cutting broach, it will weaken the balance at that point, and the centrifugal force will cause the balance to open out still more (Fig. 253). Consequently the balance will be larger in diameter during the long arcs, resulting in a slower rate.

So that if the watch loses PU, the two holes referred to can be opened, which will cause a losing rate DU, with the relative fast rate PU. The dotted lines indicate position of arms during long arcs.

Fig. 253. Centrifugal force positional adjustment. Dotted lines indicate position of arms during the long arcs.

The Isochronism Test is not to be confused with the positional test, although some of the positional adjustments can be employed to rectify it. The word isochronism means " occupying equal time," and to test this condition in connection with watches proceed as follows. Wind up the mainspring fully and note the error after, say, 3 hours (always dial up) ; if it is + 3 seconds it indicates that if the isochronism is correct it should be + 24 seconds after 24 hours, that is, provided the watch gains at the rate of 1 sec. per hour. Make an observation after the expiration of another 3 hours, and the error is + 6 seconds. Observations should be made every three hours, i.e., wind and set at 9 a.m., observe at 12 noon, 3 p.m., 6 p.m., and at 9 a.m. the next morning ; then wind and set at 6 p.m. and observe at 9 a.m., 12 noon, 3 p.m. and 6 p.m. We have thus observed the watch for six periods of three hours, equalling 18 hours, which is usually sufficient.

The times of observation can be split up as best suits an individual programme. The object is to take the rate at frequent and regular intervals during the 24 hours, especially the first 3 hours and the last 3 hours. It may be found that the rate fluctuates, as, for instance : 1st 3 hours +3, 2nd 3 hours +8, 3rd 3 hours +14, and 24 hours +46 ; a total of 22 seconds in excess of what it should be. In this case an adjustment can be made to the curve of the overcoil. Instead of drawing the curve nearer to the centre, open it so that the curve is further from the centre. Alternatively, the index pin adjustment can be used. The other forms of adjustment described when adjusting in positions would not be suitable, and if either of the above adjustments upset the PU positional adjustments, there are other positional adjustments which can be introduced to correct this. The +22 seconds quoted is rather much, and in such circumstances it would be advisable to seek further for a cause before making any adjustment. For instance, observe the arc of vibration of the balance when the mainspring is fully wound and also when it is say 20 hours down. If there is a big discrepancy seek the cause.

The mainspring or a faulty depth in the train or a faulty action of the escapement may be the cause of the trouble : these sections have been dealt with under their separate headings. If you are satisfied that the movement itself is not at fault, then make the adjustment to the overcoil of the balance spring or the index pins. The fusee helped to overcome the isochronous error, as the force of the mainspring was equalised and a more or less constant arc of vibration of the balance maintained. The curve of the overcoil should and will overcome it, and the use of the index pin adjustment is useful.

An important point with all watches is that they should run for a much longer period than that actually required : a 24-hour watch should run for at least 36 hours. This is a manufacturer's problem, and at the factory it is quite a simple matter to achieve. It makes the task of rating much easier and at the same time more satisfactory.

Another adjunct which helps with the rating is the stop work to the mainspring. The best part of the mainspring is used and a more even flow of power assured.

After having adjusted the watch DU and PU it may be necessary to adjust it PR and PL. Such an adjustment is usually associated with a fine watch. A great deal of time can quite easily be expended on these adjustments and the quality of the movement must, in the first place, warrant the time spent. Another and most important factor is that the movement must be capable of responding to such treatment.

To cite a definite instance again, we might have a watch with a rate of +5 sec. DU +10 sec. PU and then test it PR and find the error is +15 seconds, that is + 5 seconds in excess of the PU reading. There are several reasons why this may happen and they will give us a clue to the correction. In the first place meticulous care must be observed with regard to the condition of the balance staff pivots. If they are *very slightly* oval that *may* be the cause of the trouble. Whatever the cause, the adjustment or correction must not interfere with the PU adjustment.

Pursuing our reasoning, make sure the inside of the balance staff holes are perfect ; the slightest roughness here can account for anything. Another possible cause may be the want of poise of the lever. Some levers

The table below is taken from an American journal and was compiled by C. T. Higginbotham. It forms a ready calculation of the daily error of a watch. Fractions of a second have not been considered and the calculations are to the nearest second. Accumulated error can be very deceptive. A wearer may use the watch for, say, 30 days and then finds that the watch is 9 minutes slow, an appreciable amount, but when thought of in terms of seconds per day, i.e., 18 seconds per day, it is not quite so alarming ; further, the watchmaker can better estimate the amount of adjustment necessary when considering 18 seconds per day than 9 minutes in 30 days.

Total Error	1m.	2m.	3m.	4m.	5m.	6m.	7m.	8m.	9m.	10m.
Days Run	s.	m. s.	m. s.	m. s.	m. s.	m. s.	m. s.	m. s.	m. s.	m. s.
2 ..	30	1 0	1 30	2 0	2 30	3 0	3 30	4 0	4 30	5 0
3 ..	20	40	1 0	1 20	1 40	2 0	2 20	2 40	3 0	3 20
4 ..	15	30	45	1 0	1 15	1 30	1 45	2 0	2 15	2 30
5 ..	12	24	36	48	1 0	1 12	1 24	1 36	1 48	2 0
6 ..	10	20	30	40	50	1 0	1 10	1 20	1 30	1 40
7 ..	9	17	26	34	43	51	1 0	1 9	1 17	1 26
8 ..	7	15	22	30	37	45	52	1 0	1 7	1 15
9 ..	7	13	20	27	33	40	47	53	1 0	1 7
10 ..	6	12	18	24	30	36	42	48	54	1 0
11 ..	5	11	16	22	27	33	38	44	49	54
12 ..	5	9	15	20	25	30	35	40	45	50
13 ..	5	9	14	18	23	28	32	37	42	46
14 ..	4	8	13	17	21	26	30	34	39	43
15 ..	4	8	12	16	20	24	28	32	36	40
16 ..	4	7	11	15	19	22	26	30	34	37
17 ..	4	7	11	14	18	21	25	28	32	35
18 ..	3	7	10	13	17	20	23	27	30	33
19 ..	3	6	9	13	16	19	22	25	28	32
20 ..	3	6	9	12	15	18	21	24	27	30
21 ..	3	5	9	11	14	17	20	23	26	28
22 ..	3	5	8	11	14	16	19	22	25	27
23 ..	3	5	8	10	13	16	18	21	23	26
24 ..	2	5	7	10	13	15	17	20	22	25
25 ..	2	5	7	10	12	14	17	19	22	24
26 ..	2	5	7	9	12	14	16	18	21	23
27 ..	2	4	7	9	11	13	16	18	20	22
28 ..	2	4	6	9	11	13	15	17	19	21
29 ..	2	4	6	8	10	12	14	17	19	21
30 ..	2	4	6	8	10	12	14	16	18	20
					Daily Error					

To find the Daily Error, take the column headed by the Total Error and read off the figure against the number of Days Run in the left-hand column. For a greater Total Error than is shown in the table, add the results of two or more columns together, i.e., for 23 minutes Total Error add the results of column 10 (twice) and column 3, or columns 10, 8 and 5. For an odd 30 seconds, average the results from the columns both sides of the required figure, i.e., for 6 minutes 30 seconds take the average of 6m. and 7m.

are so made that it is impossible to poise them, but we can at least improve the poise.

When the watch is PR, observe the position of the lever notch ; the ruby pin may be falling towards it or the notch may be on its side so that the ruby pin enters the notch on the side. This may give a clue, the draw of the pallet to the escape wheel may not be as strong as it should, and the ruby pin may touch very slightly as it enters.

A good deal of investigation on these lines will have to be pursued because there is no definite adjustment such as the adjustments first enumerated, to correct the PR positional error. Try the watch PL and if we find the error is + 5 seconds, it may in these circumstances be possible to adjust the pinning point at the centre to compromise ; the watch is + 10 PU + 15 PR + 5 PL, that is, taking the PU position as the mean, the difference between PU and PR is + 5 seconds and between PU and PL − 5 seconds. We could, therefore, arrange for the watch to be + 5 seconds PU + 10 PR and ± PL. Another step farther and we could alter the shape of the curve of the overcoil or alter the shape of the ends of the staff pivots and make the main vertical position to read PU ±, *i.e.*, the same as the DU or no *difference* in the rate PR to that of the DU position. We may then get ± PU, + 5 seconds PR and − 5 seconds PL.

You will note that we still have the difference of 10 seconds between PR and PL. The pinning point alteration has spread some of the PU error to the PR and PL positions but it has not removed it. The removal of the error must be effected by some constructional condition, such as a slight escapement fault, or the actual shape of the curve of the overcoil. To employ any one of the adjustments made to correct the vertical or PU error must affect the PU error itself, but, as we have seen, the errors can be camouflaged. From this brief discourse it will be appreciated that the three vertical positions adjustment can be a protracted business and therefore costly ; on the other hand, a watch may rate in all three vertical positions quickly. It can only be summed up by saying that it is a way watches have.

It is necessary to revert to temperature tests for a few moments. Most watches that are required to be submitted to temperature tests are tested in positions in the heat and the cold. For instance, PU in 85° F. and 42° F.

When you are satisfied with the normal temperature positional tests proceed to test in the heat. If the watch under test PU has a cut balance and the error is in excess of the normal PU error and also of the DU heat test, it will indicate that the balance is thrown out of poise when in heat. Such a condition is quite possible as has been pointed out when discussing temperature adjustments. In such a case nothing can be done about it, other than to change the balance.

In the case of the plain or monometal balance, the balance cannot be thrown out of poise and, other than the known positional and temperature errors, no further error should be shown as the result of the test in the vertical position in temperatures.

On each occasion it has been assumed that the PU error is slow. Should it be found that the error is fast, then reverse the instructions. For instance, open the curve of the overcoil of the balance spring ; make the balance pivots more pointed (but still round at the ends) ; fit a new balance staff with pivots larger in diameter and a pair of larger jewel holes, etc., etc.

It will be seen from the foregoing that there are seven or eight methods of adjustment if the constructional faults mentioned in the section Timing PR and PL are counted. It largely depends on the watch you are working upon as to which adjustment is used. Positional adjustment can be a lengthy business. As it would obviously not be economical to spend much time on an inexpensive watch, the repairer himself must decide each case on its merits. Not only must the question of time be considered, but the watch itself may not be worth the time ; not necessarily the intrinsic value, but it must be decided if the watch is capable of responding to positional adjustment. All watches are not.

However, having decided that the watch is capable of a better performance, proceed to deal with it, using the adjustment you think best. Say, for instance, it is a fine quality watch under repair. First see that the shape of the curve of the overcoil is as near correct as possible ; then the pinning point at the centre is checked and corrected if necessary. During the tests an improvement can be made by slightly flattening the ends of the balance staff pivots. The final touch can be given by the slightest adjustment to the index pins and so progress until the best possible result is obtained.

Positional adjustment, for the want of a better word, is " fake." A watch may be timed very closely and pass an official test such as " Kew " with high marks, but if that watch is used for twelve months and then cleaned and resubmitted to the same test, the chances of it gaining the same high marks are slight. In the first place the watch was tuned up to certain conditions, possibly to accommodate dozens of minute errors. After twelve months' running the errors increase or decrease and other errors set in. It must always be borne in mind that *absolute perfection* is impossible, and this applies particularly to watches ; watches seeming to have more than their fair share of imperfection

How to Use the Correction Charts

The following is a summary of the discussion on positional timing. This summary should prove helpful when used in conjunction with the correction charts which follow. In the event of a watch having an error similar to one of those tabulated, a reference to the table and the summary should help to solve the difficulty quickly. The text dealing with each heading of positional adjustment should be studied, and the summary and chart will at once suggest the necessary action to be taken.

1. Alteration to the shape of the overcoil of the balance spring. If the curve is made smaller or brought nearer to the centre it will cause the watch to gain in the vertical position.

2. Observe the correct pinning point of the balance spring at the centre.

3. Alteration to the shape of the end of the balance staff pivots. Flatten the ends to give the comparative gaining when the watch is in the vertical position.

4. Reduce the diameter of the balance staff pivots and fit smaller jewel holes to give the comparative gaining when in the vertical position.

5. Adjust the index pins : open the pins and adjust the balance spring to bear on one pin to make the watch gain in the vertical position.

6. Adjust the poise of the balance so that it has a heavy point at the bottom, to make the watch gain in the vertical position.

7. Open the curve of the overcoil of the balance spring, i.e., make it larger in diameter or further away from the centre, to make the watch lose in the vertical position.

8. Sharpen or make less blunt the ends of the balance staff pivots to give comparative losing when the watch is in the vertical position.

9. Fit a new balance staff with pivots larger in diameter and new and larger jewel holes to give the comparative losing when the watch is in the vertical position.

10. Open the index pins and adjust the balance spring so that it works evenly between them, to make the watch lose when in the vertical position.

11. Adjust the heavy point at the top of the balance to make the watch lose in the vertical position, having due regard to the extent of the arc of vibration of the balance as explained.

CORRECTION CHART—GAINING RATE

Positional Errors in Seconds	Total Error in Seconds	Suggested Methods of Correction	Remarks
DU +5 PU +15 } =	+ 10 PU	No. 7 or No. 2 for 1st grade watches. No. 10 or No. 11 for 2nd grade watches	The whole of the error could be removed by any one of these adjustments. The quality of the watch must be considered.
DU +5 PU +20 } =	+ 15 PU	No. 7 and No. 2 for 1st grade watches. No. 8 or No. 10 for 2nd grade watches.	No 7 and No. 2 may accomplish what is desired and finally a slight No. 5 is permissible in a 1st grade watch.
DU +5 PU +25 } =	+ 20 PU	No. 7 and No. 2. Then No. 8 and finish up with No. 10 for 1st grade watches. For 2nd grade No. 10 and/or No. 11.	No 8 may correct the remaining error, if not No. 10 will. For 2nd grade watches No. 10 or No. 11 will remove the whole error.
DU +5 PU +30 } =	+ 25 PU	No. 7 and No. 2. Then No. 8 and finish up with No. 10. For 2nd grade watches No. 10 and/or No. 11.	The above remarks apply here.
DU +5 PU +35 } =	+ 30 PU	No. 7 and No. 2. Then No. 9 and finish up with No. 10. For 2nd grade watches No. 10 and No. 11.	No. 9 may correct the remaining error, if not No. 10 will do so. For 2nd grade watches No. 10 or No. 11 will remove the whole error.
DU +5 PU +40 } =	+ 35 PU	No. 7 and No. 2. Then No. 9 and finish up with No. 10. For 2nd grade watches No. 10 and No. 11.	If the watch is not for a 3 vertical positional test a slight No. 11 could be used. For a 2nd grade watch, either No. 10 or No. 11, or a little of both, will remove all the error.
DU +5 PU +45 } =	+ 40 PU	No. 7 and No. 2. Then No. 9 and finish up with No. 10. For 2nd grade watches No. 10 and No. 11.	The above remarks apply here.
DU +5 PU +50 } =	+ 45 PU	No. 7 and No. 2. Then No. 9 and finish up with No. 10. For 2nd grade watches No. 10 and No. 11.	The above remarks apply here.
DU +5 PU +55 } =	+ 50 PU	No. 7 and No. 2. Then No. 9 and finish up with No. 10. For 2nd grade watches No. 10 and No. 11.	The above remarks apply here.

These charts should prove useful, not so much for actual reference but to illustrate the number of adjustments possible and the combination of adjustments.

CORRECTION CHART—LOSING RATE.

Positional Errors in Seconds	Total Error in Seconds	Suggested Methods of Correction	Remarks
DU +5 ⎫ PU −5 ⎭ =	− 10 PU	No. 2 or No. 3 for 1st grade watch. No. 5 or No. 6 for 2nd grade watch.	The whole error could be removed by any one of these adjustments. The quality of the watch must be the deciding factor.
DU +5 ⎫ PU −10 ⎭ =	− 15 PU	No. 1 and No. 2 for 1st grade watch. No. 3 or No. 4 or No. 5 or No. 6 for 2nd grade watch.	No. 1 and No. 2 may accomplish what is required, and finally a slight No. 5 is permissible in a 1st grade watch.
DU +5 ⎫ PU −15 ⎭ =	− 20 PU	No. 1 and No. 2. Then No. 3 and slight No. 5 if necessary for 1st grade watch. No. 5 and/or No. 6 for a 2nd grade watch.	As the error is rather big, No. 1 would prove to be fairly bold and the final adjustments made with No. 5. For the 2nd grade watch No. 5 adjustment would remove the whole error.
DU +5 ⎫ PU −20 ⎭ =	− 25 PU	No. 1 and No. 2. Then No. 4 if the error is still large ; finish up with No. 5 for 1st grade watch. No. 5 and No. 6 for 2nd grade watch.	No. 4 may correct the remaining error, if not, slight No. 5 will do so. For 2nd grade watches No. 5 will remove the whole error.
DU +5 ⎫ PU −25 ⎭ =	− 30 PU	No. 1 and No. 2. Then No. 4 and finish up with No. 5. For 2nd grade watches No. 5 and No. 6.	The above remarks apply here.
DU +5 ⎫ PU −30 ⎭ =	− 35 PU	No. 1 and No. 2. Then No. 4 and finish up with No. 5. For 2nd grade watches No. 5 and No. 6.	If the watch is not for a 3 Vertical positional test a slight No. 6 may help. For 2nd grade watches No. 5 and No. 6 either or a little of both.
DU +5 ⎫ PU −35 ⎭ =	− 40 PU	No. 1 and No. 2. Then No. 4 and finish up with No. 5. For 2nd grade watches No. 5 and No. 6.	The above remarks apply here.
DU +5 ⎫ PU −40 ⎭ =	− 45 PU	No. 1 and No. 2. Then No. 4 and finish up with No. 5. For 2nd grade watches No. 5 and No. 6.	The above remarks apply here.
DU +5 ⎫ PU −45 ⎭ =	− 50 PU	No. 1 and No. 2. Then No. 4 and finish up with No. 5. For 2nd grade watches No. 5 and No. 6.	The above remarks apply here.

CHAPTER FIFTEEN

MAKING NEW PARTS

MAKING NEW parts is a test of real skill and rightly comes under the heading of watch*making*. Watchmaking, as we know it to-day, can be classified into three categories :

1. To be able to examine and clean a watch well.
2. To be able to fit a new balance spring and time and adjust it for temperatures and positions.
3. To be able to file and turn well, to make new parts equal to the originals.

The man who can combine all three of these accomplishments is a most valuable acquisition to any workshop. The man who is able to fill any one in a really first-class manner can be classed as a first-class craftsman. It is well worth while to master all three and, of the three, making new parts needs the most practice and is perhaps the most difficult. Such work may be difficult to some, while on the other hand making new parts comes easy and is a pleasure to others. For general work the third category is not much use without the first. In some workshops it may be possible to segregate the work, but from the man's point of view it is far better to be a good all-round craftsman rather than a specialist. He can then command a good position anywhere and in any part of the world.

In this chapter an attempt will be made to show how easily new parts can be made. As with other sections, there are some things which must be taught. They cannot be picked up. We learn from the experience of others and often what may look like a difficult job is comparatively simple when once you know just how to set about it. It is not practicable to mention all the parts it is necessary to make, but a range is selected that should cover all the ground of filing, turning and polishing : It will only be a matter of application to suit the immediate requirements.

Before we start on the actual work, the polishing materials, the method of preparing them, and the medium with which they are used will first be discussed.

Oilstone Dust, for grinding steel work is a fine powder which can be purchased from the tool shop. To those who prefer it, carborundum can be used. The method of preparation is the same as for oilstone dust and it can be used in a similar manner and for the same purposes. It is convenient to use at one time about as much as can be laid on a sixpence. Place this on a block (see Fig. 254), and mix with clock oil to the consistency of cream or a little thicker. It is most important that this abrasive should not

Fig. 254. Container for polishing material.

come into contact with other polishing material. For this reason it is better to keep the oilstone dust in a separate container, and not in one of those three or two tier blocks sold for that purpose. The method of using is to dab the polisher on to the oilstone dust, except when employing laps or other similar methoas, when the oilstone dust is conveyed with the tip of a knife and then spread over the surface to be used.

The polisher employed when using oilstone dust and oil is of iron or soft steel. The polishers are made in various sizes and shapes to suit the work in hand. For arbors, such as parts of the balance staff and pinions, a polisher about 6 in. long, $\frac{1}{8}$ in. to $\frac{3}{16}$ in. wide, and $\frac{1}{16}$ in. thick is

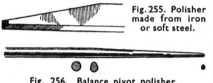

Fig. 255. Polisher made from iron or soft steel.

Fig. 256. Balance pivot polisher.

used, the active end of which is filed up as shown in Fig. 255. When making balance staff pivots a round rod about 6 in. long and $\frac{1}{16}$ in. to $\frac{1}{8}$ in. diameter is filed as Fig. 256. Such a polisher can be used for all sizes of pivots.

When polishing a flat surface by hand, with oilstone dust, a piece of plate glass about 3 in. square is used. Laps are made of iron or mild steel.

In the February, 1939, issue of the *Horological Journal*, an article on " How the Jewels in Your Watch are Made " says :—

" The basic material used in the production of artificial stones is generally ammonia alum, a sulphate of aluminium and ammonia, and is specially manufactured to get the necessary purity. The alum is first calcined in a furnace at a temperature exceeding 1,000° C. This drives off the water of crystallisation together with the sulphuric acid and ammonia, pure alumina Al_2O_3, in the form of a light white powder in an extremely fine state of subdivision remains. . . . It is of interest to note that alumina produced by the treatment of ammonia alum produces ' diamantine,' the indispensable polishing medium of the watchmaker."

Diamantine is sold in the tool shops in small bottles and it is most important to keep the bottle corked in order to exclude dust. It is a fine white powder, and is made up for use in the following manner. Take as much diamantine as will lie on a silver threepenny piece and place it on a block similar to the one used for oilstone dust. To this little heap of powder add one drop of watch oil from the medium size screwdriver. Well clean with a fine emery buff the flat pivot burnisher, wipe it thoroughly with a linen rag. Mix the oil with the diamantine, using considerable pressure ; the object is to use as little oil as possible, though it may be necessary to add another drop of oil eventually. At first the diamantine appears to be quite dry but continue to mix with the flat part of the burnisher, beating and crushing it at the same time.

Eventually a stiff paste, of about the consistency of putty, will result.

Some authorities say that a glass rod should be used to mix diamantine as steel discolours it. After mixing with the burnisher the diamantine will be of a dark grey colour but this in no way impairs its efficiency.

In use the diamantine is transferred to the polisher by dabbing the

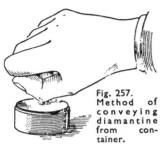

Fig. 257. Method of conveying diamantine from container.

polisher on to the diamantine, using the smallest amount consistent with effectiveness. To transfer diamantine to a lap or block, knock the knuckle of the thumb (make sure it is clean) on to the paste (Fig. 257), and then knock the knuckle on to the lap or polishing block (Fig. 257a), when sufficient should then be transferred. When not in actual use, always replace the lid of the block containing the diamantine immediately, in order to exclude dust.

The dust floating about in the air is sufficient, if it settles on the diamantine, to cause scratches.

The same polishers as were used for the oilstone dust may be employed with the diamantine. For example, when polishing an arbor after the oilstone dust has been used, the polisher is cleaned by filing, leaving a cross grain for the retention of the polishing material. Wipe the polisher on a linen rag to remove all traces of the oilstone dust and apply the diamantine. For other work, a bell-metal polisher can be used. When polishing the heads of screws by hand, use a bell-metal polisher about 6 in. long, $\frac{1}{2}$ in. wide, and $\frac{1}{4}$ in. thick. Laps are made of bell-metal. When polishing flat by hand—" under-hand polishing "—a zinc block is used, 3 in. by 2 in. and $\frac{1}{2}$ in. thick

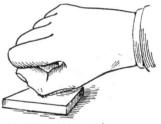

Fig. 257a. Method of conveying diamantine to polishing block.

is a convenient size (Fig. 258). Both zinc and bell-metal are used only with diamantine, they should not be used for oilstone dust. The bell-metal polisher is prepared by filing, leaving a cross grain to retain the diamantine.

Fig. 258. Zinc polishing block and paper sheath.

The zinc block is filed occasionally to keep it flat and the actual spot to be used is scraped with a knife until bright (Fig. 258a). The polishing block should always be cleaned before using. Make sheaths of stiff paper in which to keep the zinc block and bell-metal polishers, *dust must be kept away from diamantine polishing at all costs.*

Box-wood is also useful as a final polisher. It is obtainable from the

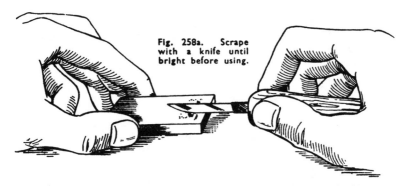

Fig. 258a.   Scrape with a knife until bright before using.

size of a piece of watch pegwood to a watch brush. As a final finish, after the metal polisher, it imparts a beautiful black polish. It is useful for arbors and heads of screws. Laps are made of box-wood when a dead flat surface is required. To redress box-wood, scrape with a knife and apply the diamantine as you would for bell-metal or zinc. A piece of pegwood, cut flat, takes the place of box-wood quite well and the back of a watch brush handle has done very good service when polishing the heads of screws and similar pieces.

Red stuff or rouge for polishing gold and brass is not much used to-day. The rouge is mixed much like diamantine, except it does not require the beating. It is used on tin polishers similar in shape to the iron polishers used for diamantine and also on a polishing block. The method of applying the rouge to the polishers is similar to that employed when using diamantine.

Water-of-Ayr or Montgomerie stone is similar in appearance and substance to slate. It can be obtained in many grades, that known as Montgomerie stone being the most generally suitable for watch work. It is sold by the tool shops in strips about 6 in. long and from ¼ in. sq. to 1 in. sq. The method of using is to dip the stone into water and rub it on to the article being treated.

If a piece of brass is to be polished with the tin polisher and red stuff, it is first prepared with Montgomerie stone. Montgomerie stone is to brass and gold what oilstone is to steel. It will be seen how both these polishing mediums can be used as the final finish. These are the principal polishing materials and polishers ; further details as to their use will be described as and when required during the making of the various parts.

The object to achieve when filing is to file flat and true. During watch repairing only small pieces come the way of the repairer, and in order better to explain the rudiments of correct filing, the making of a cock, such as a balance cock, will be considered first. Once the elementary stage has been mastered, filing small steel parts will come more easily. When filing brass use a sharp or new file, and when it is of no further use for filing brass it is then fit for use on steel.

Do not attempt to file hardened or hardened and highly tempered steel for two reasons. First, the metal will damage the file and secondly you will be unable to file it successfully.

The cock about to be made will be of brass, so use a sharp file. Take a piece of brass of about ½ in. long, ¼ in. wide, and ¼ in. thick. Lay this on a piece of cork secured in the vice. Knock into the cork two pins as indicated in Fig. 259. Hold the file as shown and file *flat* the top surface. The object

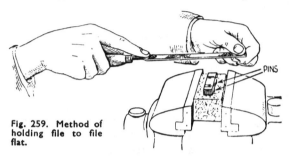

of using cork is because it gives a little, and if we bring some considerable pressure to bear on the file the piece of brass will, as it were find its own level Use long steady firm strokes with the file and remember that

Fig. 259. Method of holding file to file flat.

the cutting takes place in the forward movement.

By holding the file as indicated, an even pressure can be exerted during the whole of the stroke : you have full control over the file. If you examine a file closely you will see that it is composed of a number of teeth, all leaning away from the handle. When you come to the end of a stroke either lift the file clear of the work, or let it travel back over the surface of the work lightly, do not attempt to remove any metal on the backward stroke. Just rubbing metal backwards and forwards quickly is not filing. If you lift the file clear of the work, bring the tip smartly down on to the work before starting the forward stroke again ; this helps to assure that the file is in *full* contact with the work and avoids facets. Continue to file the top surface until all marks or unevenness have been removed. Turn over the pieces of brass and file flat the reverse surface.

When both sides are quite flat and clean—that is, clean of indentations, etc.—measure the thickness of the metal with a micrometer or a vernier gauge to ascertain that the two surfaces are parallel. Try the thickness in several different places.

Secure the brass in the vice with the sides protected by a piece of cardboard folded in two (see Fig. 260) and square up the sides or edges. If it is necessary to do a lot of filing, then make a pair of wooden jaws or chops. They are simply made. Take two pieces of wood about 1½ in. long, 1 in. wide and ¼ in. thick, an old emery buff stick answers well :

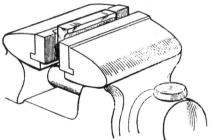

Fig. 260. Brass block held in vice between copper chops.

cut a piece of strong watch mainspring and glue this with a piece of linen to form the hinge as shown in Fig. 261. If the spring were curved

before placing it in position it will keep the chops open, so that the chops will open and close as the vice is screwed out and in.

There is no better way of learning than by actual production ; it instils the necessity of careful handling of both tools and material. Having taken

Fig. 261. Wooden chops.

the trouble to make the two faces with a good smooth flat surface it would, or should, be hurtful wilfully to mar that surface. That is how it should be, it is pride of workmanship and should apply to every part of the watch, whether you have made it or not. Heads of screws, polished surfaces, the hands of the watch, to mention only a few, are the parts most likely to suffer. The good and capable craftsman will handle every part of the watch with a care that almost amounts to reverence. The skill acquired in making new pieces will instil a due respect, and it is difficult to understand the feelings of a man who will take a piece, say a nicely finished return bar, and pass a rough file along the top surface and leave it thus. Such an act is not the work of a good craftsman, yet signs or similar maltreatment are encountered every day.

File the edges flat and true, that is, at right angles to the flat. With small pieces a better result can sometimes be obtained by holding the piece in the hand as Fig. 262. We shall now have a piece of rectangular metal, the two flat surfaces perfectly *flat*, the edges flat and true and the four angles, right angles.

This apparently simple piece of work is no mean feat for a beginner. The next stage is to file a step. Hold the piece of brass in the left hand with the first finger and thumb as a guide and let it rest on a piece of cork held in the vice, as Fig. 263. File the step with steady determined strokes, the " safe " edge of the file towards the shoulder. A pillar file,

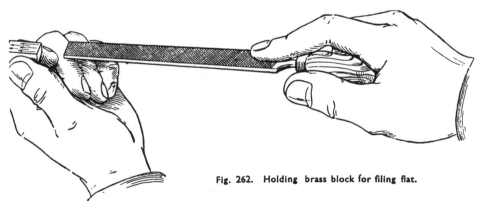

Fig. 262. Holding brass block for filing flat.

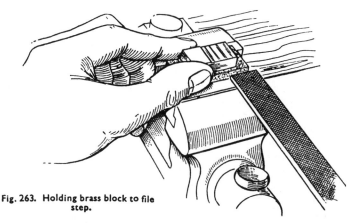

Fig. 263. Holding brass block to file step.

such as we are using, has two edges, one plain with no cutting surface, this is the " safe " edge, the other edge is serrated and will cut. Use considerable pressure on the file and train the eye on the safe edge to see that it travels perfectly straight during the whole of the stroke. Any deviation will round the shoulder. Continue filing in this manner until about two-thirds of the metal is filed away. Reverse the metal, at the same time turning it over, and file another step at the opposite end, as shewn in Fig. 264, to about half the depth of the metal. We now have a piece somewhat of the shape of a cock. To carry the work a step further file the end to shape as Fig. 265. Constructional work of this description forms excellent practice, it cultivates the ability to file flat and true. It is

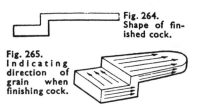

Fig. 264. Shape of finished cock.

Fig. 265. Indicating direction of grain when finishing cock.

important to note that when filing, the piece that is being filed should be made, as far as is possible, to find its own level. In this manner a flat and true surface is assured. That is why cork is used, it gives, and when it is not convenient to use cork, the piece is held in the hand as the hand also gives. Some small pieces, such as a small collet, are placed on the pad at the end of the first finger, when filing flat. Large or heavy work cannot so be treated and both hands are employed to steady the file.

It will be noticed, whether filing while the piece is in the lathe or turning or filing as just mentioned, and also when polishing, that the piece being worked is made, as far as possible, to find its own level by some means or another. Here lies the secret, or at least the greater part of it, of good craftsmanship. Good workmanship is 50 per cent. skill and 50 per cent. knowing how to hold, place, or work the piece. Practice alone will help you to accomplish this.

Had this cock or bridge been made for some special purpose, we should next drill holes for the screw and steady pins, etc. ; but as it is for practice we shall proceed to finish it. There are two or three methods of doing this. One is to finish the four flat surfaces with a medium emery buff. Use the same firm straight strokes employed when filing. A fine, straight grain should be made in the direction indicated by the arrows in Fig. 265. The same style of finish can be obtained by using the emery stone instead of the emery buff. It is considered good to use the emery buff provided the surface is fairly smooth and the job can be done quickly. If much reducing is done with the emery buff the surface tends to become rounded. In this respect the stone is preferable as considerable pressure can be exerted and a flat surface assured, but experience will teach you that the emery buff is not to be despised.

Another method of finishing brass is to stone it with Water-of-Ayr stone, having first dipped the stone in water. Use a circular motion, applying more water as required. Wash in water to clean, and a dull, matt, grainless surface results. Such a finish is ideal if the piece is to be gilt and it also can form the base of " spotting." An effective spotter is made by cutting a piece of pegwood chisel shaped. Dab the surface to be spotted with dry oilstone dust and on this revolve the peg in such a manner that the chisel end contacts the brass. A rosette will be scratched on the brass and if this process is repeated all over the surface indiscriminately until the entire surface is covered with the circular scratches, a very pleasing frosted effect will be the result. Some spotting is done at regular intervals, such as on chronometer plates, but a machine is necessary for this, and an ivory spotting piece is used to retain the oilstone dust.

Having become more or less proficient at filing flat and true in brass, it is possible to proceed with the fashioning of a click spring in steel. As a general rule working in steel is slower than when working in brass. The file should not be as sharp, so do not be impatient. Do not attempt to file hardened and tempered steel, that is, to file it to any extent ; a small alteration can be made, but when fashioning a new piece the steel must be soft. If the broken spring is available proceed as follows. Select a piece of flat steel a little thicker than the finished spring is to be. It is

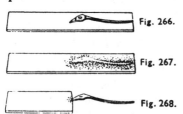

Fig. 266.

Fig. 267.

Fig. 268.

Fig. 266. Click spring ready to be " photographed " on to steel.

Fig. 267. Outline of click spring after steel strip has been blued.

Fig. 268. Click spring filed out to shape and ready to be cut off.

better if possible to select a long strip, say 6 in. long ; the reason for this will presently be seen. Clean one end of the steel with an emery buff. Heat this end slightly and smear beeswax over it, so that a thin film of wax is deposited. On this wax place the broken click spring and arrange the pieces in such a manner that the foot of the spring is furthest away from the end, Fig. 266. Before placing the spring in position remove any steady pins which may be fitted to it. Apply heat to the steel strip so that the part where the broken spring is resting turns blue in colour. When the bluing is accomplished remove from the flame and gently blow on the steel to cool. When quite cold, remove the broken pieces of the pattern click spring and we shall find that the spring has been " photographed " on to the steel. A white shape, exactly corresponding to the click spring, will be found as illustrated in Fig. 267.

Proceed to file up the new click spring. For this purpose use worn files ; the most useful are round and half-round. Do not cut the spring off the main strip. The strip of steel makes an excellent handle to hold the spring until almost filed to shape. Fig. 268 gives some indication of when it will be advisable to sever. When the spring is almost to size draw-file the sides ; this ensures an even thickness and is in reality the

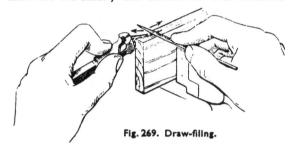

equivalent of flat filing, since it is not possible to flat-file a curved surface. To draw-file, the article is held on a wood block, the handle end of an emery buff answers well, as in Fig. 269 ; the

Fig. 269. Draw-filing.

arrows indicate the direction of the draw-filing.

When satisfied that the spring is to shape cut the spring away from the strip with a screwhead file. Finish the end while holding the spring in the slide tongs. Next drill the hole for the screw— or two holes if there are two screws—and the holes for the steady pins, if any. To do this, clamp the spring up together with a piece of brass in the slide tongs ; this will avoid breaking the drill when the hole is pierced. See Fig. 270. The spring must now be filed down to the required thickness. For this purpose use a piece of soft wood held in the vice ; again, the end of an emery buff is suitable.

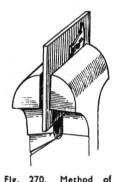

Fig. 270. Method of holding click spring with backing of brass, in slide tongs, to facilitate drilling.

Knock a short brass pin in the wood ; place the spring on the wood block with the screw hole over the brass pin (see Fig. 271). Just one or two strokes with a smooth file will suffice to make it flat, and almost the required thickness. Use considerable pressure and carry out the work slowly. It is important

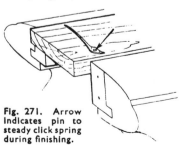

Fig. 271. Arrow indicates pin to steady click spring during finishing.

that this operation is done with a firm, steady action. Reverse the spring and repeat the flat filing so that both surfaces are flat and true.

Next countersink the screw hole to receive the screw head. If the head of the screw is chamfered, the hole needs to be chamfered with a chamfering tool, so that the head of the screw is sunk flush with the surface of the spring (Fig. 272). If the screw is square or cheeseheaded then sink the hole with a rose cutter (Fig. 273). The spring is now ready to be hardened and tempered.

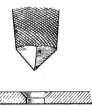

Fig. 272. Chamfering tool to sink chamfer-headed screw.

As the spring is long and thin there is considerable risk of it becoming distorted when plunged into the oil during hardening, and the risk should be minimised by binding the spring with thin iron wire as shown in Fig. 274. Such wire, known as " binding wire," can be obtained from the material dealers.

Fig. 273. Cutter to sink square or cheese-head screw.

When all the spring is a cherry red, *i.e.*, a dull red, plunge it immediately into the pot of oil and hold it there for a few moments. Remove, and unbind the wire ; now try the spring with a file to ensure that it is hard. If it is hard the file will make no impression ; it is necessary only to try the edge with a needle file. Should the file bite the metal then the process of hardening must be repeated. When sufficiently hard the spring must be tempered, and to do this boil it out in oil. Procure a small pan such as an old main spring barrel with the hole plugged and fit a wire handle to it. Place the click spring in the pan and cover it with oil ; a thick machine oil will do. Hold the pan over the flame until black smoke issues from the oil. Remove the spring from the oil ; it is now tempered. It is claimed that burning out in oil toughens the steel. Another method of tempering is to brighten one side of the hardened piece with an emery buff; place the piece on the bluing pan and

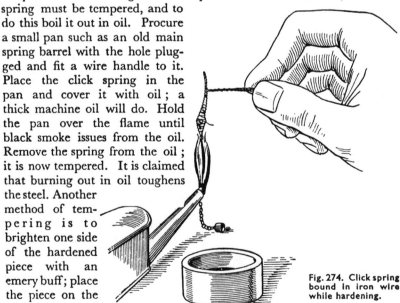

Fig. 274. Click spring bound in iron wire while hardening.

apply heat until a colour between red and blue shows, then remove it from the pan immediately, otherwise the tempering will continue past the stage required.

Any of one or more methods may be employed to finish the click spring, and we shall consider them all in order to become acquainted with them. The standard employed for any particular watch is governed by the quality of the watch itself. The new piece should be finished as the rest of the steel work. The acme of perfection is to repair a watch in such a manner that it does not look as if it has been repaired. In other words, as new ; so the new piece we have made should have the exact appearance of the original.

To obtain a straight grain the sides are first finished by stroking with an Arkansas slip. Where this is not possible, use an iron polisher charged with oilstone dust and oil, finishing with dry oilstone dust on a piece of pegwood, to give the bright satin or straight grain finish required. No matter how the top surface is finished to match to other steel work, the sides are finished with a straight grain. During the finishing of the sides the spring is held in much the same manner as when draw-filing and the action of the hand is similar. The underside of the spring is finished by placing it on the wood block with the brass pin, as we did when flat filing, but instead of the file, use an emery stone, not an emery buff ; a buff would round the surface. One or two firm strokes will quickly give the desired finish. The coarseness of the grain is controlled by the quality of the stone, so for a fine grain use a fine stone.

Before the top is finished fit the steady pins, that is, assuming it should have them. File up a piece of soft steel wire to a gentle taper and fit the pins from the top. Draw a No. 1 emery buff lengthways up and down the pin to give it a straight grain ; this will make the pin bite tighter in the spring foot and gives a finish to the steady pin. Chamfer the steady pin holes on the underside before fitting the pin. This is to ensure that burrs are removed and enables the spring to fit flat on to the plate when it is screwed home. Fit all steady pins as tightly as possible while still in the pin vice, and then cut with the nippers, leaving about 1 mm. projecting. Hold the spring on a stake and drive the pins in as far as possible with the hammer. File and stone off any superfluous metal. The underside, that is the actual steady pin, now needs to be cut short, and the ends stoned and rounded with either an Arkansas slip or a special tool made for that purpose. This tool is an *inverted* chamfer tool and is held over the end of the pin to be rounded and twirled between thumb and finger, rocking the tool from side to side while so doing.

Reverse the spring and stone the top surface with the emery stone, using the end of an emery buff as before and pressing the steady pins into the soft wood, finally making one long sweep or stroke to ensure an unbroken straight grain. Quite apart from the appearance it is advisable with all springs, if the finish is to be straight grain, to make the grain run lengthways of the spring. If you were to finish the spring with a cross grain the spring would be more inclined to break. The grain is a series of shallow nicks ; to nick a piece of metal is to invite it to fracture at that point. Having finished the sides and the top and bottom, the top edge can now be broken, that is, bevelled or chamfered. This is done

with an Arkansas slip where possible, and the iron polisher and oilstone dust where the Arkansas slip cannot be used, as Fig. 275 indicates.

Fig. 275. Finished click spring. Note bevelled edges.

The bevel on the top edge of spring is then burnished with an oval burnisher. The top edge of the screw hole is chamfered with the chamfering tool and burnished with a burnisher of a similar shape. The wheel type of chamfering tools are useful, they are also procurable with burnishing wheels the same size as the cutting wheels, see Fig. 276.

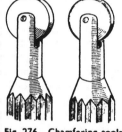

Fig. 276. Chamfering tools. Left : cutting ; right : burnishing.

If the top surface of the spring is to be underhand polished, shellac it to the end of the bolt tool, shown in Fig. 277. If the spring is fitted with steady pins it will be necessary to drill holes in the tool to receive them. Warm the end of the tool opposite the two upright screws and smear shellac on the under surface ; see that the shellac spreads, covering the surface approximately to the size of the spring to be polished. While the shellac is warm and soft press the click spring in position and immediately turn

Fig. 277. Bolt tool.

the tool over on to a piece of plate glass, a convenient size for which is about three inches square. Adjust the two end screws so that they project through by an amount equal to the thickness of the spring. Hold the tool on the glass tightly and tilt the glass up at an angle to enable you to see if the spring is in full contact with the glass, Fig. 278. It may be necessary to make further adjustments to the screws to effect this. By this time the shellac will have set. We shall now have a tripod with the click spring as one foot and the ends of the adjusting screws as the other two.

Smear a little oilstone dust and oil on the plate glass and work the click spring on this, holding the tool as shown in Fig. 279. The method of holding is very important. The first finger presses down on the tool

Fig. 278. Levelling bolt tool on plate glass.

just over the piece being polished and the thumb and second finger move the tool. The action is to move the tool backwards and forwards and also with circular and oval sweeps ; in other words, to make as many short and diverse movements as possible. Before proceeding too far examine the surface being polished. Clean the surface with pith. You may find that one part is being ground first, leaving part of the surface free of the plate glass. Further adjustment to the screws will be necessary so

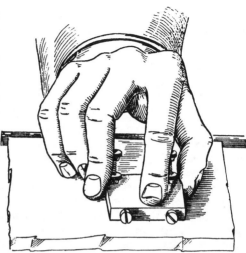

Fig. 279. Method of holding bolt tool.

that eventually the whole surface of the spring will be in contact. Proceed with the polishing until all file marks and other scratches are removed. Thoroughly clean off all traces of oilstone dust, first with a brush and then with pith.

When polishing steel the first thing to remember is that *it is essential that the surface to be polished is absolutely free from all foreign matter* : only when that state is achieved can the polishing with diamantine on the zinc block proceed. Dress the block with diamantine as previously explained and place the bolt tool with the spring attached on the block in much the same manner as when using oilstone dust and oil on glass. Hold the tool in the same manner and use the same diverse movements. Examine the surface of the spring to see that a *full* surface is being polished, making any necessary adjustments with the adjusting screws. The zinc block may not be as *dead* flat as the plate glass. When you are satisfied that the *whole surface* is in contact with the zinc block continue polishing, applying considerable pressure at first and gradually easing up until eventually hardly any pressure at all is applied. Some practice is necessary to polish well but with experience it will be possible to determine when the surface is " up," or fully polished, by the " feel." Towards the end of the polishing it should be possible to feel that the surface being polished is exceptionally smooth, almost as if the piece were not touching the block at all.

Clean the surface of the click spring with soft pith ; it should reveal a dead black velvety polish, a polish with depth, not just a shine.

To remove the spring from the bolt tool, let it drop on to the bench from a height of about 3 to 4 inches, flat, with spring uppermost and the spring will jump off. Some of the shellac may still adhere to the spring ;

to remove this, place the spring in a pan and cover with methylated spirit. Hold the pan centrally over the flame of the spirit lamp. When boiling methylated spirit is liable to spurt and ignite ; to deal with this have a flat piece of wood ready to clap on the pan, whereupon the flames will be stifled.

The edges can now be broken or bevelled, as previously explained, but in this instance the bevel should be polished and not burnished. To do this, use an iron polisher charged with diamantine ; a small-sized polisher is the most convenient. Hold the spring on the wood block in the fingers and at such an angle that the polisher will make *full* contact with the bevel. The action of the polisher is in short circular movements up and down the full length of the bevel being polished ; by so doing an even bevel is maintained.

For grey or frosted finish the spring is shellacked to the bolt tool and ground down on the glass plate. The final finish is obtained by placing on a piece of plate glass a sheet of ordinary notepaper ; on this paper sprinkle a dusting of dry oilstone dust. Now proceed to rub the spring on this paper, using much the same movements as for oilstone dust, and oil. One or two rubs will give the desired effect of a fairly bright grey or frosted finish. The edges can then be bevelled and burnished.

Whether making a click spring, return bar, return spring or click on any small piece made from steel, the same procedure is employed. It is ust a question of application.

If a piece of steel is made white by cleaning and then submitted to heat it will change colour from white to straw and then to red and on to blue ; beyond blue watchmakers are not interested. The colour does not necessarily determine the temper or hardness of the metal, but if we start with a dead hard piece of steel, that the file will not touch, and submit that to heat, then straw colour indicates a high temper suitable for the cutting edges of tools such as gravers and slide rest tools.   Red indicates a high temper, not high enough for cutting edges, but suitable for some tools, such as screwdriver blades. Red is also used by some manufacturers as the finish for screws, Longines, for instance, and also as the finish for hands. Blue is a very useful temper for watchmakers, all springs and most of the steel work in a watch is " safe " if lowered to a blue temper. Blue is also a popular colour as a finish for screws, hands and other steel work.

When soft steel or steel that has not been hardened is coloured to a straw, red or blue, the steel is still soft or without temper. When the question of colour only is considered, as a finish, the best result is obtained when the metal has first been hardened. To blue successfully proceed as follows : We shall assume it is the head of a screw that is to be blued. Harden and leave dead hard. Fit the screw up in the screwhead tool and stone the end of the head and also the sides with an Arkansas slip, clean off in benzine and brush well, make sure the slot is clean. Polish the end of the head, first with the bell-metal polisher and then with the box-wood slip or the back of the handle of a watch brush, as explained previously. It is advisable when polishing prior to bluing, to use the diamantine a little more moist than you would otherwise use it, and also to polish for the minimum of time. If the diamantine is dry and the polishing laboured the blue is inclined to be milky or " foxy " in appearance, it has not that clear blue so desirable. When you are satisfied with the polish, clean the screw thoroughly in benzine and brush well, particularly well, and see that the slot is clean. Do not handle the screw with the fingers as it is most important for successful bluing that the surface be clean and entirely free from grease.

Place the screw upright, with the thread in one of the holes in the bluing pan and hold over the flame of a spirit lamp. Hold the pan in the left hand and with a pair of tweezers or screwdriver in the right hand tap the handle of the pan near the pan itself. This will cause the screw to jump up and down slightly and by so doing the heat is more evenly distributed. Watch the screw carefully, it will change colour to straw and then red. At this point remove the pan from the flame, the colouring will continue without additional heat. Immediately it is the required blue, remove the screw from the pan, otherwise the tempering will continue and may leave the screw green. The required blue comes immediately after the red and that is why it is advisable to remove the pan from the flame at that stage so as to catch the screw in time.

CHAPTER SIXTEEN

TURNING

WHEN LEARNING to turn it is advisable to start with the turns (Fig. 280). There are two reasons for this : in the first place, turning in the turns is

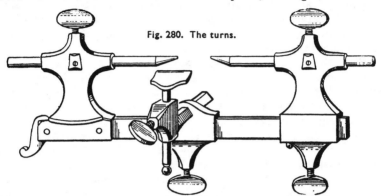

Fig. 280. The turns.

slower, which is desirable for the beginner and secondly, the work is simpler ; simpler in the sense that it is easier to achieve accuracy.

Fig. 281. "Blue" balance staffs.

Turning done in the turns is worked between the centres, while work in the lathe is invariably held in some form of chuck. There are one or two points to watch to ensure accurate or true turning. Even if the work is between centres in the lathe, it is propelled by the lathe, and the cutting is quicker. So to start with we shall concentrate on the turns. Incidentally, some of the finest turning is done on the turns. The schools in Switzerland teach on the turns first ; we cannot afford to despise this excellent example in spite of it being a primitive method.

First learn to turn well and cultivate speed afterwards. We shall talk at some length on lathe work later.

It is usual to buy balance staffs in the rough (Fig. 281) from the tool shop. They are known as " blue staffs." They are ready hardened and

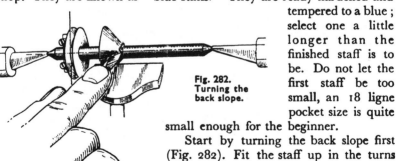

Fig. 282. Turning the back slope.

tempered to a blue ; select one a little longer than the finished staff is to be. Do not let the first staff be too small, an 18 ligne pocket size is quite small enough for the beginner.

Start by turning the back slope first (Fig. 282). Fit the staff up in the turns as illustrated in Fig. 283. Split ferrules can be purchased in various sizes. Select a suitable ferrule and secure it to the staff and wind the horsehair once round the pulley. Horsehair is purchased in hanks from the tool shop and is to be preferred to cotton thread as it does not fray. If horsehair is not

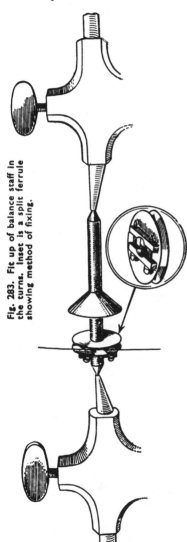

Fig. 283. Fit up of balance staff in the turns. Inset is a split ferrule showing method of fixing.

available then use cotton thread waxed with beeswax. The bow with which the horsehair is used is made of whalebone and when purchased is usually too stiff. The bow should be of such strength that it will hold the hair taut without breaking it, and yet have enough give to allow it to slip round the pulley of the ferrule should the graver, through miscalculation, be dug a little too deep into the work. This slipping makes for safety, since if the hair does not slip the work will either break or be put out of truth. The balance staff is fitted between the runners with *no endshake*, but at the same time it must be free. Make the runners secure and apply just a spot of oil to each pivot.

The position of the T rest is important. It should be at such a height that when the graver is in position the cutting edge is just a shade above the line of centres of the work, see Fig. 284. If the cut is made below

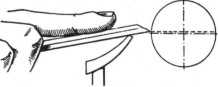

Fig. 284. The correct position of graver for turning.

the line of centres there is a risk of breaking the work or making it run out of truth. If the cut is much above the line of centres full advantage is not taken of the cut. The graver wedges the metal off, as it were, and when we visualise this the foregoing will be apparent. The illustrations (Fig. 285) should make this point quite clear. The next observation is that the T rest should be as close to the work as possible, so as to prevent chattering of the cutter. If, for instance, the T rest were half an inch away from the work, that part of the graver from the T rest to the work would be inclined to give and as a result a movement of chattering would be experienced. (See Fig. 286.) On the other hand, if the T rest were too close it would not be possible to hold the graver firmly and at the same time see the work (Fig. 287). Experience will teach the correct distance to place the T rest from the work.

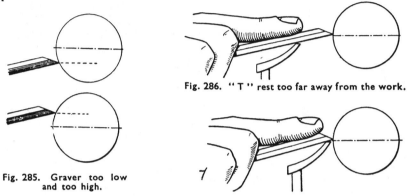

Fig. 285. Graver too low and too high.

Fig. 286. " T " rest too far away from the work.

Fig. 287. " T " rest too close to the work.

Before starting to turn first look at the gravers. It is important that they be sharp and free from a feather edge. To sharpen or whet hold as Fig. 288, and trace an oval shape on the stone using considerable pressure. It takes some little practice to whet a graver well. For all ordinary turning use a Turkey or Indian stone and oil, or a fairly fine carborundum and no oil. If for fine turning, *i.e.*, smooth surface, finish the whetting on an Arkansas stone with oil. After the face of the graver has been whetted just give one rub on the stone to each of the two sides of graver (A and B, Fig. 289), holding it flat on the stone while so doing (Fig. 290). Finally, dig the point of the graver into soft

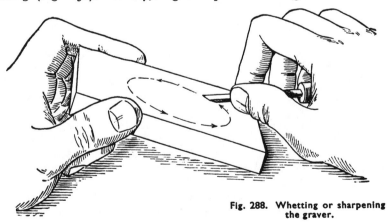

Fig. 288. Whetting or sharpening the graver.

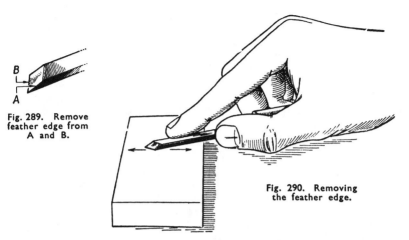

Fig. 289. Remove feather edge from A and B.

Fig. 290. Removing the feather edge.

wood, such as the leg of the bench, to ensure that all feather edges are removed. To test the graver for sharpness dig the point lightly into the thumb nail (Fig. 291) and if it drags then all is well. It is important to remove feather edges, otherwise the work will be burnished, the graver will not cut and a burnished surface can be difficult to remove in some circumstances.

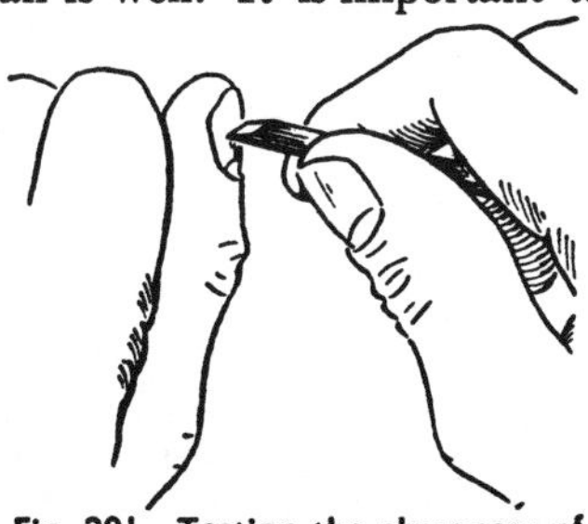

When turning with the bow, cuts are made on the down stroke only, as the work is revolving towards you. On the completion of each downward stroke the graver is held away from the work and as the bow is moved upward the work is free to revolve backwards. A little practice

Fig. 291. Testing the sharpness of the graver.

and ability to present the graver to the work on the downward stroke only, will become quite natural. To start turning hold the bow in the up position, apply the graver to the work and present that portion of the graver near the point first. Hold the graver *very firmly* down on to the T rest, the graver must not move or give to the work, the work must give to the graver. The illustration (Fig. 292) shows the part of the graver to use when making the work true in the round.

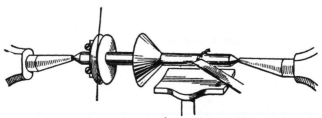

Fig. 292. Turning with edge of graver at an oblique angle.

To understand what turning really is visualize a large piece of metal between the centres with the proportional power to make it revolve, assuming the work is oval and we wish to make it perfectly cylindrical. We would find it impossible to turn true by holding the cutter by hand, the work would just push the cutter away. The diameter of the work may be reduced, but it would still maintain its original oval shape. In such an instance the cutter must be held in a slide rest and then the work would be forced to give way.

Returning to our balance staff, if the work is oval, for instance, the graver will cut in two places only, as the cylinder develops so a fuller cut is made and when perfectly true in the round a full cut is taken.

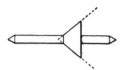

Fig. 293. Indicating flat or straight face of back slope.

Proceed to turn the back slope of the staff until perfectly true and the slope itself a straight taper, *i.e.*, the surface should be flat and not curved (Fig. 293). While the staff is fitted up in the turns finish off the back slope and polish it ; the reason for this will be explained later. To polish, use the polisher (Fig. 255, on p. 164), damping it with oilstone dust and oil. Work the bow up and down quickly and at the same time move the polisher backward and forward so that the work revolves against the direction of the polisher, *i.e.*, the polisher should not travel with the work.

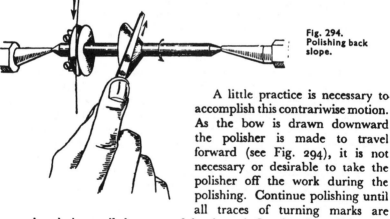

Fig. 294. Polishing back slope.

A little practice is necessary to accomplish this contrariwise motion. As the bow is drawn downward the polisher is made to travel forward (see Fig. 294), it is not necessary or desirable to take the polisher off the work during the polishing. Continue polishing until all traces of turning marks are removed and also until the taper of the slopes is flat, *i.e.*, the polisher has made full contact with the surface being polished. When satisfied that the surface is perfectly smooth, clean off with pith to remove all traces of the oilstone dust. To do this effectually, make the work revolve and hold the pith up to it, occasionally cut a thin piece of the pith away to present a clean surface ; *absolute cleanliness is essential.* Clean the polisher by wiping it with a clean linen rag, re-file the acting part of the polisher cross grain, and also lightly file the knife edge on the tilt (see Fig. 295).

Charge the polisher by just dabbing it on to the diamantine ; it is only necessary just to damp it. Now proceed to polish the slope, using the same strokes as when polishing with the oilstone dust. Use a little pressure in the initial stages, gradually easing off ; experience will generate the ability to " feel " the surface and know when a full polish is accomplished. Clean off with pith and a rich *black* polish is left, not just a shine, but a polish with depth, devoid of scratches or grain. Do not be satisfied until this is achieved, it is possible and it's quite simple ;

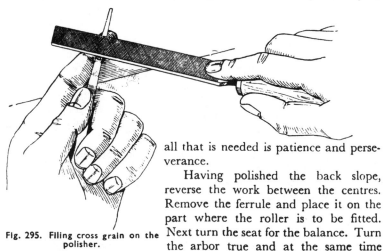

all that is needed is patience and perseverance.

Having polished the back slope, reverse the work between the centres. Remove the ferrule and place it on the part where the roller is to be fitted. Next turn the seat for the balance. Turn the arbor true and at the same time

Fig. 295. Filing cross grain on the polisher.

true up the shoulder upon which the balance is to rest and, if anything, very slightly undercut. The balance must seat flat (Fig. 296). If this shoulder is slightly rounded the balance may rock and will not run true when riveted in position. When cutting into the shoulder, make sure that part of the polished slope is cut away, this will give the effect of extra sharpness or flatness to the slope (see Fig. 297). The arbor, or body of the staff, is first turned true in the round and then reduced to a slight taper until the balance fits. The fit must be comfortably close (a push fit), it

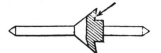

Fig. 296. Balance seating, indicating slight undercut. (Illustration exaggerated.)

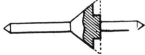

Fig. 297. Dotted lines indicate cut into back slope.

should not be necessary to force the balance home, and it should not fit too easily. If the fit is too easy the balance may run out of true in the round when riveted in position and if too tight the arm of the balance may be distorted when driven right home and riveted. A good test as to the fit is that, if the balance is held up with the staff in position, before riveting, it will not fall out ; it should fit just friction tight.

Having turned the seat for the balance, next turn the arbor for the balance spring collet. The diameter will be smaller than or the seat of the balance and, when the balance is in position, mark a shade above the balance arm on the arbor to determine where the undercut to accommodate the rivet of the balance is to come. This mark will therefore be a shade further from the back slope than the thickness of the balance arm. Turn the arbor to a slight taper until the balance spring collet fits to within about twice the depth of the collet from the rivet. When turning a long arbor use the full cutting edge of the graver. Undercut

Fig. 298. Running graver along the arbor to make smooth.

for the river using the same graver well whetted (Fig.299). Sometimes it is an advantage slightly to tilt the graver when removing the feather edge on the stone, it adds strength to the cutting edge, but when preparing the graver for undercutting keep it flat on the stone, otherwise the effective cutting point will be less pointed, as in Fig. 300, which is somewhat exaggerated to illustrate the result of tilting the graver.

Now polish the arbor with oilstone dust and oil, using the same polisher as for the back slope. Polish until the balance spring collet fits to within a distance equal to the thickness of the collet from the rivet. The illustrations, Fig. 301, show the position of the balance spring collet on the

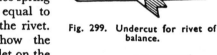

Fig. 299. Undercut for rivet of balance.

Fig. 300. Facet formed through tilting graver when removing feather-edge.

arbor after turning and oilstone and diamantine polishing.

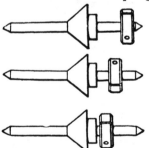

Fig. 301. Top : arbor turned to let collet on. Middle : polished with oilstone dust. Bottom : polished with diamantine.

Next clean and re-file the polisher, charge with diamantine and polish the arbor until the collet fits almost up to the rivet, remembering that the collet is to be pressed home to make it fit perfectly tight when the balance is finally assembled in the movement. During the polishing with oilstone dust and diamantine the top of the rivet will also become polished and this is desirable, because when the balance is riveted in position the polished surface will make a good finish.

Mark the arbor at the termination of the collet when it is pressed home against the rivet. It is from this point that the formation of the top pivot starts. Some movements are so designed that a short arbor is required before the pivot is made, but generally speaking the pivot is formed immediately above the balance spring collet. From here onwards we must start taking measurements. If the old staff is available and it was the correct size we can use it as a gauge.

If for some reason it is not desirable to use the old staff as a model when taking measurements for balance staff, it will be necessary to take the measurements from the movement. The handiest gauge to use is the vernier (as Fig. 115). First remove both the top and bottom end stones of the balance staff, screw the balance cock into position, making sure that it is parallel with the bottom plate. Now is the time to put it right if it has been bent up or down to accommodate a mal-fitting staff. Next take the measurement from the outside of the top and bottom jewel holes, allowing just a shade in addition for the protrusion of the staff pivots. The next measurement is the position of the balance ; screw the pallet cock into position and measure from the outside of the lower balance hole to the top of the pallet cock, and add to this measurement the amount necessary for the freedom of the balance of the pallet cock ; this measurement marks the position of the seat for the balance. Now measure from the lower balance hole to the top of the lever notch and add sufficient for the freedom of the impulse roller of the lever and also add the thickness of the same roller ; this gives the position of the seating for the roller. These are the main measurements, the rest is fitting. The top part of the staff forms itself automatically, being controlled by the height of the balance spring collet, the remainder providing the top pivot.

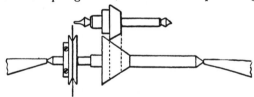

Fig. 302. Measuring for position of bottom pivot.

To proceed with the staff : reverse the ferrule on the staff and fit up in the turns so that the arbor for the roller can be dealt with (Fig. 302). Usually it will be necessary to cut into the polished back slope to let the roller on high enough. Here again this is desirable as it adds to the sharp effect of the turning. Turn the arbor, first for truth with the cutting edge of the graver near the point and then to a gentle taper until the roller fits, to within a distance from the back slope equal to the length of the roller ; that is, assuming the roller originally touched the back slope on the old staff. When once you have turned the arbor true move the graver up and down on the T rest to ensure a gentle taper with no ridges (Fig. 298).

The shoulder of the back slope should be perfectly square with the arbor. To cut this shoulder square hold the graver as Fig. 303 and see that no pip is left in the angle. The arbor is then polished with oilstone dust and oil, as before, until the roller fits to within half its length from the back slope. When the polisher is near the shoulder of the back slope make sure that the strokes of the polisher are in line with the shoulder. Some little practice is necessary to accomplish this. Shut the left eye and train the right eye along the edge of the polisher contacting the shoulder and concentrate on that edge to keep it straight and steady, slight divergence will cause the shoulder to become rounded (Fig. 304). When the polisher is away from the shoulder move it up and down the arbor fairly quickly and, while moving it backwards and forwards, impart a slight circular movement, round and round and up and down. This is to break the grain and form an arbor with no ridges. The bow is worked with equal speed at the same time but in the reverse direction, as explained previously. The polisher is then prepared and charged with diamantine and the arbor polished until the roller almost fits up to the back slope, leaving just sufficient for the final tap which will make it fit tightly when finally assembled.

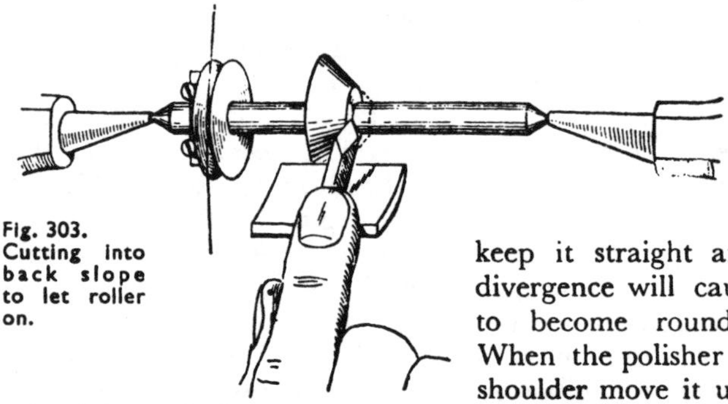

Fig. 303.
Cutting into back slope to let roller on.

The same care is exercised when near the shoulder during the polishing with diamantine as was observed when using oilstone dust. Sufficient oilstone dust and diamantine finds its way to the knife edge of the polisher to polish the shoulder ; with practice it will be found quite a simple matter to turn and polish a shoulder square, so that it will have the appearance of being lapped. Once this has been mastered the back of learning how to turn has been broken. Place the ferrule on the end of the roller arbor (it does not matter if the arbor is marked as we shall turn it away when making the bottom pivot) and reverse the staff between the centres so that the top pivot can be made. Hold the old staff to the new one and mark the position for the end of the top pivot by holding the point of the graver at that position and

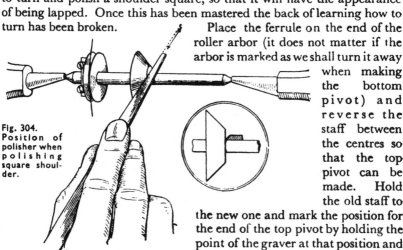

Fig. 304.
Position of polisher when polishing square shoulder.

turning a light line, check up again before making the parting cut. (Fig 305). Turn the end off to length using the point of the graver so as to leave a conical pivot (Fig. 306). Finish the conical pivot off with an Arkansas slip,

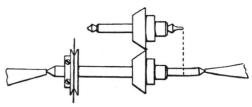

Fig. 305. Measuring for position of top pivot.

indicated by an arrow in the illustration (Fig. 307), which is self-explanatory.

As a rule the top pivot is formed immediately after the spring collet seating, as already mentioned, so we shall proceed to make the

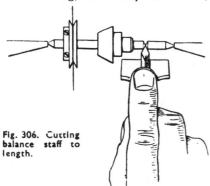

Fig. 306. Cutting balance staff to length.

top pivot. Turn the back slope to the pivot as shown in Fig. 308. If there is sufficient length this slope can be turned to a long taper, in which case it is polished, first with oilstone dust and oil and finally with diamantine. Watch that the shoulder is kept clean and square. Should there not be length enough for a long back slope, then it is customary to leave it unpolished from the graver. In these circumstances the graver is whetted on an Arkansas stone so that a fine cut can be made. Before actually making the final cut as the finish, just moisten the graver in the mouth. With the finely whetted graver just catch the edge of the spring

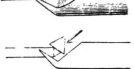

collet arbor, not only does it give sharpness to the arbor but assists when placing the balance spring collet in position. (See Fig. 309.) Arrow indicates the final cut.

Now turn the actual cone part of the pivot. To be correct the cone should form two-thirds of the length of the pivot, i.e.,

Fig. 307. Runner to form conical pivot. *Bottom:* arrow indicates triangular Arkansas slip.

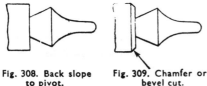

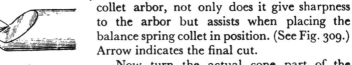

Fig. 308. Back slope to pivot.

Fig. 309. Chamfer or bevel cut.

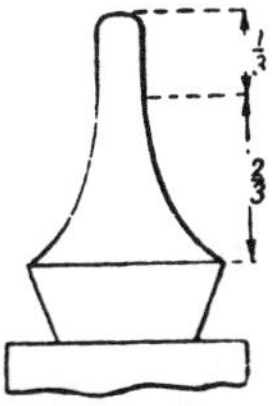

Fig. 310. Correct shape for balance staff pivot.

Fig. 311. Graver point shaped to turn staff pivots.

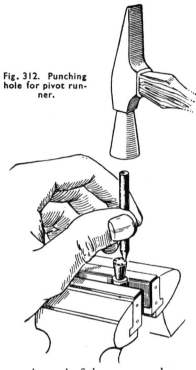

Fig. 312. Punching hole for pivot runner.

two-thirds shaped and one-third parallel (Fig. 310) ; it is calculated that the strongest pivots are so made. When turning the pivot, shape the end of a graver as shown in Fig. 311 and keep it especially for this purpose. It will not be possible to turn the pivot small enough in the existing runner so a runner is made especially for that purpose. Procure a piece of steel rod to fit the turns and about 4 inches long. Make the ends flat and square to the body. Hold the rod in the vice between copper or brass chops and, with a fairly sharp centring punch, punch a series of dots round the edge, not too deep (Fig. 312). Stone the end of the runner to remove the burrs thrown up by the punch and turn to the shape illustrated in Fig. 313. Turn so that some of the holes punched almost break into the turning, the necessity for this will be appreciated presently. Harden and temper the end of the runner, clean up with an emery stick and it is ready for use. To make the runners for the turns a lathe must be used.

Fit the staff up in the turns, selecting a hole in the new runner that will bring the pivot as far forward as is required and turn the pivot to shape and size ; the pivot should not fit into the balance cock hole at this stage.

Fig. 313. Pivot runner.

If you find that the pivot is buried in the hole in the runner and it is not possible to turn it, just stone the runner away with an Arkansas slip until the hole is near enough to the edge (Fig. 314). Having turned the pivot it should now be polished. Use the pivot polisher (Fig. 256, p. 164) charged with oilstone dust and oil.

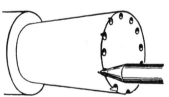

Fig. 314. Showing holes punched on extreme edge.

For this purpose the runner (as Fig. 315) is used and the pivot is laid on the runner and held in position with the polisher. To make this runner select a piece of steel rod about 4

Fig. 315. Pivot polishing runner.

inches long that will fit the turns. Make the end square and flat, and then drill a series of holes at about the same distance from the outer edge and to a depth equal to about the length of a pivot plus one third. The end of the runner is now turned down, leaving a series of pivot beds, that is, a sort of round-bottomed grooves. The size of the beds depends upon the size of the drills used. The end of the runner is then hardened and tempered and cleaned up with an emery buff, and is ready for use. The action of the polisher is the same as when polishing the arbor and, in addition, the polisher is slightly twisted so that you have in effect the motion of twisting the polisher up the cone of the pivot. In this manner the grain is broken and the possibility of ridges forming eliminated.

Continue polishing the pivot thus until it just starts to fit the hole in the balance cock. Clean the same polisher, re-file, giving it a cross grain, and re-charge with diamantine. Use the same runner, first cleaning it well with a rag followed by pith. Use the same motion as was employed when polishing with oilstone dust. Several strokes with the polisher will impart the black polish desired and the pivot should fit the hole comfortably. An important point to watch when polishing balance pivots is to see that the part of the pivot which should be parallel is kept so (see Fig. 316). When polishing pivots the inclination is to make them bullet

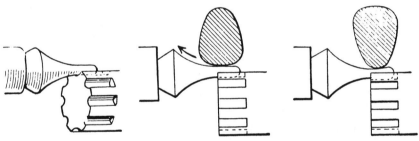

Fig. 316. Pivot resting on runner

Fig. 317. Correct size polisher and indicating movement of polisher.

Fig. 318. Polisher too small, forming "bullet" end to pivot.

headed and this is largely due to the fact that the polisher is not twisted or turned during the process of polishing and also to the fact that the small part of the polisher is used when the larger end would be

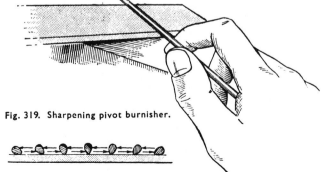

Fig. 319. Sharpening pivot burnisher.

more suitable. The illustration (Fig. 317) depicts the correct part of the polisher in use and also the small part causing the bullet head (Fig. 318).

Clean the pivot and the bed with pith and burnish, employing the same motion. The burnisher is the same shape as the polisher and quite simple to make. After filing to the required shape harden the active end and leave it dead hard. The business side is dressed or sharpened on a medium emery stick, using the movement as indicated in Fig. 319. Before using the burnisher, smear the active surface with a little oil. The burnisher will form a hard skin on the surface of the pivot and make it more durable. The end of the pivot is finished when the staff is completed and will be dealt with later.

In order to facilitate handling the staff to turn the bottom pivot the balance is next riveted on. Remove the ferrule and place the staff on a steel stake, first making sure that the surface of the stake is clean and

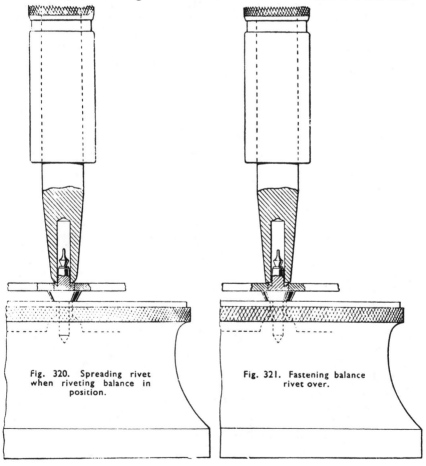

Fig. 320. Spreading rivet when riveting balance in position.

Fig. 321. Fastening balance rivet over.

free from dust. Place the balance in position and press home flat on to the seat. Select a hollow punch that fits comfortably over the balance spring collet seat so that it will spread the rivet (as Fig. 320). One or two taps with the light hammer will be sufficient to spread the rivet. Then select a flat polished end hollow punch to finish the rivet (as Fig. 321). Now fit on to the balance the ferrule made especially for that purpose and set up between the centres of the turns (as Fig. 322), or the Squire's runner (Fig. 323) can be used. Now for the bottom pivot. Present the old staff to the new one to determine where the end of the pivot is to be and proceed in exactly the same way as when making the top pivot or, if working to measurements, measure off.

The staff is almost complete, the roller is fitted into position and a gentle tap with the light hammer is sufficient to drive it home up to the shoulder of

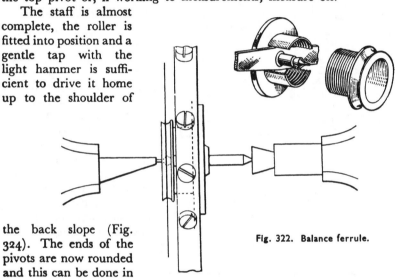

the back slope (Fig. 324). The ends of the pivots are now rounded and this can be done in

Fig. 322. Balance ferrule.

the jacot tool or in the turns with a runner made especially for the purpose (see Fig. 325). The ferrule is now fitted to the balance. Select a hole in the runner that fits the pivot freely and fit up the staff in the turns (as Fig. 326). The lantern runner (the one with the holes) is made secure in such a position that the balance staff is parallel with the bed of the turns. This is important, otherwise it may be the cause

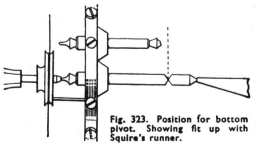

Fig. 323. Position for bottom pivot. Showing fit up with Squire's runner.

of the pivot breaking. Bring the lantern runner up so that the staff has endshake between the runners ; the pivot projecting through the hole must not be allowed to bind on the cone part of the pivot. Apply oil to both pivots. Sharpen the flat burnisher on a medium

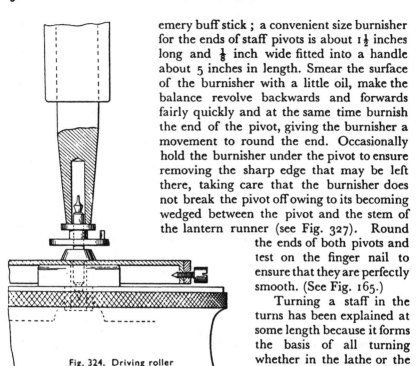

Fig. 324. Driving roller home.

emery buff stick ; a convenient size burnisher for the ends of staff pivots is about $1\frac{1}{2}$ inches long and $\frac{1}{8}$ inch wide fitted into a handle about 5 inches in length. Smear the surface of the burnisher with a little oil, make the balance revolve backwards and forwards fairly quickly and at the same time burnish the end of the pivot, giving the burnisher a movement to round the end. Occasionally hold the burnisher under the pivot to ensure removing the sharp edge that may be left there, taking care that the burnisher does not break the pivot off owing to its becoming wedged between the pivot and the stem of the lantern runner (see Fig. 327). Round the ends of both pivots and test on the finger nail to ensure that they are perfectly smooth. (See Fig. 165.)

Turning a staff in the turns has been explained at some length because it forms the basis of all turning whether in the lathe or the turns, *and the importance of practising first on the turns cannot be too strongly stressed.*

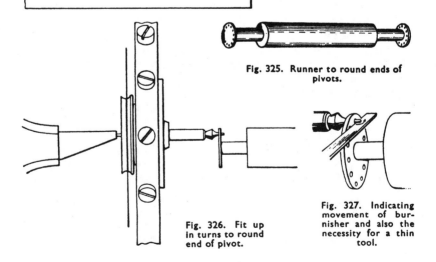

Fig. 325. Runner to round ends of pivots.

Fig. 326. Fit up in turns to round end of pivot.

Fig. 327. Indicating movement of burnisher and also the necessity for a thin tool.

CHAPTER SEVENTEEN

THE LATHE AND ITS USE

IT IS now time to give attention to turning in the lathe and lathe work generally, but before doing so it is necessary to discuss the lathe itself. There is little doubt that the lathe is one of the watchmakers' most valuable tools, it is speedy and efficient, not only speedy in accomplishing the work but, with the various accessories, the fit up of the work is carried out in an expeditious manner. The illustration here (Fig. 328) is of the simple lathe comprising the bed, headstock, tailstock and T rest ; the accessories will be explained as required to do the work in hand.

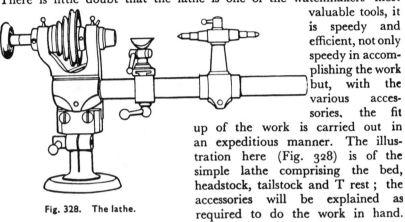

Fig. 328. The lathe.

When purchasing a new lathe buy the best possible and one of the popular makes so that accessories are easily come by. Handle the lathe with great care, do not force any of the fixing screws, finger tight is all that is needed in a well-cared-for lathe. This also applies to the draw-in centre of the headstock. If, for instance, a split or wire chuck is used, it should not be necessary to force the draw-in centre to tighten the work in the chuck ; if the work is not held securely by finger tightness then change the chuck, not only will the thread of the chuck and the draw-in centre be saved but also the work will be more accurate. Occasionally, say once in 12 months, take the lathe to pieces and clean all the bearings, see that the oil channels are clean and free from old oil. Reassemble and oil.

When assembling, the headstock should have no endshake at all, but at the same time it must be quite free. To adjust the endshake the grub screws that hold the cone-shaped bearing are loosened, and if it is required to lessen the play between the two fittings of the headstock this cone bearing is pressed inwards. To do this place a piece of wood over one end—the handle of an emery buff answers quite well—and give it a light blow with the clock hammer. If it is necessary to ease the spindle because the cone bearing is too tight, place the handles of two emery buffs over the smaller pulley, one on each side, making the buffs meet at one end, and strike both buffs with the hammer ; this will cause the end of the pulleys to strike the inside of the cone bearing and so drive it out. Take great care not to drop the lathe, but if by accident it does have a fall, test immediately for truth.

To test, place in a split chuck a piece of steel rod with a conical end ; the conical end must be perfectly true. Place one of the male runners in the tailstock and bring the two points together : they should coincide exactly if the lathe is true. If the points or centres do not coincide there is not much you can do about it other than to return the lathe to the maker as the cause may be due to several reasons—the bed not at exact right angles to the headstock, the headstock not planted square on its bed, the tailstock not square or slightly twisted—matters beyond the average

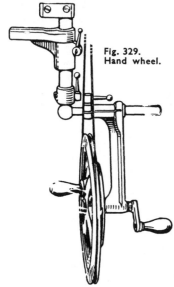

Fig. 329.
Hand wheel.

watchmaker's powers or equipment to correct, so do not waste your time, it may only make matters worse ; it's a tool maker's job.

The lathe can be driven in three ways, by hand, foot or by motor. In the first of these methods the hand wheel is used (Fig. 329) and it has much to commend it, especially for the beginner, as turning is slower and greater control can therefore be exercised. The foot wheel (Fig. 330) needs more practice than the hand wheel and has the advantage that it frees the other hand. The other hand is, in some instances,

Fig. 330.
Foot wheel.

useful for steadying the hand holding the cutting tool. Men who are used to the foot wheel would not, as a rule, change to other methods.

The motor driven lathe (Fig. 331) should be the objective of all beginners ; there is little doubt it is the most efficient method. The hand wheel has, to some extent, the disadvantage that it is liable to make the lathe vibrate when worked at speed. The foot wheel does not suffer this disadvantage but it takes some practice to operate it satisfactorily. The motor seems to have no disadvantages and it is not tiring but, and this is a big but, it is fast. The actual speed can be regulated in most

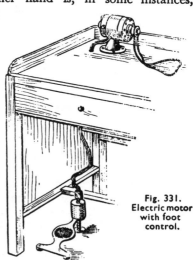

Fig. 331.
Electric motor
with foot
control.

models by foot control but even so the cutting is fast, and special practice is necessary. This is mentioned as a warning, especially to beginners. Metal is reduced very quickly both by cutting and polishing and the risk of breaking is also greater ; a slight dig, due to a jerk, and the work is either broken or made out of true.

Fig. 332. Split chuck.

As an example it is proposed to describe turning a new balance staff in the lathe and for this purpose the split chuck, sometimes referred to as a wire chuck or a collet, will be used.

The split chuck, as shown in the illustration (Fig. 332), grips only at the end of the chuck. If the piece gripped by the chuck is of the same diameter as the hole in the chuck the grip will be by the whole of the parallel part of the chuck intended for that purpose. Therefore if the piece is a good fit, then a slight screw to draw the chuck into the cone part of the headstock will hold the work firmly and, more than that, it will hold it in such a manner that pressure applied during cutting will not cause it to move ; this is most important.

Take a look at the illustration in Fig. 333. Here the chuck has been forced open to receive the work, with the result that only the back of the parallel grip holds the work, which is most unsatisfactory. Pressure

Fig. 333. Split chuck forced open.

applied during cutting will cause the work to move, with the result that the work will run slightly out of true. In addition to this, a chuck so treated will be ruined for future use.

Another point to consider is that if, after turning the projecting end it is then required to reverse the work in the chuck or, as may be necessary, another and smaller chuck, the work is almost sure to run out of true. The ability to turn true in the split chuck after reversing the work, even if the correct size chuck is used, is always a debatable subject. Men who turn between centres maintain it is not possible, whereas the split chuck men claim it is ; in any case, work turned in the chuck is true enough for most commercial purposes. But more of this anon. To revert to the correct size of chuck : if the chuck is not large enough, the work will not be held sufficiently tight without forcing the draw-in rod and so forcing the thread of both the chuck and the rod. *It will be seen that it is most important to select the correct size of chuck.*

In making a balance staff, it is proposed, for the purpose of instruction, not to use a " blue " staff. Select a piece of steel wire the diameter of which is as large as the hub of the staff. Blue steel wire can be used, *i.e.,* hardened and tempered, or soft steel can be used, hardening and tempering when the blue staff stage is reached. Be particular to use the correct sized chuck and allow the minimum length of wire to project. First turn down to let the roller on and then turn the back slope of the balance seat. Polish both the roller arbor and the back slope.

Just a word here about the quality of the finish. The finish should be the same as would be supplied by the manufacturer of the movement. If the quality of the movement calls for a fully polished staff, it is so finished, and if the quality is a grey finish, the staff is left as from the

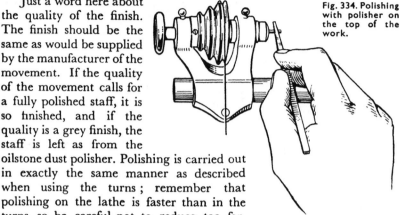

Fig. 334. Polishing with polisher on the top of the work.

oilstone dust polisher. Polishing is carried out in exactly the same manner as described when using the turns ; remember that polishing on the lathe is faster than in the turns, so be careful not to reduce too far.

There are two methods of holding the polisher, one is on top of the work as Fig. 334, and the other is underneath as Fig. 335. The T rest is removed during polishing. Personal preference may dictate the adoption of one method in preference to the other, but the choice is immaterial.

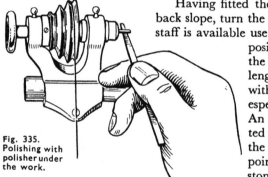

Having fitted the roller and finished the back slope, turn the bottom pivot. If the old staff is available use this as a guide for the position of the pivot. Cut the arbor to the correct length and turn the pivot with the graver which is kept especially for that purpose. An ordinary graver is whetted in the usual manner and the left-hand edge of the point is rounded off on the stone, and finally finished

Fig. 335. Polishing with polisher under the work.

on the Arkansas stone, so that a fine cut can be made.

The first four illustrations in Fig. 336 show the progressive stages of turning for the lower part of staff, and the remainder illustrate the turning of the upper portion after the staff is reversed in the lathe. The pivot can be polished with the same polishers as were used when making the staff in the turns or it can be finished in the jacot tool (Fig. 337), which will be described later.

Having completely finished the lower part of the staff, reverse it in the lathe. It will be necessary to select another chuck with a smaller hole. If the staff does not run true, slightly loosen the chuck and hold a piece of pegwood, the end of which is flattened, under the staff. and make the headstock revolve in reverse at some speed and while it is in motion tighten up the chuck (see Fig. 338).

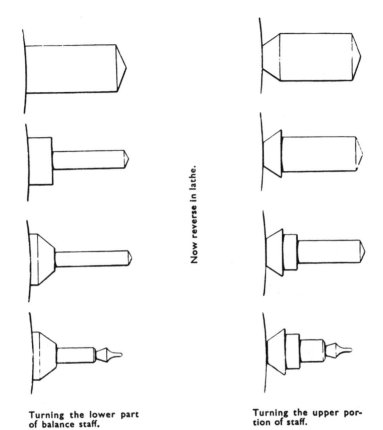

Now reverse in lathe.

Turning the lower part of balance staff.

Turning the upper portion of staff.

Fig. 336. Eight progressive stages in turning a balance staff in the lathe.

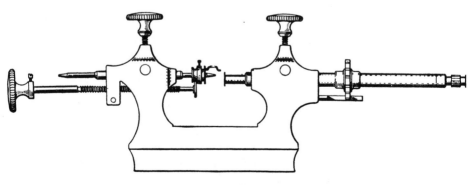

Fig. 337. Jacot tool.

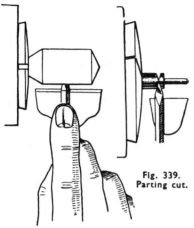

Fig. 338. Truing staff in split chuck.

Fig. 339.
Parting cut.

Turn away as much as possible that part which will not be required. To do this use the point of the graver (as Fig. 339), and make the cut approximating the position of the end of the top pivot. Reasonable care must be exercised as the staff in the chuck is weak, although it has the support of the shoulder bearing hard against the face of the chuck. We now turn the seat for the balance. If anything, slightly undercut the actual seat to ensure that the balance seats flat, cutting into the back slope ; this adds sharpness, as already pointed out. The old staff, if available, should be used as a gauge. Reduce the arbor until the balance fits, friction tight, down on to its seating ; it is not necessary to polish this seating. Mark the exact position for the top of the pivot and cut away. Turn the arbor for the balance spring collet and well undercut for balance rivet. Turn the top pivot and finish it off.

Remove the staff from the lathe and, assuming for a moment that the pivots were polished and burnished, it only remains to round and burnish the ends. First of all rivet

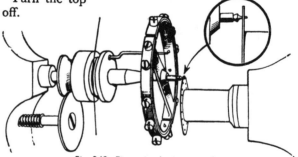

Fig. 340. Fit up in the jacot tool.

the staff on to the balance and fit up in the jacot tool as shown in Fig. 340. Select a hole in the lantern end runner that fits the pivot loosely and bring the runner up to the pivot so that its face does not touch the cone of the pivot, apply oil to both pivots. The small flat burnisher is used, exactly the same procedure is pursued as when using the turns, already explained.

The illustration in section (Fig. 341) shows the balance seating undercut in comparison with the straight dotted line. (Undercut somewhat exaggerated.)

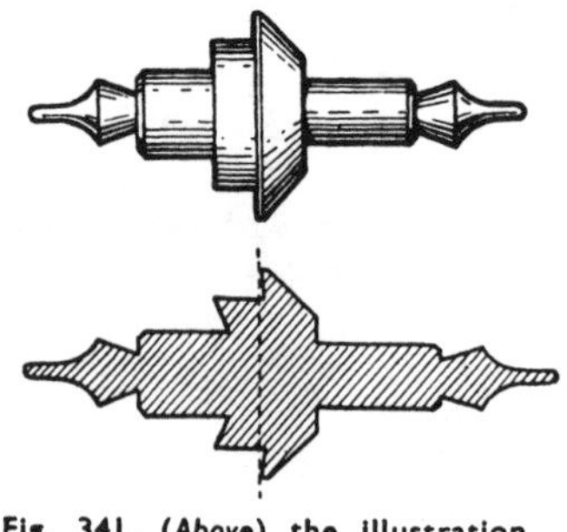

Fig. 341. (Above) the illustration shows the finished staff, and (below) the same in section.

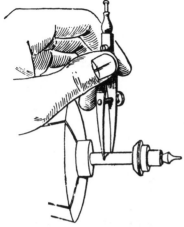

Fig. 342. Pinion callipers.

Instead of removing the partly finished staff from the chuck in order to turn the other end, the staff can be finished with one fixing in the chuck. This system is in principle the same as employed in the factories mass producing staffs in automatic machines. It has much to commend it ; a staff so made must be true.

The procedure is this : Allow the piece of steel—it must be blue steel, as we cannot harden and temper it afterwards—to project from the chuck an amount approximately the length of the finished staff. Turn the top part of the staff first. Let the balance on and then the balance spring collet and finally turn the top pivot. Now turn the lower part. It will be necessary to take the measurement of the arbor for the roller and for this purpose use the old staff and I am of the opinion the best tool for this purpose is the pinion callipers (Fig. 342). The tool illustrated in Fig. 343 is used to turn the lower part of the staff. It is made from an old pillar file

Fig. 343. Cutter made from an old file.

and is sharpened or whetted with a fine carborundum slip. The cutting edge for turning the pivot is finished on the Arkansas stone, a fine cut being essential as the final finish is by the burnisher only. To sharpen or whet, the tool is held in the left hand and the slip is used as one would

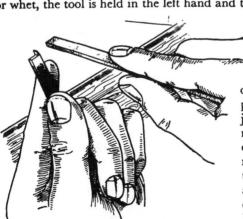

Fig. 344. Method of sharpening special cutter.

use a file (Fig. 344).

The illustrations (Fig. 345) should be self-explanatory of the whole procedure of making the staff. The pivots are polished in the jacot tool, in fact, they are not polished but burnished only. Select a bed on the runner of the jacot tool so that the pivot rests in the bed a little more than half its diameter (see Fig. 346). Bring the runner up so that only the parallel part of the

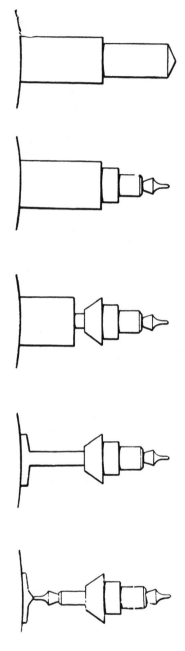

Fig. 345. Five stages of making staff without removing from chuck.

pivot rests in the bed ; the cone must be free. The jacot tool pivot burnisher has the left edge on both sides of the burnisher rounded, and should be used with this rounded edge towards the radius at the root of the pivot so that this radius is polished simultaneously with the pivot (see Fig. 347). To sharpen or remake the burnisher use the copper or lead faced wood block in the manner illustrated in Fig. 348. The block is dressed with dry carborundum powder, not too coarse. Hold the burnisher as shown and draw it up and down the block in firm steady strokes. If the burnisher

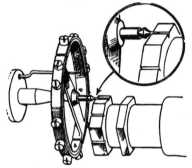

Fig. 346. Jacot tool runner, showing correct bed for pivot.

has a rounded edge, give it a twist on the last inch of the stroke so that this portion is also remade (Fig. 349).

Apply oil to the pivot in the left-hand runner and smear oil on the burnisher and proceed to burnish the pivot, applying some little pressure. With this form of pivot polishing the reducing is fairly rapid when compared with the system as used in the turns, so try the pivot in the jewel hole after a little burnishing and continue testing at frequent intervals to ensure that the pivot is not made too thin. In addition to the downward pressure, apply a little pressure to the left so that the round edge of the burnisher contacts the cone of the pivot and burnishes it at the same time. When the pivot is burnished to size, fit up in the lantern runner and burnish the end as previously explained.

There is yet another system of turning a balance staff. After the staff is partly turned in the split chuck as explained in the first method, remove from the chuck and cement up in a wax chuck so that the upper part of the staff can be turned.

First of all the wax chuck. Fit up in the split chuck a piece of brass

Fig. 347. Jacot tool pivot burnisher, note rounded edges.

slightly larger than the greatest diameter of the staff to be turned (see Fig. 350). Turn the end flat and true and also turn the body true in the round. Cut a conical hollow in the end ; it is important that the end of the cone is free from a pip and to do this bring the T rest round to face the end of the work (see Fig. 351). Hold the graver very firmly down on to the rest and start the cut as near the centre as you can judge, you will immediately

see if a pip is to develop—a small circle will appear. If this is so, move the graver forward or backward slightly to cut the pip out, proceed to cut a hollow sufficiently deep to take the lower part of the staff, as Fig. 353. This is known as " catching the centre." The necessity for avoiding a pip is shown in the illustrations (Figs. 352-4).

Fig. 348. Method of sharpening pivot burnisher.

Warm the chuck while still in the lathe. The wax chuck should not be removed from the split chuck once it has been turned If for some reason it has been removed, make quite sure it is true by re-turning with the graver, paying special attention to the point of the cone. Pack the hollow with shellac and apply more heat until the shellac is quite soft, and then place the partly finished staff in position and hold the end yet to be

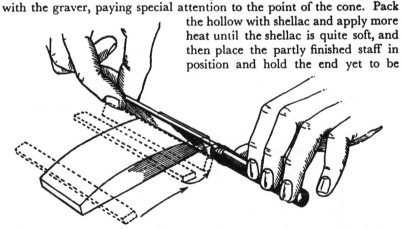

Fig. 349. Showing the twist of the pivot burnisher to remake the rounded edge.

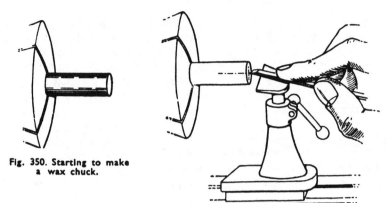

Fig. 350. Starting to make a wax chuck.

Fig. 351. Catching the centre, for the wax chuck.

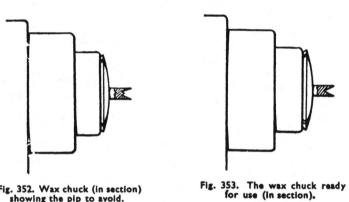

Fig. 352. Wax chuck (in section) showing the pip to avoid.

Fig. 353. The wax chuck ready for use (in section).

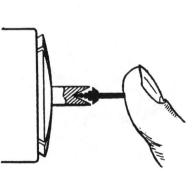

Fig. 354. Truing the balance staff in the wax chuck.

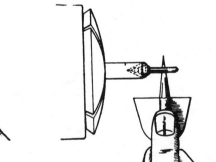

Fig. 355. Final truing with a piece of pegwood.

turned by the pad of the first finger-tip (see Fig. 354), revolving the headstock fairly rapidly and at the same time applying a little pressure to the staff so that the pivot is forced well into the point of the cone. While so doing blow on the chuck to cool and set the shellac. The staff should run almost true and to make quite sure apply a little heat, only sufficient to enable the staff to move, and while in this state hold the pegwood as illustrated in Fig. 355 to make perfectly true, as explained

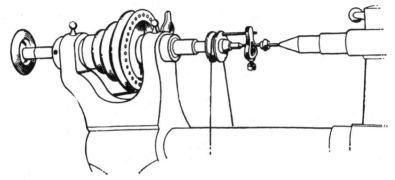

Fig. 356. Balance staff fit-up between centres.

when dealing with the split chuck. Hold the pegwood in position and keep the lathe moving until the shellac is quite set. The upper part of the staff is now ready for turning.

To remove the staff when finished, take the wax chuck from the lathe and apply a little heat to the end of the chuck furthest from the staff and pull the staff out when the shellac is soft enough to release it. If this procedure is adopted there is no risk of softening the staff. To remove the shellac boil out in methylated spirit as explained elsewhere.

The perfect method is turning between centres. This system may take a little longer and can be reserved for precision work such as staffs for a chronometer or a fine quality pocket watch. Use a blue staff and attach to it a carrier and fit up in the lathe as illustrated in Fig. 356. A friction pulley can be used as a safety piece (Fig. 357). The object is that the line passes over the friction or safety pulley

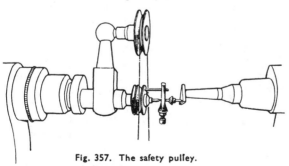

Fig. 357. The safety pulley.

and is adjusted so that it bears on the pulley operating the carrier, the pressure of the line being such that if undue pressure is brought to bear on the work being turned the motion will be arrested and so, maybe, save a staff. If for instance the graver digs a little deeper than it should, there is the risk of the work either breaking or becoming out of true, but with the friction pulley the work would cease to revolve, thereby obviating the risk. The actual making of the staff between centres is precisely the same as described when using the turns, the only difference being that the work rotates in one direction only, as with all lathe work.

Before further discussion on turning in the lathe, it is as well to consider the question of truing the balance : to true a solid balance in the round is not always a simple matter. The best way of discovering where a balance is out of round is to spin it in the callipers (Fig. 358) with the guide close to the edge. The Americans favour the callipers illustrated in Fig. 359. The staff pivots fit *through* the holes and the

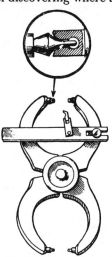

staff rests on the conical part of the pivot, and this arrangement has much to commend it. Further, the balance is not removed from the callipers during manipulations to make it true ; this needs some skill and practice and it is advisable to start on some old balances first, so as to become accustomed to the strength of the pivots. In any case, the actual manipulations of the balance itself are the same, whether used with the Ameri-

Fig. 358. Callipers and guide.

Fig. 359. American style callipers.

can or the English style callipers. With the latter the balance is removed for manipulation.

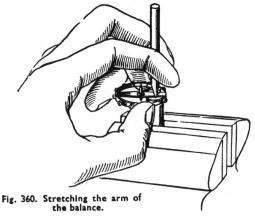

Fig. 360. Stretching the arm of the balance.

Should the balance prove out of round at the position of the arm the short side can be stretched. Place the balance upside down on the stake, and with a rounded edge chisel-shaped punch give the short arm a tap at the position indicated in illustration Fig. 360.

Should, however, the balance be out of round by reason of the balance staff hole being out of

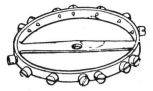

Fig. 361. Note balance staff hole in balance out of centre.

Fig. 362. Step chuck.

centre (as shown in Fig. 361), then the only method of truing is to remove the staff and " catch " the hole true. In order to do this, select a step chuck (Fig. 362) into one of the steps of which the balance comfortably fits. Having first removed the balance screws, if there are any, fit up in the lathe as Fig. 363. Bring the T rest to face the balance and with the cutter held firmly on the rest, catch the side of the hole until a full cut is made. It may be necessary to fit another staff or if economy has to be studied, fit a collet to the balance to accommodate the old staff. In a low-grade watch the balance being out of round need not be considered, provided it is in poise. A balance out of round is unsightly and it is better, from a workmanship point of view, for it to be in round.

Fig. 363. Catching hole true in balance.

There is another point, but it is not worth considering when dealing with moderate grades of watches, and that is dynamic poising. Dynamic poising is poising while in motion, and a balance out of round and in poise statically may be out of poise when in motion. From an engineer's point of view this will set up vibration and cause wear at the bearings, but from the time-keeping aspect I do not think it calls for our attention. The balance is comparatively light and the effect of wear at the pivots because of the want of dynamic poise is negligible, but when timing a watch in five positions it may be necessary to consider it.

To revert to the truing, if the balance is out of flat, it can usually be bent with the finger nails. Assuming one of the arms is bent, hold the balance as Fig. 364 and, by pushing the thumb nail of the right hand up and holding the rim of the balance down with the tip of the first finger, the

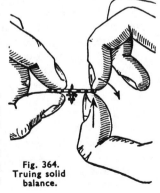

Fig. 364. Truing solid balance.

rim will be forced down. A little practice on these lines and you will soon become experienced as to where to apply the pressure.

The cut or compensation balance is treated in much the same manner as the solid balance as regards stretching the arm to true in the round, and also catching the hole in the centre so that it is concentric with the rim. The cut balance is more suscept-ible to being out of round than the solid balance, quite apart from the two adjustments just mentioned.

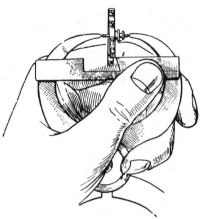

Fig. 365. Showing cut balance out of flat.

To deal with truing in the flat first : hold the balance in the callipers as Fig. 365, so that there is no endshake and bring the guide to the edge of the rim. Move the balance round slowly and note where the unevenness is. If it is as Fig. 365, hold the balance near the arm and lift

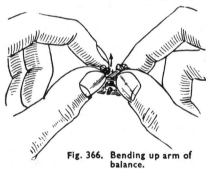

Fig. 366. Bending up arm of balance.

the limb of the balance up, higher than it is intended to be as it will naturally spring down again. The amount of lift depends upon the hardness or softness of the balance ; go cautiously until the temper of the particular balance is discovered (see Fig. 366). If the balance is true from the arm and then dips down as the cut or free end is reached, hold the balance in the brass or copper lined pliers and bend the limb up (Fig. 367).

To make true in the round, hold in the callipers and adjust the guide so that it points to the outer edge of the rim of the balance (Fig. 368). In this instance the whole of the limb is bent inwards, and should be corrected by holding the balance in the left hand and carefully pulling out the limb with the nail of the first finger of the right hand (Fig. 369).

If there is a kink in the balance rim, the tool illustrated in Fig. 370 is useful. Assuming the balance is kinked as Fig. 371. Place the balance flat on a stake with a hole to take the roller, etc. ; straddle the tool as Fig. 372 and sway the tool to the left, as indicated by the arrow, to bend the limb out. We now

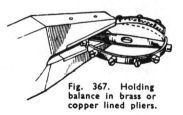

Fig. 367. Holding balance in brass or copper lined pliers.

move the tool along so that the prong straddles the balance at the termination of the kink (Fig. 373) and sway it to the right, to bring the limb back. It may be necessary to make one or more bends, but this is the method and *practice alone can make perfect.*

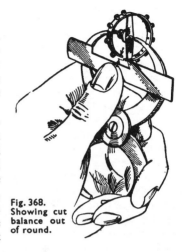

The turning of a centre pinion incorporates the fitting of the cannon pinion. In addition to this, the general principle of procedure applies to all pinions, 3rd, 4th and escape, only the shape of the arbors differing. First, knock the old pinion out and pass a cutting broach through the hole in the centre wheel to remove any burrs that may be there. Fit the pinion up in

Fig. 368. Showing cut balance out of round.

the lathe, using a split chuck, and grip the pinion by the head, *i.e.*, the leaves. If the correct size chuck is selected, requiring little drawing in to tighten, the leaves will not be damaged.

Reduce the head to the approximate length and then turn a shoulder

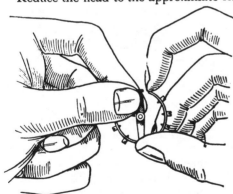

to receive the wheel. When cutting the leaves to reduce the head to length hold the graver as illustrated in Fig. 374. The graver is held very firmly down on to the T rest and the cuts are light, otherwise the point of the graver will be broken off continually. When the body of the pinion is reached, the leaves can sometimes be broken off by crushing with the nippers (Fig. 375).

Fig. 369. Bending limb of balance out.

Fig. 370. Tool for truing balance.

Fig. 371. Kinked balance (somewhat exaggerated to illustrate).

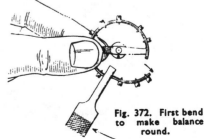

Fig. 372. First bend to make balance round.

Turn the arbor true and smooth and turn the seating for the centre wheel, holding the graver to the leaves (as Fig. 376).

The shoulder is turned to a taper, so that when the wheel is driven on the leaves cut slightly into the wheel. Reduce the leaves until the wheel is about $1\frac{1}{2}$ times its thickness from the seating ; this ensures a good tight fit and at the same time the wheel is not likely to be thrown out of round. Turn the superfluous pinion away and cut an undercut for the rivet. Remove the pinion from the chuck and place, rivet side up, on a flat stake, with a hole just large enough to

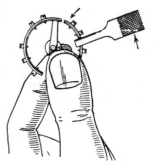

Fig. 373. Final bend to make true in the round. (Stake not shown.)

receive the arbor, so that the pinion head rests on the stake. Drive the wheel home to its seating with a hollow flat-end punch (as Fig. 377).

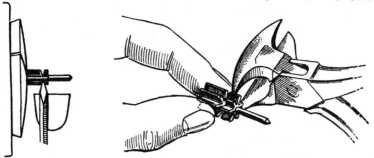

Fig. 374. Hold graver to catch leaves only.

Fig. 375. Nip off leaves.

Finally, rivet over in the manner employed when riveting the balance staff, and replace in the split chuck so that the cannon pinion arbor can be

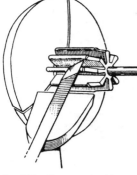

Fig. 376. Turning shoulder to receive wheel.

turned. If the arbor is a long one, bring up the female runner in the tail stock to support it. Usually rough pinions are supplied with conical ends, but if this pinion is not so finished, turn a conical pivot on the end to receive the runner.

A male runner is the one with a point and the female runner is the one with a blind conical hole drilled into the end (see Fig. 378). The fit-up in the lathe will appear as illustrated in Fig. 379. First reduce the arbor to form the lower pivot, leaving a slight shoulder to keep the wheel free of the plate. Use the old pinion if possible, as a guide to the positions of the various shoulders. The illustration (Fig. 380) is of the finished pinion

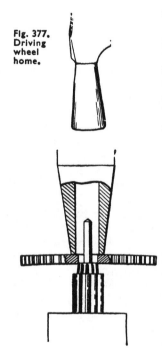

Fig. 377.
Driving
wheel
home.

and will help to show at what we are aiming.

The arbor should now be turned down to fit the cannon pinion, leaving a shoulder for it to rest upon. It is advisable, to facilitate fitting, to round broach the inside of the cannon and push out the pip or pips placed there to form the snap ; they can be punched back again later on. Turn the arbor to a slight taper with the graver, until the cannon

Fig. 378. *Left :* male runner. *Right :* female runner.

fits, say, half-way down. The taper should be about the same as the taper of a cutting or round broach. Polish the arbor with the iron polisher and oilstone dust and oil, until the cannon fits comfortably down on to its shoulder ; it should not be a tight fit, reliance being placed upon the pips for the friction tightness. If the cannon fits at all tightly before the pips are made it will have the tendency to ride up when the hands are

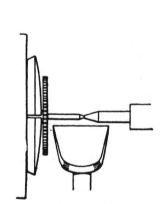

Fig. 379. Showing female runner
support.

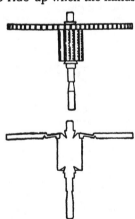

Fig. 380. *Top :* finished centre
pinion. *Bottom :* in section to
show undercuts.

set. This is because the spring effect of the pips on the body of the cannon is not as strong as the friction caused by a tight fit ; the pips will not be able to hold the cannon down and it will ride up if rotated. It is

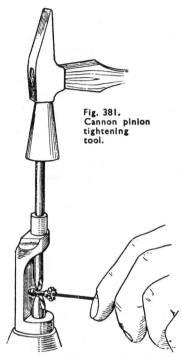

Fig. 381.
Cannon pinion
tightening
tool.

important, therefore, that the cannon should fit with no tightness or slackness. If it fits slackly it will rock from side to side and this movement is accentuated when the tip of the minute hand is observed during the setting of the hands. It is not necessary to finish the arbor further than the grey finish. Now re-punch the pips in the cannon, and to do this file up a piece of brass wire to fit the cannon, file a flat along one side and fit the wire into the cannon so that the flat side comes where the pip is to be punched. If there are to be two pips, one each side, then file two flats and arrange so that the pips face the flats. Dealing with one pip first, hold the cannon in the tool (Fig. 381) and lower the chisel-shaped punch on to the body of the cannon in the position where the pip was originally, give a slight tap on the punch to raise a slight pip on the inside of the cannon.

If the tool (Fig. 381) is not avail-able, then hold in the vice a piece of brass that fits in the turned part of the cannon (Fig. 382).

Fit the cannon on to the arbor, it will be found to fit tightly, and press straight down ; do not twist the cannon, and make sure it is seated hard on to its shoulder. Then hold the wheel steady and with the brass nose pliers cause the cannon to revolve on the arbor three or four times. Pull the cannon straight off, do not twist it if it can possibly be avoided. Examine the arbor : the pip should have scored a ring which marks the position of the snap. Had the cannon been twisted when placing in position or re-moving it the ring would not be so defined. Turn the arbor at the

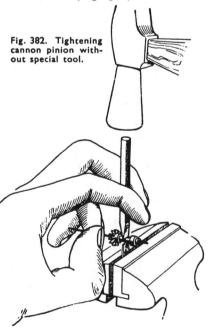

Fig. 382. Tightening cannon pinion with-out special tool.

position of the ring (as Fig. 383). Press the cannon on to the arbor again and you should feel the snap; if, however, it is not pronounced enough, turn the nick in the arbor a little higher as indicated in illustration (Fig. 384). The dotted lines show where the new cut is to be made. It may now be necessary to make the pip more pronounced or deeper. Try the cannon on again and you should be able to feel and maybe hear the snap. The cannon fitted in this manner will not ride up.

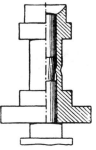

Fig. 383. Indentation of cannon shows where to turn for snap.

Fig. 384. Dotted lines indicate where to turn if snap is insufficient.

If the cannon pinion had two pips, one on each side, then a chisel-shaped punch is used to replace the flat end punch in the tool, and if no tool is available the cannon is reversed on the brass piece in the vice and an indentation made with the chisel punch. The illustration (Fig. 383) shows the cannon in section with the pip somewhat exaggerated to indicate the process.

The arbor is next shortened to length. Place the cannon in position and mark so that the arbor is flush with the top of the cannon. Stone the end as flat as possible, but not dead flat, and polish with the bell-metal polisher and diamantine.

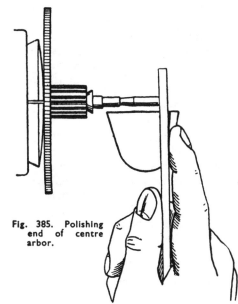

Fig. 385. Polishing end of centre arbor.

The fit-up in the lathe to polish the end of the centre arbor is as Fig. 385. In a fine quality movement, especially English, you will find that the end of the cannon pinion is polished hollow and the centre arbor is of such a length that it meets the bottom of the hollow—a very nice piece of workmanship (Fig. 386) and quite easy to accomplish. It is worth mentioning here, as the procedure could be put to other uses.

Fig. 386. Finished end of cannon and centre arbor.

Fig. 387. Cannon pinion on turning arbor, but *not* projecting.

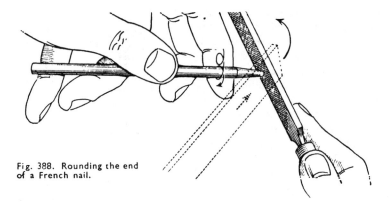

Fig. 388. Rounding the end of a French nail.

Fit the cannon on to a turning arbor so that it just sticks on to the end without the arbor projecting (Fig. 387). Procure a piece of iron wire—a French nail answers well—and round the end, an exact round is not important ; twirl the wire between the thumb and first finger of the left hand and pass a fine file over the end to round it (Fig. 388). Now place the bow on the ferrule of the arbor and hold the pivot in the hole of a runner or one of the holes usually found at the side of the jaws of the vice. These holes are placed there for use such as this and also for drilling. Charge the rounded end of the iron wire with oilstone dust and oil and place it on the end of the cannon as illustrated in Fig. 389. Revolve the arbor rapidly and apply a little pressure to the wire and at the same time move the wire up and down a little and also twist it slightly between the thumb and finger, a perfect round hollow will result. To polish, clean the end of wire and re-file and charge with diamantine by just knocking the end on to the diamantine block. Clean the cannon in benzine and brush and pith well to remove all traces of oilstone dust. Repeat the operation as before and we shall have a beautifully polished hollow.

To revert to the centre pinion : Undercut into the body of the pinion at the rivet end so that the arbor at the back of the lower pivot is conical in

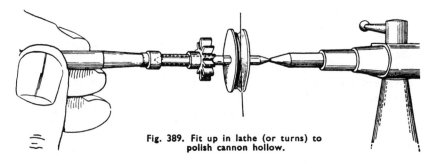

Fig. 389. Fit up in lathe (or turns) to polish cannon hollow.

shape. This undercutting used to be a fine art and the object was to make it as deep and narrow as possible. From a purely technical point of view the object of the undercut is to prevent the oil of the pivot from creeping away. To make the undercut use the point of the graver and as you get deeper whet the graver so that it becomes narrower ; the illustration (Fig. 390) shows the procedure and the dotted lines indicate the eventual shape of the graver. Reverse the pinion in the split chuck ; another chuck will be necessary with a smaller hole. Turn the upper part of arbor and polish it, first with oilstone dust and then diamantine. Next turn top pivot, cut to length, and polish, followed by undercutting top end of the pinion head in a similar manner to the lower end. You will have noticed that in *all* turning the polishing is com-

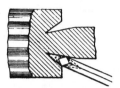

Fig. 390. Cutting the undercut. Dotted lines indicate varying shapes of graver.

pleted before another cut is made. I have mentioned it before and it's worth repeating because we cut into the polished surface and by so doing extra sharpness is effected ; it's an illusion but an effective one.

We are now ready to face the ends of the pinion head. Fit a ferrule on to the wheel (Fig. 391). The facing tool is simply made from an old iron door key, a piece of iron rod or a French nail ; the illustrations (Fig. 392) show what is wanted. The business end of the tool (A) is filed flat and then charged with oilstone dust and oil by dabbing the end on to the oilstone dust block. Fit the bow on to the ferrule and hold the facing tool on to the end of the pinion head as shown in Fig. 393.

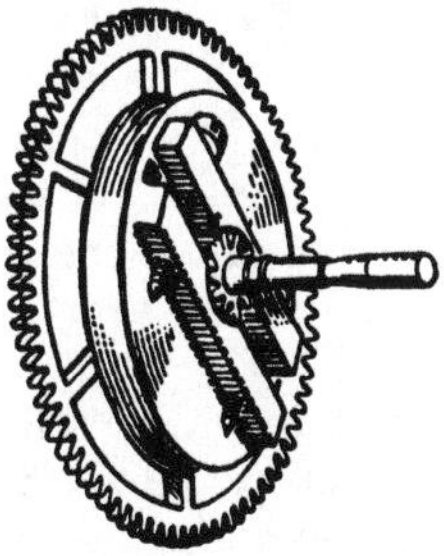

Fig. 391 Ferrule in position

A female runner can be used in the turns or the tailstock of the lathe. The facing tool is held in the left hand. Make the pinion revolve quickly and apply a little pressure on the facing tool and at the same time slightly twirl it backward and forward. The tool is held as steady as possible but the flatness of the face is not dependent upon this ; as with all polishing, the work finds its own level if held in the correct manner. About a dozen strokes of the bow will be sufficient, clean off with pith and inspect the face ; it should be dead flat and the whole surface ground to a grey finish ; if it is not so, continue with the oilstone dust. The grinding will remove any roughness left by the riveting and the tool may touch the brass wheel and this will give it the desired finish. When the face is satisfactory, clean in benzine and

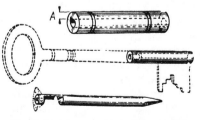

Fig. 392. Facing tools : *top, iron rod; middle,* from a key ; *bottom,* from a nail.

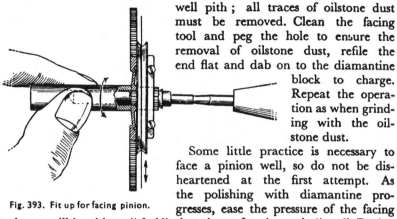

Fig. 393. Fit up for facing pinion.

well pith ; all traces of oilstone dust must be removed. Clean the facing tool and peg the hole to ensure the removal of oilstone dust, refile the end flat and dab on to the diamantine block to charge. Repeat the operation as when grinding with the oilstone dust.

Some little practice is necessary to face a pinion well, so do not be disheartened at the first attempt. As the polishing with diamantine progresses, ease the pressure of the facing tool, you will be able to " feel " when the surface is nearly " up." During the final strokes of the bow it may be noticed that the tool will squeak ; this is a signal that the polishing is almost complete. Continue with the bow, easing the tool off still more until the action has the " feel " of velvet and the job is finished. Clean off with pith and a beautiful " black " polish should be revealed, not just a shallow shine but a polish with depth. We now reverse the wheel and face the lower end of the pinion head. Clean off well and polish with diamantine as before. Facing has taken much longer to describe here than to do ; with practice it is a speedy operation.

There are one or two points to be discussed in connection with making a winding shaft. Select a piece of blue steel wire the diameter of which is a little greater than the largest part of the shaft. Fit up in a split chuck in the lathe, first allowing a small part of the wire to project, and turn a conical pivot on the end. Then allow as much wire to project as the shaft is to be long, measuring from the threaded part to the portion of the shaft that fits into the movement. If the shaft is at all long it may be necessary to bring the tailstock into use with a female runner, to steady the work. We turn down the shaft so that it fits tightly into the movement, thus forming the shoulder that works between the plates.

Before much reduction has taken place turn the pivot on the end and polish with oilstone dust and diamantine so that it fits snugly into its hole. Make sure to leave the pivot as long as possible, so that when the shaft is in the hands set position the pivot is still in its hole. If the movement is side set the length of the pivot is not so important. Continue to turn the shaft until it fits tightly between the plates. Polish the portion that will operate in the plates with oilstone dust and diamantine until it is free.

Turn down the shaft to fit the crown wheel. Polish and finish the portion for the crown wheel only ; it is not necessary to polish the whole of the arbor. Next mark the position the castle wheel will occupy and turn a small nick at this point. We shall now have the shoulder for the crown wheel to work upon and from the termination of this shoulder to the shoulder of the pivot of the shaft is to be filed square for the castle wheel to slide up and down. The illustration (Fig. 394) should make this clear.

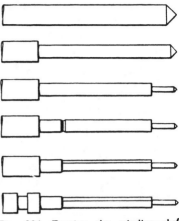

Fig. 394. Turning the winding shaft. From top, blue steel ; first shoulder ; pivot ; nick for square ; square filed ; groove for pull-out piece.

Lock the headstock of the lathe by the pin on the spring piece which fits into the holes on the side of the largest pulley. Replace the T rest with the roller rest (we shall consider the single roller first). Bring the roller up to the work and make sure that it is parallel with the shaft and also almost level with the top of the shaft. Usually the roller is best placed about ¼ inch from the work, but this largely depends upon the size of the shaft being made. Hold a fine, fairly sharp, flat file firmly on the roller rest with the safe or non-cutting edge against the nick already cut (Fig. 395). Move the file backward and forward two or three times without touching the shaft, apply some little pressure on the file to keep it flat on the roller rest. When you have acquired the feel of the file gradually tilt the file on to the shaft until you touch the shaft and then give a firm steady forward stroke. Use a worn file.

Remember that the shaft is hardened and tempered steel, and so must be filed slowly. Make two or three full strokes with the file and then move the headstock round exactly a quarter of a turn. The count plate on the pulley will be marked to indicate the quarters. Once the headstock is fixed proceed to file another flat and, as far as possible, file the same amount as before. Continue thus until all four flats are filed. The square should be a slight taper towards the pivot and, to effect this, place a piece

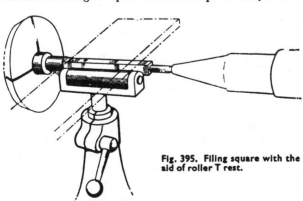

Fig. 395. Filing square with the aid of roller T rest.

of notepaper under the shoe of the roller rest at the end nearest the headstock, before the rest is made secure, this will cause the roller to tilt slightly and so produce the desired taper (Fig. 396). The square of the shaft should not present a full square yet, the corners should still show part of the original cylindrical shaft and this will form a guide as to the truth of the square (Fig. 397).

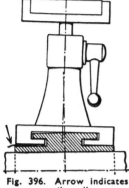

Fig. 396. Arrow indicates paper to tilt roller rest ; to facilitate filing taper.

If the square is true the four corners or edges should all present the same curvature ; if they do not, file the offending flat or flats until all the edges are equal. Then continue to file each flat in turn, just a little to each flat, until the edges are sharp. You may be sure then that the square is at least fairly true. Try the castle wheel on the shaft and, if necessary, continue to file the flats until the castle wheel fits on to the shaft about halfway up. Even if the corners are not sharp, the work may be considered good, because this will depend upon the size of the square in the castle wheel. We now remove the shaft from the chuck and cut to the approximate length ; turn a cone on the end that is to be tapped for the button. Place in the headstock a female runner and bring the tailstock up with another female runner, fit the shaft freely between these centres. Polish the flats with the iron polisher charged with oilstone dust and oil (Fig. 398).

Fig. 397. Winding shaft with square not fully filed.

Hold the polisher as one would hold a pencil, using a little pressure and giving a circular backward and forward motion to the polisher, moving up and down the whole length of the flat at the same time. In this manner a perfectly flat surface will be maintained ; move the shaft round with the fingers to the next flat and polish that in a similar manner, and so on until all the flats have received treatment. Try the castle wheel

Fig. 398. Shaft free between centres so that when polishing it finds its own level.

on occasionally and proceed with the polishing, a little to each flat at a time, to keep the square true, until the wheel fits to about its own length from the shoulder. When this is achieved, clean the shaft in benzine and well pith to remove all traces of oilstone dust ; clean the polisher and re-file and charge with diamantine. Replace the shaft between the centres and repeat the operation, polishing all four flats until the castle wheel fits freely up to its shoulder. The flats may not be highly polished and free from scratches but this is unimportant, they will get scratched when the shaft has been withdrawn a few times and the castle wheel has slid up and down the shaft.

The next step is to cut the groove for the pull-out piece. Hold the shaft as far into the movement as possible, screw the pull-out piece so that the nib presses fairly hard on to the shaft, and give the shaft a turn or two. This will mark the shaft where the groove is to be cut. Use the tool illustrated in Fig. 343 to cut the groove, first of all whetting

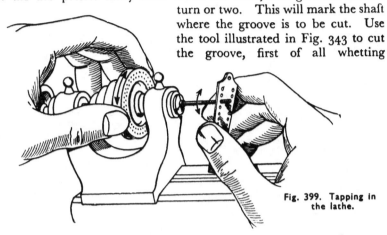

Fig. 399. Tapping in the lathe.

the cutting edge square with the carborundum and not at an angle as was used when turning the balance staff. Before cutting the groove allow just a shade for freedom, *i.e.*, the groove is cut a little above where the mark was made.

To cut the thread for the winding button, reverse the shaft in the chuck and grip it by the part that works between the plates. If making the shaft from blue steel, it will be necessary to soften the button end before cutting the thread. Having decided the size of the thread either by the old shaft or the thread in the button, turn the shaft down so that it fits the hole in the screw plate two holes larger than the one we shall use to make the thread. Turn the end of the shaft to a taper so as to form a lead when making the thread.

Watchmakers' screw plates do not as a rule *cut* the thread, no metal is removed, the thread being burred up. I mention this because this fact, in conjunction with the hard metal, calls for great care when tapping or making the thread. Hold the screw plate in the right hand and the pulley of the headstock in the other, apply plenty of oil and work the headstock backward and forward and at the same time work the screw plate in a similar manner. You will soon experience the friction of the tapping; if care is not exercised the shaft may be twisted off, so go cautiously. The first five or six threads will not be full and as the full threads are made the drag will be greater. The illustration (Fig. 399) shows the procedure. It now only remains to cut the threaded end

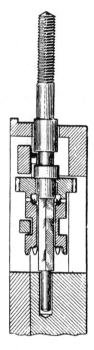

to length, which is dictated by the position of the button when the movement is in its case and the shaft is finished. As with all new parts, the shaft is finished to match the quality of the movement ; the shoulder that works between the plates, the crown wheel shoulder and the pivot are polished with diamantine in any case, but the rest of the shaft can be left grey from the oilstone dust. The illustration (Fig. 400) shows the finished shaft in the plate and the clearances, etc., are indicated.

The double roller T rest (see Fig. 401) is used in the following manner. The file is held firmly, and contacting *both* rollers at the same time. The whole of the roller part of the rest is then lowered on to the work and when the file touches lower just a little more. If you now file, keeping the file always in contact with the roller nearer to you, the file will eventually make contact with the second roller when the work has been filed down. In this manner a dead flat surface must ensue, and an equal amount will be filed from each flat.

Fig. 400. Shaft in position. Note endshake, position of termination of square and freedom of pull-out piece nib.

Fig. 401. Double roller T rest.

The parts we have made in the lathe, the balance staff centre pinion and winding shaft cover practically all turning operations met with in the average workshop. We have dealt with turning true, polishing, facing and filing. *It is now a matter of practice, plenty of practice.* Making new parts cannot be taught by books alone ; the procedure can be explained and it is for the student to apply it ; as I have said before, turning takes more practice than filing and of the two it is the more important to the watchmaker.

Fitting a new pivot is not done in first class work, but there are some circumstances when it has to be tolerated, where economy is a consideration or when the new part in the rough, such as a pinion, is unobtainable, and it is therefore necessary to deal with the subject.

In fitting a new pivot to a pinion, first of all stone the old pivot away flat to the arbor with an Arkansas slip. It is better not to reduce the temper of the piece being pivoted, but some pinions are so hard that it is practically impossible to drill them. In these circumstances draw

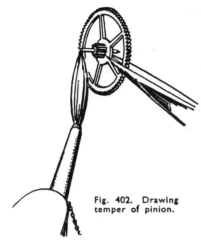

Fig. 402. Drawing temper of pinion.

the temper a little. Hold the pinion so that only the end to be drilled contacts the flame of the spirit lamp, let the end touch the edge of the flame and hold it there until the colour changes to a blue. (See Fig. 402.) This will discolour the pinion a fair way up but we shall remove that presently. Select a runner of the pivoting tool (Fig. 403) with a hole that fits the drill we are to use. The size of the drill should be a little larger than the new pivot we are to fit. The trumpet end of the runner will fit over the arbor of the pinion and as the drill is a close fit in the hole this forms the centring of the hole for the pivot. We next fit the wheel up in the tool with the bow ready for use (Fig. 404). The drill to be used for steel is rounded and the cutting edge is stoned to an acute angle ; this adds strength to the drill.

If the correct size drill is not available it is quite simple to make one. File up a piece of steel wire that fits the drillstock of the tool to the shape shown in Fig. 405. Hold the end on a flat stake and, with the flat-faced steel hammer, flatten the extreme end (as Fig. 406). If the drill is of reasonable size file the end to the shape shown in Fig. 407. Should the drill be so fine

Fig. 403. Pivoting tool.

that it will not stand up to the file, shape the end with an Arkansas slip after it is hardened and tempered. To harden the drill hold the end in the flame of the spirit lamp until it is cherry red and immediately plunge in oil. Try with a file to make sure that it is hard, then clean one of the flats with an emery buff. Hold the drill so that the stock contacts the edge of the flame and directly the brightened flat becomes a straw colour withdraw sharply from the heat and wave in the air to prevent further tempering (Fig. 408). If the drill is a fine one the hardening can be effected by air cooling ; make the end red as before and directly it is of the required colour withdraw smartly from the flame, and this sudden chilling is usually sufficient to harden. Care must be exercised with fine drills as the tip soon becomes white-hot and there is the risk of burning the metal. The tempering is effected in the same manner as already explained but much greater care must be taken or the business end will become soft and therefore useless as a drill. The blade of the drill is then stoned with an Arkansas slip (as Fig. 407).

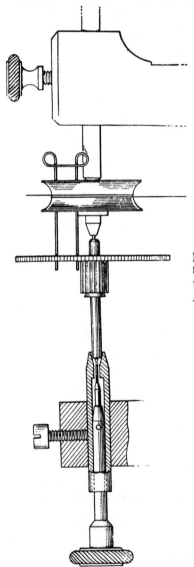

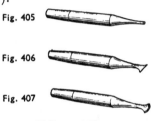

Fig. 405

Fig. 406

Fig. 407

Making a drill.

We are now ready to drill. Apply plenty of oil (clock oil) to the trumpet runner and also a little to the other pivot. Apply a little pressure

Fig. 408.
Tempering
drill.

to the drillstock and make the work rotate slowly. It is essential that the drill should cut all the time ; you will be able to feel the cutting and if you are not satisfied with the progress examine the drill for hardness and shape, etc. To use a drill that does not cut is a danger, because the hole becomes burnished and this burnished surface can be most difficult to remove. If for some reason the hole does become burnished it can sometimes be removed by flattening the end of the drill. Use the drill

Fig. 404. Fit up for pivoting, showing trumpet end and drill in position.

until the burnished surface is removed and then re-shape the drill and proceed to drill the hole. While drilling rotate the drillstock just a half-turn each way, this assists the truth of the drilling. Remove the drill occasionally and clean to remove swarf (cuttings), apply more oil and drill until the hole is about 1½ to 2 times in depth the length the new pivot is to be. This rule does not hold good when drilling up for a seconds pivot.

The new pivot we file from a piece of blue steel wire. Select a piece a little larger than the new pivot is to be and file with a fine file to a gentle or gradual taper. Reduce until the end enters the hole in the pinion to about half the depth of the hole, then draw file so that it will grip well. It may be necessary to stone the end as the draw filing will reduce the diameter a little ; leave the end that goes into the hole flat, so as to ensure the fullest contact with the side of the hole. Peg the hole in the pinion with a pointed pegwood to ensure that it is free from swarf. Dip the end of the wire in dry oilstone dust, sufficient will adhere to key into the sides of the hole. Cut the wire to about a quarter of an inch in length ; place the pinion on a stake and lightly tap the pivot into position (Fig. 409). By tapping lightly you will be able to drive the pivot fully home with little fear of splitting the pinion arbor. When the pivot is quite home cut off with the nippers almost to length. The new pivot is finished in the jacot tool. Select a bed on the runners so that the pivot projects above the surface of the runner a little less than half its diameter (Fig. 410). First rub the pivot down with the pivot file, reduce the pivot thus until it fits its hole tightly. Clean the bed and the pivot with pith and burnish the pivot with the pivot burnisher to finish and so that it is free in its hole. The necessary freedom of pivots has been dealt with in Chapter 4.

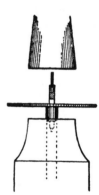

Fig. 409. Driving new pivot into position.

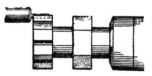

Fig. 410. Indicating correct size bed in jacot tool.

A more refined way to finish the pivot is first to grind it with oilstone dust and oil and then finish with diamantine, finally burnishing. I feel that pivoting is improvised and does not warrant a lengthy process to finish ; filing and burnishing answers quite well and is used extensively by the Swiss to make pivots generally.

The end of the pivot is finished in the lantern runner in a similar manner to that employed when rounding up the staff pivots as previously explained. The end of the pivot is first rounded off with an Arkansas slip. The new pivot is now finished and if it proved necessary to draw the temper we remove the discoloration in the following manner :—

Pour into a glass or chinaware vessel a little hydrochloric acid. A convenient size for the vessel is about the diameter of a penny and about ⅛ inch high, and the acid should half-fill such a container. Hold the pinion in the tweezers so that the part to be dealt with hangs downwards, immerse the affected part in the fluid for a second or two and then immediately rinse in cold water, running water for preference. Then immerse in liquid ammonia for about one minute to ensure that the acid is killed, rinse again in water and dry off in boxwood dust or killed lime for about an hour. The fumes from the hydrochloric acid are corrosive and should therefore be treated with respect ; furthermore, the acid will burn the skin if it makes contact.

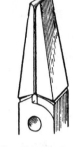

Fig. 411. Pliers to straighten balance staff pivots.

The illustrations showing the straightening of pivots apply to balance staff pivots and train wheel pivots. Generally speaking, a parallel train pivot will not straighten, and it is fortunate that these pivots do not often get bent ; the seconds pivot (the pivot on which the seconds hand is fitted) is the exception and usually this pivot will respond owing to its length.

Procure a pair of flat-nose pliers and file all the serrations from inside the jaws, making them quite smooth. Round off the inside edges of the end of the jaws with a file, and file the outside of the jaws down so as to make them thinner and narrower. Study the illustration (Fig. 411) well, 50 per cent. of the success rests with the tool ; we want the pliers to be firm and yet to be delicate and responsive to the touch.

Fig. 412. Kinked balance staff pivot.

Examine the bent pivot with the double eyeglass and if a kink or double bend is observed it is wellnigh impossible to straighten it out satisfactorily (Fig. 412). If the bend is a smooth single bend there is a good chance of success. Warm the ends of the pliers, hold the balance in the left hand and grip the pivot with the pliers in such a manner that, as the pliers are drawn away, the end of the pivot touches the inside of one jaw on one side and the base of the cone on the other. The pivot is not gripped tightly and then straightened in one movement ; it is gradually straightened by what would appear to be pulling the pivot out (Fig. 413). What we are doing is to utilise the method we should employ if we were to straighten a piece of wire between the first finger and thumb. Heat the ends of the pliers occasionally and proceed in this manner, slowly, until the pivot is straight. The sliding movement of

Fig. 413. Straightening balance staff pivots.

the smooth jaws will not have marked the pivot unduly, but it should be burnished in the jacot tool to make sure of a perfectly smooth surface.

Keep the jaws of the pliers in good trim by cleaning off the discoloration caused by heating with a fine emery buff, and use these pliers solely for the purpose of straightening pivots.

To revert to the lathe : the slide rest is a valuable accessory, and there are many uses to which it can be put ; two of them will be considered here. First to face a plate, such as turning out the inside of a barrel cover. If possible it is better to fit up the barrel cover in a step chuck, as described when centring the hole in the balance. The other method is to stick the cover on to a wax chuck or plate. If the cover is thin there may be no alternative as a thin plate will not stand up to the cutter without support at the back. The disadvantage of sticking it up is that you cannot be certain that it is flat owing to the varying thickness of shellac between it and the plate.

Fig. 414. Wax chucks.

To deal first with the wax chuck (Fig. 414). Fit the chuck up into the headstock and warm it with the spirit lamp. Smear a little shellac over the surface and apply more heat until the shellac is quite fluid, and then place the barrel cover in position and press it hard against the chuck to make it as flat as possible. Use the back of a watch brush for this purpose and make the headstock revolve slowly while so doing, this will help to keep it flat (Fig. 415). Before the shellac sets remove the watch brush and place the T rest square to the barrel cover (Fig. 416). Sharpen a piece of pegwood to a blunt point and make the end round so that it will fit the hole in the barrel cover. Hold the peg firmly on the T rest with the rounded end in the hole, causing the headstock to revolve fairly quickly and in this

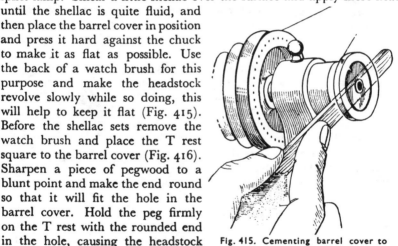

Fig. 415. Cementing barrel cover to wax chuck.

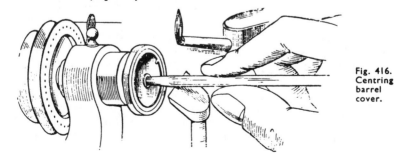

Fig. 416. Centring barrel cover.

manner bring the cover central. If a wax chuck is not available, cement the cover on to a piece of brass and fit this up in the mandril in the lathe. To make true or central, drill a hole in the brass plate large enough to take the centring rod of the mandril so that it contacts the hole in the barrel cover and then make tight the dogs holding the plate when this is accomplished (Fig. 417).

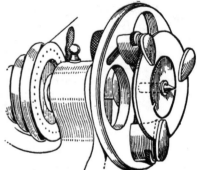

Fig. 417. Centring barrel cover on plate in mandril.

All is now ready to commence turning. The most useful shape slide rest cutter is as Fig. 418. Engineers use various shaped cutters with certain angles of rake for clearance, and watchmakers' lathe catalogues illustrate such cutters, but for the

Fig. 418. Slide rest cutter.

requirements of the watch repairer the one illustrated answers for most purposes. The cutter itself is locked in the slide rest by means of the screw placed there for that purpose. There are two points to watch when setting the cutter in position ; one is to see that it is the correct height, i.e., a shade above the line of centres (Fig. 419), and the other point to watch is that the cutter is secured as firmly to the slide rest as possible. Also keep the cutter short ; we want as little as possible to project from the slide rest. This is most important, otherwise we shall get chattering. Chattering occurs if the cutter is not held firmly, which results in the work being cut in short jerks and is obvious by the noise made while cutting and in the uneven surface of the work being cut. If the cutter, when

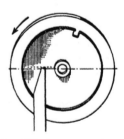

Fig. 419. Cutter set above line of centre.

placed in the slide rest, is not high enough it is packed on the underside with thin strips of brass or other metal (Fig. 420). The cutter is not very likely to be too high if it has been ground correctly ; the fault, if any at all, is generally to err on the low side.

Bring the slide rest along the bed up to the work so that the cutter almost touches the work and make secure. As the work revolves towards you the cutter also traverses the surface towards you. Operate the

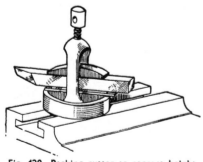

Fig. 420. Packing cutter to correct height.

handle (A) to bring the cutter towards the centre and in the exact position the cut is to be made (Fig. 421), which in this instance is as shown in the illustration (422). Make the headstock revolve and operate the

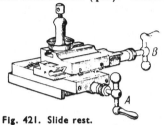

handle (B) until the cutter makes contact with the barrel cover and starts to cut, then operate the handle (A) in the opposite or anti-clockwise direction so that the cutter is drawn towards you. Proceed thus, turning the handle (A) slowly while the work is revolving fairly quickly until the cutter is almost to the required position at the edge. It is impossible to make a clean

Fig. 421. Slide rest.

cut shoulder at this edge, so withdraw the cutter clear of the work and operate the handle (A) so that the cutter is as Fig. 423. Make the cutter contact the work again and then draw it towards you as before making the work revolve in the opposite direction ; if the cutter has been made to con-

tact the work to the same depth as when turning from the centre, no metal will be cut away when the cutter reaches the part that has already been turned. A smooth surface will thus be turned ; if a square end cutter is used and the whole of the end made to contact the work a square shoulder could

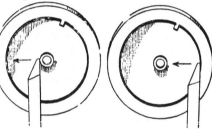

Fig. 422. First cut. Fig. 423. Second cut.

be cut both at the centre and the edge with one setting, but the chances are the surface cut would tend to be ridged, the cut being jumpy, not exactly chattering, but it would not, in all probability, be as smooth as the result of the two cuts described.

Another method of holding the work is in the step chuck (Fig. 362, p. 205). Of the two methods this is perhaps the best but, as explained, it has its limita-

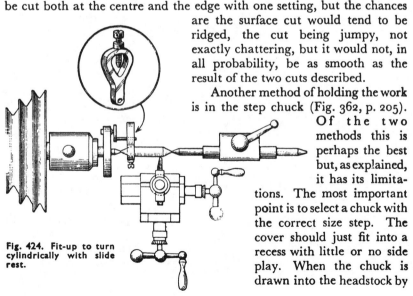

Fig. 424. Fit-up to turn cylindrically with slide rest.

tions. The most important point is to select a chuck with the correct size step. The cover should just fit into a recess with little or no side play. When the chuck is drawn into the headstock by the centre rod a slight turn of the rod will tighten the cover in the chuck. If this is observed, the cover will run truer than if some considerable tightening of the chuck were necessary to make it grip the barrel cover. Slide rest turning is precisely the same in principle as when using the graver for cylindrical turning, and this more particularly applies to light work, such as the watchmaker's, than perhaps to the heavy work of the engineer where it is possible to take extraordinary measures to secure rigidity of both the work and the cutter.

The slide rest can also be utilised for cylindrical turning, such as a barrel arbor, for example. The work is fitted up in the lathe either in

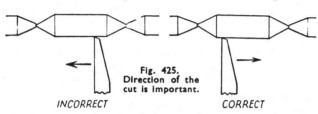

the split chuck with support at the tail-stock or between centres. In the latter case a carrier is at-

Fig. 425.
Direction of the cut is important.

INCORRECT   CORRECT

tached to the work and the fit-up is as illustrated in Fig. 424. Other than the position of the work the procedure is similar to that explained when turning out the barrel cover, the cutter is drawn across the work with the point of the cutter always following. If the point of the cutter is made to traverse forward there is the risk of it chattering. The illustration (Fig. 425) should make this point clear.

The screw-head tool is an accessory to the lathe and it is also a tool to be used without the lathe. We shall consider its use in conjunction with the lathe first (Fig. 426).

This tool is used primarily as a lapping device, supplied with three laps : one each of iron, bell metal and boxwood. To polish a screw-head

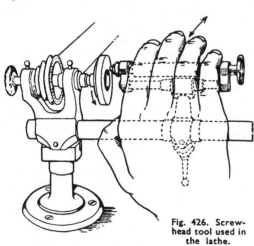

Fig. 426. Screw-head tool used in the lathe.

flat, for instance, the screw is secured in the stock of the screw-head tool by its thread ; it is important to see that the head of the screw is flat against the end of the chuck in the stock. Secure the iron lap in the lathe and charge it with oilstone dust and oil. Secure the screw-head tool fairly near to the lap. The stock is arranged so that is slides up and down its own bed. Apply a little oil to this bed and also to the bearings of the screw-head stock. Make the headstock of the lathe revolve moderately quickly, roll the palm of the hand on the stock of the screw-head tool and at the same time persuade it towards the lap so that the head of the screw contacts it. In this manner the end of the head will be ground flat. The stock is made to revolve comparatively slowly when compared with the lap and this, combined with the position of the head on the lap, breaks up the grain and so ensures a flat surface. If the head of the screw were central with the lap this condition would not exist and the possibility of a flat surface would, at least, be more uncertain.

When a full surface has been ground, replace the iron lap with the bell-metal one charged with diamantine ; clean the head of the screw to remove all traces of oilstone dust and proceed to polish the surface, using similar movements as when grinding. The final finish is given with the boxwood lap charged with diamantine and used in the same manner. Not only can screws be polished in this manner but the end of the barrel arbor and any piece that can be held in the chuck of the screw-head tool.

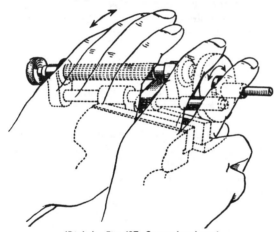

(Right). Fig. 427. Screw-head tool.

The same tool as used in the lathe is not employed when polishing by hand; the principle is the same but the procedure is different. The tool as Fig. 427 is used. Fit the tool up in the vice and secure the screw in the stock.

Charge the iron lap with oilstone dust and oil and hold as shown. Make the stock revolve backward and forward and at the same time revolve the lap backward and forward, a little faster than the stock and push it down on the head of the screw. In this manner the head of the screw is ground flat. Apply a little oil to the bearings of the stock and also to the arbor upon which the lap revolves. Replace the iron lap by the bell-metal one and proceed to finish the head as described before.

To finish the rounded heads of screws or other parts, whether in the lathe or the hand-operated screw-head tool, the procedure is the same. If in the lathe, the roller rest for the polisher is fitted on and the piece to be polished is secured in a split chuck in the headstock of the lathe. The polisher rest in the hand-operated tool is the roller rest nearest to you in Fig. 427.

Secure the screw in the stock as for lapping. It is usually sufficient to prepare the surface to be polished with an Arkansas slip, rolling the stock with the left hand and resting the slip on the roller rest, working the slip backward and forward against the head of the screw ; if the two-way movement is employed as indicated in the illustration (Fig. 427) a good surface will be obtained. Hold the slip on the side of the head to finish that surface ; a clean circular grain is thus obtained and no further finish is necessary. Finishing the sides of the heads of screws equally applies when the top of the head is lapped flat. Clean the screw well, charge the bell-metal polisher with diamantine and proceed to polish the surface, using the same two-way movement employed when using the Arkansas slip. The bell-metal polisher is about 7 inches long, ½ inch wide and ¼ inch thick. The final finish is given with a boxwood polisher, of about the same size as the bell metal, charged with diamantine.

A good substitute for the boxwood is the back of the handle part of an ordinary watch brush. The bell metal polisher is remade by filing, leaving a cross grain, and the wood polisher by scraping with the bench knife lengthways. The curvature to the head can be made quite round, or, if the stone and subsequently the polishers are held to keep the head as flat as possible, a slightly rounded surface will be made, known as a " tallow " head.

The oilstone dust and oil is transferred to the lap by scooping up a little on the tip of the bench knife and smearing it over the surface of the lap with the tip of a finger. The diamantine is transferred to the laps and the polishers by the thumb knuckle, as explained when polishing underhand.

The accessories to the lathe are legion. There are devices for accomplishing almost everything and while they are fascinating to see, and maybe to own, there are many for which the average watch repairer has little use, but in order to make this chapter as complete as possible the majority will be discussed and comment made upon their usefulness to the watch repairer.

The " Tip-over " T rest (Fig. 428) is useful when a good deal of turning is to be done. It can be tipped over out of the way while measurements are made or polishing is being done and when the rest is turned over again it will not be necessary to re-adjust it.

Fig. 428. " Tip-over " T rest.

There are chucks for every purpose. The most useful are universal chucks, brass chucks, and lantern chucks. Universal chucks possess reversible jaws (Fig. 429), enabling a ring, such as a watch case bezel, to be held or, when the jaws are reversed, the steps so formed are useful for holding a watch plate when fitting a new centre hole and for other similar jobs.

Brass chucks (Fig. 430) are used in the split chuck, made especially

Fig. 429. Universal chuck.

for that purpose, to hold the threads of screws and other pieces where it is necessary to protect the surface. They are not suitable for turning balance staffs and pinions or other pieces where absolute accuracy is essential.

Fig. 430. Brass chuck.

Lantern chucks (Fig. 431) are made of bronze with a steel screw centre. They are used to hold such pieces as a ratchet wheel with barrel arbor combined, where it is necessary to polish the end, or a large screw so that the end can be polished. They do not hold the work accurately enough to be used for turning. The small steel lantern chucks (Fig. 432) are useful for holding small screws to enable the ends to be polished, or a seconds hand so that the pipe may be shortened with an Arkansas slip.

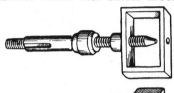

Fig. 431. Lantern chuck.

Fig. 432. Small Lantern chuck.

Drilling : No lathe is complete without some form of drilling device. The system illustrated in Fig. 433 is virtually the pivoting tool, but for small work I prefer the hand tool used with the bow as previously explained. For larger work, the system here illustrated is excellent. Say, for example, that it is desired to drill up a barrel arbor for the ratchet wheel screw ; the procedure is as follows.

Before the square is filed for the ratchet wheel to fit on to, select one of

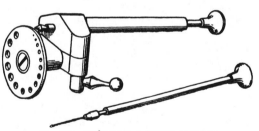

Fig. 433. Self centring drilling accessory.

the chamfered holes in the drilling plate that will allow the end of the arbor to sink into it, but taking care that the hole in the plate is not large enough for the arbor to project. The hole should be about the size of the drill we are to use. The idea is that the chamfer acts as a centring piece so that when the drill makes contact with the arbor it will drill centrally. The drill is fitted into the rod and the whole contrivance is brought up to the arbor which is held in a split chuck in the headstock. The tailstock is made secure and then slight pressure is brought to bear upon the centring plate and that piece made secure. Supply plenty of oil to the chamfer hole and place the drillstock into position. Cause the headstock to revolve fairly slowly and apply some little pressure to the drillstock and occasionally twist it slowly. Proceed to drill, removing the drill occasionally to see that it is cutting and applying a little more oil before replacing. This accessory can be used for a number of purposes, such as drilling up for a pivot too large for the bow pivoting tool drill, to make bouchon wire, and so on.

If the centring device just described is not available, drilling can be carried out quite effectively in the following manner. Secure the piece to be drilled in the headstock : if it is of the rod type use a split chuck ; should it be a plate, such as a barrel cover, fit up in the step chuck.

Catch the centre first, with the graver as explained when making the wax chuck. Retain the T rest in the same position and fit the drill into the pin tongs. Adjust the T rest so that the drill is level with the hole to be drilled (see Fig. 434). Make the headstock revolve and hold the drill up to the work, applying some little

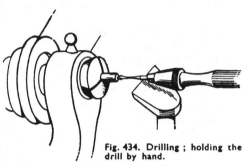

Fig. 434. Drilling ; holding the drill by hand.

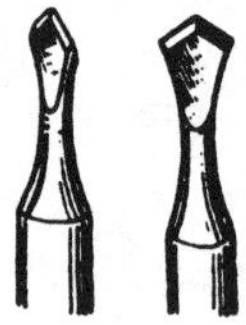

pressure. Make the drill revolve slowly, about half a turn. When drilling brass the drill is shaped as Fig. 435. Experience will teach when you are drilling straight ; in fact, it is not possible to drill otherwise, because the drill will break if it is not held square to the work and any depth of hole is to be drilled.

Fig. 435. Shape of drill for drilling brass.

The drilling tailstock (Fig. 436) can be used for the same purpose, i.e., when drilling without the centring plate. For repetition work the tailstock with lever is useful (Fig. 437).

For topping or rounding up I favour the hand tool ; you are able to feel the work. Should you, however, have a large quantity of wheels to top then the tool shown in Fig. 438 is admirable, but for the average watch repairer such a tool is, I feel, unnecessary.

The average watch repairer so rarely needs to cut a wheel himself that the wheel cutting accessory here illustrated (Fig. 439) is not absolutely essential. It used to be

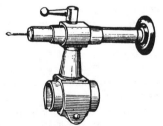

Fig. 436. Drill held in tailstock.

said that if you live in the backwoods you must take *everything* with you ; that does not necessarily hold good to-day, the post brings most things to the door. Further, some lathe accessories take quite a deal of time to fit up and, generally speaking, it is not worth while for one

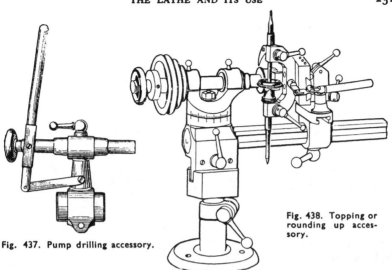

Fig. 437. Pump drilling accessory.

Fig. 438. Topping or rounding up accessory.

job a year; for repetition work it's another story. The same remarks apply to the lapping equipment as to the wheel cutting accessory, one so rarely requires it (Fig. 440).

If it is not possible to procure a new ratchet wheel that is interchangeable, then one in the rough state can be purchased from the material dealer, and fitted and finished as follows, remembering that such wheels are supplied soft. First file the wheel to the thickness of the old wheel; knock a short brass pin into the handle end of an emery buff held in the vice and place the wheel in position so that it is free to revolve (Fig. 441). File down the surface with a pillar file, and during the filing the ratchet wheel will revolve, the file being inclined to slip about. This is just what is wanted, because in this manner an even thickness can be maintained. When the wheel has been reduced to the required thickness, open the square hole so that it fits the square of the

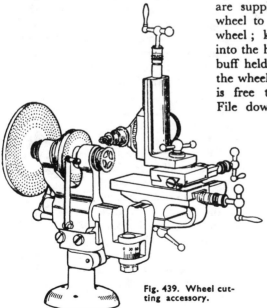

Fig. 439. Wheel cutting accessory.

barrel arbor tightly, using a three-square needle file and filing each of the four sides of the square in the wheel separately. It is not possible to file a good square hole with a four-square file, even if you use one side of the file only; the three-square enables you to get into the corners and make a clean job (Fig. 442). When the wheel is fitted and no more filing is necessary, it can be hardened and tempered.

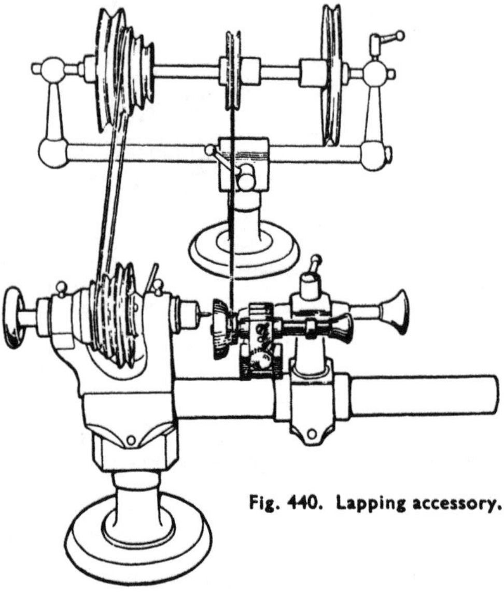

To finish, replace the wheel on the emery buff with the brass pin and, with an emery *stone*. not

Fig. 440. Lapping accessory.

Fig. 441. Wheel held by a pin while being made thinner.

the emery buff, give one or two firm strokes so that a clean straight grain finish is effected; it may be necessary to secure the wheel with another brass pin, this one engaging in between two teeth, to prevent the wheel from revolving. Reverse the wheel and remove this last-mentioned pin. Stone with the emery stone the surface presented, which will be the top of the

wheel. The wheel may revolve during this stoning, but that does not matter, the aim being to obtain a smooth surface with all file marks removed. Now take a new emery buff and, controlling the wheel with the finger and thumb of the left hand, draw the corner only of the edge of the buff across the centre of the surface of the wheel in a straight line, work the buff backward and forward in this manner in deliberate steady strokes and at the same time cause the wheel to revolve slowly. Continue this process while the wheel makes

Fig. 442. To file square hole use three-square file.

several revolutions, and scratch thin straight lines straight across the centre of the wheel (Fig. 443). In this manner, an agreeable snailing effect will be given to the wheel. The coarseness of the snailing, which should be similar to the transmission wheel, is controlled by the coarseness of the emery buff.

If the adjacent steel work is a matt finish the wheel should be

Fig. 443. Producing a straight snailing effect.

finished in a similar manner. Remove all file marks with the stone as mentioned before. Place a piece of thick notepaper on a sheet of plate glass, and on this paper smear a little oilstone dust and oil. The wheel is held down on to the paper with the rounded end of a piece of pegwood, the underside of the wheel uppermost, and polished underhand, tracing larger movements than those described when speaking about underhand polishing. At first employ some little pressure and ease off as the polishing or grinding proceeds.

Encourage the wheel to revolve during this process as it helps to break up the grain. To do this it may be necessary to twirl the pegwood slightly ; on the other hand, as the pressure is eased the wheel may revolve automatically. Finished in this way the surface will be a dull grey matt. If a bright matt finish is desired, in order to match the other steelwork, sprinkle a little dry oilstone dust on to a clean dry part of the paper. After the oilstone and oil treatment is completed, clean the wheel in benzine and dry off. Then proceed to use the dry oilstone dust in a manner similar to that employed when using it with oil.

Rust is one of the watchmaker's enemies. Manufacturers have combated the problem by plating and this appears to be very effective, but it limits the style of finishing and affects the appearance generally. From a purely utilitarian point of view it is serviceable, the steel work does not rust. Other manufacturers have made some steel parts from stainless steel, to achieve the same end—stainless steel being non-corrosive —but there are difficulties in manufacture ; stainless steel does not drill or turn well. It is difficult to work. Many watches have, and no doubt will continue to have, their steel work made from steel that is liable to rust. With most parts of a watch movement the steel work is so slight that it is not possible or essential to remove all traces of rust. We shall take one or two parts as examples.

If a steel balance spring is rusted there is not much you can do about it other than to fit a new one. If the watch is not a fine one, one from which a good rate is expected, light spots of rust can be removed, or perhaps it would be more accurate to say, almost removed. Rust, if it has been corroding for some time, causes pitting, and to remove the effects of rust entirely it is necessary to remove all the pits, and with the balance spring this is not possible. Take a sharp instrument, such as the tip of the bench knife, and lightly scrape the affected parts. This will discolour the spring but that is unimportant. Dip a pointed pegwood in oil and carefully rub the part scraped. I am afraid there is little more that can be done. When it comes to a rusted index, there is more material to work upon.

Stone with the emery stone as much as possible, and if it is not possible to remove all the pits, rub them well with a piece of brass. Use a corner of the brass and press it well into the affected part, the brass will fill the holes or pits in and thus hinder, if not entirely eliminate further corrosion. The index is then polished underhand in the bolt tool as previously explained. When polished you may be able to see the small brass spots, but this is to be preferred to rust pitting.

If badly rusted little can be done to save a rusted pinion ; slight rust, can, however, be treated. To remove rust from the leaves first pick the rust away with a tool made from an ordinary sewing needle stoned to a chisel shape. Then charge a pointed pegwood with oilstone and oil and work this up and down the length of the leaves. Clean well in benzine and charge the pegwood (first resharpened to remove all traces of oilstone dust) with diamantine and work this up and down, the peg will eventually take the shape of the leaves and all parts will be polished. The arbor of the pinion is ground with the iron polisher and oilstone dust and oil and finished with diamantine. If you are treating a part where pressure cannot be applied to fill the pits, such as an escape wheel, copper can be used instead of brass ; a piece of copper wire answers well.

The procedure in general is to remove the rust if possible ; if not, remove as much as possible and then fill in, if any pits are left, with either brass or copper. Finally, polish the part as it was originally.

CHAPTER EIGHTEEN

THE ENGLISH LEVER

WHEN THINKING of English watches one is inclined to consider the fusee watch only, but the English makers have produced going-barrel watches in vast quantities and, as for many years to come English watches will be in need of repair, it is fitting that some consideration should be given to them here. Watch manufacturing in England is not yet dead, far from it, but the modern English watch will never be far removed from the Swiss design. The chapters dealing with the Swiss watch, therefore, equally apply to the English. This still leaves us with the older type of English movement, especially the fusee, and it is with this older type of hand-made movement that this chapter deals. The instructions here are brief, but sufficient for the purpose : repairing English watches needs a book to itself.

The enthusiastic watch repairer will read this chapter with interest because it tells of watchmaking at its best. I have yet to see an English hand-made watch that is not a pleasure to inspect. It must be admitted that some of these watches give even good watchmakers some trouble to rate moderately well, but I am concerned at the moment only with craftsmanship. Even with some of the lower grade hand-made movements you will find good turning, polishing, facing of pinions, undercutting, etc., and in the fine quality movement will be found craftsmanship which commands respect, for it has never been surpassed and rarely equalled.

The functioning of the various parts such as the escapement, depths of the train and the mainspring are, in the main, the same as the Swiss or, to put it the correct way round, the Swiss is similar to the English. In this respect, the English watch came first. The method of procedure is a little different when examining and comparing the English with the Swiss.

In an English ¾-plate going-barrel watch the examination should start with the escapement. Try the shake on the banking, also the balance endshake, and then remove the balance spring. Some of the balance spring collets are solid rectangular steel and, to remove them, hold the collet with a stout pair of brass tweezers in the right hand. Holding the tweezers firmly, twist the balance clockwise and the tweezers anticlockwise, at the same time gently pulling the balance away from the collet (Fig. 444). Next examine the staff pivots to see if they are bent ; replace the balance in the movement and screw the balance cock into position.

Usually the action of the escape teeth on the pallets is not visible, the pallet cock being in the way, so test the locking in the following manner. Hold the movement in the left hand as shown in the illustration (Fig. 445), this will leave the thumb free to move the balance. With a pointed pegwood apply slight pressure to the 4th wheel in the forward

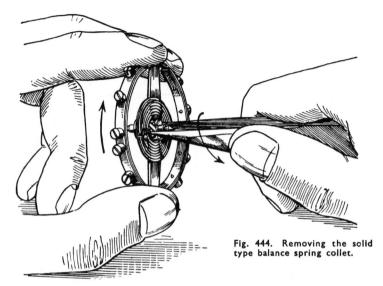

Fig. 444. Removing the solid type balance spring collet.

direction. Lead the balance round slowly with the thumb until the ruby pin engages in the lever notch and, when the lever starts to move, press the thumb against the bottom plate of the movement to steady it. It will then be found that the balance can be moved a little way in either direction without the thumb actually moving along the side of the plate. In this manner it is possible to impart a very steady movement to the balance.

Continue rotating the balance until a tooth of the escape wheel has dropped, and at this precise moment release the balance suddenly by just levering the thumb so that it is upright. The thumb does not leave the plate, but the tip which has been operating on the balance is now free of it (Fig. 445 as dotted line). If the locking is good the balance will swing smartly round until the ruby pin strikes the other side of the lever, the pressure on the 4th wheel having given the extra impulse. The balance will return so that the

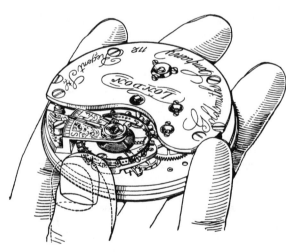

Fig. 445. Correct way to hold the movement.

ruby pin is about to enter the notch again. At this juncture bring the thumb forward to arrest the balance and lead it as before to unlock on the other pallet. Repeat this until all 15 teeth are tested on each pallet stone. This test only discloses whether the locking is safe, it does not reveal a locking that is too deep ; that will be dealt with later. If the locking is shallow, *i.e.*, it mislocks, the balance will not receive its impulse, but the guard pin will bind on the roller and so hold the balance or retard its motion. It is always advisable to try several teeth on the same stone before you decide that it does mislock. The locking may be very light, and a slight backward movement of the balance may give the impression of mislocking.

Before going further it would be as well to describe how to correct mislocking should it occur. With the Swiss exposed pallet stones, it is simple, but it is not so simple with the English. The stones are set in flush with the steel part of the pallets, so first try the side shake of the pallet staff pivots, and also the escape pinion pivots : a new and closer fitting jewel hole may correct the locking. If the wheel mislocks on both pallet stones a larger escape wheel may correct it.

It cannot be ascertained until the escapement has been examined further, which will follow in due course. For the moment we shall assume that the locking is safe.

To check the run to the banking, the lever is wedged by placing a thin slip of cork under the tail (Fig. 446) and the procedure of this test and its correction is exactly similar to that employed when examining the straight line Swiss escapement already explained.

The test for angle is then made, employing the method of observing the movement of the lever by the motion of the ruby pin after the drop of the escape tooth on to the pallet, as explained when dealing with the Swiss escapement. The correction for angle is, however, different from the method employed when adjusting the Swiss

Fig. 446. Lever wedged with cork.

escapement. The English escapement has the pallets pinned to the lever by two pins, usually of brass. To move the lever to the correct position fix the pallets in the tool as shown in Fig. 447 and, with a piece of brass wire as a punch, tap the lever into the position required.

Many of the English watches are fitted with the ratchet tooth escape wheel (Fig. 448), and this requires more inside and outside shake than the club tooth. In other words, the ratchet tooth needs more drop than the club tooth, the reason being that greater latitude is necessary in order that the back of the teeth are clear of the front part of the pallets as they move down into the wheel. The club tooth, on the other hand, is cut away at the back so that the pallet is immediately free (Fig. 449). The arrows indicate the freedom.

Reverting to the locking, the inside and outside shake may reveal

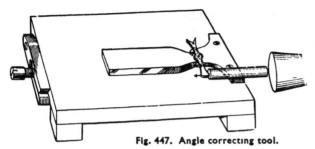

Fig. 447. Angle correcting tool.

that the escape wheel is too small. Fitting a larger wheel will c o r r e c t m i s-locking on both stones, but if, on the other hand, the escapement is correct in other respects and it mislocks on one or both stones, it indicates that the pallets must in some way be brought nearer to the escape wheel. One method of effecting this is to fit a new pair of pallets with the part where the stones are set a shade longer. This is not always convenient or even possible to-day : pallet making is practically a lost art in England. The best thing to do is first to examine the pallet jewel holes to see if they

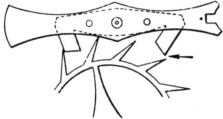

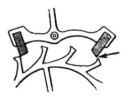

Fig. 448. Ratchet tooth escapement.   Arrow indicates drop.

Fig. 449. Club tooth escapement.   Arrow indicates drop.

are the usual English type, *i.e.*, set into brass collets and the collets fitting into a recess.   It is possible that a small dot has been made on the brass setting : sometimes one dot on the balance hole, two dots on the pallet hole and three on the escape wheel. These dots should face similar dots on the part into which the jewel is set. It may be that the setting of the hole is not exactly round and the hole has been placed into a

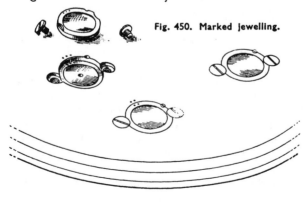

Fig. 450. Marked jewelling.

certain position to accommodate the locking. What may have happened is that, in order to bring the pallets nearer to the escape wheel, the edge of the brass setting has been filed for part of its circumference and the opposite edge burnished to spread the metal. This has the effect of pushing the hole to one side, and it is therefore necessary to indicate its position (Fig. 450). Escapement makers do not admit that this statement is correct, but say the jewel holes are so marked to ensure their correct replacement in their respective settings. The amount of adjustment possible by this means is slight, but then the amount necessary may also be slight. Another method is to stretch the escape wheel teeth a little. Place the wheel on a flat stake in the staking tool and use a flat-ended punch, apply frequent and light taps to the punch and make the wheel revolve continually while so doing.

When testing for the run to the banking pay particular attention to a deep locking; if none, or very little run, do not adjust the banking pins until satisfied that the locking is not at fault. If there is suspicion in this direction fit up the escape wheel and pallets in the depthing tool. Adjust the tool so that the distance between the two pairs of runners is the same as the distance between the escape and pallet holes, and the locking can then be accurately observed. If the locking is too deep, the teeth can be topped, and not only does this correct the locking but it increases the run to the banking. To top the teeth, fit up in the turns as Fig. 451,

Fig. 451. Topping the escape wheel teeth.

bring the T rest up close and square to the wheel and hold an Arkansas slip firmly down on to the rest. Rotate the wheel slowly, in the downward direction only, and lever the Arkansas slip over until it touches the teeth of the wheel. Do not move the stone other than for the return movement but hold it firm and steady to the wheel. The stone is made to contact the wheel when it is travelling in the one direction only; one downward stroke of the bow is usually sufficient to reduce the teeth enough for another test to be made to ascertain if the locking is corrected.

Fortunately the depth of the locking does not often call for adjustment in an English watch, and this can be attributed mainly to the fact that it is difficult for the locking to be tampered with by the enterprising yet inexperienced watch repairer. This is just as well, as it is not so simple to correct as the Swiss exposed pallets. The teeth of the ratchet escape wheel are more frail than the club teeth and are liable to wear. Other than this, except perhaps a wide pallet hole, little is likely to go wrong with the locking.

The best method of comparing is to clean the movement and, as the operation proceeds, discuss the differences that exist between the English and the Swiss.

Having examined the escapement, the parts should be prepared for cleaning. The escape wheel is brightened by immersion in cyanide ; the balance is treated in a similar manner as explained previously. The tops of the endstone settings are polished before placing them in the benzine pot. Sharpen a piece of pegwood to a short point, dip it into the *dry* diamantine and work this round the chamfered part of the setting. The top is polished by burnishing. Old watch jewellers used to polish the tops on a tin block with red stuff, underhand. It is claimed that the polish lasts longer than burnishing, but on the whole I have found burnished settings most satisfactory.

To burnish, lay the endstone on the handle end of an emery buff held in the vice. Clean a flat burnisher on a fairly fine emery stick—o or oo—wipe well with a clean rag, apply just a trace of oil and smear it over the surface. Bring the burnisher down on to the setting with some little pressure, this will cause the setting to sink slightly into the soft wood of the buff handle and so hold it secure. Proceed to burnish, using firm steady strokes, two or three fairly heavy ones and then lighten the pressure for one or two strokes ; lift the burnisher carefully off the work, as the setting may adhere to the burnisher, and examine, and a beautiful dead flat polished surface should result. Not only are the endstone settings to the escapement treated in this manner, but all the jewel hole settings and also the bush to the top barrel pivot. All English watches are not the same ; a great many have endstones to the lever and escape wheel, screwed-in jewel holes, and a screwed bush to the top barrel pivot. When the jewel hole settings have been polished it is advisable to replace them immediately and place the plate in the benzine pot.

Now for the train. Invariably the barrel is fitted with stop work and more often than not the boss of the finger piece forms the top pivot. Usually the finger piece is marked with a dot, and the square of the barrel arbor is similarly marked, or one corner of the square may have a nick cut into it and the finger of the finger piece should point to this nick or dot. It is important that the finger piece is fitted on to the arbor so that these markings coincide. The reason for this is that during manufacture the pivot is turned true on the arbor when in that particular position and to change it round to another square afterwards may make the barrel run out of true. The mainspring is set up in a similar manner to that of the Swiss watch.

The movement is now dismembered and most of the parts

are in the benzine. The majority of English movements are gilt, so when the plates and bars are removed from the benzine and dried with a clean linen rag, they are brushed with a clean soft brush, using a circular movement to avoid scratching.

Other than the fusee itself the examination of the fusee movement is similar to that of the going-barrel. It is the fusee that is at present under consideration.

The fusee clicks are liable to wear and often need to be replaced. In order to do this it is necessary first to take the fusee to pieces. Sometimes copper wire is used to pin up the fusee and, if such is the case, hold the fusee in the left hand as shown in Fig. 452 and give the lower pivot of the fusee a smart blow with the brass hammer. This will shear the copper pin and so release the cap, the piece of copper wire left in the fusee arbor can then be pushed out. The maintaining-power wheel is lifted off and to this the two fusee clicks are fitted. If a brass pin has been used to pin up, push

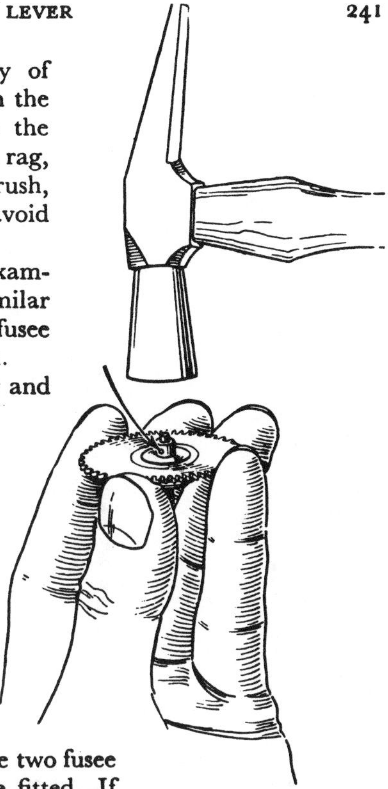

Fig. 452. Removing fusee cap. Arrow indicates the pin.

the pin out with the point pusher, operating on the small end of the pin.

The worn click or clicks can be removed by punching out. Place the maintaining-power wheel on a stake with a hole large enough to receive the click and give a light tap to the rivet of the click with a small flat-ended punch, whereupon it will easily come away (Fig. 453). These clicks are only very lightly riveted as will presently be seen. File a long pivot on the end of the click wire (Fig. 454), and file so that the pivot comes in the position as indicated in the illustration (Fig. 455), the pivot should comfortably fit the hole in the maintaining-power wheel. Cut the click wire, leaving

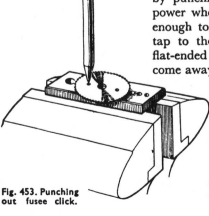

Fig. 453. Punching out fusee click.

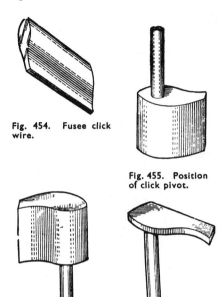

Fig. 454.   Fusee click wire.

Fig. 455.   Position of click pivot.

Fig. 456.   Click on the end of pivot.

Fig. 457.   Click almost ready for fitting.

the click on the end of the long pivot as Fig. 456. The click is now thinned and trimmed up with needle files until it fits into position (Fig. 457). File the top of the click flat so that it is a shade below the ridge on the maintaining-power wheel and finish the top with the polisher and oilstone dust and oil. (Fig. 458.) Place the click in position, turn the maintaining-power wheel upside down on to a flat steel stake and nip the long pivot off as near the wheel as possible (Fig. 459).

While still holding the wheel down on to the stake, file the end of the pivot almost flush with the wheel and finally give the end of the pivot one or two light taps with a round faced hammer to rivet it. The burr thrown up by the filing is almost sufficient to hold the click but the *light* riveting makes quite sure. Try the click to see that it is quite free and that the click spring can operate it satisfactorily. If the click,

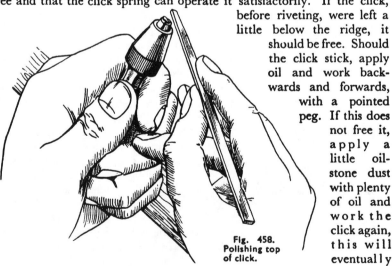

before riveting, were left a little below the ridge, it should be free. Should the click stick, apply oil and work backwards and forwards, with a pointed peg. If this does not free it, apply a little oilstone dust with plenty of oil and work the click again, this will eventually

Fig. 458. Polishing top of click.

make it perfectly free. After oilstone dust has been used the wheel must be particularly well cleaned with benzine. Use a stiff watch brush dipped in benzine and scrub round the click. Every trace of the abrasive must be removed.

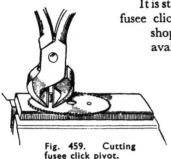

Fig. 459. Cutting fusee click pivot.

It is still possible to purchase fusee click wire in some tool shops, but if none be available, proceed in exactly the same manner, using a rectangular rod. The rod should be of such dimensions, that when the pivot has been filed ready to shape up the

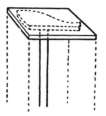

Fig. 460. Click filed from rectangular steel. Dotted lines indicate the original piece of metal and the finished click.

click to fit into position, a not undue amount of filing is necessary. Before starting to file the click will be as Fig. 460 and, as the click is thin, the shaping will present no difficulty. The clicks are not hardened ; this applies to the click wire as well as to the hand fashioned click.

Some fusee ratchets are made of steel and these are usually to be found in the ⅜-plate movement. They are solid with the fusee square and held in position by three screws threaded into the fusee. Should such a ratchet be worn, which is rare, the procedure was to fit an entirely new piece. To-day such parts are not procurable and the best treatment is to fit a new ratchet to the old arbor. First remove the ratchet from the fusee and fit up in the split chuck in the lathe. Hold the arbor by the pivot top, and turn the ratchet to about one-third its diameter and half its thickness (Fig. 461). Select a ratchet of the correct size and cut a recess into it so that the ratchet just reduced in size fits into it tightly (Fig. 462), making sure the wheel is the right

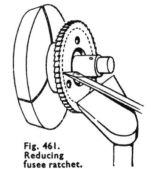

Fig. 461. Reducing fusee ratchet.

Fig. 462. New ratchet recessed to fit fusee piece.

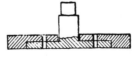

Fig. 463. New ratchet in position.

way round. Reduce the new ratchet to the correct thickness, drill holes and rivet the two pieces together (Fig. 463).

Brass ratchets are much more likely to wear, but they are certainly more easily replaced. Remove the old ratchet by prising up with the bench knife (Fig. 464). Remove the two pins which hold the ratchet : sometimes they can be pulled out, but if this is not possible, turn them down flush in the lathe. Make a dot in the fusee near the outer edge, at

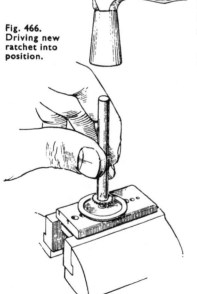

Fig. 464. Prising up old brass ratchet.

right angles to the original pins (Fig. 465). Select a new ratchet and open the hole in the centre with a cutting broach until it fits the fusee arbor tightly. Remove burrs with a file and drive the ratchet on to the arbor until it seats flat on to the fusee. Again, make sure it is the right way round (Fig. 466). Next drill two holes opposite the dot : by marking the fusee it was ensured that the holes will not run into the old ones. File up and fit well-fitting brass pins and drive home, leaving the ends flat and square so that they grip for the full length of the pin (Fig. 467). Cut the pins off close to the ratchet with the nippers. Fit up in a split chuck in the lathe and turn the top surface of the ratchet to the correct thickness, which is determined by the height of the ridge of the maintaining-power wheel ; it should be a little lower, for the same reason as observed when fitting the click. The centre of the ratchet is cut

Fig. 465.
Arrow indicates dot to give position of new pins.

out to free the boss of the maintaining-power wheel. It is not necessary to rivet the pins. The finished job is shown in Fig. 468.

While dealing with the fusee it is as well to clean and reassemble it.

Fig. 466.
Driving new ratchet into position.

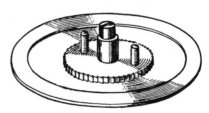

Fig. 467. Pins to hold new click.
Inset shows square end to pin.

If the pivots are cut they can be re-polished. The sides of the square are polished with the iron polisher and oilstone dust and oil and left grey. Should burrs be thrown up due to the key being too large or worn, hold the square on a flat steel stake and tap each side of the square with the flat-faced hammer

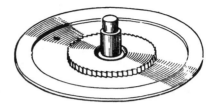

Fig. 468. The new ratchet fitted.

in order to make it as square as possible without reducing the square unduly. This is better than reducing the square to remove the burrs. Finish grey as before. The end of the square is polished with diamantine. Hold the fusee in the screw-head tool and touch the top of the square with an Arkansas slip to remove burrs and polish with the bell-metal polisher charged with diamantine, finish off with boxwood and diamantine. The four top edges are broken, *i.e.*, slightly chamfered or bevelled with the Arkansas slip (Fig. 469), giving the sharp finish so desirable. Clean all parts in benzine.

Apply a spot of oil to each of the clicks, two spots to the teeth

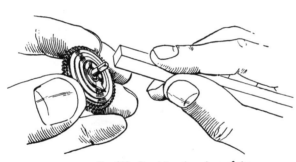

Fig. 469. Breaking the edges of the fusee square.

of the ratchet and a little to the arbor upon which the maintaining-power wheel works. Place this wheel in position and then the great wheel, apply a little oil to the recess in which the cap works and some to the centre where the great wheel revolves. Place the cap in position, making sure that it is the right way round ; the hole running through it must coincide with the hole in the arbor. File up a long tapered copper pin and pin up tightly. Cut the pin close to the cap with the bench knife (Fig. 470).

Hold the fusee in the left

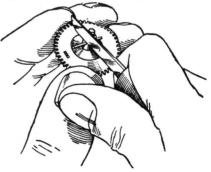

Fig. 470. Pinning up the fusee.

hand by the great wheel and turn the cone part of the fusee by the square, it is important that it be quite free but without any side play. Now reverse the direction of the fusee to ensure that the maintaining-power spring operates.   This can be checked by observing the pin which operates in the elongated hole on the underside of the great wheel

Fig. 471. Indicating pin of maintaining-power spring.

(Fig. 471). If the fusee is pinned too tightly the spring will not be able to move the fusee back. This can be corrected by holding the fusee as in Fig. 452, and giving the bottom pivot a light tap with the brass hammer ; sometimes a knock with the back of a watch brush is sufficient. Adjust in this manner until the fusee slides back under the power

of the maintaining-power spring ; the fusee must be free, and there must be no side or up-and-down play of the great wheel, otherwise there will be trouble with the maintaining-power detent when the movement is assembled.

The rest of the movement is cleaned in the usual way. The chain is cleaned by winding it once round a piece of pegwood held in the vice (Fig. 472), applying a little oil where indicated by arrow, and working the chain backwards and forwards until it is quite supple. Rinse in benzine and brush well to dry. Hold the chain as in Fig. 473 and pass quickly through the flame of a spirit lamp to burn off any hairs or fluff that may be ad-hering to it. Burning off is very important,

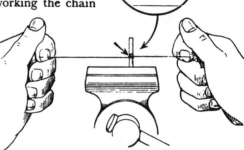

Fig. 472. Cleaning fusee chain.

especially with the ¾-plate, because the balance runs near to the chain and a hair touching the balance at various times can be a difficult fault to eradicate when rating.

One form of hook to the mainspring it may be necessary to fit is the square hook. Other than this, the procedure of hooking a mainspring is

Fig. 473. Burning off fusee chain.

much the same as explained for the Swiss watch.

Select a piece of rectangular soft steel, a shade larger than the size of the hole in the barrel. Steel rods used to be sold by the tool

shops especially for this purpose and were known as " hooking-in steel."
File the end so that it fits the hole in the barrel comfortably—it is

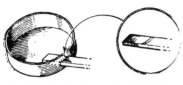

important to fit at an angle as indicated
in Fig. 474—and finally clean all four
sides with the Arkansas slip. Hold the
rod in position in the barrel and, with a
pointed scriber, mark a line from
the inside and the outside on the steel,
this will indicate the height or thickness
of the hook. Remove the rod and hold

Fig. 474. Indicating angle of "hooking
in " steel before marking.

in the sliding tongs so that the jaws expose only the
part that was projecting into the barrel. A pivot is filed
on this end as in Fig. 475. The position of the pivot
is important : it should be more to the forward part
of the hook, the tendency is not then to wrench out
the hook.

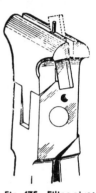

Shape the end of the mainspring and drill a hole
as Fig. 476. Rivet the partly finished hook on to the
spring (Fig. 477), leaving a slightly rounded rivet, not
filed off flush ; we want a little support here. Next
cut the hook a little above the line scratched, that is
the part that was projecting outside the barrel. File the
top of the hook smooth and remove the burrs from
the four top edges. Bend the spring with the brass-
n o s e d

Fig. 475. Filing pivot
for square hook.

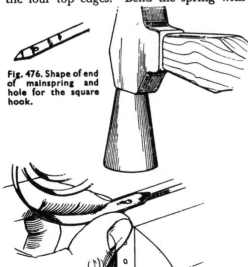

pliers to the approximate
curvature of the inside of
the barrel, Fig. 478. Wind
the spring in the mainspring
winder and bring into
operation the lever to

Fig. 476. Shape of end
of mainspring and
hole for the square
hook.

Fig. 478.
Bend main-
spring to
curve of in-
side of barrel.

engage the hook, as Fig. 479.
Bring the barrel up to the
spring with the hole opposite
the hook, carefully release
the click and allow the
spring slowly to unwind.
The hook should enter the
hole in the barrel but sometimes a little persuasion is

Fig. 477. Riveting square hook to mainspring.

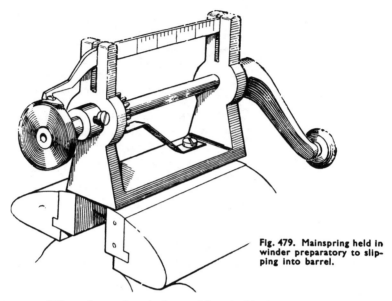

Fig. 479. Mainspring held in winder preparatory to slipping into barrel.

necessary. When the spring is in position hold the barrel in the left hand and tap with the back of a watch brush, near the hook, thus causing the hook to seat well home. File the hook down with a fine file, taking care not to touch the barrel with the file, and finally stone with an Arkansas slip to ensure the removal of all burrs. Now remove the spring from the barrel to finish the top of the hook. Hold the end of the spring flat on the handle end of an emery buff held in the vice and, with the polisher and oilstone-dust and oil, polish the top surface (Fig. 480). Clean off and polish with diamantine. The spring is now ready to be placed finally in the barrel, as previously explained.

The movement having been cleaned, it is ready for assembly. The centre wheel, fusee, detent, barrel, centre, 3rd and 4th wheels are placed

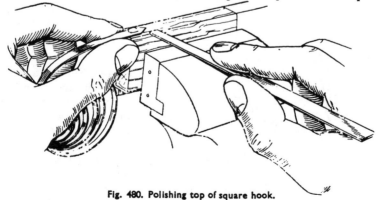

Fig. 480. Polishing top of square hook.

in position, but not the chain. Place the barrel ratchet and click in position and turn the barrel and the fusee so that the hooking of the chain is facing the outer edge. Hook the chain first on to the barrel, making sure it is the correct hook (Fig. 481), then place the first finger

of the left hand so that the chain can be brought over and rest on the back of the finger. Hook the other end of the chain to the fusee, stretch the finger out so that the chain is taut (Fig. 482) and wind the chain on to the barrel. If the movement is held with the ratchet click at the top it will fall to the ratchet. The illustration is of a full plate movement and the procedure is precisely the same for a ¾-plate movement.

Fig. 481. Fusee chain hooks. *Left*, barrel hook ; *right*, fusee hook.

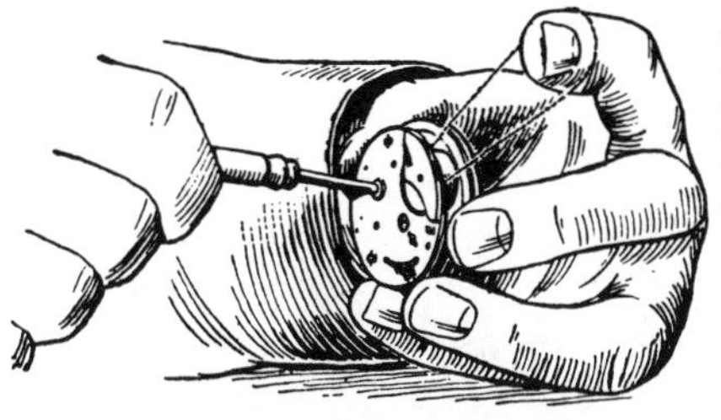

Fig. 482. Method of holding chain during fitting.

Withdraw the finger and continue to wind until all the chain is wound round the barrel, and also until it has pulled the fusee round and the chain is taut. To start with, set the mainspring up three-quarters of a turn and tighten the barrel click. Next adjust the chain on the barrel so that the coils are equal distances apart, this is quite easily effected with a pointed peg. Screw the adjusting rod (Fig. 483) on to the fusee square and wind up fully.

Wind slowly and observe carefully that the chain is riding accurately in the fusee grooves. Also observe that the stop piece acts satisfactorily. The chain lifts the stop iron so that the stop piece on the fusee butts squarely on the end when the chain is fully wound on to the fusee. Hold the movement firmly (Fig. 484) and allow the train to run down ; this will cause the adjusting rod to rotate, and the idea is to adjust the sliding weight on the rod to such a position that the unwinding will *just* lift the weight. If the weight comes up too quickly, move the weight further from the square. The power of the mainspring should just lift the weight when fully wound. When this is accomplished allow the mainspring to unwind, and at each revolution of the fusee the weight should be lifted with the same ease or speed until all the chain is again on the barrel. If the mainspring will not lift the weight at the last turn set it up a little more, and should the last turn be stronger than the first, the spring was set up too much in the first instance. Accurate adjustment may not prove possible owing to the curve of the fusee being incorrect ; in this case make the adjustment as good as possible.

Fig. 483. Adjusting rod.

The procedure with the full plate is exactly similar to the ¾-plate with the exception that when assembling the 3rd wheel is omitted.

The escapement is assembled under the same plate as the train and it would not run down when wound if all the train were in position. After the fusee adjustment has been made the 3rd wheel is placed into position by removing the the bar as in Fig. 485. When assembled with the escapement in position in the ¾-plate movement, and in the full plate, observe the maintaining-

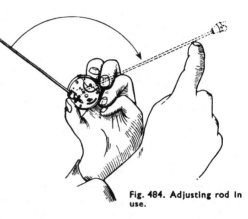

power wheel closely at the point where the detent operates. Wind the mainspring up two or three clicks and release the key. If the maintaining power is in order you will see the detent gather up three or four teeth of the maintaining-power wheel, so that when the watch is wound in the future the train will

Fig. 484. Adjusting rod in use.

not be reversed during winding, the maintaining-power spring keeping the train going in the forward direction during the time taken to wind it up.

When the fusee watch is assembled and it is wished to set it to the exact time, *after* it has been allowed to run down fully, you will find that

Fig. 485. Showing the bar of a full plate movement with the 3rd wheel removed.

the train will not start to move forward immediately it is wound. The train of the going-barrel movement moves forward immediately a little power is applied to the mainspring and, to accomplish this with the fusee movement, it is necessary to wind it in the direction opposite to that of winding the mainspring, so that the maintaining-power spring is wound up. A slight movement of the key is all that is necessary. The maintaining-power spring only takes 3 to 5 teeth of the maintaining-power wheel to wind it up.

One last word about fusee movements. Make sure a fusee dust cap is fitted on to the fusee square. Watch keys harbour dust and this dust can be ejected into the top fusee hole and so cut the pivot. To repair and clean a fusee movement is a nice piece of work and the time taken should be from four to six hours, for which, before 1914, 4s. to 6s. was paid to the watchmaker—an interesting comparison with conditions obtaining to-day.

When taking a fusee movement to pieces it is not possible to let the mainspring down as is the case with the going-barrel movement. The procedure is to remove the escapement and let the train run down, first cutting a long chip of pegwood to wedge into the 4th wheel, then removing the escape wheel and pallets. Remove the chip carefully and use it to touch the 4th wheel to act as a brake so that the train does not run down suddenly, as it may cause damage. Then loosen the barrel ratchet click screw, place a key on the barrel square and let the set-up part of the spring down. With the full plate the balance is first removed ; wedge the 4th wheel, unpin the top plate (or unscrew if screws are fitted) near the pallets only, lever the plate up just sufficient to remove the lever, and again make the plate secure. Let the train run, using the chip as a brake as before, and then let the set-up part of the mainspring down.

CHAPTER NINETEEN

FRICTION JEWELLING

WHEN IT was discovered that a jewel could be finished on its outside edge to be circular in form and having its circumference exactly concentric with its hole, so that when accurately fitted into the plate it would hold itself in position by friction alone, a most important advance was made in watch construction ; it meant that the watch was simpler, more accurate, and less costly to make and, what is still more important to this treatise, infinitely easier to repair than with the older methods of setting jewels by rubbing in or fitting screw-held ring settings.

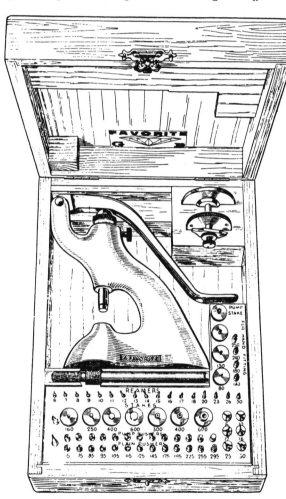

Fig. 486. Friction jewel-setting equipment.

In order to assure some of the older craftsmen who may question the efficiency of a jewel hole held by its own pressure, it should be understood that modern engineering practice readily accepts a theory of friction tight positioning, referred to variously as push-fit or press-fit. In the case of the jewel hole it is a press-fit in the plate. That is to say, the hole in the plate is a trifle smaller than the outside diameter of the jewel, there being a certain amount of elasticity in the metal which will give when the jewel is pressed into position. The pressure of the jewel against the metal of the plate is sufficient to retain it in position for an indefinite time, particularly as there is practically no end pressure on a jewel bearing. As it takes a pressure of 15 lbs. to remove a correctly fitted friction jewel, it is very unlikely that a jewel will be displaced in ordinary wear or during repair of the movement when cleaning the jewels with pegwood.

The great advantage a friction-held jewel has over an ordinary rubbed-in setting is that it is more likely to be set upright. Jewels are supplied with the outer circumference accurately sized and the sides parallel with the axis so that, provided the hole in the plate is correct to size, the jewel can only be set dead square.

In the majority of instances when setting a rubbed-in jewel hole, the part to be jewelled is shellacked on to a wax chuck and the seating for the new jewel turned out. It is possible at this point for a number of errors to creep in ; it may not be dead flat on the chuck, and in all probability it will not be, as was discovered when dealing with the wax chuck. Even slightly out of flat will cause the jewel to be set at an angle. Further, there is not the same control over the endshake when compared with the friction-set jewel. Another important point in favour of the friction-set jewel is the speed with which it can be fitted.

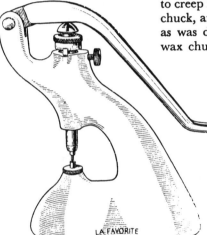

Fig. 487. Jewel-setting press.

It would be as well to discuss the jewel - setting tool before attempting to use it. *La Favorite* appears to be popular in Switzerland, and is supplied with a number of accessories such as anvils, punches and the like. I am indebted to the makers for the majority of the illustrations in this section.

The illustration (Fig. 486) shows the equipment of which the press (Fig. 487) is an essential part. The anvils or stakes, some of which are flat and solid and others hollow, fit into the lower part of the tool. Punches or pushers of various sizes, some flat and others hollow, fit into the stock used in the upper part of the tool (Fig. 488). Some of the hollow punches are self centring (Fig. 489) and the one illustrated is for pressing the balance jewel hole into position. Reamers for opening the hole in the plate prior to fitting the jewel are accurately sized and the size stamped on the side, such as 109, which indicates 1·09 mm.

Some makes of reamers are marked 1/100 mm. larger than actual size ; the user should check this by measuring before use.

Other accessories will be discussed as required during the fitting of a jewel. The jewels are supplied with straight and olive holes for the train wheels, and balance staff holes are also obtainable olive formed. Brass buchons or chatons are also procurable, so that a brass non-jewelled hole, such as a centre hole, can be re-bushed in a similar manner to that employed when fitting a jewel hole. The illustration (Fig. 490) shows the accessories supplied with each tool.

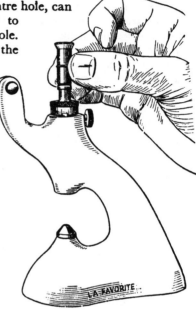

The first thing to do before replacing any jewel hole is to set the tool so that the endshake of the part that works in the jewel hole is correct, and to do this proceed in the following manner. Fit a flat stake into the lower part of the tool and place the piece to be jewelled—say the centre and third wheel bar—upside down on the stake so that the inside or under-side of the jewel is uppermost. Fit one of the pushers, i.e., the flat-ended piece used to press the jewel home, into the stock in the upper part of the tool. Adjust the micro-meter screw adjustment at the top

Fig. 488. Showing the stock to which the pushers are fitted.

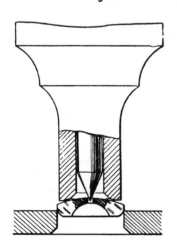

Fig. 489. Self-centring pusher.

of the tool so that the pusher just touches the face of the jewel when lowered. This forms a stop and limits the move-ment of the pusher, ensuring that the new jewel will be pressed in to the same depth as the original. Now is the time to correct the endshake should it be necessary. If the original jewel is not smashed but just cracked, chipped, or the hole too large, it will be possible to test the endshake, and should it be necessary, for instance, to increase the endshake, then the screw adjustment is set so that the pusher can be pressed lower. To do this it will be necessary to remove the bridge from the stake and here the micrometer screw will be

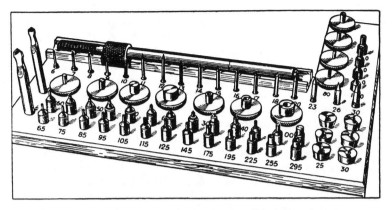

Fig. 490. The accessories supplied with the tool.

useful, as the amount of the increase of endshake can be estimated. On the other hand, if the original jewel is smashed and bulges, remove it or, if the jewel is missing, adjust the pusher so that it corresponds with the estimated position of the original jewel face. There are two or three ways of setting a jewel, some are set from the top or outside and some are rubbed in from the inside ; discretion must be used when estimating the position of the face. However, having adjusted the stop for the endshake, fix it by the knurled screw and then push out the old jewel with a piece of pegwood.

Place the bridge on the stake and fit a broach or reamer into the upper part of the tool and open out the hole to remove the old jewel

seating and setting. When the reamer has finished cutting continue rotating it in the hole until the round part of the reamer makes full contact with the hole to its full depth, thus ensuring that the hole is opened to an *exact* size, which is most important. When cutting away an old setting it may be necessary to change the reamer for another, one or more sizes larger, to ensure that a sufficient parallel surface on the side of the hole is made available to grip the jewel. It is advisable to change the reamers one size larger only each time, to avoid the likelihood of making the hole out of centre.

It may so happen that, after opening the hole to remove the original setting, a jewel of sufficient diameter may not be available. Should this prove the case proceed as follows. Brass rings or " chatons " are obtainable graduated in the same way as the jewels, *i.e.*, the outside and inside diameters noted in ·01 mm. steps. Note the size of the last reamer used and select a brass ring of an outside diameter ·01 mm. larger. Fit the jewel into this ring and then press the ring-set jewel into position as if it were an ordinary jewel hole. It

Fig. 491. Chamfering tool.

may be necessary to open the hole in the bridge rather larger than would be the case if a jewel only were to be fitted, otherwise the brass ring would be so thin as to prove unworkable.

The next step is lightly to chamfer both sides of the hole to remove any burrs which may be thrown up. The chamfer on the inside of the bridge will act as a lead when pressing in the new jewel. Fit the chamfering piece (Fig. 491) up in the tool and use it to remove the burrs, especially the inside one, in preference to doing it by hand, to ensure that the chamfer will be true with the hole.

Note the size of the last reamer used, which will be found stamped on the side, and select a jewel with a hole the correct size for the pivot and outside diameter 1/100 mm. *larger* than the reamer. For instance, if the last reamer is marked 70, which is 0·70 mm., then the jewel will be taken from the bottle marked 70 (0·70 mm.). Actually, if the reamer marked 70 were to be measured it may be found to be only 0·69 mm., *i.e.*, 1/100 mm. smaller in diameter than the corresponding jewel hole. Place the bridge on the stake with a hole in it large enough to clear the other side of the jewel should it project, though as small as possible in order to give the maximum support to the surrounding metal : it takes 35 lb. pressure to insert the new jewel and care must be taken that the metal is not distorted. Stand the new jewel, bottom up, over the hole in the bridge, and the necessity for the chamfer will readily be appreciated. Lower the flat-faced pusher on to the jewel and with the lever exert a gentle, steady, but firm pressure which should be continued until the stop arrests further

Fig. 492.
Rubbed-in type of jewel hole.

movement, when the job is done, no further finish being necessary.

The illustration (Fig. 492) shows the original rubbed-in set jewel ; in this case it is a balance jewel, but the procedure is the same. Fig. 493 shows the reamer about to enter the hole, Fig. 494 cutting the hole open and Fig. 495 the round part of the reamer making contact. Fig. 496 demonstrates a hollow pusher pressing in the jewel hole, but for a flat-faced jewel a solid pusher answers equally well. If the jewel has a rounded face the hollow pusher is essential, as the pressure is exerted on the outer diameter of the jewel and the risk of crushing is avoided. The pusher as illustrated in Fig. 496 will answer quite well, and there are also self-centring pushers of this description but these are not essential. The illustrations (Figs. 497-498) show the broaching or reaming of the hole in the tool.

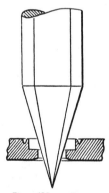

Fig. 493.   Reamer about to enter the setting.

When it is desired to replace a friction jewel with another, the procedure is similar to that already described. The endshake is taken care

of and the stop fixing screw tightened. The old
jewel is pushed out and, as it takes a pressure of
15 lbs. to do this, it is advisable to remove it in
the tool. Select a stake with a hole that will just
receive the old jewel, use a long pusher fitted into
the stock and press out the jewel with the lever.
By this means an upright steady pressure is
assured and, as good support is given to the
metal surrounding the jewel, there is no fear of
distortion. Next select a reamer that fits the hole
tightly and pass this through. If the reamer is at
all free select the next size larger and enlarge the
hole slightly to ensure that it is the *correct* size.
The secret of success is that the hole *must be
exactly* 1/100 *mm. smaller than the jewel.* The actual
fitting of the jewel is the same as before.

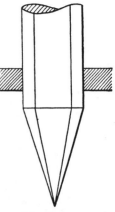

Fig. 494. Reamer cutting
old setting away.

Now to upright a hole. We shall consider a
balance jewel hole; the procedure is the same
for a train jewel except for the setting of the

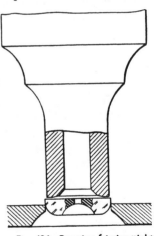

stop. For conveni-
ence it is better to
upright from the
lower jewel and to
fit a new top jewel.
First remove the
balance cock and
lay it, right way
up, on the stake
in the tool ; adjust
the micrometer
screw so that the
pusher—this time
the special hollow
balance jewel
pusher (Fig. 489)
—just contacts the
upper face of the

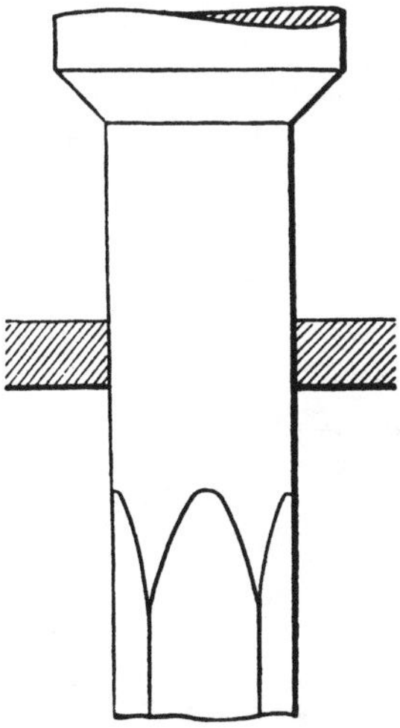

Fig. 495. Round part of
reamer in full contact.

Fig. 496. Pressing friction-tight
jewel into position.

jewel. The endshake of the balance is determined by the end-stone
and as the end-stone almost touches the jewel hole from the top we take
our measurement from there. Remove the old jewel, screw the cock on
to the bottom plate, and remove the lower balance end-stone. Fit the
attachment illustrated in Fig. 499 into the tool and arrange the plate
in such a position between the dogs that the pump centre fits into the
lower balance jewel hole, and then make the dogs secure. Select a
reamer a little smaller than the hole in the cock and fit this up in the
stock, lower into the hole and see if it is possible to start cutting.

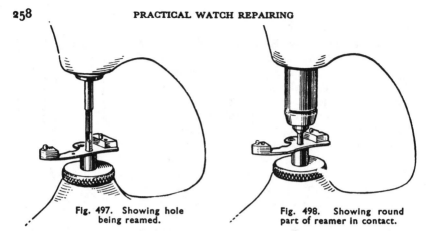

Fig. 497. Showing hole being reamed.

Fig. 498. Showing round part of reamer in contact.

As the top hole is not upright or in alignment with the lower hole cutting may start on one side of the hole. Continue in this manner, changing the reamer for the next size larger, until a full cut is made, at which point the hole must be upright. Remove the plate from the tool and fit up in place of the dog attachment a flat stake with a hole in it, unscrew the balance cock from the bottom plate and pass the same reamer through the hole until the round part makes full contact. It was not possible to do this when the cock was screwed to the plate, because

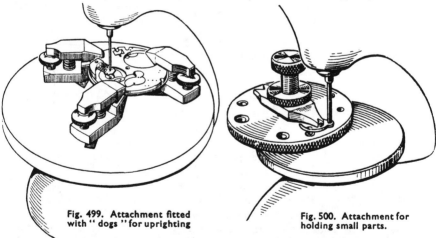

Fig. 499. Attachment fitted with "dogs" for uprighting

Fig. 500. Attachment for holding small parts.

there was not sufficient depth. Chamfer both sides as before and press the new hole in from the outside, that is from the opposite way in which the train hole was fitted. In this manner the correct endshake is assured.

The fitting of a balance jewel is covered by the instructions on uprighting a hole. To fit a jewel to a small piece, such as a pallet cock or an end-stone to an end-stone piece, use the attachment as illustrated in Fig. 500, which is self-explanatory. Exactly the same procedure is employed to fit an end-stone as for a jewel hole.

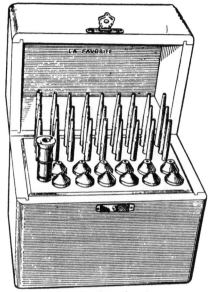

Fig. 501. Set of stakes and punches useful for many purposes.

By employing a set of stakes and punches, illustrated in Fig. 501, *La Favorite* can be used as a staking tool. When so used the lever handle is removed (*see* Fig. 502). This tool can also be used for such jobs as fitting hands (Fig. 503) and also for fitting unbreakable glasses (Fig. 504).

There are two methods of setting a rubbed-in jewel hole. One is by using the lathe, another is by using a hand tool. The former method will be dealt with first.

As repair work is being dealt with, it is assumed that the hole being fitted is a replacement.

First remove the old hole by pushing it out with a piece of pegwood ; push it out the way it went in as this will help to lift up the burr or setting which held it in position. Wax up the piece on the wax chuck in the lathe and make central. Open out the setting with a burnishing tool (as Fig. 505). Hold this tool first at an angle and then gradually bring it up so as to push back the metal previously rubbed over to hold the jewel secure, making the headstock revolve slowly while so doing. When the seat for the new jewel is free and square (Fig. 506) select a jewel hole the correct size for the pivot and also one that fits the setting comfortably. Smear a little oil over the surface of the jewel so that when it is placed in position it will hold there while the setting is being rubbed over again. To burnish the setting over use the same burnishing tool, but this

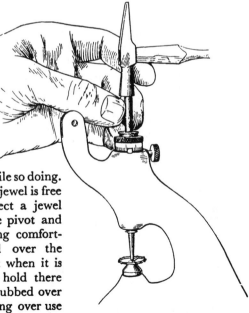

Fig. 502. Riveting a balance staff.

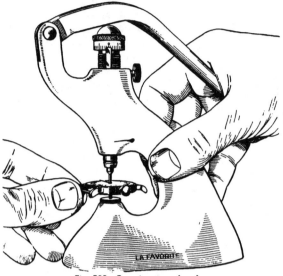

Fig. 503. Pressing on a hand.

time use it the other way round. The illustration (Fig. 507) shows the procedure. Some jewels are set by just rubbing the metal over the edge of the jewel ; a gulley has not been cut so that the metal immediately beside the jewel can easily be burnished over. In this case the tool (as Fig. 505) is used to open out the setting, but a rounded end burnisher is used to

rub the metal back again to hold the jewel secure (Fig. 509).

A set of tools made especially for the purpose (Fig. 511) is used when hand setting a jewel. The old hole is pushed out as before and the setting is opened by unscrewing the prong of the tool so that it is tight in the setting. To do this, hold the tool (of the correct size) upright in the setting and while there unscrew the prong until it binds and then revolve the tool between the fingers (Fig. 512). When the tool feels free open a little more and so on until the old setting is brought up and the seating is free

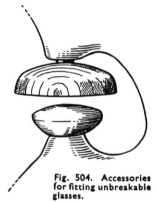

Fig. 504. Accessories for fitting unbreakable glasses.

Fig. 505. Opening a setting on the lathe.

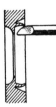

Fig. 506. Ready for the jewel.

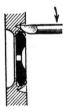

Fig. 507. Rubbing over the setting.

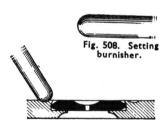

Fig. 508. Setting burnisher.

Fig. 509. Burnishing a setting.

Fig. 510. Stages in making the jewel-setting tool.

to receive the new jewel. To re-set the jewel use the complementary tool to close the metal in over the jaw. Adjust the prong so that the ends fit over the setting and twirl between finger and thumb applying some little downward pressure so that the metal is rubbed or burnished over (Fig. 513). A trace of oil on the acting surfaces of the tool sometimes facilitates the operation.

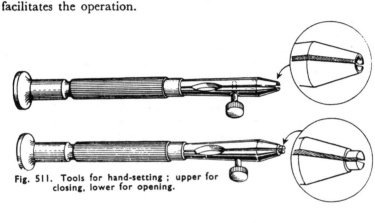

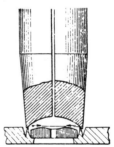

Fig. 511. Tools for hand-setting ; upper for closing, lower for opening.

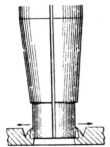

Fig. 512. Opening a setting with the hand tool.

Fig. 513. Closing a setting with the hand tool.

CHAPTER TWENTY

SHOCK-RESISTANT JEWELLING

THE SHOCK-RESISTANT watch cannot be looked upon as a novelty, in the sense that it is a passing phase. There is little doubt that it does serve a useful purpose and has come to stay. This sounds curious because Breguet (1747-1823) used a form of shock-resisting device, the "parachute," but after him little, if any, attention has been given to this safeguard.

During the last 20 years the idea has been revived and we now find a good percentage of the watches leaving Switzerland fitted with some form of shock-resisting device. The balance staff and the staff jewel holes are the most vulnerable parts of a watch and most liable to damage as the result of a blow or fall, so it is these parts which receive attention.

It is true that broken balance staffs are to be met with in shock-resistant watches, but there must have been many moments in the life of those same watches where the staff has been saved by the resilience of the balance bearings. Not only is it desirable to protect the staff pivots from breakage but also from damage. A watch not fitted with any shock-resistant device may, as the result of a slight jar or blow, receive damage to the balance pivots that will not actually stop the watch, nor even seriously disturb the timekeeping, but the wearer is conscious that the timekeeping is not just the same as it was. Not sufficient to complain of, perhaps, but not so consistent.

If you examine the staff pivots of that watch very carefully through a strong eye-glass you may find a slight facet on what should be the rounded end or, if the balance is spun in the calipers, one or both of the pivots slightly bent. There is little doubt that had the balance been fitted with some shock absorbent device this damage would not have occurred and the good reputation of the watch would have been sustained.

There are several systems of shock-resistant devices in use to-day and in the main the principle is the same. That is, the bearings of the balance are held in position by a spring and the fitting is so shaped that even if the watch receives a sideways jolt the bearings will give and then slip back to their original positions. If the concussion is beyond a certain limit, the balance staff is so designed that a shoulder near each pivot comes into contact with a solid part of the shock-resistant fitting and the pressure is taken off the staff pivots and transferred to a more substantial part.

The makers of the movement give certain dimensions to the manufacturers of the shock-resistant device, who then supply the component parts which consist of balance jewel holes set into specially designed rings or "chatons," end-stones, springs to hold the jewels into position, and the cups or blocks on to which the shoulders of the balance staffs butt or bank if the shock exceeds certain limits.

The precautions to be observed by the watch repairer are : To see

Fig. 514. The "Incabloc" is distinguished by the shape of the spring holding the top end-stone.

Fig. 515. The "Incabloc" components : A, the block, or seating ; B, end-stone ; C, holding spring ; D, jewel hole ; G, staff ; H, pivot.

Fig. 516. The complete "Incabloc" assembly, showing upper and bottom jewels. References as Fig. 515, and E, spring clip ; F, balance cock ; I, bottom Incabloc assembly.

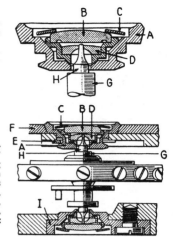

that all the parts of the shock-resistant device are scrupulously clean. The cup into which the jewel hole with its ring fits must be free from oil, dirt, burrs, etc., so that there is no fear of the jewel hole fitting sticking on its seating. When the components are assembled just touch the under-side of the jewel hole with the tweezers and exert a little pressure both laterally and longitudinally, and upon release of the pressure the jewel should spring back smartly to its original position. If it does not, dis-assemble and examine for burrs, roughness or dirt ; the jewel with its fittings must be free to act smoothly if the device is to be effective.

Oil is applied to the jewel holes only, and in the normal manner as explained in the chapter on cleaning and oiling. Apart from the main advantages of the shock-resisting system a great advantage is that it dispenses with the small jewel screws.

It is proposed to examine three of the more popular systems used in Switzerland : Incabloc, Parechoc and Shockresist.

" Incabloc " (Fig. 514) by the Universal Escapement Ltd., La Chaux-de-Fonds, Switzerland. Fig. 515 shows the component parts of this system and Fig. 516 the complete assembly. " Parechoc " (Figs. 517 and 518) by Parechoc S.A., Le Sentier, Switzerland. Figs. 519 and 520 show the component parts and Fig. 521 the assembly. Fig. 522 shows the shoulder of the balance staff banking on the end of the block when the watch receives an endwise shock and Fig. 523 when it receives a sideways shock.

Shockresist (Fig. 524) by Fabrique Ericmann—Schinz Neuville, Switzerland. This system relies upon the spring setting of the jewel hole (Fig. 525) and the spring cap to the end-stone (Fig. 526) for its resilience. When a certain degree of movement has been reached, due to a shock, the shoulder on the balance staff contacts the block as in the two previous systems.

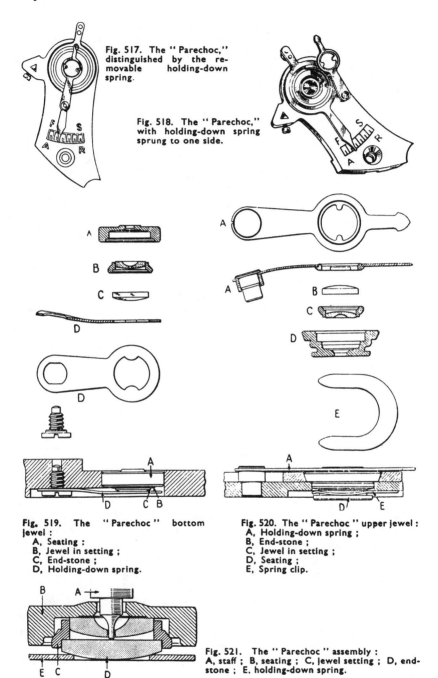

Fig. 517. The " Parechoc," distinguished by the removable holding-down spring.

Fig. 518. The " Parechoc," with holding-down spring sprung to one side.

Fig. 519. The " Parechoc " bottom jewel :
  A, Seating :
  B, Jewel in setting :
  C, End-stone :
  D, Holding-down spring.

Fig. 520. The " Parechoc " upper jewel :
  A, Holding-down spring ;
  B, End-stone ;
  C, Jewel in setting ;
  D, Seating ;
  E, Spring clip.

Fig. 521. The " Parechoc " assembly :
A, staff ; B, seating ; C, jewel setting ; D, endstone ; E. holding-down spring.

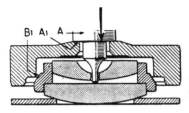

Fig. 522. An endwise shock brings the shoulder of the staff A, against a small boss A1, on the " Parechoc " seating.

Fig. 523. A sideways blow brings the staff A, against the side of the hole A2 in the seating. The jewel setting is displaced as shown at C1, C2, but the design of the chamfered edge and the holding-down spring makes it self centring.

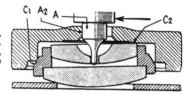

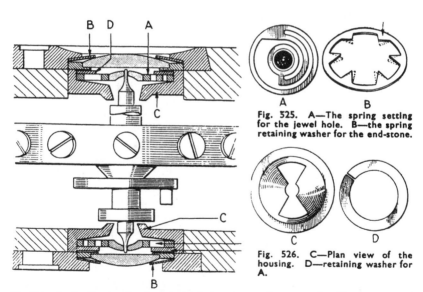

Fig. 525. A—The spring setting for the jewel hole. B—the spring retaining washer for the end-stone.

Fig. 526. C—Plan view of the housing. D—retaining washer for A.

Fig. 524. In the Shockresist the jewel-hole is set in a spring mount A. This is positioned vertically by washer D. The end-stone is retained by the spring washer B. These components are assembled in the housing C. While the jewels have a sideways movement and the end-stones are free to move vertically, it will be seen that movement in any direction will bring the special shoulders of the staff against C, protecting the pivots from shock.

CHAPTER TWENTY-ONE

MAGNETISM AND DEMAGNETISING

THE WATCH repairer is primarily interested in removing magnetism, *i.e.*, demagnetising. The modern watch, fitted with non-magnetic parts to the escapement, is not affected by magnetism, the steel parts, such as the mainspring, keyless mechanism and the pinions are, however, susceptible, but these parts when magnetised do not affect the rating of the watch. Even if these steel parts were considerably magnetised it is very doubtful if the rate would be affected. The mainspring will be the part most affected and the clinging or sticking due to magnetism will be small when compared with the strength of the pull of the spring and it is doubtful whether the clinging is more than that due to thickened oil.

The rate of a watch fitted with a steel balance spring, steel roller and lever is affected when magnetised, and the balance spring is the most vulnerable part. A slightly magnetised balance spring can be a troublesome fault to elucidate ; the watch, when in wear and subjected to external vibration, may suddenly gain a few seconds due to the coils of the balance spring occasionally sticking together. When the balance spring is more or less badly magnetised, the coils stick together permanently (until demagnetised) and the watch gains considerably. The lightly magnetised balance spring is sometimes a difficult matter to detect. It may not affect the lightest compass and is therefore not readily observable. To test for magnetism the very small light compass, the type which is almost a toy, is the best, the needle of this type of compass is very light and responds better to small lightly magnetised parts than the more robust and scientific instrument type of compass needle.

Every watch you handle, except the non-magnetic, should be tested for magnetism. Make it a habit, even if you have the watch for alteration of the index only, to test with the compass first, as magnetism may be the cause of the trouble and nothing to do with regulation at all.

Wind a piece of brass wire round the body of the compass and leave a short end sticking up as this forms a convenient means of placing the compass where wanted. Place the compass on top of the balance cock directly over the top balance end-stone (Fig. 527), wind the watch so that the balance vibrates, and observe the needle. If the watch is magnetised the needle also will vibrate backwards and forwards and sometimes it will make

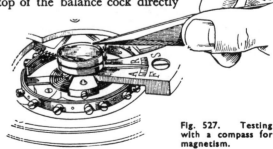

Fig. 527. Testing with a compass for magnetism.

a complete revolution and even spin round at some speed. If the needle remains stationary it does not always indicate that the movement is free from magnetism, the needle may have stuck. Give the compass a light tap with the tweezers, and if there is still no response, twist the movement slowly round, keeping it horizontal. If the movement is free from magnetism the needle will remain stationary and the pointed end will continue to point in the same direction, that is, to the magnetic north. Should the needle move round with the watch it does not, even then, necessarily indicate that magnetism is present. In these circumstances the needle may suddenly swing round and point to the north ; if it does not, lift the compass up off the balance cock and replace. Should the needle still have the appearance of sticking it may be that the keyless work and mainspring are magnetised and are forming the attraction, so much so that any slight magnetism in the escapement is not strong enough to influence the needle.

Place the compass flat on the bench and hold the edge of the watch, near the keyless work, to the needle and observe if there is any movement. Magnetism here will repel or attract the ends of the needle. If the needle

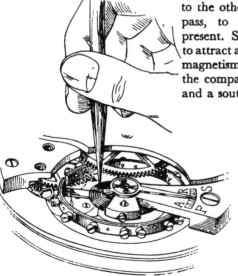

is only attracted and it is not possible, by presenting the edge of the movement to the other end or point of the compass, to repel it, no magnetism is present. Should it be possible, however, to attract and repel the compass needle, magnetism is present. The needle of the compass is a magnet with a north and a south pole, and a ferrous metal which is not magnetised will attract the needle.

The harder the metal the more difficult it is to induce magnetism in it, *and it is more difficult to remove ;* soft iron, on the other hand, does not retain magnetism. After demagnetising try with the compass on the balance cock again as magnetism is not always removed at the first attempt. Another test to make quite sure that the

Fig. 528. Pressing coils of balance spring together to test for magnetism.

balance spring—the most important part—is quite free, is gently to press the coils together with a pointed piece of pegwood (Fig. 528) and if there is no trace of sticking it can safely be assumed that magnetism is not present. Should, however, the coils have a tendency to stick together, then either the spring is magnetised or oil is present, and to make sure, first clean the spring in benzine and then again press the coils together.

Some watches are very reluctant to relinquish their magnetism, especially in the balance spring, and the best way to deal with that is to remove the spring from the balance and wrap it in a screw of tissue paper (Fig. 529) and demagnetise. Another method is to smear a little vaseline on to a piece of card, such as a visiting card, and on to this stick the balance spring and then pass it into the demagnetising coil.

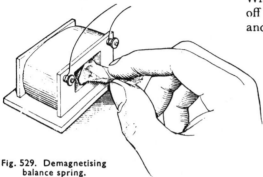

When demagnetised, clean off in benzine. If the balance spring is placed in the machine with no protection, there is a very real risk of the spring becoming tied in knots because, to demagnetise, the subject must first be magnetised and the sudden movement caused by the magnetism overcomes the resistance of the spring and the coils are thrown into confusion.

Fig. 529. Demagnetising balance spring.

In general there are two kinds of demagnetising machines, one using A.C. (alternating current) and the other D.C. (direct current). The active part of the machine, as far as the watchmaker is concerned, is the coil, and it is into this coil the article to be demagnetised is placed. The procedure is to place the article inside the coil and hold it there so that it does not touch the sides. Switch the current on and then slowly draw the article out and away from the coil and, when at arm's length, switch off the current (see Fig. 530). Test with the compass, and if the article is not free from magnetism, the operation should be repeated. Sometimes a more effective method is to draw the article smartly out of the coil, but generally the slow movement is the more satisfactory. Another hint is to hold the article in the coil for a moment or two with the current on (you will be able to feel the effects of magnetism, the article vibrating slightly) and then slowly withdraw it. The following is a description of suitable A.C. and D.C. machines for which I am indebted to Hillyard T. Stott, A.M.Inst.R.E., who is well qualified to speak on such matters.

1. *Alternating-magnetic-field from Alternating-current Mains.*

We need a coil, and can most conveniently energise it from the mains by means of a transformer, at low voltage. A " bell-ringing " transformer can be used, for the power with which we are concerned is only small. A transformer with a 4-, 5-, or 6-volt secondary could also be obtained from a wireless receiver ; it need not even be removed from the receiver, but wires could be brought out from a set

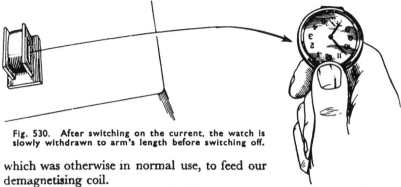

Fig. 530. After switching on the current, the watch is slowly withdrawn to arm's length before switching off.

which was otherwise in normal use, to feed our demagnetising coil.

Since the field is strongest inside the coil, we provide space there to take the parts with which we wish to deal. The writer has frequently used an old 100-turn plug-in tuning-coil from an old-fashioned type of wireless set, to produce the field required. But for those who wish to make up proper and permanent equipment, Fig. 531 gives constructional details of a practical and inexpensive coil for 4-6 volts. The " bobbin " or former is made from thin wood—plywood scraps are very suitable— and is either glued together, or secured with brass pins. It will be seen from the drawing that it uses two cheeks or plates each 2 in. by 4 in., and two pieces each $2\frac{1}{4}$ in. by $1\frac{1}{8}$ in.

It is wound with double-cotton-covered copper wire, No. 24 s.w.g., which is 0·02 in. dia. About 140 yds. are required, and this has a weight of 0·7 pound. In practice, $\frac{3}{4}$ lb. is wound on to the bobbin and the resistance comes out at a shade over 9Ω so that it passes about 0·5 amp. at 4·5 volts ; and about 0·675 amp. at 6 volts. Any transformer which can provide 1 amp. even for short periods will suffice. The bobbin may be fed at 8 or 12 volts for a minute or so at a time, which will give an even stronger field, and it will be seen, later, that a matter of a minute or so at a time is all that is needed. The cost of the energy used is too small to be worth working out. Wind on the wire evenly, leaving 2 in. sticking out through the commencing hole. About 60 turns will go to the layer, and the total number of layers is less than ten. Keep the turns tight. At the end of the wind, bring it out through the second small hole. If desired, the whole bobbin and winding may be impregnated with shellac-varnish (shell-lac dissolved in methylated spirit to the consistency of milk), but in

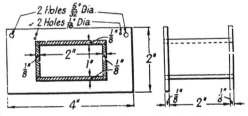

Fig. 531. The bobbin for a demagnetising coil ; plywood or thin oak is very suitable material. All dimensions in inches. Glue together, or assemble with brass pins. A suitable base-plate of similar material may be fitted, after winding.

any case it is desirable to varnish the bobbin and to cover the winding with a layer of tape or silk, and varnish over this. Cellulose enamel or lacquer is also quite suitable.

Fit two 4 B.A. terminals, or nuts and bolts to act as terminators, and clean and clamp the ends of the winding firmly. A base plate of wood, about 5 in. by 3¼ in., may be fitted, which will enable the coil to be screwed down in a permanent position.

The coil will run quite cool, only heating up a little if run for long periods together, and is connected up as shown in Fig. 532. It is assumed that the main-socket switch will be used, or a switch can be fitted in one of the mains connection-leads. For the latter, pieces of lighting-flex are quite suitable.

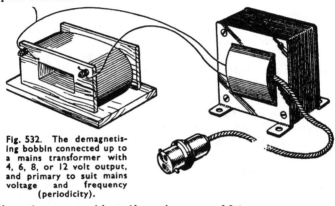

Fig. 532. The demagnetis-ing bobbin connected up to a mains transformer with 4, 6, 8, or 12 volt output, and primary to suit mains voltage and frequency (periodicity).

2. *Alternating-current without Alternating-current Mains.*

In the absence of A.C. mains, if we have means of generating current, a small A.C. generator will serve. If it provides about 1 amp. at a voltage between 4 and 12 volts the bobbin can be fed direct. But with a generator of higher output voltage, a suitable transformer must be used.

If there are no means of generating current, or only of direct current—and this at low voltage—or battery current is available, alternating-current can be produced by means of a vibrator. This will need a special transformer with a double primary-winding and a suitable output-secondary. Fig. 533 shows the connections. Radio manufacturers, or suppliers of vibrators, would no doubt furnish the special transformer needed. It may even be possible to get, for high-voltage direct-current mains, high-voltage vibrators, and the output from these is then treated, for this work, as A.C. mains in Fig. 532.

3. *No Electricity of any kind available.*

An alternating magnetic field is still required, so it must be produced by means of a rapidly rotating magnet. A bar-magnet is easiest to deal with, but a horse-shoe magnet may give a slightly stronger field, weight for weight. The simplest arrangement is made by converting a

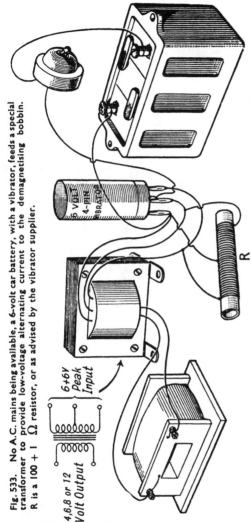

Fig. 533. No A.C. mains being available, a 6-volt car battery, with a vibrator, feeds a special transformer to provide low-voltage alternating current to the demagnetising bobbin. R is a 100 + 1 Ω resistor, or as advised by the vibrator supplier.

6+6V Peak Input

4,6,8 or 12 Volt Output

small grinder, removing the stone, and fitting a clamp to the spindle, using brass or wooden parts, as shown, and brass nuts and bolts or screws. Figs. 534 and 535 show both methods, and typical details. But much depends upon what magnets are available ; one from an old magneto would be very suitable. The fittings must be firm and strong, and poising is essential.

Speeds of at least 1,500 r.p.m. of the magnet are required to give a 25 c/s A.C. field (3–5 turns of the handle per second, with average gearing), and centrifugal forces would rapidly cause flimsy constructions to fail—and possibly cause damage to persons or property ! Treadle-drive would be very convenient in some cases.

A word of caution is necessary about the watchmaker's bench and permanent magnets. Any permanent magnet which may be lying about may easily cause the very trouble which has to be cured, and the rotating - magnet demagnetiser is no exception when it is stationary. So set it up, and keep it, at some distance from the main work-area. Five or six feet should be considered a minimum. Large magnetic compasses, and magnetised tools, are all to be considered, and tools, consequently, should be kept free from all traces of self-magnetism. With the system described, this is easy.

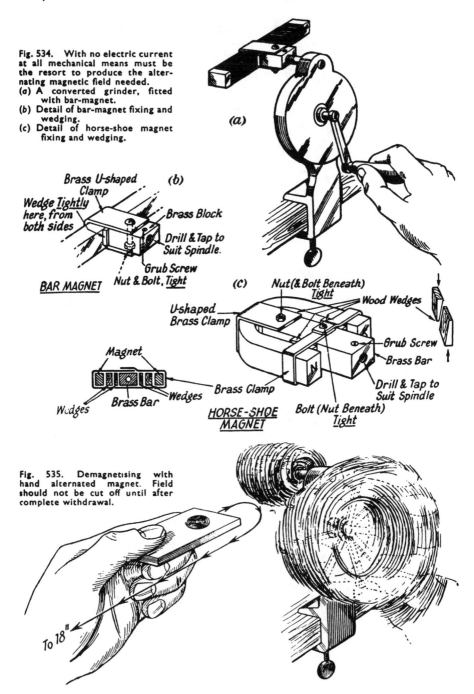

Fig. 534. With no electric current at all mechanical means must be the resort to produce the alternating magnetic field needed.
(a) A converted grinder, fitted with bar-magnet.
(b) Detail of bar-magnet fixing and wedging.
(c) Detail of horse-shoe magnet fixing and wedging.

(a)

(b)

Brass U-shaped Clamp

Wedge Tightly here, from both sides

Brass Block

Drill & Tap to Suit Spindle.

Grub Screw Nut & Bolt, Tight

BAR MAGNET

(c) Nut (& Bolt Beneath) Tight

Wood Wedges

U-shaped Brass Clamp

Grub Screw

Brass Bar

Magnet

Wedges

Wedges

Brass Bar

Brass Clamp

Drill & Tap to Suit Spindle

HORSE-SHOE MAGNET

Bolt (Nut Beneath) Tight

Fig. 535. Demagnetising with hand alternated magnet. Field should not be cut off until after complete withdrawal.

To 18"

CHAPTER TWENTY-TWO

WATER-RESISTANT CASES

THE PURPOSE of this chapter is not to discuss the many methods introduced from time to time, of keeping moisture out of a watch case, although
the main types are reviewed later, but rather to consider the general
principle of the water-resistant watch case and how to make the miscalled
water-*proof* case more efficient.

Many ingenious designs of watch case introduced over the past 20
years have claimed to protect the movement from damage by immersion
in water, while what is mainly required is protection from the ingress
of moisture generally present in a humid atmosphere. The different
construction of a case necessitated by it being resistant to normal
humidity and resistant to the ingress of water under definite immersion
at a stated depth or pressure is vast indeed, and it will be as well to study
the methods of testing in order to focus attention on the requirements of a
thoroughly water-*proof* watch.

It is advisable to avoid as far as possible the use of the word water-
proof in connection with watch cases. There can hardly be degrees of
proofing in the same way as there can be degrees of resistance ; therefore,
it is better to follow the lead given by the trade in America in condemning
the indiscriminate use of the word water-*proof*. From experience I find
there are very few watch cases which may be called water-*proof*, and the
term water-resistant should be used in preference in order to avoid giving
a guarantee which may become misleading. To deter users of watches
which, even though they may possess a high power of resistance to the
ingress of water in conditions in which watches obviously should not be
used, wearers should be schooled into regarding the matter in its proper
light, and to realise that ordinary water-resistant cases have been invented
and designed to protect the movement from the entry of moisture in
general wear or in cases of accidental immersion ; never for deliberate
soaking which is certain to damage the movement in time, unless excep-
tional measures are taken in the construction and assembly of the case.
An absolute water-proof case can be made, but for all ordinary purposes
this is not necessary. The water resistance of the case can be tested in
two ways, the first being pressure by submergence at various depths and
the second by resistance to immersion under conditions of a vacuum.

The submergence test is usually carried out both in shallow and deep
water. Shallow is regarded as up to a depth of three feet and deep water
between three feet and thirty feet, but it is usual to test the watch at a
depth of 10 feet and it is agreed that if a case passes that test it will stand
up to both the shallow and the deep tests. In certain respects the shallow
water test is more searching than the deep water test, the reason being
that with some systems of glass fitting the additional pressure of the deep
test improves its sealing properties, and it has been found that a case

which passes the deep test may not always pass the shallow or lighter pressure test. Testing in the pressure chamber (Fig. 536) is more natural because when the case is submerged in water it is subjected to pressure only. It is agreed that the ten feet depth of water is the best average, being equal to a pressure of 4·3 lbs. per square inch.

In testing, the case is screwed up tightly, the winding button replaced and the case is suspended in the testing machine in the manner illustrated. The knob at the base of the machine is screwed up increasing the water pressure to equal the depth decided for the test ; in the case of ten feet the dial should indicate 4·3 lbs. pressure. Usually the case is left in the testing chamber for a period of 60 minutes. If it stands the pressure for one hour it will usually stand up to 12 hours or 24 hours. It is not sufficient merely to dip the case in water and withdraw it immediately, even if it is lowered to the required depth ; many ordinary snap - back - and - bezel cases with no pretensions to water resistance will stand up to that. When the testing time is completed, unscrew the knob to relieve the pressure and remove the case. The knob at the top is for screwing down the cap of the instrument. Dry the outside of the case well to

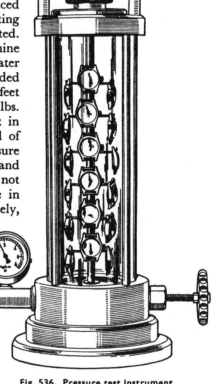

Fig. 536. Pressure test instrument.
(Makers : *La Centrale*).

make sure no water is present, then open the case and examine the interior for traces of moisture.

For the vacuum test the case is prepared and immersed in the same manner as in the pressure chamber, see Fig. 537. In this test, however, the pump is operated to reduce the air pressure in the space between the surface of the water and the top of the chamber and the pumping is continued until the dial indicates the vacuum required for the test. Usually the dials are graduated to indicate by 1 inch of mercury. 4·3 lbs. pressure equals 8·776 inches fall of mercury ; 8·776 inches is equal to ten feet submergence in water. Refer to table for other data.

WATER PRESSURE TABLE

Depth of Water	Lbs. per sq. inch	Inches of Mercury	Millimetres of Mercury
1 foot	·43	·8776	22·29
2 feet	·86	1·7552	44·58
3 ,,	1·29	2·6328	66·87
4 ,,	1·72	3·5104	89·16
5 ,,	2·15	4·3880	111·45
6 ,,	2·58	5·2656	133·74
7 ,,	3·01	6·1432	156·03
8 ,,	3·44	7·0208	178·32
9 ,,	3·87	7·8984	200·61
10 ,,	4·30	8·7760	222·90
11 ,,	4·73	9·6536	245·19
12 ,,	5·16	10·5312	267·48
13 ,,	5·59	11·4088	289·77
14 ,,	6·02	12·2864	312·06
15 ,,	6·45	13·1640	334·35
16 ,,	6·88	14·0416	356·64
17 ,,	7·31	14·9192	378·93
18 ,,	7·74	15·7968	401·22
19 ,,	8·17	16·6744	423·51
20 ,,	8·60	17·5520	445·80
21 ,,	9·03	18·4296	468·09
22 ,,	9·46	19·3072	470·38
23 ,,	9·89	20·1848	512·67
24 ,,	10·32	21·0624	534·96
25 ,,	10·75	21·9400	557·25
26 ,,	11·18	22·8176	579·54
27 ,,	11·61	23·6952	601·83
28 ,,	12·04	24·2528	624·12
29 ,,	12·47	25·4504	646·41
30 ,.	12·90	26·3280	668·70

Directly the dial indicates the required vacuum, observe the watch case closely. If it leaks, bubbles will appear at the faulty parts of the case and eventually rise. If a bubble appears but does not grow bigger and eventually leave the case and rise, the case does not leak at that point. What happens in this test is that the air inside the watch case is at the same pressure as the air outside the chamber and as the pressure inside the chamber is relieved by the partial vacuum, air inside the case tries to rush out. This test is very speedy; if no bubbles appear in three or four minutes the case can be regarded as resistant to water in the conditions of the test.

The practical difference in the two methods is that if the watch is tested with the movement complete, it is necessary with the pressure test to unscrew the case to ascertain if water has penetrated. As it has been found from experience gained by testing many thousands of cases that it is essential for the sealing ring (washer) to be changed for a new one every time the case is unscrewed, it looks as if there can never be any certainty that the case is water-proof. It may appear extravagant to fit a new sealing ring every time the case is opened, but the construction of cases of this type calls for handling in this manner.

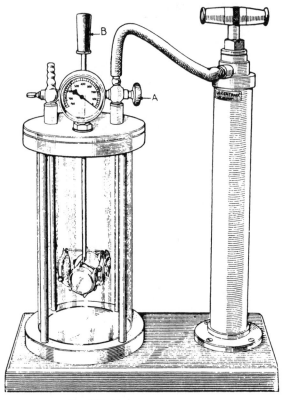

Fig. 537. Vacuum test instrument.
A : Valve to release the vacuum.
B : Handle for lowering watches
into tank. (Makers : *La Centrale*.)

The difficulty can be overcome by employing the vacuum test, and here the vacuum chamber proves its worth. If the complete watch is tested in the vacuum chamber and no bubbles appear, the case is proof. Should bubbles form, remove the watch at once and well dry the case. Water will not have entered, but the case should have attention and be tested again. If the watch were allowed to stay in the water until the bubbles stopped forming, water will immediately penetrate at the points where the bubbles formed.

From the foregoing the use of the pressure chamber at all might be questioned. Generally, if the case passes the vacuum test it will pass the pressure test, but there are odd instances when this is not so. The vacuum chamber sets up a different set of conditions, the case is trying to explode, as it were, and the effect of the pressure chamber is to force water into the case.

These tests have been discussed at some length in order to demonstrate the difficulty of issuing a guarantee that a so-called water-resistant case really keeps out water in all conditions, particularly if the watch is only in for repair. Water enters the case via the winding shaft and pendant sleeve, at the joint between the glass and the bezel, and at the joining of the back.

There are three popular types of button and pendant. The screw button and pendant, originally invented by A. L. Dennison as long ago as 1871, is used in various forms to-day and it is important that the wearer is instructed in the method of screwing down the button after winding or hand setting, and to ensure that the button is screwed up as tightly as possible. Should the button overturn through wear on the screw thread, the only remedy is to return

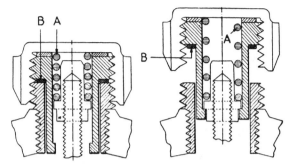

Fig. 538. The Rolex screw button.
Left, closed. *Right,* Open ready to wind or set hands.
A : Helical spring.   B : Sealing washer.

the case to the maker to have a new pendant and button fitted. (Fig. 538.)

Another popular style is a pendant containing a gland or sleeve of a plastic substance. In this system a tube of a clinging type of plastic material is set into the pendant, the plastic known as Neoprene answers well for this purpose. The pipe of the winding button makes contact with the gland and so excludes water (Fig. 539). The friction between winding button and gland is inclined to make the winding of the mainspring seem stiff; but it is not advisable to alter this condition, otherwise the efficiency of the seal will be impaired. If, however, it is essential to ease the pipe of the winding button, on no account attempt to secure clearance by opening the hole in the plastic gland but reduce the button pipe or shank. The winding can sometimes be eased by applying a little lanoline or vaseline to the pipe of the button.

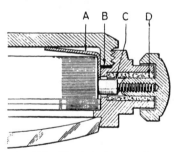

Fig. 539. Gland set into pendant.
A : Spring ring round movement to hold it in position.
B : Plastic on soft metal sealing washer.
C : Winding shaft.
D : Gland set into pendant.

The precaution for the wearer to take with this system is to reverse the winding button a little after winding, the reason being that the button can cling so much that the recoil of the click will not operate. When the mainspring is wound tightly and allowed to remain in this state it will pull on the barrel hook and cause the balance to knock the banking, making the watch go fast.

The third system fits the plastic sleeve in the button; a plastic ring is fitted on the inside of the winding button which makes contact with the outside surface of the pendant. (Fig. 540.)

Most modern cases are fitted with this type of button, the winding being easier than in the case of the plastic gland type described above.

The majority of glasses fitted to water-resistant cases are of unbreakable plastic material, many of which are liable to shrink in course of time. The fitting of the snap-in type depends upon the amount of outward pressure exerted by the glass in the groove of the bezel. (Fig. 540.) The danger of this method of fitting is that as the glass shrinks it becomes loose and obviously is no longer a water seal. A film of rubber solution run round the groove in the bezel before the glass is inserted may lengthen the life of the seal. It is always advisable to fit a new glass to all cases of this type when the watch is under repair.

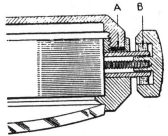

Fig. 540. Gland set into button.
A : Plastic or soft metal sealing washer.
B : Gland set into button.

A very successful system of glass fitting is illustrated in Fig. 542. The glass is held in position by a screw ring which forces the glass against a compressible plastic ring which is also in contact with the case. The advantage of this system is that if the glass shrinks the flange is still in contact with the plastic ring and so excludes the water.

There are many variations of the system of fitting a glass by means of a retaining ring. The illustration (Fig. 541) shows one such fitting ; it is effective and does not suffer if the glass shrinks. It is also suitable for shaped glasses and the press-in type of case as distinct from the screw back.

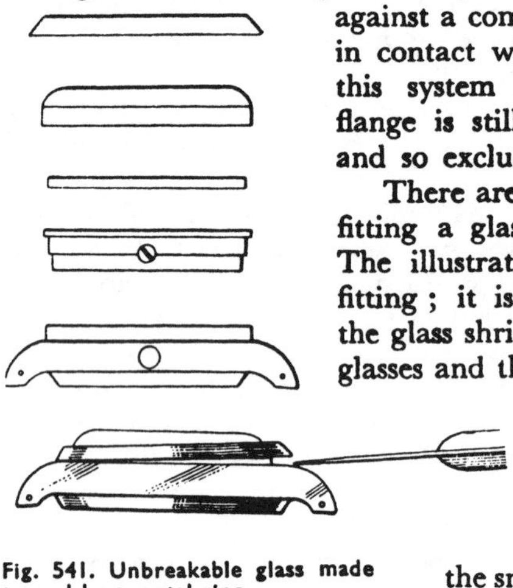

In the main there are three systems of dealing with the back of the case, the screw-on back, the back held on by screws, and the snap-on back. Fig. 542 shows a case where the back is a thin large screw which seats on a soft metal or plastic ring to provide a seal. As has been explained above, this ring should not be used twice if a perfect seal is to be expected. When repairing a watch it may not always be possible to fit a new ring. There are literally hundreds of different

Fig. 541. Unbreakable glass made to seal by a metal ring.

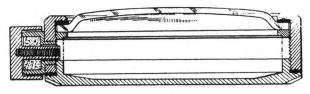

Fig. 542. A specially shaped unbreakable glass to exclude water.

sizes of cases and it would be impossible to keep a stock to suit all. Therefore, the next best thing is to smear the edge of the back that seats on the sealing ring with a little vaseline and beeswax (two parts vaseline, one part beeswax melted together). The unfortunate position

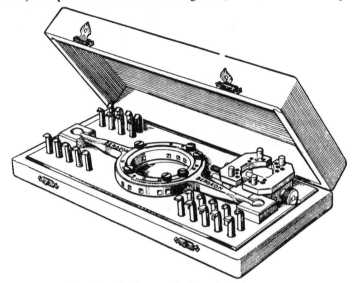

Fig. 543. The Bergeon, Swiss, universal case opener.

created by lack of standardisation and uniformity in the styles of cases, which call for many different sizes and designs of keys or spanners to unscrew them, can be overcome by using a tool such as is illustrated in

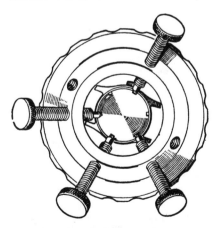

Fig. 544. The De Vries, American, universal case opener.

Fig. 545. Press-in type of water resistant case.

Fig. 543. It is universal and opens the great majority of cases. Illustration (Fig. 544) shows another tool of American make which appears to be very efficient in this direction.

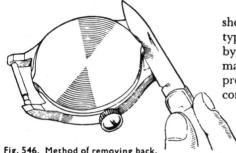

Fig. 546. Method of removing back.

The illustration (Fig. 545) shows one of many of the press-in types of case. They are opened by holding the case in such a manner that the two thumbs can press on the glass. Exert some considerable pressure and the case will come apart. Hold close to the bench so that the watch has not far to fall. Care must be exercised when opening the snap-on type of case with a knife. If the blade is inserted too deeply there is a risk of damaging the sealing ring. Most of these cases are provided with a lip to the back and if the blade of the knife is placed under the lip only and not inserted into the case and the case is levered apart, using the shoulder of the strap lug as a fulcrum, no damage can be done to the ring (Fig. 546).

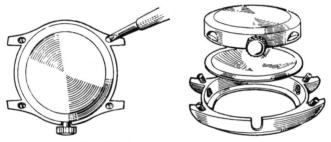

Fig. 547. Case held together by screws.

There are many variations of the device in which the back is held on by screws. Fig. 547 shows one of the most popular. There are no special precautions to be taken other than general care ; if the edges are bruised or nicked the back may leak at that point.

In some water-resistant cases it is necessary to detach the button before it is possible to remove the movement. This system consists of a button and stem which is snapped on to the shaft (Fig. 548) and, before attempting to remove the movement from the case, it is first necessary to remove the button. To do this place a watch bag (chamois leather or linen) *over* the button and, with the ordinary cutting nippers, grip between

Fig. 548. Snap-on button and stem.

the button and case (Fig. 549), and carefully apply pressure as if about to cut off the pendant. The button will come away quite easily and safely, damaging neither the case nor the button. If the button projects far from the case and it is not possible to lever the button off with a single

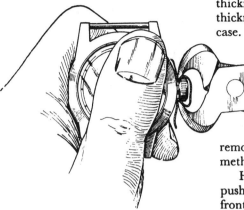

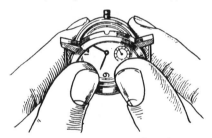

Fig. 549. Removing snap-on button and stem. Note padding between case and nippers.

Fig. 550. Removing case from frame.

Fig. 551. Removing distance ring which allows movement to drop out of case.

thickness of fabric, double the thickness between the button and case. There is on the market another system where the button is just knocked on to the shaft direct, the shaft is in one piece ; you will find the removal of the button by this method equally effective.

Having removed the shaft, push the case through from the front, so that it is released from the frame holding it (Fig. 550). Then remove the unbreakable glass by levering it up with the blade of the bench knife ; lift the distance ring off the dial and the movement will drop out of the case (Fig. 551).

To re-assemble, reverse the procedure ; finally snapping the stem back on to the shaft. Make sure the tongue of the shaft coincides with the slot of the stem before applying pressure. The correct position will be indicated when the hands can be set by a turn of the button, as the shaft was left in the hands-set position after detaching the button.

The friction-tight button can be knocked on by a smart blow with the back of the watch brush ; crude, perhaps, but effective. Alternatively, if the button is inserted into the sleeve and turned until it is felt to engage, it can be pushed home by pressure against the edge of the bench. Test the junction by pulling out the button for handsetting.

Never guarantee a case water-*proof*. It should be water-*resistant*, to the extent of being splash-proof or safe for a momentary immersion, but above all things discourage the wearer from the belief that watches can be made *proof* at all times against soaking in water. They were never intended for this use and, however good, should never deliberately be subjected to it. After repair, whenever possible, fit new sealing rings to the case. Failing this, apply vaseline and beeswax, as advised above, to the seating. If the glass is of the ordinary sprung-in type fit a new one, first applying rubber solution to the bezel groove. With the plastic gland in the pendant apply lanoline or vaseline to ease the winding if necessary. Never open the plastic gland. Advise the wearer to reverse the button after winding. Make sure the back is screwed up tightly before you hand the watch over to the wearer, or if it is one of the press-on type, make sure it is pressed home as far as it will go. Advise the wearer at all times that his watch, water-proof or otherwise, is a precious precision instrument needing constant care if it is to give good service.

CHAPTER TWENTY-THREE

THE BULOVA ACCUTRON TUNING FORK WATCH

A. L. BREGUET first used a tuning fork as a controller of timekeeping in a clock in the 19th century. A means of using a tuning fork in a watch was invented by Max Hetzel, a Swiss electronics engineer, in 1950. It was developed in the USA by him as the chief physicist of the Bulova Watch Co. By 1959, mass production of the Accutron watch was started. The Accutron movement is made in America and at the Bulova factory in Bienne, Switzerland. It is also used in the Universal Unisonic watch.

In 1958, a licence was granted to Ebauches S.A., Switzerland, to manufacture the movement, so tuning fork watches are also being sold under various other brand names.

I am indebted to the Bulova Watch Co. for the information regarding servicing which follows.

THE MOVEMENT

The mechanism consists of 12 moving parts as compared with about 20 in the normal manually-wound watch.

As the gear train is following and not driven, there can be practically no wear. Oil is necessary at the bearings, but the condition of the oil does not influence the timekeeping. Furthermore, as the battery which drives the watch runs down, it does not adversely influence the vibrations of the fork. A time does come, however, when the watch will stop because of lack of power.

There are two sections of operation in the Accutron movement. The mechanical components consisting of (1) the indexing or motive mechanism and the gear train: and (2) the electronic and electromagnetic components, comprising the battery, electronic circuit, and tuning fork.

The motive mechanism, which transmits the motion of the tuning fork to the gear train, forms a most important part of the mechanical part of the movement. It consists of parts so small that their functioning cannot be checked with an eyeglass. A microscope is essential for this purpose. If the microscopic examination calls for adjustment, this can be accomplished with the aid of an eyeglass.

A microscope of reasonable quality is satisfactory, provided it meets the following specification: 20-30 diameters magnification; fairly wide field; at least 2 inches working distance. (The typical biological or metallurgical microscopes are not suitable. They have short working distances and give inverted images.)

TOOLS REQUIRED

Special tools and equipment can be acquired from the Bulova Watch Co., London, and in addition to the microscope the kit consists of:—

1. Voltmeter, Fig. 552
2. Movement holder, Fig. 553
3. Locking-ring spanner.
4. Finger-post wrench.

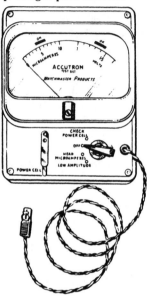

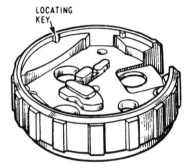

Fig. 552.   **Fig. 553.**

The voltmeter set provides

1. A "recess" marked "Power Cell" to hold the battery during testing.

2. A meter reading either volts or microamperes, indicating the correct value by a section marked "OK".

3. A four-position master rotary switch for selecting the various test conditions as—

Position 1—Check battery

    "   2—Off

    "   3—Read microamperes

    "   4—Low amplitude. (In this position the meter supplies the reduced voltage to the movement during the indexing or motive mechanism adjustment.)

4. A two-wire lead with a spring clip for attachment to the movement, correctly positioned in the movement holder.

5. A black screw, directly below the centre of the meter scale, for returning the meter hand to zero.

TO REMOVE MOVEMENT FROM
CASE

1. Use special spanner.
2. Remove locking ring.
3. Lift hand setting handle to aid removing back.
4. Lift back straight up and away from case.
5. If gasket is pulled up in removing the back, remove the gasket. If however it remains in the case, it is not necessary to remove it for regulation purpose.
6. The movement can now be removed from its case. Regulation can be accomplished without removing the movement or the battery from the case. See Fig. 554.

Special points to observe

When removing the hands, exercise care not to turn centre-seconds pinion forward or force it backward, since this will damage the motive mechanism.

The post, spring and jewel assemblies on the tuning fork (the motive pallet spring), and on the pawl adjusting bridge (the pawl pallet spring) are very delicate. Handling of these assemblies should be kept to a minimum, and should be done, when necessary, with the greatest care. If either spring is damaged or either jewel is separated from its spring, the entire assembly must be replaced by a new one. The jewels cannot be recemented or the springs replaced, except in the factory. An Accutron movement must

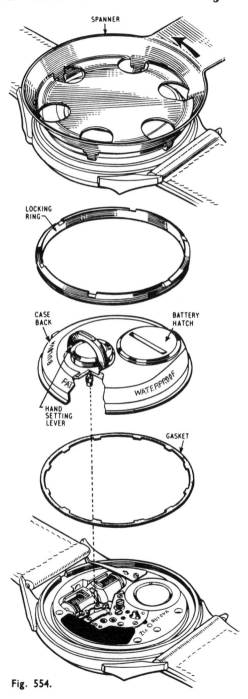

Fig. 554.

PROBLEM	POSSIBLE CAUSES (in order of probability)	DIAGNOSIS PROCEDURE	REMEDIAL ACTION
Gaining or losing a few seconds per day	Abnormal wearing habits or Improper regulation		Regulate, see page 288
Stopped (No hum)	1. Exhausted battery	Check battery voltage. If low or no voltage, battery is exhausted	Replace battery
	2. Faulty electronic circuit	If voltage is normal, check current. If no current, electronic circuit is faulty	Replace complete coil assembly
	3. Mechanical blockage of tuning fork	If current is high, check if tuning fork is blocked	Find blockage and remove it
	4. Faulty electronic circuit	If no blockage of tuning fork, electronic circuit is faulty	Replace complete coil assembly
Stopped (Sweep second hand does not turn but fork hums)	1. Exhausted battery	Check battery voltage. If voltage is low, battery is exhausted	Replace battery
	2. Motive mechanism maladjustment	If voltage normal, open case, remove movement, expose motive mechanism, and examine under microscope. Check ratchet jewel engagement.	Readjust indexing mechanism if necessary
	3. Mechanical blockage of train	If jewels appear normal, check train freedom. Train may be blocked.	Find mechanical blockage and remove it.

Symptom	Probable cause	Test	Remedy
	4. Dirt on index wheel	If train is free, and ratchet jewel engagement is correct, tap movement lightly with pencil to increase fork amplitude, while observing closely with eyeglass. If ratchet wheel rotates once and then stops again, this is evidence of dirt in ratchet wheel teeth.	Clean entire movement as described.
	5. Damaged teeth on index wheel	If symptoms persist after cleaning, ratchet wheel has been damaged.	Change ratchet wheel
Gaining or losing excessively	1. Tuning fork not free	Open case, remove movement and check current. If current too high, examine for obvious foreign material interfering with free vibrations of tuning fork.	If foreign matter is observed, remove same and recheck to see that current is normal.
	2. Defective coil	If current too high and no evidence tuning fork is not free, expose motive mechanism, disengage pawl jewel and check current again. If current remains high, coil assembly is defective.	Replace complete coil assembly.
	3. Mechanical interference in train	If current drops within "OK" range or below in 2, above, cause is excessive train friction.	Find interference and remove it.
	4. Foreign material clinging to magnetic elements	If current is "OK" in 1, above, and rate is many seconds per day slow, check for loose screw or other matter clinging to a tuning fork magnet.	Find foreign matter and remove same.
	5. Motive mechanism maladjustment	If current is "OK" in 1, above, motive mechanism may be out of adjustment.	Check and readjust motive mechanism as necessary.
	6. Dirt in index wheel teeth	If current and motive mechanism adjustment have been found correct, there may be dirt in ratchet wheel teeth.	Clean entire movement.

not be demagnetized or exposed to any high strength magnetic field. Anything affecting the permanent magnets on the tuning fork will seriously affect the timekeeping of the watch.

If it is necessary to remove the tuning fork for purposes of cleaning, keep the fork away from anything made of steel e.g. tools, steel watch parts, etc.

The magnets on the tuning fork are extremely powerful and will have the tendency to attract small steel pieces. Also the fork can be attracted to large steel articles, either of which may damage the fork. The teeth of the ratchet or motive wheel and the jewel pallets are not oiled.

Do not bend the tines of the tuning fork. If the tines become misaligned, or the fork damaged in any way, the fork must be replaced with a new one.

Detecting faults

1. Gaining or losing a few seconds a day.
2. Gaining or losing an excessive amount, i.e. one or more minutes per week.
3. Stopped.

Unlike conventional watches, where regulation can be effected to correct fairly big errors, the tuning fork watch is so designed that normal wearing conditions will not affect the timekeeping more than a few seconds a day. If the error is more than one minute a week, the watch requires servicing, not regulation.

The method of diagnosis consists of proceeding whereby you progressively narrow down the section of possible malfunction. Having determined from your own examination or the owner's description whether the watch has stopped, how much it is gaining or losing and whether the hum of the tuning fork is audible, you are already on your way toward localizing the source of the trouble. If the hum is audible it can be concluded that the electronics circuit is operating and the fork is vibrating. If the battery voltage is correct, it indicates the fault is somewhere beyond the fork, maybe in the motive linkage or the gear train which connects the motive mechanism with the hands. If the hum is not audible it is ample indication that there is some malfunction in the battery, in the electronic circuit, or that the fork is mechanically blocked.

The procedure shown in the servicing table further narrows down the possible causes until the correct source of the trouble is located.

PROCEDURE FOR REGULATION

The tuning fork regulators are serrated to make them easier to rotate and to serve as a calibration. See Fig. 555. The serrations of each regulator form 7 divisions (4 projections and 3 indentations). Each of these divisions is equal to 2 seconds per day; in other words, rotating one of the regulators a distance equal to one division changes the rate of timekeeping by 2 seconds per day.

Regulation for as little as $\frac{1}{2}$ second per day can be made by rotating one of the regulators $\frac{1}{4}$ division. The amount of movement of a regulator can be gauged by reference to the dot on top of each cup fixed to the two tines of the tuning fork.

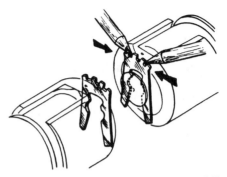

In order to allow greater latitude for regulation, either one or both of the regulators can be rotated in making a correction e.g. a correction of 4

Fig. 555.

seconds per day can be made either by rotating one regulator 2 divisions or by rotating each regulator 1 division.

Since there are 7 divisions on each regulator and as each division is equal to 2 seconds per day, it would be possible to make a correction of more than 28 seconds per day. Using a pointed piece of peg-wood, the regulators are moved towards the centre of the movement to make the watch gain, and, conversely they are moved towards the edge of the movement to make the watch lose.

To check electronic circuit

Place the movement, dial side down, in the movement holder with the battery recess adjacent to the notch in the side of the holder. Some models require the hands and dials to be removed. See page 294.

With the battery in the recess of the voltmeter test set, connect the spring clip at the end of the lead to the movement so that the centre finger is touching the contact in the centre of the battery recess. Fig. 556.

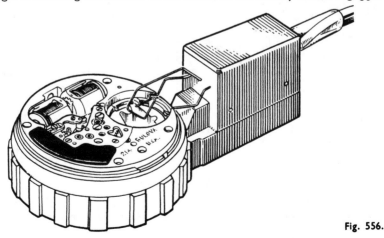

Fig. 556.

Turn the voltmeter to "Read microamperes" position. The battery is now connected to the movement through the test set and the meter will give a reading of currents on the left hand scale. (It may be necessary to tap the movement lightly to start the tuning fork vibrating.) The current reading should be in the "OK" position of the scale (4.5 to 7.0 microamperes). If it is, the electronic circuit is operating satisfactorily.

Should the movement be warmer than room temperature, owing to the heat of the bench lamp, this may cause a higher than normal current. If the reading is slightly higher than "OK", leave the movement for $\frac{1}{2}$ hour at room temperature, away from the rays of the bench lamp, and re-check the current.

Index or motive mechanism

The motive mechanism is perhaps the most important and certainly the most delicate part of the movement.

It is essential to use the microscope to examine it; even a strong eye glass is not sufficient. The fine ratchet tooth wheel of 300 teeth is stepped forward by a fine spring with a jewel pallet secured to it at the rate of 360 vibrations of the tuning fork per second. Remove the safety bridge to expose the motive mechanism (Fig. 557). The design of the mechanism

is such that, when correctly adjusted, the amplitude of the tuning fork vibration can vary from just over 1 ratchet wheel tooth to just under 3 teeth without affecting operation. This is controlled by the alignment and depth of engagement of the pallet jewels and their interrelation. First, the alignment of both pallets is checked and, if necessary, adjusted, then the engagement of the ratchet pallet is checked, and, if necessary, adjusted.

Finally, the relation between the two jewels is observed. The procedure is as follows.

Fig. 557.

1. Loosen ratchet guard screw, and turn guard away, being careful not to damage the pallet springs, which runs through the guard, then tighten screws. (Fig. 558).

2. Looking at the movement under the microscope, make sure the ratchet jewel is engaged with the ratchet wheel. (The pawl pallet must be engaged with the ratchet wheel, so that during the check for engagement of the motive pallet—see section 3—the wheel will not travel backward.) If it is not engaged, rotate pawl bridge cam until it is brought into contact with the wheel.

3. Check to be sure that each pallet spring is straight and that both

pallets are centred on the ratchet wheel. (See Fig. 559.) If the motive pallet is not central it can be corrected with the pallet spring post tool, which fits on to the pallet spring post, located on the tuning fork. Place the tool over the end of the post and gently press it in the correct direction to centre the pallet on

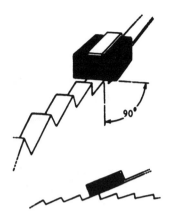

Fig. 559.

PAWL SPRING POST

Fig. 560.

the wheel, by slightly bending the post. (See Fig. 560.) The pawl pallet can be centred by bending the pallet spring with tweezers. Each pallet should be perpendicular to the plane of the wheel. This can be corrected by lightly grasping the pallet spring, near its base, with tweezers, and slightly twisting. Be careful not to touch the pallet jewels. 4. Check the engagement of the motive pallet by pulling back the tine of the tuning fork to which the pallet spring is attached with a pointed piece of pegwood. See Fig. 561. Count the number of

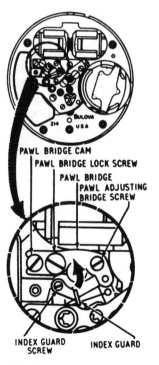

PAWL BRIDGE CAM
PAWL BRIDGE LOCK SCREW
PAWL BRIDGE
PAWL ADJUSTING BRIDGE SCREW

INDEX GUARD SCREW   INDEX GUARD

Fig. 558.

teeth the motive pallet drops off before the pallet pulls away from the ratchet wheel. The pallet should drop off 5 to 8 teeth. If the number of teeth is smaller than 5 or greater than 8, the engagement can be modified by gently pressing the motive pallet spring, near the end where it is secured, toward or away from the wheel, using a blade of the tweezers or a needle. After this adjustment, the engagement should be re-checked. See Fig. 562.

Fig. 561.   Fig. 562.

5. Loosen pawl bridge lock screw slightly; leave pawl adjusting bridge screw tight.

6. Disengage pawl pallet completely by rotating pawl bridge cam until the cam end of the bridge is at its maximum distance away from the ratchet wheel. See Fig. 563. Then examine the pawl pallet under the microscope; it should not be touching the ratchet wheel and not more than one-half its thickness away from the wheel. This distance can be adjusted by pressing gently (in or out) on the pawl pallet spring, as described when adjusting the motive pallet engagement, section 4.

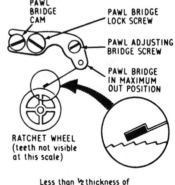

Fig. 563.

7. With the battery in the recess on the test set, turn the rotary switch to the "Low amplitude" position. Attach the test set to the movement with the spring clip and the tuning fork should begin to vibrate. If it does not, tap the movement lightly and the fork will start and the current will read on the scale at the lower end of the "OK" area, or slightly below.

8. Rotate the cam very slowly, either clockwise or anticlockwise, until the movement begins to run, by reason of the motive pallet

causing the ratchet wheel to rotate. This can be observed without the microscope. Continue to turn the cam until the ratchet wheel stops; continue still further until you reach the point where the wheel starts to rotate continuously. At this point the adjustment is complete and the tension of the motive pallet spring is correct.

9. Tighten pawl bridge screw and check the tightness of the pawl adjusting bridge screw. The train of wheels should continue to run, but if not, the adjustment must be made again.

10. Disconnect the test set spring clip from the movement.

11. Loosen ratchet guard screw and turn guard into position and make secure, taking care not to damage motive pallet spring or the pawl pallet spring. Tip the movement into a suitable position and observe with the microscope the clearance between the motive pallet spring and the guard. With the guard in position, the motive pallet spring should pass through a point slightly inside the centre of the slot in the guard, see Fig. 564. The spring should not touch either side of the slot. If it does, bend the guard up or down slightly to centre the spring and at the same time make sure the pawl pallet spring is free of the guard.

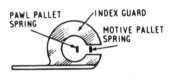

Fig. 564.

12. Replace safety bridge and make secure.

Checking freedom of the train

The safest and most convenient method of checking the freedom of the train is, with a pointed piece of pegwood, to pluck or to twang the tine of the tuning fork to which the motive pallet spring is attached. The fork will then vibrate for a few moments and the train will rotate—if it is free. This check can be observed with an eyeglass. If no motion of the gearing is apparent when the tine is plucked, it is evident there is some obstruction, assuming the motive linkage has been checked, as noted in the servicing table procedure. If the obstruction cannot be seen, the movement must be taken to pieces and cleaned.

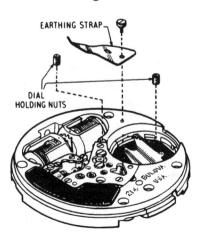

Fig. 565.

To dismantle movement

Remove earthing strap (see Fig. 565) so that movement can be placed in holder. Then remove the two dial holding nuts. Fit movement in

holder dial up.   Remove hands, dial, hour wheel and cannon pinion.
Then remove setting wheel spring and minute wheel spring screws.

Remove minute wheel and setting wheel.   Make sure not to turn
centre seconds pinion backward or forward.   Now place movement dial
down in holder and remove safety bridge. See Fig. 566. Loosen ratchet
guard screw as explained in section 11, page 293. Now fit movement
in holder, bottom plate uppermost. Remove shock bridge and remove
the two tuning fork screws. See Fig. 567. Turn movement over in holder

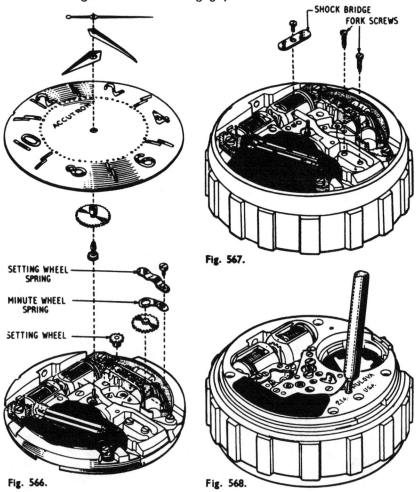

SHOCK BRIDGE
FORK SCREWS

Fig. 567.

SETTING WHEEL
SPRING

MINUTE WHEEL
SPRING

SETTING WHEEL

Fig. 566.

Fig. 568.

and with a metal punch, tap on the base of the tuning fork. See Fig. 568.
Reverse the movement and lift fork at the base until it is in a vertical
position. See Fig. 569. Then remove the coil lead retainer plate, held by
two screws.

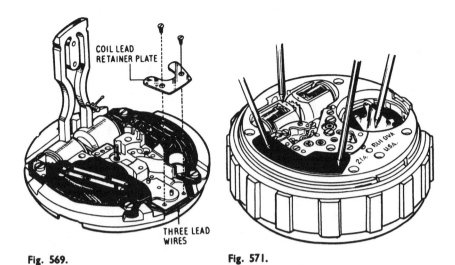

COIL LEAD
RETAINER PLATE

THREE LEAD
WIRES

Fig. 569.   Fig. 571.

Now lower fork carefully, do not force down. Next remove the four coil form screws. See Fig. 570. Lift the movement from the holder and place it over the movement, and rotate until the notch on the edge of

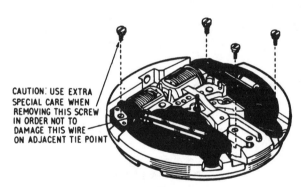

CAUTION: USE EXTRA
SPECIAL CARE WHEN
REMOVING THIS SCREW
IN ORDER NOT TO
DAMAGE THIS WIRE
ON ADJACENT TIE POINT

Fig. 570.

the bottom plate fits into the notch of the holder. Invert the complete assembly and, with pegwood, push down on the coil assembly at several points, thus disengaging the coil and fork assembly. See Fig. 571.

The movement can now be removed from the holder, leaving the coil and fork assembly in the holder. The coils can be removed from the fork by gently spreading the coils apart. The remainder can be dismantled ready for cleaning in the manner employed when cleaning a spring-driven movement. Remove pawl adjusting bridge and pallet spring assembly. The pawl bridge is not tapped and will come out with the bridge. See Fig. 572. Remove end stone jewels by applying horizontal pressure to the U shaped spring, allowing lip of spring to emerge from under the bezel. The spring can then be tipped up and the endstone removed.

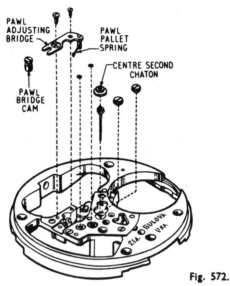

Fig. 572.

The electronic circuit, tuning fork and the pawl adjusting bridge must not be cleaned in a machine. These pieces are just dipped into a benzine bath and then placed on tissue paper to dry.

Re-assembly

Since a watch of this description should be repaired by an experienced watchmaker, it is only necessary to say that the movement is assembled using the description to dismantle in reverse. The train is oiled in the conventional manner, but very sparingly. *The motive ratchet wheel and the motive pallet and the pawl pallet are not oiled.*

The coil and fork assembly are placed in the slots of the movement holder. The bottom plate is placed over the holder, making sure key in bottom engages in notch of holder. Hold the holder and bottom plate together in the hand and press through holes to partially seat the assembly in the bottom plate. Lift base of fork to the vertical position and replace coil lead retainer plate. Check position of the three lead wires to make sure the delicate insulation will not be damaged when the retainer plate is screwed down.

Lower fork carefully and press firmly in position with a piece of pegwood. Apply pressure to base of fork only; avoid contact with the tines. Replace tuning fork screws. Replace shock bridge and screw down. Check to see fork is free to vibrate—that the coils fit into the cups at the end of the tines without touching, and that nothing is in contact with the tines at any point. The rest of the assembly should be obvious.

When the battery is replaced, the tuning will start to vibrate, but if it does not, a light tap on the edge of the watch case will start it off.

A few hints

Make sure the contact spring on the battery cover makes good electrical contact with the battery.

Oil sparingly where oil is necessary.

The tuning fork must never be prized up. Follow the instruction for its removal implicitly.

Make sure the motive ratchet wheel has the correct amount of end-shake. No endshake can cause excessive gaining.

ACCUTRON WITH DATE. MODEL NO. 218

Fundamentally the mechanism of the 218 is the same as the movement described. The battery is enclosed under the back of the case and the hands are set by means of a winding button as in a normal spring driven watch.

It is important to note the parts are not interchangeable with the other model; even the battery is a different size. The back of the case is unscrewed in the normal manner and the hand setting shaft is removed as illustrated in Fig. 573. The date mechanism is dismantled as follows:—

1. Remove date trip spring by collapsing open end sufficiently to slide into recess above trip arm until loop end is clear of its recess. Spring may then be withdrawn from date bridge. See Fig. 574.

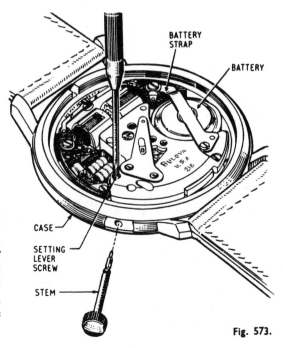

BATTERY STRAP

BATTERY

CASE

SETTING LEVER SCREW

STEM

Fig. 573.

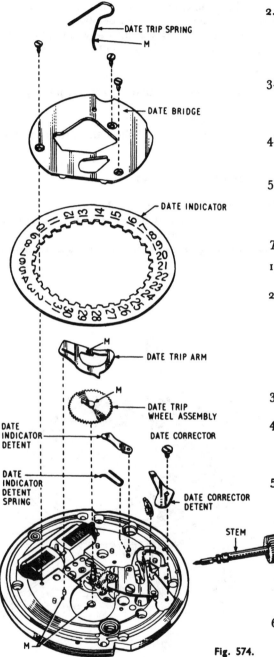

Fig. 574.

2. Remove date bridge (three screws). Caution: Lift with care to avoid loss of date indicator detent spring.

3. Remove date indicator detent spring, date indicator detent and date ring indicator.

4. Remove date trip arm and date trip wheel assembly.

5. Remove date corrector detent (one screw).

To reassemble and oil

1. Replace date corrector detent (one screw).

2. Oil date and trip wheel pivot at (M) and replace date trip wheel assembly and date indicator trip arm. Use lubricant sparingly.

3. Oil sparingly, date trip arm pin at (M).

4. Replace date indicator ring, date indicator detent and its spring.

5. Replace date bridge (three screws).

Note: Make certain date trip arm is not trapped between pillar plate and date bridge before tightening screws.

6. Apply a small amount of oil at (M) to lower end of date trip arm.

7. Replace date trip spring by collapsing open sufficiently to permit insertion into date bridge recess above date trip arm, then slide loop end into recess, making certain that upper end spring snaps into cutout.
8. Oil sparingly indicator trip arm at (M).
Use Moebius OL 207 special oil with molybdenum disulphide.
Bulova emphasize the sparing use of oil.

CHAPTER TWENTY-FOUR

WATCH TIMING MACHINES

A TIMING machine, also called a "rate recorder", has become an essential adjunct to the watch repairer's equipment. It is speedy and decisive and an enormous help.

Not only does the machine help when regulating a watch, but it also detects escapement faults.

It is useful when making an adjustment to a watch in wear by the owner. Suppose the observation is that the watch is gaining two minutes a week. Before making any alteration to the index, test the watch on the machine. According to the owner's reading, it should show a gain of approximately 17 sec per day, in which case the index is moved to slow until the reading is as near no error as possible. Normally the error shown on the tape should be up to +30 sec because the average wearer has a personal error of about 30 sec per day slow.

If, however, the error of the watch while being worn was, say, 30 sec per day slow and the reading on the machine showed plus 10 sec, then the personal error of the owner was greater than average and the index should be adjusted to make the watch gain 40 seconds a day, and so on.

The information which follows has been kindly supplied by the manufacturers of the Vibrograf timing machine, and also the manufacturers of the Greiner machine. The English agents for Greiner Electronic Ltd. Langenthal, Switzerland are Greiner Electronic (Great Britain) Ltd., 182 Upper Richmond Road, Putney, London, S.W.15.

The English agents for Reno S.A. (the manufacturers of the Vibrograf), La Chaux-de-Fonds, Switzerland are Convair Time and Electronics Ltd., 81–89 Farringdon Road, London, E.C.1.

THE GREINER RATE RECORDER

The machine illustrated in Fig. 575 is the

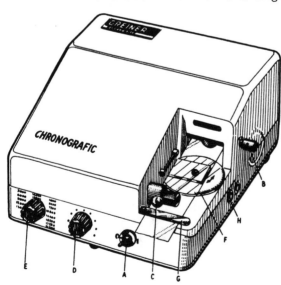

Fig. 575.

simplest and least expensive of the Greiner timing machines and is known as Chronografic. Details of the machine are: (A) Main power switch; (B) Motor starter; (C) Paper feed lever; (D) Volume control; (E) Watch heat selector; (F) Measuring dial; (G) Cutting edge to off paper; (H) Earphone socket.

Should there be a slight electrification effect when touching the unearthed instrument or the microphone, pull the main plug out and re-insert in inverted position and the harmless effect will disappear.

The following are graphs given by Greiner.

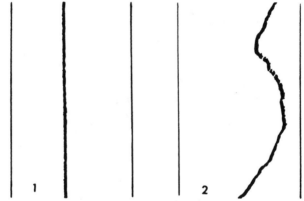

(1) Watch in excellent condition.

(2) Fault in centre wheel and third wheel pinion. Average rate 30 seconds fast in 24 hours.

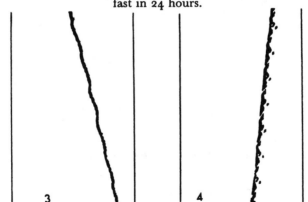

(3) Fault in third wheel and 4th wheel pinion. Average rate 25 seconds slow in 24 hours.

(4) Escapement fault on one pallet stone. Average rate 10 seconds slow in 24 hours.

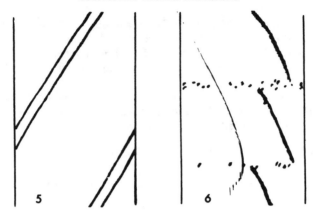

(5) Out of beat. Average rate fast 70 seconds in 24 hours.

(6) Periodically knocking.

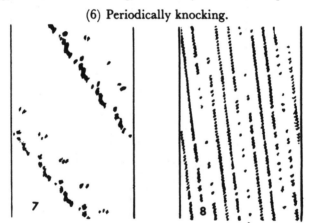

(7) Watch needs to be cleaned. Amplitude of balance too small (poor action).

(8) Trace of Bulova Accutron watch—tuning fork mechanism—Rate is slow 13 seconds in 24 hours.

Besides helping to check the rate and detect defects, a watch timer is the ideal instrument for the periodic testing of stocks, whether of watches or clocks.

THE VIBROGRAF B100 RATE RECORDER

Fig. 576 shows the new Vibrograf B100. Details are:

1. Movable dial to read accurately the gain or loss of the watch's timing; 2. Printed recording on paper: a means of checking the precision of the watch and detecting any faults; 3. Lever for paper speed control. The slow speed is for observations over a long period, therefore doubling

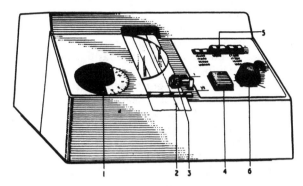

Fig. 576.

the precision of the reading; 4. Push button system for starting and stopping paper movement; 5. Push button system for selecting the right frequency; 6. Knob for starting the machine and for regulating volume.

The Vibrograf can be used to test movements equipped with escapements other than the jewelled-lever escapement (Roskopf, cylinder, detent, tourbillon, etc.).

Electric watches are also easy to test, although it should be borne in mind that the normal microphone records only their mechanical functions. A special induction microphone can be supplied on request, for recording the electric impulses.

There are other means of recording the electrical impulses of watch and clock movements, but for these it is advisable to follow the instructions of the watch supplier, or else consult the Vibrograf technical service department.

To obtain a usable trace with electric tuning fork timepieces, an adaptor is required.

The Vibrograf can also be used with an earphone for acoustic controls.

Here are some notes for the watchmaker who wishes to get the best service out of his Vibrograf.

When the apparatus is installed, make sure that it is in a firm position and far enough away from any noises which could influence the microphone (motors, typewriters, compressed air, ultrasonic machines, etc.). Also, see that the cooling system works properly, i.e. that the air-holes are not blocked.

Bear in mind that the information given by the traces (as regards rate) is inaccurate when the watch is badly placed on the microphone.

Find the best degree of amplification by starting at minimum volume and increasing the amplification control until the correct trace appears. If scattered marks appear instead of a line, the machine is not properly set for the number of vibrations of the watch; the correct setting must be found by operating the push buttons for frequency selection.

When interpreting a Vibrograf trace of unusual appearance, remember that a watch may have several defects at the same time, each one having its own particular influence on the trace.

Avoid preconceived ideas when interpreting the trace. Some watchmakers are inclined to take it for granted that the balance is out of poise, some are always imagining that the jewels are scratched or broken, or that parts of the watch are worn out, while others lay the blame chiefly on magnetism. Such tendencies are likely to cause errors of judgement.

To be able to draw valid conclusions on the subject of isochronism, it is necessary to make several recordings in the horizontal position, gradually increasing the degree of mainspring wind: e.g. one turn, two turns, four turns, and fully wound.

Faulty poise of the balance does not affect the rate in horizontal positions. In vertical or oblique positions, it causes an isochronal error.

Recordings should be made before and after each adjustment; it is then possible to see, by comparing the two traces, whether the adjustment has had the desired effect.

Interpretation of traces recorded by the Vibrograf.

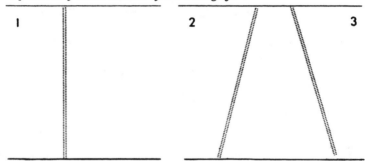

(1) *Running accurately*

When the movement is running accurately, the trace takes the form of either one or two straight lines parallel with the edges of the paper.

The position of the trace in relation to the edges of the paper is of no importance.

(2 and 3) *Gain right and loss to the left*

The slant of the trace is the exact indication of the amount the watch is gaining or losing at the time of the test. This value can be read in figures (i.e. in seconds and minutes) on the reading-scale. A right-hand slant signifies gain, a left-hand slant loss.

Correction: In order to obtain the best possible rate under normal conditions of wear, the correction must allow for the rate in different positions. In other words, it is not always advisable to make the trace perfectly parallel with the paper.

For the same reason it is better to carry out the examination with the mainspring two-thirds wound, or to make two measurements, each at a different degree of wind.

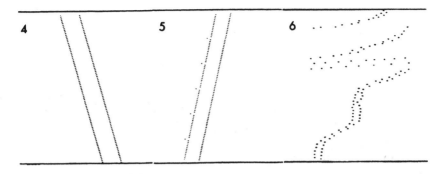

(4) *Bad beat*

Bad beat is the result of an unequal duration of the two vibrations which make up the oscillation. The two traces appear on the Vibrograf separated by a gap.

The importance of this defect can be estimated only by taking into consideration the amplitude of the balance and the characteristics of the recording apparatus.

Correction: The escapement is set into beat, preferably by turning the collet on the balance staff, until the traces are sufficiently close together. If the movement is equipped with a mobile studholder, the operation can be carried out directly on the microphone.

(5) *Damaged tooth on escape wheel*

When an irregularity recurs in every fifteenth mark on one of the trace lines, this means that one of the fifteen teeth of the escape wheel is damaged.

The irregularity sometimes appears on both traces of the trace.

Correction: Change the escape wheel.

(6) *Balance knocking*

The appearance of the trace in this case is that of a "staircase".

However, as knocking is not always continuous, the trace may also be composed of normal branches and completely irregular branches whose scattered marks correspond to the vast gain caused by the knocking.

This sort of trace is sometimes produced by an escapement which "catches".

Correction: Replace the mainspring by another one of weaker strength.

(7) *Faulty escapement or damaged pallet stone*

The reading is composed of two traces, one of which is regular, and the other badly printed with the marks out of alignment.

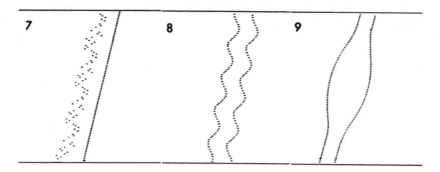

This signifies that only one of the two pallets of the escapement is working properly.

Correction: Check the impulse-pin, the pallets, the guard pin and the unlocking angle which may be too slight on one of the pallets.

(8) *Escape wheel out of round*

The reading consists of two traces with waves occurring at regular intervals. If there are fifteen marks between the maximum point of one wave and that of the next, we may conclude that the escape wheel which has, in most cases, fifteen teeth, is out of round.

A trace, similar though irregular, may be produced by severe sideshake of the pivots.

Correction: Check the sideshake of the pivots and if necessary change the escape wheel, or the jewel hole or holes.

(9) *Variation in balance amplitude*

When there is a variation in the distance between the two traces, this signifies that the amplitude of the balance varies, as a result of an isochronal error.

Correction: Check the bearings of the balance, the oiling, and all the causes of amplitude variation.

(10) *Dirty escapement or irregular transmission*

A completely irregular trace is the result either of a dirty escapement or of irregular transmission due, for instance, to lack of oil.

In this case it is advisable to continue the recording for some time and to see whether the trace presents more precise characteristics.

Correction: Clean and oil the movement, check the sideshake of the pivots, and see that the wheel train functions properly. Demagnetise the movement.

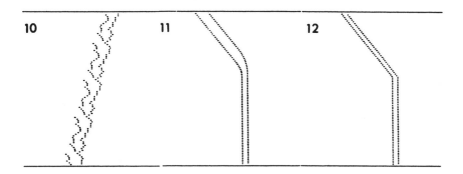

(11) *Balance-hairspring not isochronous*

When the rate indicated by the trace differs widely between the horizontal and vertical positions, or between the various degrees of mainspring wind, this means either that the isochronism is inadequate or that the play of the hairspring between the curb-pins is too great.

Correction: Check whether the play of the hairspring is not too great, whether the escapement functions normally and whether the balance bearings are in a good state.

The problem of isochronism is very important and at the same time very complex. It is therefore advisable to consult page 155. Also the book "Practical Watch Adjusting" by D. de Carle (N.A.G. Press).

(12) *Balance not in poise*

If the trace swerves sharply during the changeover from the horizontal to the vertical position, or the other way round, it means that the balance is not in poise.

This defect is sometimes combined with an isochronal error.

Correction: Bring the balance into poise, or else replace it by a sprung balance that is already counted, pinned and poised (sprung balances of this kind are nowadays on the market). If there is also an isochronal error, proceed as indicated in Section 11.

(13) *Excessive sideshake of pallet-staff or balance pivots, or defective train*

When the trace takes the form of an irregular wavy line, it is usually the result of excessive sideshake on the pallet-staff or balance pivots, or of a defective train, or a combination of these defects.

Correction: Check the sideshake of the pivots and replace the faulty parts of the wheel train, if any.

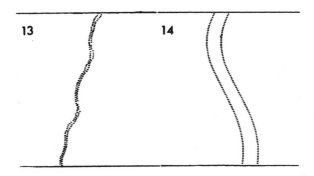

(14) *Variation in running of balance, poor transmission, loss of amplitude.*

If the trace is a long wavy line, it generally means that the balance is running irregularly owing to a variation in the driving power.

In order to detect the cause of the defect accurately, continue the recording over a long period, if possible at a slower paper speed. The frequency of the maximum points of the wavy line will indicate the faulty train.

Correction: In every case it is advisable to begin by dismantling the movement and cleaning and oiling it thoroughly; then check the side-shake of the pivots and the state of the bearings.

Replace any part that the trace shows to be defective.

SOME OF THE 101 REASONS LIKELY TO CAUSE A WATCH TO STOP

DIRT AND NEGLECT

1. The existence of dust and dirt.

2. A hair wedged in some part of the case.

3. Sometimes *slight* rust on pinions, especially small watches.

4. Rust generally.

5. Failure to wind fully (ladies are especially prone to this) or to wind at all.

6. Winding shaft ; the castle wheel square cutting the plate allowing the shaft pivot to project through and to touch the barrel or some other part that should be free.

7. The castle wheel touching the intermediate wheel, due to the check action of the keyless work being faulty.

HANDS AND DIAL

8. Hands not free of each other or fouling the dial or the glass.

9. Motion work, including the intermediate wheel, not free.

10. Loose dial ; it may thus work to one side and bind the hands.

11. Hand work so loose that they fail to carry. This may cause apparent intermittent stopping.

12. Loose minute wheel stud.

13. Cannon pinion riding up and binding motion work.

MAINSPRING

14. Mainspring not free in the barrel.

15. Dry or dirty mainspring.

16. Broken mainspring.

17. Click spring failure.

18. Barrel out of upright, accentuated when the mainspring is fully wound.

19. Barrel hook projecting and touching some other part.

20. Ends of " T " hook on mainspring too long ; projecting from barrel and fouling centre wheel or plate.

21. Mainspring slips, so that watch stops before full period.

22. Shoulders, or boss, inside barrel (at centre) too large, causing mainspring to bind.

23. Barrel cover off ; due to a fall or careless assembly.

24. Crook end of return spring touches side of barrel.

TRAIN

25. Lack of endshake to the train wheels.

26. Loose jewel holes.

27. A screw misplaced, binding on some other part that should be quite free.

28. Bent teeth on the wheels or barrel.

29. A pivot may fit its hole too well and that part minutely out of upright would bind. This can cause intermittent stopping.

30. Faulty depths, especially the fourth wheel and escape pinion.

31. Bent train wheel pivot, especially the fourth if fitted with

seconds, causing the seconds hand pipe to rub the sides of the seconds hole in the dial.

32. Cracked or chipped jewel hole, when the crack or chip is inside the hole.

33. Worn pinions, causing locking.

34. Train holes too wide.

35. Any pinion loose in its wheel.

36. A cracked pinion leaf; the centre pinion is subject to this, caused when the mainspring breaks.

37. Worn pivots, which soon cause locking or binding in certain positions.

ESCAPEMENT

38. Insufficient shake of the lever on the banking.

39. No endshake to the lever.

40. The roller fouls the lever.

41. Loose end-stones.

42. Loose pallet stone or stones.

43. Loose ruby pin.

44. The ruby pin too long, it may touch the guard pin.

45. Too much oil to the top lever pivot. A likely cause especially in very small watches.

46. Loose roller.

47. Separate rollers out of alignment.

48. The escape wheel mis-locks on the pallets.

49. Safety roller touching lower balance jewel setting or end-piece screw.

50. Broken staff.

51. Loose guard pin.

52. No endshake to the balance.

53. Excess of shellac on pallets or ruby pin.

54. Bent staff or pivots.

55. Staff " mushroomed," *i.e.*, the ends spread, generally due to being crushed.

56. Cracked balance end stone, especially if the pivot works in or on the crack.

57. Screw loose on balance and touches another part.

58. Lack of freedom of the balance spring, it may touch the balance arm when dial down.

59. Projecting free end of balance spring fouling balance.

60. Balance spring stud through too far and touches the balance when the watch is D.U.

61. Loose balance spring collet.

62. Loose balance spring stud.

63. Balance spring badly caught up.

64. Balance spring fouls centre wheel.

65. Balance spring loosely pinned.

66. Timing collet on balance too large or out of position and touches pallet cock.

67. Curb pins or block too low, touching balance.

68. Balance fouls pallet cock or pallet cock screw.

69. Balance staff pivots too short.

70. Ruby pin too short.

71. Excessive shake on the roller.

72. Loose banking pin or pins.

73. Broken or missing ruby pin.

74. Index over too far ; fork touching centre wheel.

75. No inside or outside shake of the escape wheel teeth.

76. Escape wheel teeth (or tooth) touches the belly of the pallets.

77. Ruby pin binds in notch.

OIL AND OILING

78. The presence of thickened oil.

79. Omitting to oil some or all parts.

80. Oil evaporating altogether in some places causing seizing or firing up, the centre wheel pivots are subject to this.

81. Over oiling generally, this may not cause stopping immediately, but as the oil deteriorates it can cause stopping, especially the suction or adhesion of the minute wheel.

CASE AND GENERAL

82. The case, when shut, touches the balance cock and so binds the balance.

83. Back of the case or the dome pressing on the centre pivot, or other vulnerable part.

84. Case screw or screws worked out and lodged in movement ; or head broken off and lodged in movement.

85. Badly fitting case which wrings the movement.

86. Thin, lightly made case giving insufficient protection.

87. Unbreakable glass soft or thin and presses on to hands when the watch is in wear.

88. Previously botched repairs.

89. The watch may be badly magnetised.

90. Broken tooth of ratchet or any keyless wheel, preventing the watch from being wound.

91. Faulty negative setting sleeve ; may be at hands set position.

92. Button loose, unable to wind.

93. Hands loose and not carrying, giving appearance of watch having stopped.

A STANDARD OF WORKMANSHIP

FOURTEEN POINTS OF HOROLOGICAL SERVICE

1. Always maintain the highest standard. Your reputation depends upon each individual job ; you will probably try to explain away a temporary lapse, but the chances are that you may not have the opportunity to do so.

—

2. Watches should be repaired so that they have the appearance of being new. If you fit a new part and are unable to fit interchangeable material, make the part to match the rest of the watch, so that even the maker would have difficulty in telling the difference.

—

3. Do not change the character of the watch. If the manufacturer left the watch screws with flat white heads or coloured them red or blue, and you find it necessary to replace a screw or to restore one, finish the screw in the original style.

—

4. All scratched or mauled screws and steel work should be restored as new. If necessary, polish the centre of the minute hand, *i.e.*, the boss, flat, underhand. If the original style of the watch dictates a coloured boss, restore as when new.

—

5. If it is necessary to fit new hands, make sure they are the correct style. For preference fit the hands as supplied by the manufacturer of the movement ; the style of the hands gives character to the watch. Should you fit one new hand only, make sure it matches the other in style, *i.e.*, a spade minute hand and not a moon minute hand with a spade hour hand ; also see that the new hand has the same weight or degree of boldness as the existing one. Another point denoting good workmanship is always to fit an English seconds hand to an English watch. An English seconds hand has a solid centre ; some of the very old English watches have a seconds hand with a gold centre, but these are rare. A word about glasses : if the bezel is made for a crystal glass do not fit a lunette and if made for a flat glass do not fit a raised one, and so on.

—

6. Make sure the movement is really clean, without smears or finger marks.

—

7. See that the dial and the glass are clean without dust or finger marks.

—

8. Clean the inside of the case well, especially round by the joints, and pass through the flame as explained in a previous chapter. Polish the outside of the case ; this is the only part the customer sees. See that the bow of a pocket watch is tight ; it takes only a moment to tighten it with the bow-pliers. Watch cases set with stones should be washed out to make the stones as bright as possible.

—

9. It is the watchmaker's responsibility to see that the case is as dust-proof as possible. With gem set watches it is a good plan to run a *little* white wax round each setting ; a piece about the size of a pinshead, picked out with the point of a knife. Apply the wax to the back of each setting, the girdle of the stone, not on the culet. Apply the minimum of heat to the front of the case so that the wax runs round the stone to fill in any holes. Too much heat makes the wax run over the stone detracting from its beauty. If you have any doubt of the fitting of the glass, especially if it is a shaped glass, run a little very thin cement round the edge, Seccotine or Le Page's glue answers well ; add water to make the glue thin, it then penetrates and is not unsightly. If the case itself does not fit well and is likely to let in dust, apply a film of wax to the snapping edge so that the case closes on to this film of wax. One part beeswax and three parts vaseline or petroleum jelly, heat together to mix. It is the watch repairer's *duty* to see that dust cannot easily enter ; you cannot blame the wearer.

—

10. When the watch is finished and ready to hand to the customer the index should be in the centre and the movement running to time. See that the watch is fully wound and set to the correct time, even if you had the watch for some quite small job. Watches should always be handled with extreme care ; in the customer's presence be very particular on this point. Remember, a watch is a precious thing to the owner and he will appreciate your consideration. If the owner had not previously viewed the watch as the delicate instrument that it really is, quite apart from its intrinsic value, greater care may thus be suggested by your example. Wipe the case with a chamois leather and hand it over as if it were something rare, and as if you are especially interested in that particular watch. The watch is one of many to you ; it may be *the only one* to the owner.

Invite the customer to bring it back, say in a week's time, to check the rating and to make any adjustments necessary to suit wearing conditions. Discourage interference with your work ; you have repaired the watch and are proud of it and want to see it giving satisfaction. Remember that you are one of the best watch repairers and the most capable person to handle the watch. Be jealous of your reputation, it is always a sign of good workmanship and service.

—

11. Whenever necessary explain the working parts of the watch in language as non-technical as possible to the customer. A new balance

staff, for instance, has pivots finer than the smallest needle, etc. Modern doctors explain the working of the human system to their patients, that is, the part immediately needing treatment ; it makes everybody happy and so it can be with a watch. Let the customer see your mechanical diffi- culties ; do not be plaintive, you may lose his interest or convey the impression that you are working up for a high charge.

—

12. Reputations are made and lost by what other watch repairers say about your work. Never give another man an opportunity to disparage your workmanship. Read paragraph No. 1 again ; it is vital.

—

13. Learn all you can ; you have never finished learning, read all there is to be read on watchmaking, and there is quite a lot of it. Above all, put into practice all the good stuff you read. You will readily recog- nise what is good ; experience teaches that.

—

14. Finally, do not run down another horologist's work, even if it leaves something to be desired. If the condition of a movement is in question, treat the matter diplomatically ; describe what you can do to improve it, do not give an opinion that somebody else has done a poor job. Be prepared to stand by your own results ; that is your reward.

INDEX